Peter Nolan

coping with

CAPITAL FLOWS

in

east asia

Nomura Research Institute, Ltd. (NRI), established in 1966, is Japan's largest and most comprehensive private-sector research organization. It offers a wide range of services, including public policy research, investment and financial research, management consulting, contract research and regional planning. The company is also Japan's leading supplier of systems consulting, integration and operating services.

NRI has a staff of 2,700 and operates globally through offices in Tokyo, Yokohama, Osaka, New York, Washington, D.C., San Francisco, London, Frankfurt, Paris, Zurich, Sydney, Hong Kong, Singapore, Taipei and Seoul. NRI also manages the Nomura School of Advanced Management, one of Japan's foremost centres for management training, and is affiliated with the Tokyo Club Foundation for Global Studies, a non-partisan foundation supported by Japanese industry to promote better understanding in Japan of world issues.

The **Institute of Southeast Asian Studies** (ISEAS) was established as an autonomous organization in 1968. It is a regional research centre for scholars and other specialists concerned with modern Southeast Asia, particularly the multi-faceted problems of stability and security, economic development, and political and social change.

The Institute is governed by a twenty-two-member Board of Trustees comprising nominees from the Singapore Government, the National University of Singapore, the various Chambers of Commerce, and professional and civic organizations. A ten-man Executive Committee oversees day-to-day operations; it is chaired by the Director, the Institute's chief academic and administrative officer.

coping with CAPITAL FLOW in east asia

Edited by
C.H. KWAN
DONNA VANDENBRINK
CHIA SIOW YUE

NRI Nomura Research Institute
Tokyo

ISEAS Institute of Southeast Asian Studies
Singapore

Published jointly by

Institute of Southeast Asian Studies & Nomura Research Institute
30 Heng Mui Keng Terrace 1-10 Nihonbashi
Pasir Panjang Chuo-ku, Tokyo 103
Singapore 119614 Japan

First reprint 1999

Cataloguing in Publication Data

Coping with capital flows in East Asia / edited by C.H. Kwan, Donna Vandenbrink and Chia Siow Yue.
(ISEAS current economic affairs series, 0128-2114)
1. Capital movements—East Asia.
2. Monetary policy—East Asia.
I. Kwan, C. H., 1957-
II. Vandenbrink, Donna,
III. Chia, Siow Yue.
IV. Series.
HG3891 C75 1998 sls97-106016

ISBN 981-230-015-5 (soft cover)
ISBN 981-230-016-3 (hard cover)

ISEAS on the Internet: http://www.iseas.edu.sg/pub.html

Typeset by Superskill
Printed in Singapore by Seng Lee Press Pte Ltd

Contents

List of Tables

List of Figures

Acknowledgements

The publication of this book was made possible through the generous funding of the research project by the Tokyo Club Foundation for Global Studies. The editors would like to thank Mr Shozo Hashimoto, President of the Tokyo Club, for writing the forward.

Many people associated with Nomura Research Institute (NRI) and the Institute of Southeast Asian Studies contributed in different ways to this publication. The editors express appreciation for their input and support.

List of Contributors

Emilio T. Antonio, Jr.	University of Asia and the Pacific, Philippines
Bhanupong Nidhiprabha	Thailand Development Research Institute, Thailand
Edward K.Y. Chen	Centre for Asian Pacific Studies, Lingnan College, Hong Kong
Dongchul Cho	Korea Development Institute, Korea
C. H. Kwan	Nomura Research Institute, Japan
Manuel F. Montes	Institute of Southeast Asian Studies, Singapore
Emilio S. Neri, Jr.	University of Asia and the Pacific, Philippines
Raymond C.W. Ng	Centre for Asian Pacific Studies, Lingnan College, Hong Kong
Ong Hong Cheong	Institute of Strategic and International Studies (ISIS) Malaysia
Mochammad Rosul	Center for Policy and Implementation Studies, Indonesia
Teresa V. Taningco	University of Asia and the Pacific, Philippines
Amina Tyabji	National University of Singapore, Singapore
Ya-Hwei Yang	Chung-Hua Institution for Economic Research, Taiwan
Zhao Jinping	Development Research Center of the State Council, People's Republic of China

Foreword

When the Tokyo Club Foundation for Global Studies was deciding on a research theme for its annual joint project by the members of the AT10 network of East Asian think-tanks, capital flows were a major policy issue for the countries of the region. In the 1990s many of the countries represented in the research network had been the focus of vast international investment and capital movements. They had managed to maintain financial and economic stability and continue their enviable growth following the Mexican Crisis of 1994-95. But was Asia really different from Latin America? What were East Asian governments doing to ensure that the benefits of capital inflows were maximized and their problems controlled? How were they handling the threat of inflation, given stable exchange rate regimes and strong capital inflows? These were the issues that we hoped to understand when we asked the AT10 researchers to investigate their countries' experiences with capital flows in the 1980s and 1990s. The results, which the researchers presented at a conference in Tokyo in January 1997, form the main chapters in this volume.

This research could not have been more timely for, even as the conference papers were being compiled, the region was struck by a crisis that sent currencies plunging, turned off the spigot of capital inflows, strained businesses dependent on foreign debt, exposed weaknesses in banking systems, and sent several countries to seek international rescue packages. The turmoil is not over yet and the full extent of its impact on the region's economies remains to be seen.

Given these developments, the Tokyo Club delayed publication in order to ask each contributor to comment on the Asian crisis from the midst of the turmoil. The AT10 researchers' perspectives on what has happened in their countries since July 1997, how the authorities have coped with the situation, and what lessons can be learned are added as updates to the original chapters. In addition, Dr Manuel F. Montes of the Institute of Southeast Asian Studies kindly contributed his synthesis of the currency crisis in Southeast Asia.

Shozo Hashimoto
President
Tokyo Club Foundation for Global Studies

February 1998

1

Coping with Capital Flows in the Asian Countries

C. H. Kwan

An increasing inflow of foreign funds has helped Asian countries to achieve high economic growth by allowing them to invest more than they save, but at the same time it has created new problems. Volatile capital movements may create macroeconomic instability, and massive inflows may push up real exchange rates, with adverse effects on exports. Indeed, the Mexican crisis in late 1994 through early 1995 and Thailand's currency devaluation in the summer of 1997 had repercussions among many Asian nations. Making the best use of the inflow of funds for economic development while checking possible side effects has become an important policy issue for these countries. This chapter discusses how Asian countries coped with capital inflow up to 1996. Analysis of the latest currency crisis in Asia prompted by the reversal of capital flow follows in the next two chapters.

PROGRESS TOWARDS LIBERALIZATION OF CAPITAL TRANSACTIONS

Countries liberalize international capital flows in order to raise economic efficiency and enhance growth potential. These ends are realized by lowering interest rates through such means as arbitrage between domestic and foreign interest rates, intensified competition, and higher productivity in the financial sector.

Capital account liberalization in Asia has been accelerated by three additional factors. First, the trend toward liberalization and internationalization in money and capital markets in the world economy has reduced the effectiveness of controls on capital movement by individual countries. The liberalization of capital transactions is in essence a mere acceptance of the current situation as a *fait accompli*. Second, many countries have responded to external pressure (notably from the United States) by opening their money and capital markets and removing foreign exchange controls. Third, the liberalization of external transactions has become a prerequisite for admission to some international organizations. For example, South Korea submitted a schedule of capital liberalization in preparation for admission to the OECD. China is liberalizing trade and foreign exchange regulations in expectation of securing membership in the World Trade Organization (WTO).

To prepare for liberalization of capital account transactions, rapid progress has been made in some Asian countries toward currency convertibility for current account transactions. Indonesia and South Korea gained IMF Article 8 status in 1988, followed by Thailand in 1990, the Philippines in 1995, and China in 1996. This step obliges these countries to remove restrictions on current account payments. Incidentally, Hong Kong, Japan, Singapore, and Malaysia were accorded IMF Article 8 status as early as the 1960s.

Some Asian nations have been earnest about fostering offshore markets in order to develop their domestic financial markets and facilitate overseas fund raising. Asian offshore markets are characterized by looser regulations with regard to interest rates, reserve requirements, withholding taxes on interest, and foreign exchange controls than their onshore counterparts. Hong Kong and Singapore, the early starters, have established themselves as major international financial centres. They have been followed by Malaysia's Labuan market (established in 1990) and Thailand's Bangkok International Banking Facility or BIBF (established in 1993), both of which have shown impressive development and are gaining in importance as channels for raising funds abroad. More recently, Taipei and Shanghai have announced their own plans for international financial centres in an attempt to catch up with these front-runners.

Asian stock markets are also being opened to the outside world. South Korea began to open its securities market in January 1992, when it permitted non-residents to invest directly in Korean stocks as part of its plan to promote the gradual expansion of its capital market. Taiwan also approved the acquisition of local stocks by foreign institutional investors in 1991 subject to certain conditions. In China, which is moving rapidly along the path toward a market economy, a stock exchange was set up in Shanghai in December 1990, followed by a second one in Shenzhen in July 1991. Investment in Chinese stocks by non-residents has been facilitated with the listing of more and more Chinese enterprises in Hong Kong and New York, in addition to the listing of B-shares of Chinese enterprises (shares intended for foreign investors) in the two domestic stock markets. Asian countries that are less restrictive toward investment in their stock markets by foreigners, such as Hong Kong, Singapore, Malaysia, Thailand, the Philippines, and Indonesia, have tried to further enhance their attractiveness to foreign investors by strengthening their supervisory systems and promoting computerized transactions.

The deregulation of foreign direct investment in Asian countries is also well under way. China's acceleration of its reform and open door policy since 1992 has prompted other Asian countries to focus on improving their investment environments. As a general trend, their policies toward foreign capital have begun to converge. China has made great progress in opening more regions as well as industries and sectors to foreign investors.

ASEAN nations have responded to these moves by China by taking steps to encourage investment by foreign companies, including measures to address domestic structural problems and to accelerate industrial upgrading. In a series of measures implemented since June 1993, Indonesia has basically removed restrictions on investment by foreign companies, requirements concerning capital movement, and regulations governing minimum amounts of investment. Preferential treatment of export processing zones has been expanded. Malaysia and Singapore have cut corporate taxes. As a means of enhancing its overall attractiveness to foreign investors, ASEAN admitted Vietnam, Laos, and Myanmar into its camp and promoted the establishment of the AFTA (ASEAN Free Trade Area). All of these efforts help expand and deepen intra-regional economic co-operation. Meanwhile, South Korea, a typical NIE, has also increased the number of industries in which foreign companies can invest and is reinforcing incentives in order to accelerate technology transfer.

RAPIDLY INCREASING CAPITAL INFLOWS

Led by private investors, inflows of funds into Asia expanded sharply between 1990 and 1996 (Table 1.1). Factors on the receiving side contributing to this upsurge included the progress of trade and capital liberalization, Asia's continued high economic growth and macroeconomic stability, and the emergence of new frontier economies, including China. Factors on the investing side included business recessions in developed countries and the consequent decline in international interest rates, the shift to overseas production by Japanese enterprises due to the yen's appreciation, and the liberalization of capital outflow in Asian NIEs and their emergence as creditor nations.

TABLE 1.1
Net Private Long-term Capital Flows to Developing Countries by Country Group, 1990–96
(US$ billions)

	1990	1991	1992	1993	1994	1995	1996*
All developing countries	44.4	56.9	90.6	157.1	161.3	184.2	243.8
Sub-Saharan Africa	0.3	0.8	–0.3	–0.5	5.2	9.1	11.8
East Asia & the Pacific	19.3	20.8	36.9	62.4	71.0	84.1	108.7
South Asia	2.2	1.9	2.9	6.0	8.5	5.2	10.7
Europe & Central Asia	9.5	7.9	21.8	25.6	17.2	30.1	31.2
Latin America & the Caribbean	12.5	22.9	28.7	59.8	53.6	54.3	74.3
Middle East & North Africa	0.6	2.2	0.5	3.9	5.8	1.4	6.9
Top country destinations							
China	8.1	7.5	21.3	39.6	44.4	44.3	52.0
Mexico	8.2	12.0	9.2	21.2	20.7	13.1	28.1
Brazil	0.5	3.6	9.8	16.1	12.2	19.1	14.7
Malaysia	1.8	4.2	6.0	11.3	8.9	11.9	16.0
Indonesia	3.2	3.4	4.6	1.1	7.7	11.6	17.9
Thailand	4.5	5.0	4.3	6.8	4.8	9.1	13.3
Argentina	–0.2	2.9	4.2	13.8	7.6	7.2	11.3
India	1.9	1.6	1.7	4.6	6.4	3.6	8.0
Russia	5.6	0.2	10.8	3.1	0.3	1.1	3.6
Turkey	1.7	1.1	4.5	7.6	1.6	2.0	4.7
Chile	2.1	1.2	1.6	2.2	4.3	4.2	4.6
Hungary	–0.3	1.0	1.2	4.7	2.8	7.8	2.5

Notes: * preliminary data. Country groups are classified according to the World Bank's Debt Reporting System. Private flows include commercial bank lending guaranteed by export credit agencies. Country ranking based on cumulative 1990–95 private capital flows received.
Source: World Bank. 1997. *Global Development Finance*. Vol. 1.

Combined long-term and short-term net inflow of funds into Asia amounted to $130.8 billion (8.9 percent of GNP) in 1996, much greater than Latin America's total of $78.3 billion (4.9 percent of GNP). The expansion of funds flowing into Asia was accompanied by a major change in the composition of those funds. Official assistance toward developing countries slowed down due to economic recession and fiscal constraints in the developed countries. This slowdown contrasted with an active move among private investors to seek higher returns in the Asian region. This trend was reflected in the replacement of public funds by private sector funds, which accounted for about 96 percent of the long-term net inflow of funds into Asia in 1996. It should be noted that non-debt funds such as direct investment and equity investment, accounted for the majority of total private sector funds (Figure 1.1).

FIGURE 1.1
Composition of Private Capital Flows in East Asia and Latin America

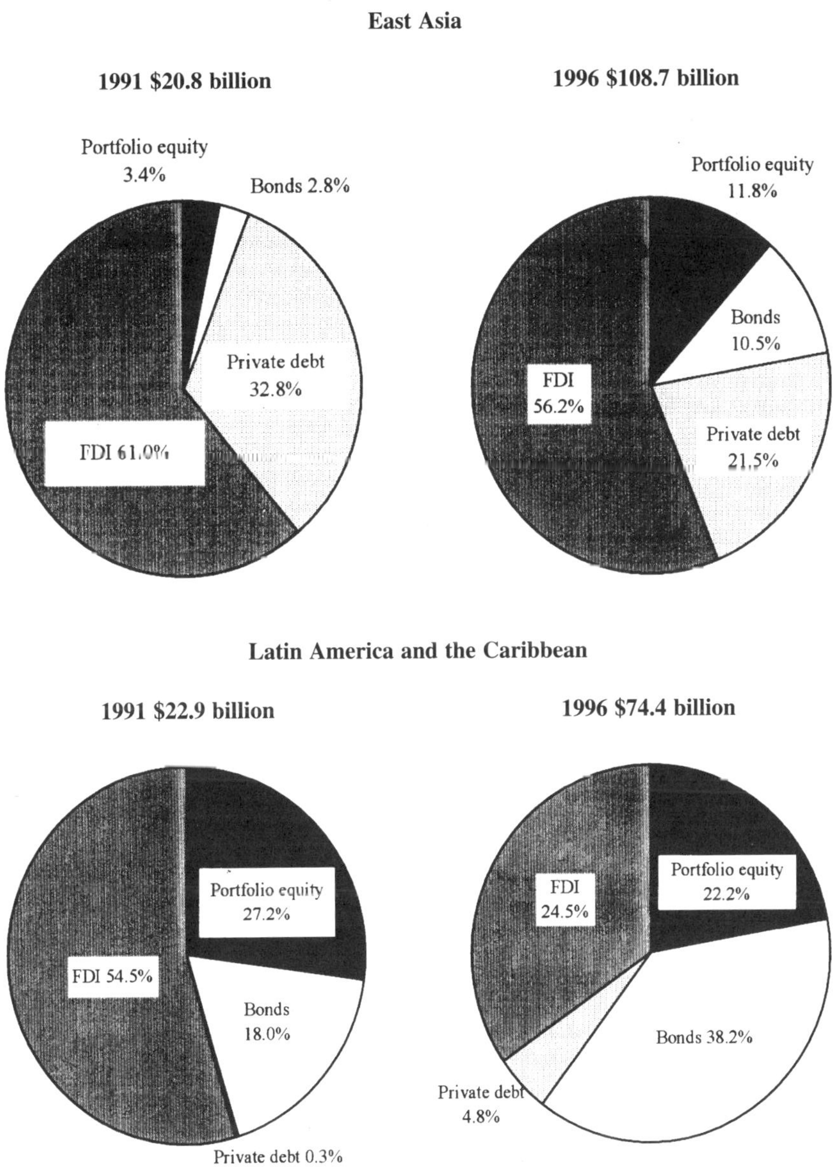

Note: Country groups are defined according to the World Bank's Debt Reporting System.
Source: World Bank, *Global Development Finance*. Vol. 1, 1997.

The rapid increase in direct investment in Asia since the beginning of the 1990s was a major source of funds supporting Asia's economic development. Unlike other forms of fund inflows, direct investment is the most stable source of funds and can directly help to expand production capacity because it has low market liquidity and because it reflects long- and medium-term corporate strategies. Net inflow of funds through direct investment in Asia amounted to an estimated $61.1 billion in 1996. This represents 56.2 percent of net long-term private fund inflows into Asia and 55.8 percent of direct investment in the entire developing world.

The yen's appreciation in the first half of the 1990s acted to revive direct investment by Japanese companies in Asia. In terms of its importance to Japanese companies, the Asian region changed from an export-production base into a market for finished products. Reflecting this shift, the investment boom was concentrated in China rather than in the Asian NIEs and the ASEAN countries, in sharp contrast to the previous boom after the Plaza Accord of 1985. Emerging multinational corporations in the Asian NIEs (mostly owned by overseas Chinese) also turned their eyes toward China instead of the ASEAN countries. Direct investment in China amounted to $42.3 billion in 1996 and accounted for 69 percent of the inflow of direct investment into Asia.

As Asian stock markets develop and become more and more open to foreign investors, stock investment has become an important channel for the inflow of funds into Asia. The inflow of funds into Asia through stock markets soared from only $700 million in 1988 to $18.1 billion in 1993. Since the Mexican crisis in late 1994, however, it slowed to an estimated $12.9 billion in 1996.

AVOIDING THE DUTCH DISEASE

A sustained increase in the inflow of funds could weaken the export competitiveness of the host country by pushing up its real exchange rate through either an appreciation of the nominal exchange rate or higher inflation. This phenomenon is analogous to the so-called "Dutch disease," in which the discovery of some natural resource, such as oil, tends to drive up the real exchange rate and cause the domestic manufacturing sector to shrink (see Appendix).[1] By lowering interest rates and boosting the money supply, inflow of funds similarly pushes up domestic demand and the real exchange rate. The appreciation of the real exchange rate in turn increases the production of non-tradable goods (services) at the expense of tradable goods (manufacturing). The reverse takes place when the resulting deterioration in the current account balance prompts foreign investors to withdraw their funds. In some Latin American countries, appreciation and devaluation have occurred in cycles, causing real exchange rates to fluctuate widely.

In the Dutch disease model, the stability of the real exchange rate is an important factor determining macroeconomic stability. Until the currency crisis in the summer of 1997, real effective exchange rates in Asian countries had remained relatively stable despite active capital movement, in sharp contrast to the wide fluctuation of real effective exchange rates in Latin America (as measured by J. P. Morgan's Trade Weighted Currency Index).

Four factors helped Asian countries to avoid the Dutch disease in the face of massive capital inflows. First, a large proportion of the inflow of funds into Asia was in the form of direct investment. The resulting increase in production capacity and thus aggregate supply helped curb upward pressure on real exchange rates. In contrast, the inflow into Latin America includes more speculative, short-term funds which tend to increase consumption and reduce domestic savings as asset prices increase to create a bubble economy. Thus, capital inflow acted as a supplement to domestic savings in Asia but as a substitute for domestic savings in Latin America.

Second, prudent management of fiscal policies also ensured economic stability in Asian countries. Indonesia, Thailand, and Singapore, for example, based their macroeconomic policies on fiscal austerity. This implies an increase in government sector savings, which worked to pull down interest rates and exchange rates and to weaken the pressure for fund inflow.

Third, in Asian countries, as compared with Latin American countries, a large part of the inflow of funds tended to help expand imports rather than domestic demand (thus reducing the income multiplier effect). This was particularly true for direct foreign investment which induced imports of capital equipment and parts from investing countries such as Japan.

Finally, since Asian nations loosely link their currencies to the dollar, the appreciation of the yen since 1985 held down effective rates. However, fluctuation in the exchange rate of major currencies (notably the yen) against the dollar has destabilized effective exchange rates. The sharp depreciation of the yen against the dollar since mid-1995 led to over valuation of the Asian currencies in effective terms, paving the way for the currency crisis that erupted in the summer of 1997 (see chapter 2).

POLICY OPTIONS IN THE SHORT TERM

In the short term, measures available to Asian countries to minimize the side effects of rapid capital inflow include (Figure 1.2):

- tightening regulations on capital transactions to prevent the inflow of funds,
- allowing local currencies to appreciate to reduce inflationary pressure,
- intervening in the exchange market to stabilize exchange rates (to maintain fixed rates) while at the same time offsetting (sterilizing) the resulting increase in the money supply through monetary policy intervention, and
- intervening in the exchange market without sterilization.

In practice, Asian countries often employ combinations of these measures. These countries fall into four groups according to the weights they put on the four options: (1) strictly regulating capital transactions (China), (2) tolerating exchange rate appreciation (Singapore), (3) targeting exchange rate and money supply objectives simultaneously through sterilized intervention (Malaysia, Thailand, and Indonesia), and (4) stabilizing exchange rates without resorting to sterilization (Hong Kong).

Restrictions on Capital Inflow

In countries where the liberalization of capital transactions is still at an early stage, the quantity and form of incoming funds have been subject to strict institutional regulation. The inflow of funds is thus checked before it touches shore, insulating the domestic economy. In countries where capital liberalization has reached an advanced stage, capital movement is sometimes regulated in emergencies through temporary measures, notably by regulations targeting overseas fund raising by the banking sector. An apt example of the former group of countries is China, which still maintains strict regulations on a wide range of capital transactions, whereas a typical example of the latter group is Indonesia, where inflow and outflow of funds are free in principle. Malaysia and Thailand lie somewhere in between.

Capital inflow can be controlled by either direct or indirect measures. Direct measures include restrictions on the acquisition of domestic securities or bank deposits by non-residents and overseas fund-raising activities, forward foreign exchange transaction, and open foreign exchange positions of banks. Indirect measures include taxing short-term overseas borrowings and imposing higher reserve requirements and withholding taxes on bank deposits by non-residents.

FIGURE 1.2
Policy Options to Cope with Capital Inflow

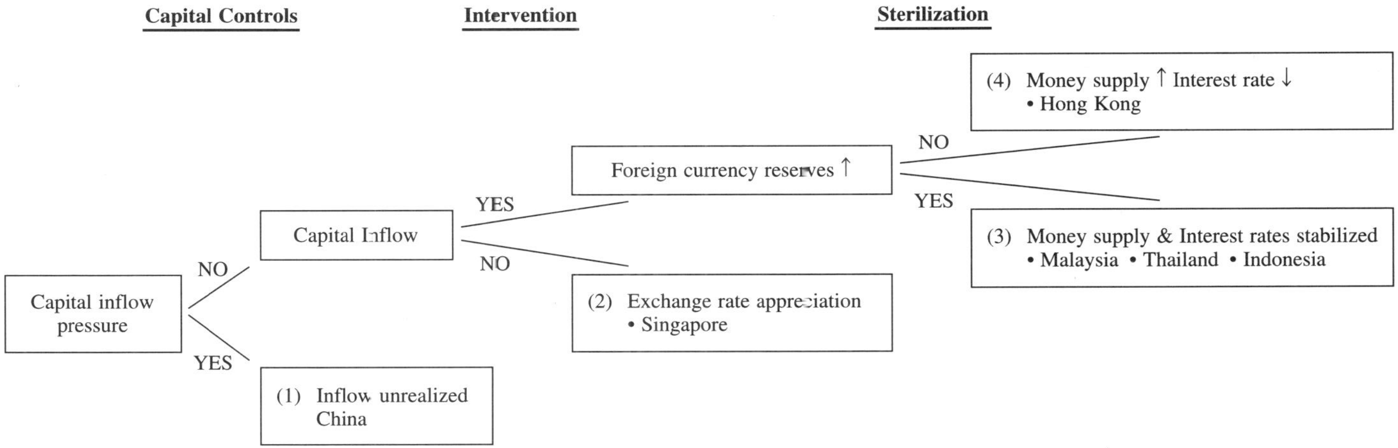

Type of Transaction	Market Means (Indirect)	Regulatory Means (Direct)
International	• Intervention • Exchange rate appreciation • Widening exchange rate band	• Quantitative control and tax on residents' overseas fund raising and non-residents deposits and securities acquisitions • Ceilings on banks' net open foreign exchange positions
Domestic	• Open market operations • Central bank securities issue • Reserve requirements • Official discount rate operations	• Window guidance • Ceiling on lending by sector

Exchange Rate Policy

When monetary authorities choose to cope with capital inflows without using capital controls, they face the choice between stabilizing the exchange rate by intervention or allowing it to appreciate. Although most Asian currencies are pegged loosely to the dollar, exchange rate policy still plays an important role in achieving macroeconomic objectives such as price stability and external balance.

A cross section comparison among East Asian countries shows that there is a stable trade off relation between inflation rates and exchange rates (Figure 1.3). Countries with currencies appreciating against the dollar, such as Japan, Taiwan, and Singapore, have low inflation rates, while countries with currencies depreciating against the dollar, such as China, Indonesia, and the Philippines, have high inflation rates. The former group of countries, which have strong preferences for price stability, are more likely to allow their currencies to appreciate as a mean to cope with capital inflows.

To curb speculative capital flow, some Asian countries have widened the band for exchange rate fluctuation while maintaining a fixed-rate or a crawling peg system. A wider band increases the risk of short-term investment by foreign investors compared with a purely fixed exchange rate system. So long as potential investors are convinced that the exchange rate can be kept within the band, however, long-term investment (foreign direct investment, for example) would not be adversely affected. Widening the band for exchange rate fluctuation also weakens the synchronization of domestic and foreign interest rates, enhancing the effectiveness of monetary policy. Indeed, although the Malaysian ringgit has shown irregular fluctuations in the short term, it has been relatively stable over the long term, suggesting that the government may be targeting an implicit exchange rate band.

Intervention without Sterilization

The Mundell-Fleming model suggests that under a fixed exchange rate system with perfect capital mobility, monetary policy has no impact on domestic interest rates or on output (Appendix). Uncovered interest rate parity holds and domestic interest rates synchronize with their counterparts overseas. Under such circumstances, there is little room for sterilization.

This is illustrated by the case of Hong Kong, which has pegged its currency (the Hong Kong dollar) to the U.S. dollar since October 1983 and

FIGURE 1.3
Correlation between Inflation and Exchange Rates

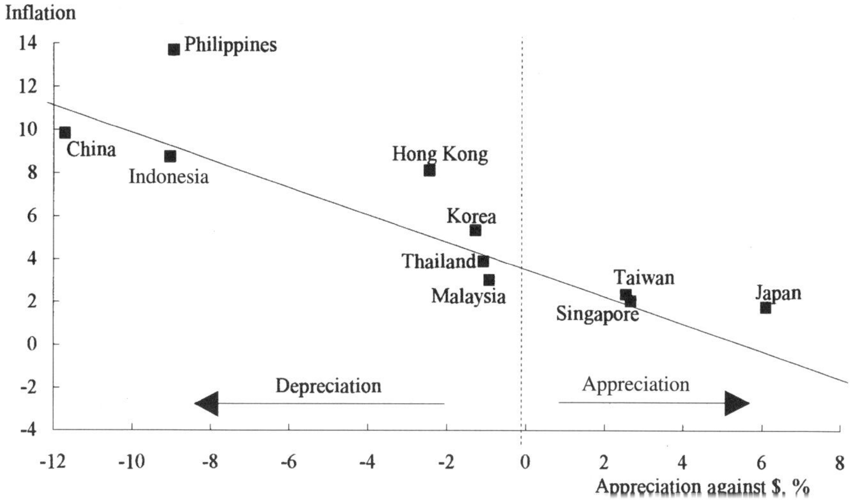

Note: Annual average for the period 1982–94
Source: Compiled by Nomura Research Institute based on official statistics.

has maintained no capital controls. Interest rates in Hong Kong follow U.S. trends very closely, reflecting arbitration between the two markets (Figure 1.4). An inflow of funds to Hong Kong will lead to an increase in the money supply (and foreign exchange reserves) without affecting domestic interest rates.[2]

More generally, in most Asian countries where uncovered interest parity does not hold, unsterilized intervention implies lower interest rates and a weaker exchange rate than in the case of sterilized intervention, as suggested by the portfolio balance model (Appendix). Intervention without sterilization is therefore more inflationary and less preferred as a means to cope with capital inflow in those countries.

Sterilized Intervention

Until 1996 intervention designed to stabilize exchange rates in the face of massive capital inflow had led to a rapid increase in the foreign exchange reserves of Asian countries (Figure 1.5). The resulting increase in high powered money might cause the entire money supply to swell through the credit multiplier effect. The rise in foreign exchange reserves, however, did not lead to a proportional increase in the money supply, thanks to sterilization efforts by Asian monetary authorities.[3]

High powered money increases with an increase in either net domestic assets (domestic factor) or foreign exchange reserves (overseas factor) of the central bank. In almost all Asian countries, the contribution of the overseas factor to the growth rate of high powered money was strongly negatively correlated with the contribution of the domestic factor. Thus the two tended to offset each other. This phenomenon indicates that the monetary authorities of those countries largely succeeded in sterilizing increases (decreases) in high-powered money resulting from increases (decreases) in foreign currency reserves by reducing (expanding) net domestic assets accompanying capital inflow (outflow).

Needless to say, the instruments of sterilization in a broad sense coincide with the monetary policy instruments used to control money supply. Indirect measures for this purpose include open market operations, issuance of central bank securities, transfer of public deposits from private banks to the central bank, official discount rate operations, and manipulation of reserve requirements. Direct measures include window guidance and moral suasion.

FIGURE 1.4
Synchronization between Hong Kong and U.S. Interest Rates

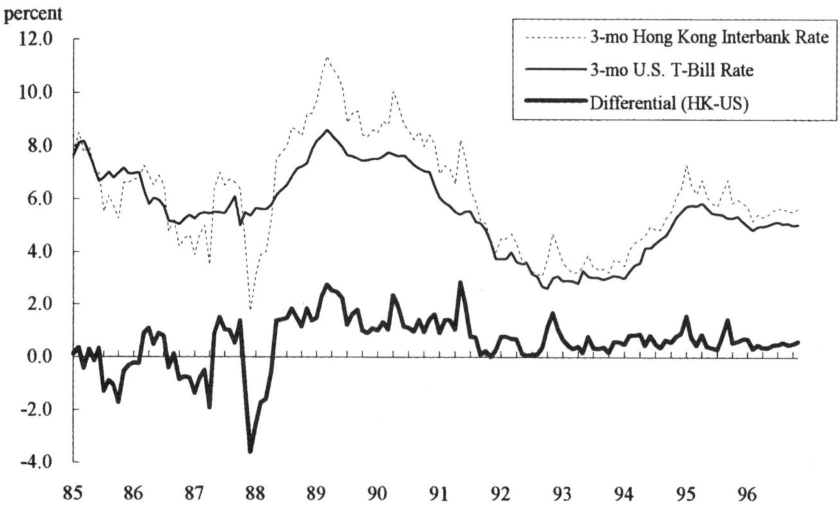

FIGURE 1.5
Balance of Payments and the Increase in Foreign Exchange Reserves in Asia's Major Debtor Countries

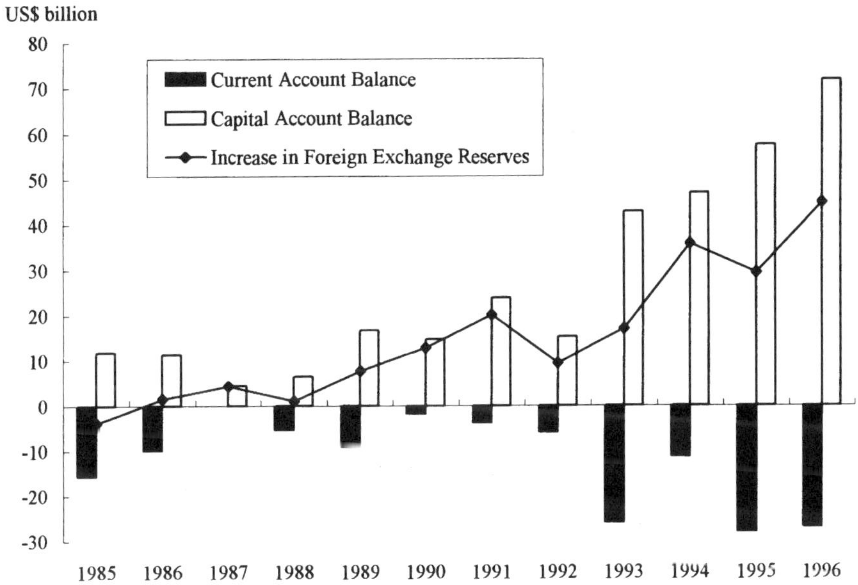

Note: Total of China, Indonesia, Malaysia, the Philippines, and Thailand. Foreign exchange reserves of China excluding holdings by the Bank of China.
Source: Compiled by Nomura Research Institute based on International Monetary Fund, *International Financial Statistics*.

Apart from achieving macroeconomic stabilization, sterilized intervention is also intended to maintain the health of the financial system by keeping bank lending from expanding as a result of inflow of funds. When the financial system is weak because of inadequacies in banks' risk appraisal and liquidity control, excessive liquidity generated in the course of capital inflow can result in expanded lending to speculative activities in real estate and stock markets. In that case, sterilization of the inflow of funds is an effective means of preventing the bad debts and bank failures that could result from a reverse flow of funds and the bursting of a bubble economy.

The effectiveness of sterilization (or simply the ability to control the money supply) is proportional to the scope for domestic interest rates to deviate from overseas interest rates and for interest rates in the banking sector to deviate from open market rates. On one hand, as suggested by the portfolio balance model, when there are restrictions on capital flow and/or when domestic bonds are poor substitutes for foreign bonds, uncovered interest parity between domestic and foreign interest rates does not hold and sterilized intervention would be highly effective in controlling the domestic money supply. Poor substitutability between domestic and foreign bonds usually reflects the presence of various risks (exchange rate risk and country risk, for example). The risk premium required to equalize the attractiveness of domestic and foreign bonds for investors depends on the relative supply of various assets, including domestic money. On the other hand, when interest rates in the banking sector are tightly regulated and/or when direct financing through open securities markets and indirect financing through the banking sector are poor substitutes, sterilization by tightening credit availability in the banking sector would be effective in controlling the money supply.[4] Poor substitutability between bank loans and securities usually reflects the high costs of arbitration between the two sectors for both investors and borrowers. Small- and medium-sized companies, for example, have no access to fund raising in the securities market and have to rely on bank loans as their major source of external funds.

EVALUATING VARIOUS POLICY OPTIONS

Should Restrictions on Capital Flow be Introduced?

The introduction of ad hoc restrictions on capital inflows may not be desirable for the following reasons. First, it is difficult to distinguish speculative funds from funds that are linked more directly to productive activities. Second, the costs of monitoring may be high and investors usually can find ways to bypass those restrictions. Third, some overseas investors may suffer unexpected losses resulting from such restrictions, and this may have an adverse effect on their confidence in the host country's economic policy. To reduce such side effects, restrictions should be limited to new transactions and removed as soon as possible.

Currency Appreciation Versus Sterilized Intervention

Several factors influence the key choice between whether to stabilize exchange rates through sterilized intervention or to allow exchange rates to appreciate. First, since there is a trade off between exchange rates and prices, exchange rate appreciation should be tolerated if price stability is given a higher priority as a policy objective. Asian countries can be divided into two groups according to whether they give priority to internal or external equilibrium. The first group includes countries that tend to control import prices by raising the value of their currencies to combat higher inflation. This policy stance is seen among creditor nations with ample foreign exchange reserves, such as Taiwan and Singapore (Figure 1.6). The other group includes countries that tend to focus on external equilibrium and cope with the erosion of competitiveness resulting from higher inflation by devaluing their currencies. This policy stance is conspicuous among debtor nations, such as Indonesia, the Philippines, and South Korea (Figure 1.7).

Second, some countries have chosen to peg their exchange rates to a specific currency in order to enhance the credibility of monetary policy. For example, Hong Kong has pegged its currency to the U.S. dollar since October 1983 in order to maintain market confidence prior to and following the 1997 reversion of sovereignty to China, at the cost of high inflation. This contrasts with Singapore, a country known for stable prices, which has successfully held down inflation by adopting a more flexible exchange rate policy. In between, Thailand had pegged the baht to a basket consisting of major currencies until the shift to a managed float system in July 1997, while Indonesia has adopted a crawling peg system in which the rupiah is allowed to depreciate against the dollar at a steady rate.

Third, in countries highly dependent on international trade, domestic prices move more in tandem with changes in overseas prices and exchange rates (purchasing power parity holds). In the case of Singapore and Hong Kong, it is difficult to keep real exchange rates at artificially low levels. This lessens the advantages of applying exchange rate policies to maintain competitiveness (and eventually current account balance).

Fourth, the scope for discretion in monetary policy (by altering domestic interest rates) is narrow in open economies with free capital mobility and high in countries with restrictions on capital transactions. A typical example of the former group is Singapore which has little choice but to rely on exchange rate appreciation to achieve price stability. South Korea and China belong to the latter group and enjoy more room in achieving exchange rate and interest rate targets simultaneously.

Criteria for Choosing the Optimal Policy

The optimal policy response differs depending on whether the capital inflow is temporary or sustainable over the long term. In the case of short-

FIGURE 1.6
Inflation and the Singapore Dollar Rate

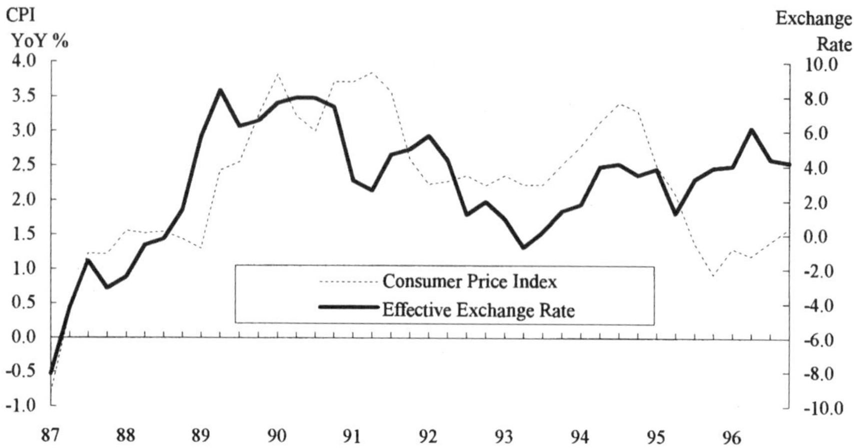

Source: Compiled by NRI based on IMF, *International Financial Statistics*.

FIGURE 1.7
Current Account Balance and the Korean Won

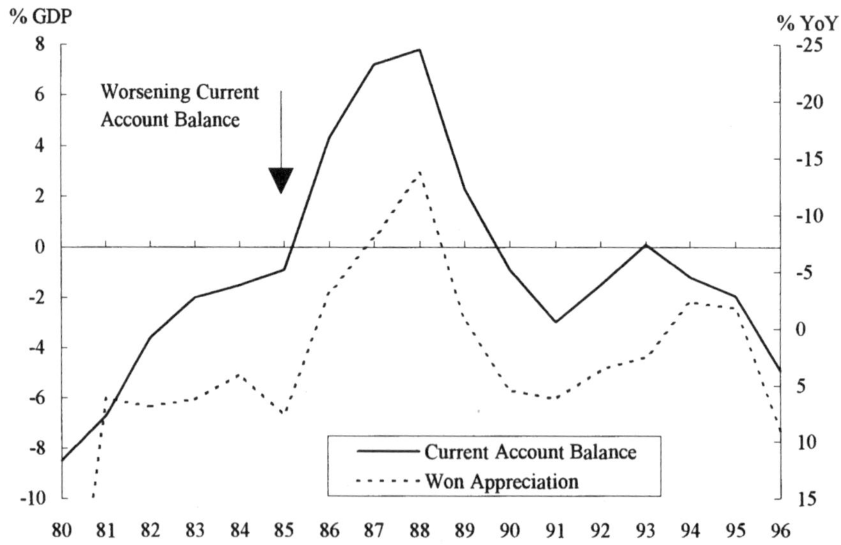

Note: Current account balance is expressed as a share of GDP. Won/dollar exchange rate is expressed as year over year change at the end of each year.
Source: Compiled by NRI based on IMF, *International Financial Statistics*.

term speculative inflow, sterilized intervention to stabilize both the exchange rate and money supply is desirable. At the same time, widening the band for exchange rate fluctuation should enhance the effectiveness of monetary policy while deterring speculative inflow. In the case of sustained inflow, the resulting appreciation of the real exchange rate can take the form of higher inflation or currency appreciation. The optimal trade off will depend on the policy objective (preference for price stability or external balance) and on the economic structure (openness of capital and goods markets) of the country concerned. At the same time, fiscal tightening should help reduce upward pressure on the real exchange rate.

The currency crisis that hit most of the countries in East Asia during 1997 and 1998 served to confirmed the major implications of this analysis. The origins of the crisis and its lessons for coping with capital flows are discussed in the next two chapters.

Notes

1 The analogy between the effect of capital inflow and the Dutch disease has been drawn by Corbo and Hernandez (1994).

2 Hong Kong's exchange rate system is a form of currency board system. The Government's Exchange Fund promises to issue and redeem the Hong Kong dollar at the parity rate (US$1=HK$7.8) to an infinite amount. Under this "passive intervention" mechanism, the parity rate can be maintained automatically. The implication of an inflow of capital for the money supply, however, is the same as "active intervention" in the foreign exchange market.

3 Sterilization is also used to cope with an expansion of foreign exchange reserves and money supply resulting from rising current account surpluses, as in Taiwan and South Korea in the latter half of the 1980s.

4 See Fry (1993) and Dooley and Chinn (1994).

References

Corbo, V. and L. Hernandez. 1994. "Macroeconomic Adjustment to Capital Inflows". *Policy Research Working Paper* No. 1377. Washington: The World Bank.

Corden, W. M. and J. P. Neary. 1982. "Booming Sector and De-industrialization in a Small Open Economy". *Economic Journal* 92 (December): 825–48.

Dooley, M. P. and M. Chinn. 1995. "Financial Repression and Capital Mobility: Why Capital Flows and Covered Interest Rate Differential

Fail to Measure Capital Market Integration". National Bureau of Economic Research *Working Paper* No. 5347.
Fry, M. 1993. "Financial Opening and Monetary Control in Pacific Basin Developing Market Economies". In *Financial Opening: Policy Issues and Experiences in Developing Countries*, ed. H. Reisen and B. Fischer. Paris: Organization for Economic Co-operation and Development (OECD).
Gartner, M. 1993. *Macroeconomics under Flexible Exchange Rates*. Hertfordshire: Harvester Wheatsheaf.
Krugman, Paul. 1994. "The Myth of Asia's Miracle". *Foreign Affairs* 73 (Nov./Dec.): 62–78.

APPENDIX

Analytical Approaches to Coping with Capital Flow

The impact of capital inflow and policy response can be analysed at three levels: the long term (when both price and quantity in the goods market adjust), the medium term (when quantity adjusts in the goods market with price remaining constant), the short term (when asset markets but not the goods market adjust). These three levels correspond, respectively, to the Dutch disease model, the Mundell-Fleming model, and the asset, or portfolio balance, model discussed below. For a theoretical analysis of the Dutch disease, see Corden and Neary (1982). The Mundell-Fleming model and the portfolio balance model are discussed in most standard textbooks on international economics. The presentation here closely follows Gartner (1993).

The Dutch Disease Model

The Dutch disease model is illustrated in Figure 1.A1, which depicts the tradable and non-tradable sectors for a small open economy. Here exports and imports are grouped together as tradable goods by assuming that the relative price between them is constant and exogenous. An increase in the relative price of the non-tradable good (which is equivalent to appreciation in the real exchange rate in this simple framework) would provide incentives for factors of production (labour and capital) to move from the tradable sector to the non-tradable sector (movement along the production possibility curve in Part a), giving rise to an upward sloping supply curve for non-tradable goods (Part b). Given a downward sloping demand curve, the equilibrium level of the real exchange rate is determined at the point where the demand curve and the supply curve intersect one another.

FIGURE 1.A1
Capital Inflow and the Dutch Disease

Production Possibility Curve

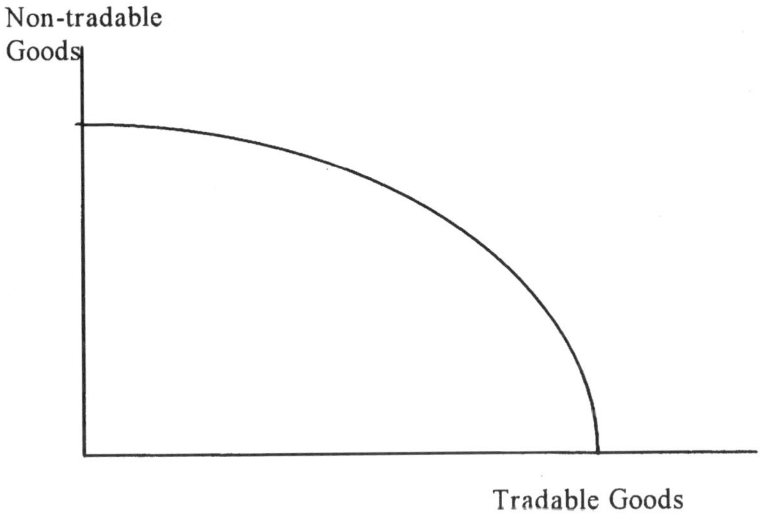

Impact of Capital Inflow

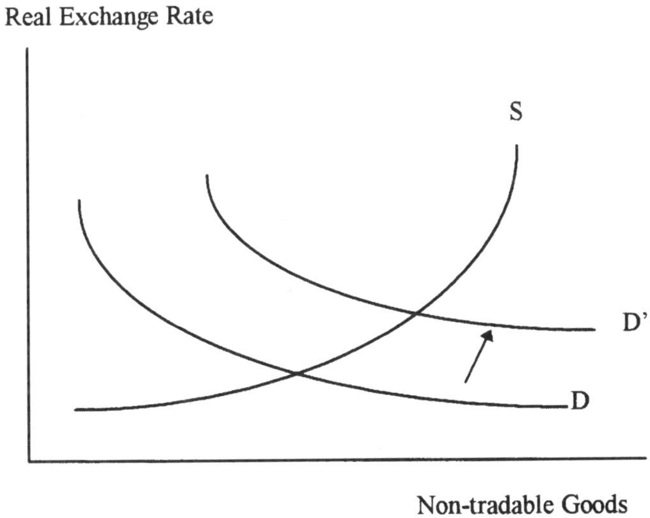

Source: Nomura Research Institute.

An increase in the inflow of funds, by raising the money supply while reducing interest rates, boosts investment and income and shifts the demand curve to the right. As a result, the equilibrium real exchange rate appreciates and the non-tradable sector expands at the expense of the tradable sector. This crowding out, however, can be avoided if the inflow of funds, also leads to an expansion of production capacity by boosting investment and shifts the supply curve to the right (not shown).

Appreciation of the real exchange rate following capital inflow can be avoided by either reducing demand or increasing supply. The former is accomplished by fiscal and monetary tightening (which shifts the demand curve to the left) and the latter requires boosting savings and productivity (which shifts the supply curve to the right). As real exchange rate appreciation can take the form of appreciation of the nominal exchange rate and/or an increase in the domestic price level (and thus higher inflation), the policy authorities have to choose an optimal combination of the two based on this trade off relation.

The Mundell-Fleming Model

The Mundell-Fleming model, which is an extension of the Keynesian IS-LM model to an open economy, has been widely used to analyse the effectiveness of macroeconomic policy when capital mobility is high. In its simplest form, it assumes 1) price rigidity in the goods market, 2) perfect capital mobility, 3) perfect substitutability between domestic and foreign bonds, 4) exogenous overseas interest rate (small country assumption), and 5) static expectations. Assumptions 2 and 3 together imply that uncovered interest rate parity holds.

In Figure 1.A2, the horizontal axis denotes output and the vertical axis denotes the interest rate. The equilibrium conditions in the goods market and the money market can be denoted by a downward sloping IS curve and an upward sloping LM curve, respectively. Based on the assumption of perfect capital mobility, the equilibrium condition for the balance of payments can be denoted by a horizontal curve FE. The equilibrium levels of output and interest rates are determined at the point where the three curves intersect. The impact of changes in the overseas interest rate and fiscal and monetary policies (exogenous variables) on domestic output and interest rates (endogenous variables) hinges crucially on the assumption concerning the exchange rate system.

In the case of a fixed exchange rate system, a decline in the overseas interest rate (downward shift in the FE curve) induces an inflow of funds until the domestic interest rate converges to the overseas level (Part a).

FIGURE 1.A2
Mundell-Fleming Model

Decline in (Foreign) Interest Rate

(a) Fixed exchange rate

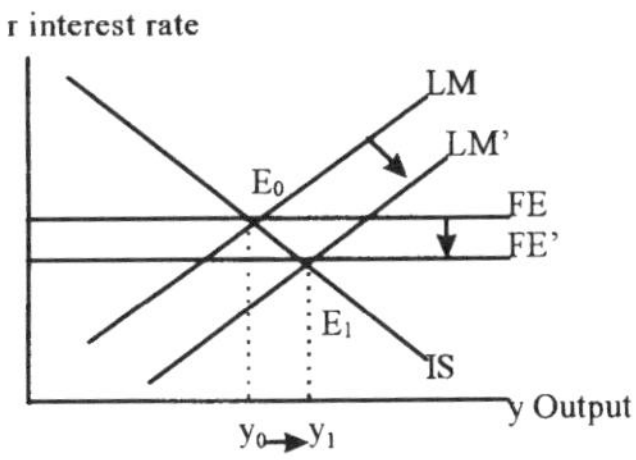

*Money supply increases as a result of capital Inflow (LM curve shifts to the right).
*Decline in interest rate stimulates output.
*Trade deficit financed by capital inflow.

(d) Flexible exchange rate

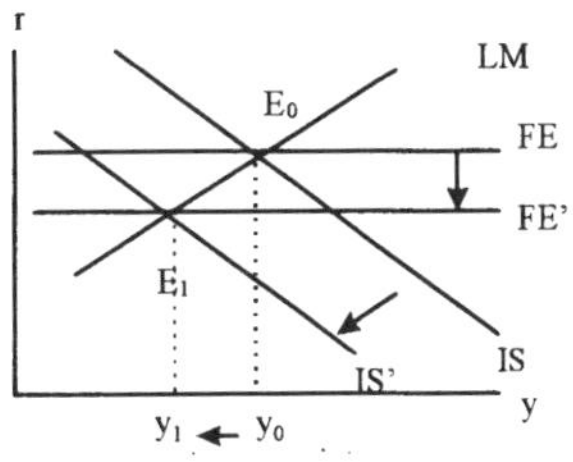

*Exchange rate appreciates as a result of capital inflow.
*Exports and output decline (IS curve shifts to the left).

Fiscal Expansion

(b) Fixed exchange rate

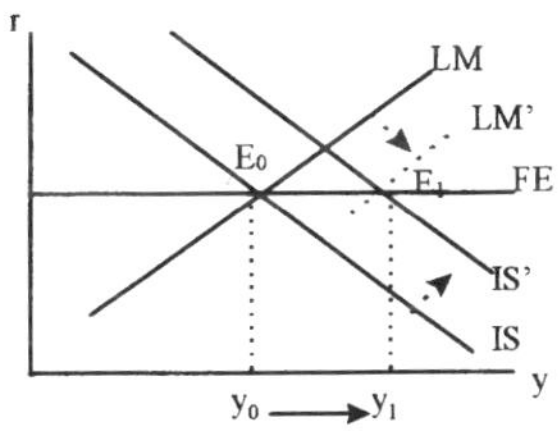

*Fiscal policy effective.
*Money supply increases as a result of capita Inflow (LM curve shifts to the right).
*Trade deficit financed by capital inflow.

(e) Flexible exchange rate

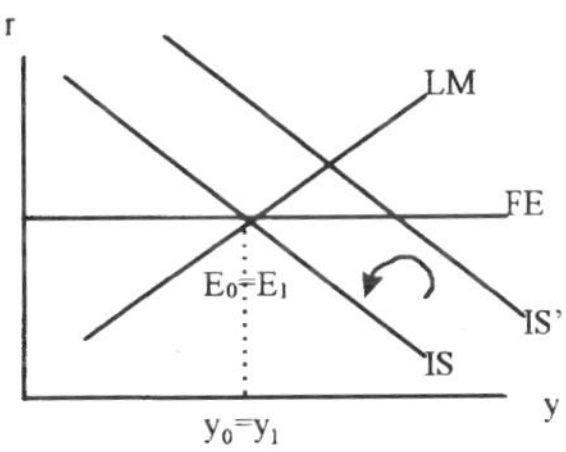

*Fiscal policy ineffective.
*Exchange rate appreciates as a result of capital inflow.
*Exports crowded out. (IS curve returns to original position).

Monetary Expansion

(c) Fixed exchange rate

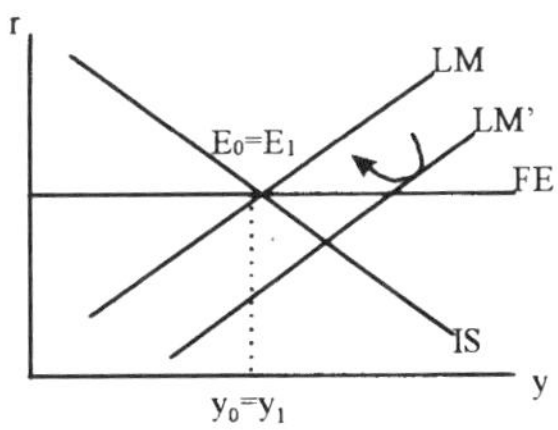

*Monetary policy ineffective.
*Monetary supply declines as a result of a capital outflow.
*LM curve returns to original position.

(f) Flexible exchange rate

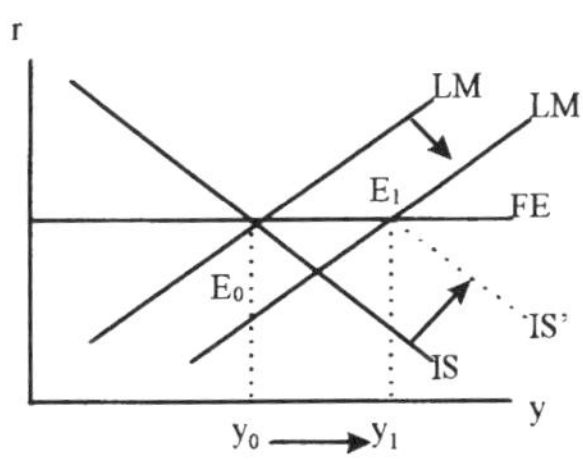

*Monetary policy effective.
*Exchange rate depreciates as a result of capital outflow.
*Exports increase. (IS curve shifts to the right).

Money supply increases in this process, shifting the LM curve to the right, while output rises as the decline in the interest rate boosts demand. Likewise, an expansionary fiscal policy (a shift of the IS curve to the right) initially puts upward pressure on the interest rate, and the resulting inflow of capital expands the money supply (shifting the LM curve to the right). Equilibrium output is attained at a higher level (Part b). Thus under a fixed exchange rate system, a decline in the overseas interest rate and an expansionary fiscal policy are effective in stimulating output. In contrast, an expansionary monetary policy (a shift of the LM curve to the right) initially puts downward pressure on the interest rate and induces an outflow of capital. As a result, money supply declines (LM curve shifts to the left) until both output and interest rate are back to the original level (Part c). The inability to reduce the interest rate in the face of perfect capital mobility cuts the link between money supply and output, rendering monetary policy ineffective. This also means that monetary policy is impotent in sterilization of the money supply as a means to cope with speculative capital flow.

The results obtained for a fixed exchange rate system are reversed for a flexible exchange rate system. First, a decline in the overseas interest rate (a downward shift in the FE curve) induces an inflow of funds, pulling down the interest rate while pushing up the exchange rate. The decline in net exports resulting from the appreciation (the shift of the IS curve to the right) more than offsets the positive effect of the lower interest rate on investment, and output actually declines (Part d). Second, an increase in fiscal spending (a shift of the IS curve to the right) puts upward pressure on the interest rate and induces an inflow of capital, which in turn pushes up the exchange rate (Part e). The positive effect of rising fiscal spending on output is fully offset by a decline in net exports (with the IS curve shifting back to the original position). Third, an expansionary monetary policy (a shift of the LM curve to the right) puts downward pressure on the interest rate and induces an outflow of capital and a depreciation of the exchange rate, which in turn boosts net exports (Part f). Thus, unlike in a closed economy, for an open economy under a flexible exchange rate system, an expansionary monetary policy boosts output through the linkage between exchange rate and net exports instead of through that between the interest rate and investment.

The Portfolio Balance Model

The portfolio balance model focuses on equilibrium in the asset market. In its simplest form it assumes 1) perfect capital mobility, 2) imperfect

FIGURE 1.A3
Effectiveness of Monetary Policy According to the Portfolio Balance Model

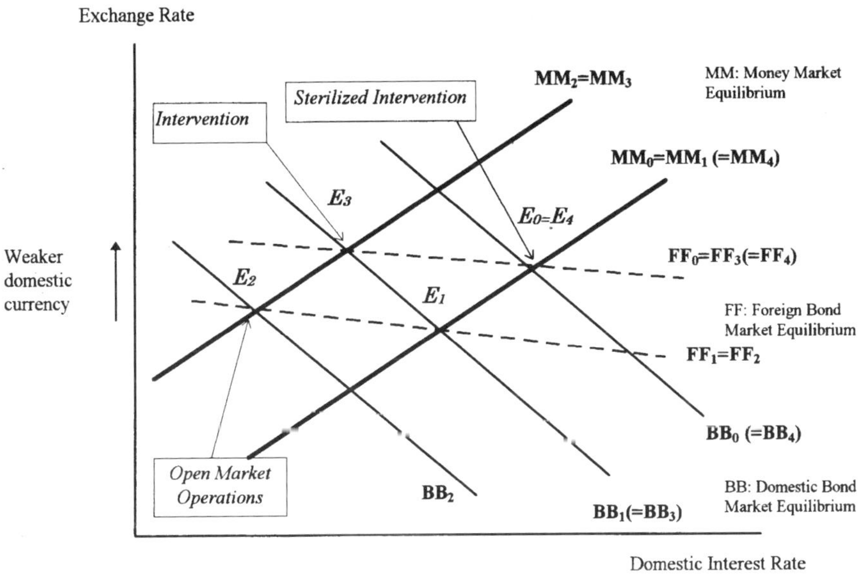

Notes: 1) E_0 denotes equilibrium before capital inflow; E_1 denotes equilibrium when local currency is allowed to appreciate; E_2 denotes equilibrium with open market operations; E_3 denotes equilibrium with intervention; and E_4 denotes equilibrium with sterilized intervention. Subscripts for MM, BB, and FF correspond to these four cases.
2) Relations among open market operations, intervention and sterilized intervention.
Exchange of assets under open market operations, intervention, and sterilized intervention is shown below:

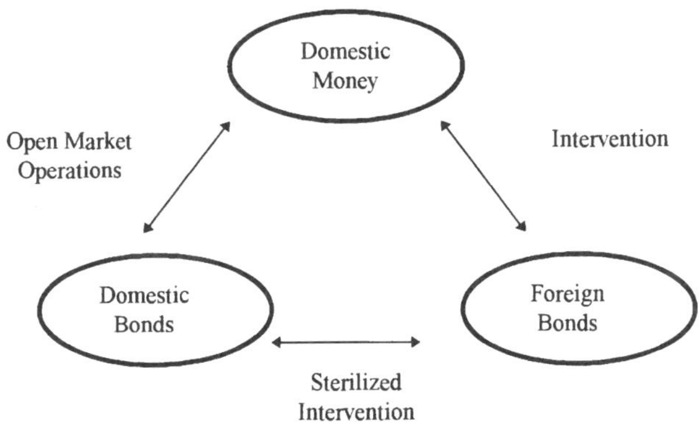

substitutability between domestic and foreign bonds, 3) an exogenous overseas interest rate (small country assumption), and 4) static (or exogenous) expectations. The assumption of imperfect asset substitution implies that uncovered interest rate parity no longer holds. The domestic interest rate (after adjusting for expectations of exchange rate changes) can therefore deviate from its overseas counterpart, the differential being the risk premium. The effectiveness of monetary policy is enhanced as this risk premium can be altered by changing the relative supply of domestic money, domestic bonds, and foreign bonds.

The basic components of the portfolio balance model are illustrated in Figure 1.A3. Given the equilibrium schedules for the money market (MM_0), the domestic bond market (BB_0) and foreign bond market (FF_0), the equilibrium level of exchange rate (r_0) and interest rate (i_0) are determined at the point where the three curves intersect one another (E_0). Capital inflow and various policy responses alter the exchange rate and the interest rate by shifting one or more of these schedules. Under a flexible exchange rate regime, an inflow of funds shifts the equilibrium point to E_1, leading to an appreciation of the local currency and a decline in the domestic interest rate.

In the context of the portfolio balance model, policy options to prevent an appreciation of the exchange rate accompanying an inflow of funds include monetary relaxation through open market operations, intervention (without sterilization), and sterilized intervention. First, monetary relaxation through open market operations (buying domestic bonds by issuing domestic money) helps to keep the exchange rate from appreciating, but the domestic interest rate would be dragged down even further (E_2). Second, intervention without sterilization (buying foreign bonds by issuing domestic money) weakens the exchange rate of the domestic currency and lowers the domestic interest rate, as in the case of monetary relaxation, but its impact on the exchange rate is relatively larger than on the interest rate (E_3). Finally, sterilized intervention (buying foreign bonds by issuing domestic bonds) weakens the exchange rate and raises the domestic interest rate, and can therefore be used to fully offset the impact of a capital inflow (E_4).

2

Asia's Currency Crisis and Its Implications for the Japanese Economy

C. H. Kwan

INTRODUCTION

The switch by the Thai government to a managed floating exchange rate regime on 2 July 1997 set off a sharp devaluation of the Thai baht that quickly spread to the currencies of neighboring countries and eventually culminated in a crisis infecting most countries in East Asia. Speculation by private investors served as a spark and deserves a share of the blame for the crisis. But more deep-rooted problems of the Asian economies constrained governments' ability to cope with external developments of the 1990s. In particular, Thailand's inflexible exchange rate regime and premature capital market liberalization hampered the responses to the weakening yen, the growing competition with China, and, of course, the massive capital flows. For most of the ASEAN countries and South Korea, the sharp currency depreciation aggravated an existing bad debt problem and brought on a credit crunch situation.

Although exports of the hardest hit countries are expected to pick up, very weak domestic demand will keep those economies in the doldrums, and economic recovery will require further financial support from overseas sources. To prevent another round of speculation, Asian countries with better economic fundamentals, notably China, should refrain from stimulating exports through currency devaluation.

Further turmoil in Asia will exert deflationary pressure on the global economy. In particular, Japan, which has developed strong ties with other Asian countries in recent years, is deemed to be most adversely affected.

Japan may be tempted to allow the yen to depreciate to stimulate its lackluster economy, but this will raise the risk of competitive devaluation among the major economic powers.

The Asian currency crisis should have taught the following lessons. First, developing countries should maintain appropriate control of capital flows until a sound banking system is in place and they should encourage FDI over short-term flows. Second, pegging to the dollar may no longer be consistent with macroeconomic stability in the Asian countries and they should pay more attention to stability against the currencies of major competitors, notably the Japanese yen. Third, to prevent the occurrence of similar crises in the future, Asian countries should maintain sound economic fundamentals, including a healthy level of foreign exchange reserves. Closer international cooperation among monetary authorities is needed to contain the contagion effect.

THE NATURE OF THAILAND'S CURRENCY CRISIS

What, then, went wrong in Thailand, where the crisis started? The Thai baht was overvalued before the devaluation, as can be confirmed by noting that Thailand's current account deficit, at about 8 percent of GNP in 1996, was comparable to that of Mexico before the currency crisis there in late 1994. The deficit build-up had taken place against a background of sharp depreciation of the yen against the U.S. dollar and growing competition with China as well as the massive capital inflows.

The Exchange-Rate Factor

Although the baht had edged down by about 4 percent against the dollar between the spring of 1995 and mid-1997 before the devaluation, the real effective exchange rate of the baht had appreciated by about 15 percent over the same period (Figure 2.1). This largely reflected the sharp appreciation of about 35 percent of the Thai baht against the Japanese yen. The exchange rate policy of pegging to a basket of currencies in which the dollar was very heavily weighted had constrained the government from allowing the baht to depreciate at a faster pace against the dollar to stimulate exports.

The slowdown of exports in most Asian countries since 1996 can largely be explained by the sharp depreciation of the yen against the dollar. Indeed, fluctuations in the yen-dollar rate have replaced the U.S. economic growth rate as the major factor determining short-term

FIGURE 2.1
The Diverging Baht

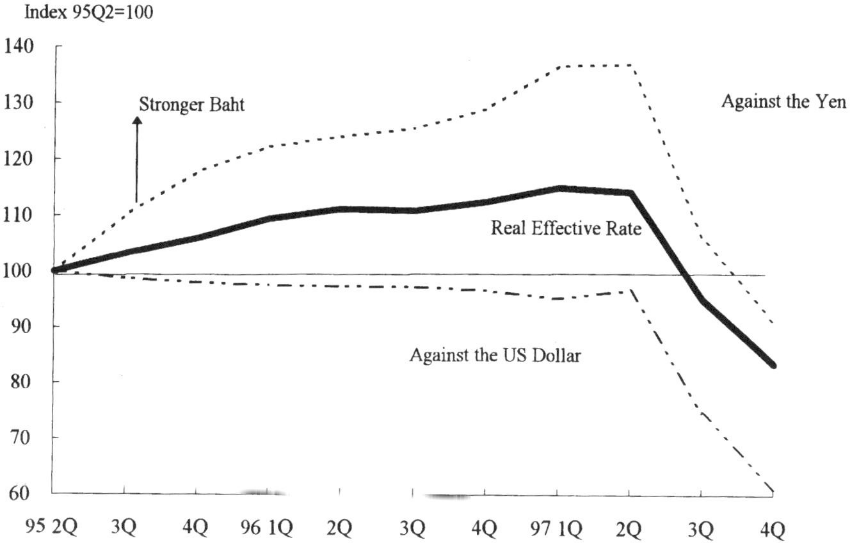

Source: Nomura Research Institute, from official statistics and *Trade Weighted Currency Index*, J.P. Morgan.

macroeconomic performance in the Asian countries since the Plaza Accord in 1985 (Kwan 1994). Given the Asian countries' exchange rate policy of pegging loosely to the dollar, a depreciation of the yen against the dollar also means a depreciation of the yen against other Asian currencies. By altering the relative prices of Japan and the other countries of Asia, it has an immense impact on the flow of international trade and investment as well as on the burden of debt repayment in the countries concerned.

A weaker yen affects economic growth in other Asian economies mainly through four channels: a slowdown in the inflow of foreign direct investment from Japan, a decline in export competitiveness with Japanese products, a reduction in the cost of imports from Japan, and in the cost of financing yen-denominated external debt. While the effects of the first two factors on the Asian economies are negative, they are partly offset by the positive effects of the last two factors.

Of these four transmission channels, the shift in export competitiveness is probably the most important in the short run. A depreciation of the yen against the dollar, by reducing Japanese export prices in dollar terms, makes Japanese exports less expensive than those from other Asian countries. As a result, exports from these countries become less competitive with Japanese products in international markets, as has been happening since 1996. The effect on exports is larger for the Asian NIEs, which have trade structures competitive with that of Japan, than for the ASEAN countries, which have trade structures complementary to that of Japan.

The hypothesis that pegging to the dollar should contribute to the economic stability of Asian countries has not been supported by theory or by experience. With their currencies pegged loosely to the dollar, economic growth has been highly vulnerable to fluctuations in the yen-dollar rate—picking up every time the yen appreciates against the dollar, and slowing down every time the yen depreciates against the dollar (Figure 2.2). Given the large impact of the fluctuation in the yen-dollar rate on economic growth, achieving macroeconomic stability requires paying more attention to stabilizing exchange rates against the Japanese yen. (This point is discussed in greater detail in the last section of the chapter.)

The China Factor

The failure of Thailand (and other ASEAN countries) to cope with growing competition from China by upgrading industrial structure may have been a major factor contributing to the region's currency crisis. In line with its level of economic development, Thailand, like other ASEAN countries, has a trade structure competitive with that of China (Figure 2.3). Competitive relations between nations can be characterized as a zero-sum game in which ones gain is the others loss.[1]

Although China accounts for only about 3 percent of Thailand's total trade, it has become an important factor determining economic performance in Thailand largely because the two countries compete with one another for export markets and inflows of foreign direct investment. Productivity growth in China's industrial sector reached nearly 20 percent a year over the last five years, far outpacing that in the ASEAN countries. The devaluation of the Chinese yuan at the beginning of 1994 also helped China expand its exports.[2] Indeed, since 1992, multinationals have favored China over the ASEAN countries as a destination to locate direct investment, while the ASEAN countries are losing share to China in international markets (particularly in labor-intensive products).

A better indicator of export competitiveness can be obtained by adjusting the real effective exchange rate to take into account changes in differentials in wages and productivity (that is, unit labor cost). The usefulness

FIGURE 2.2
The Yen-Dollar Rate and Asian Economic Growth

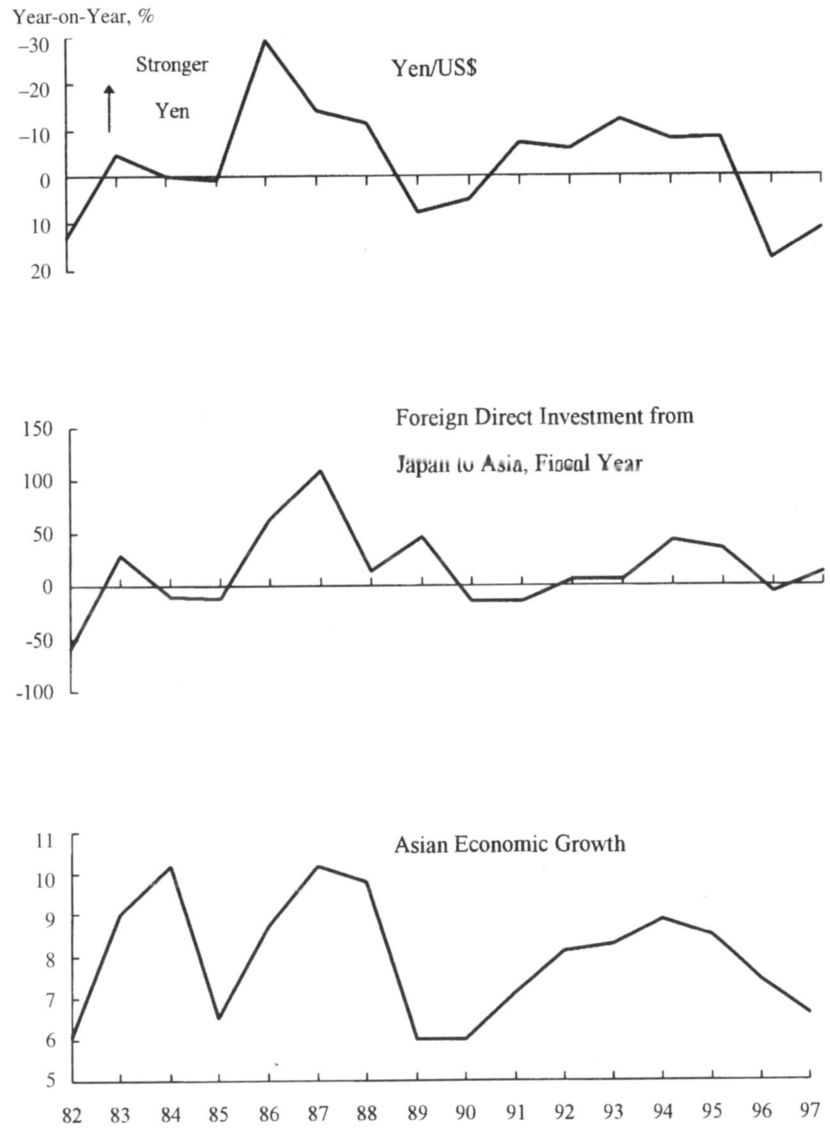

Notes: 1) Asia = NIEs + ASEAN + China.
2) Foreign direct investment for FY 1997 based on first-half figure.

Source: Nomura Research Institute, from official statistics.

of this indicator would be further enhanced if competitors' weight instead of simple trade weight were used in the calculation. By putting more emphasis on the China factor, the real effective exchange rate for the Thai baht so adjusted would imply that the over-valuation of the Thai baht had been larger than as suggested by the unadjusted index.

FIGURE 2.3
Trade Structure Correlation between China and Other Asian Countries

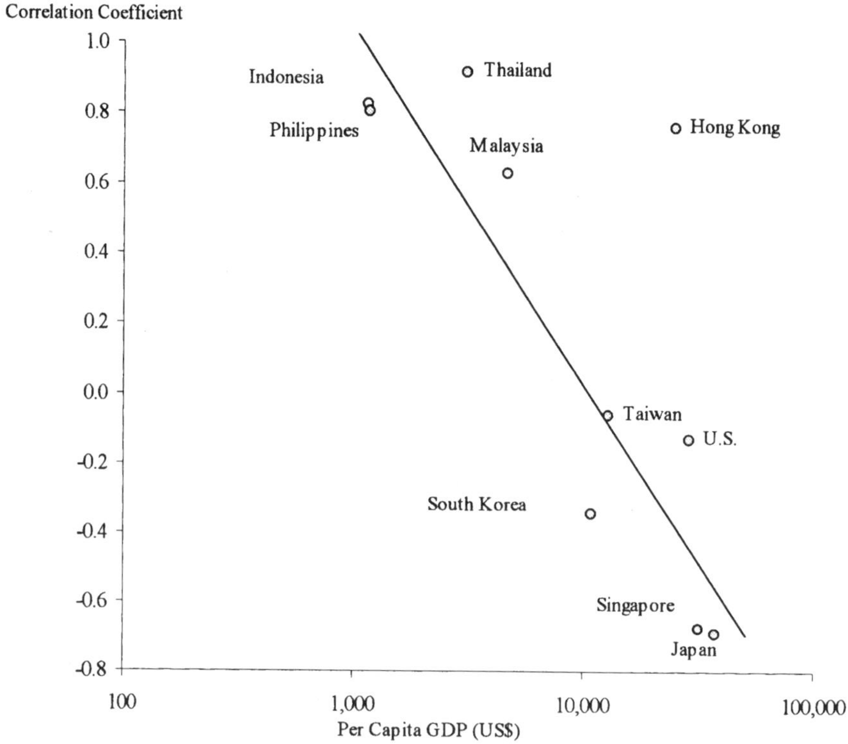

Note: The vertical axis measures the correlation between the vectors showing the specialization indexes of various commodity groups (SITC 10-category classification) for China and the corresponding country. The specialization index of a particular commodity group is defined as its trade balance (that is, exports minus imports) divided by its trade volume (exports plus imports).
Source: Nomura Research Institute from *Key Indicators of Developing Asian and Pacific Countries* (ADB, 1997).

The Capital Flow Factor

The liberalization of capital account transactions, in general, and the establishment of the Bangkok International Banking Facility (BIBF) in March 1993, in particular, had attracted massive inflows of capital to Thailand.[3] Net inflows of funds through BIBF reached $10.5 billion in 1994 (Figure 2.4). On the one hand, this made it possible to sustain the country's immense current account deficit and, on the other hand, it made macroeconomic control difficult.

Thai companies can borrow from overseas through BIBF at a lower cost than through traditional channels. For BIBF banks, transactions are exempted from reserve requirements, interest rate regulations, and foreign exchange controls that apply to domestic financial transactions, while the corporate tax rate is reduced to 10 percent from the standard rate of 30 percent. Many foreign banks without branches in Thailand have also made use of these advantages by extending loans to Thai companies through BIBF, while at the same time hoping to use BIBF as a stepping stone towards obtaining full banking licenses in Thailand.

FIGURE 2.4
Bangkok International Banking Facility (BIBF) Loans Outstanding

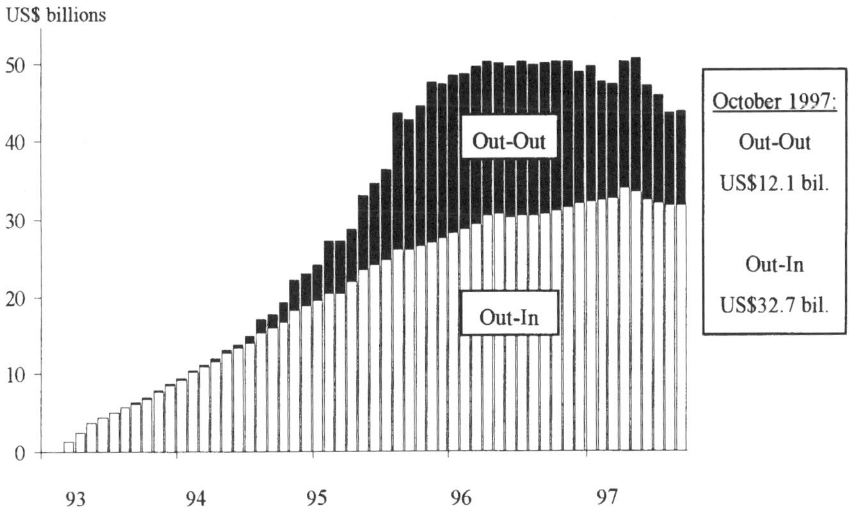

Source: Bank of Thailand.

The establishment of BIBF has made it difficult for the authorities to control the money supply. Indeed, both the banking sector and the government failed to perform the function of keeping the expansion of the bubble economy in check. The inflow of funds was more than enough to finance the current account deficit and led to rapid monetary growth despite the effort by the central bank to sterilize. Banks and financial companies under their control played an active role in channeling these short-term funds to fuel speculative activities in Thailand's stock and property markets. When the bubble finally burst in 1996, the financial system was left with massive bad debts. The situation was aggravated by investors' withdrawing their funds from Thailand and by speculative activities in the foreign exchange market in anticipation of a major devaluation of the baht.

FROM BAHT CRISIS TO ASIAN CURRENCY CRISIS: DOMINO EFFECT OR COMPETITIVE DEVALUATION

The July 1997 devaluation of the Thai baht had repercussions on most Asian currencies. The baht crisis quickly turned into an ASEAN currency crisis and, by October, into an Asian currency crisis when the Hong Kong dollar and the Korean won also became targets for speculators. The contagion effect reflects the belief among market participants that Asian countries have close ties with one another and/or they face similar problems.

Turmoil in financial markets in the region continued into 1998. From July 1997 to January 1998, the drop in the Indonesian rupiah against the U.S. dollar was over 70 percent, followed by the Thai baht, Korean won, Malaysian ringgit and Philippine peso (Figure 2.5). Even the Singapore dollar and Taiwan's NT dollar, which are supposed to be strong currencies supported by robust economic fundamentals, lost about 15 percent. Of the major Asian currencies, only the Chinese yuan and the Hong Kong dollar maintained stable rates against the U.S. dollar.

Although all Asian currencies came under downward pressure, three groups of countries can be distinguished according to the constraints facing policy authorities. The first group consists of the ASEAN countries and South Korea, which are suffering from a vicious circle of currency depreciation and accumulating bad debt. The second group includes China and Hong Kong which have resisted currency devaluation largely on political grounds. The final group is made up of Singapore and Taiwan (and probably also Japan), which allowed exchange rates to depreciate to stimulate exports.

FIGURE 2.5
Asian Currencies Follow the Baht Down
against the U.S. Dollar

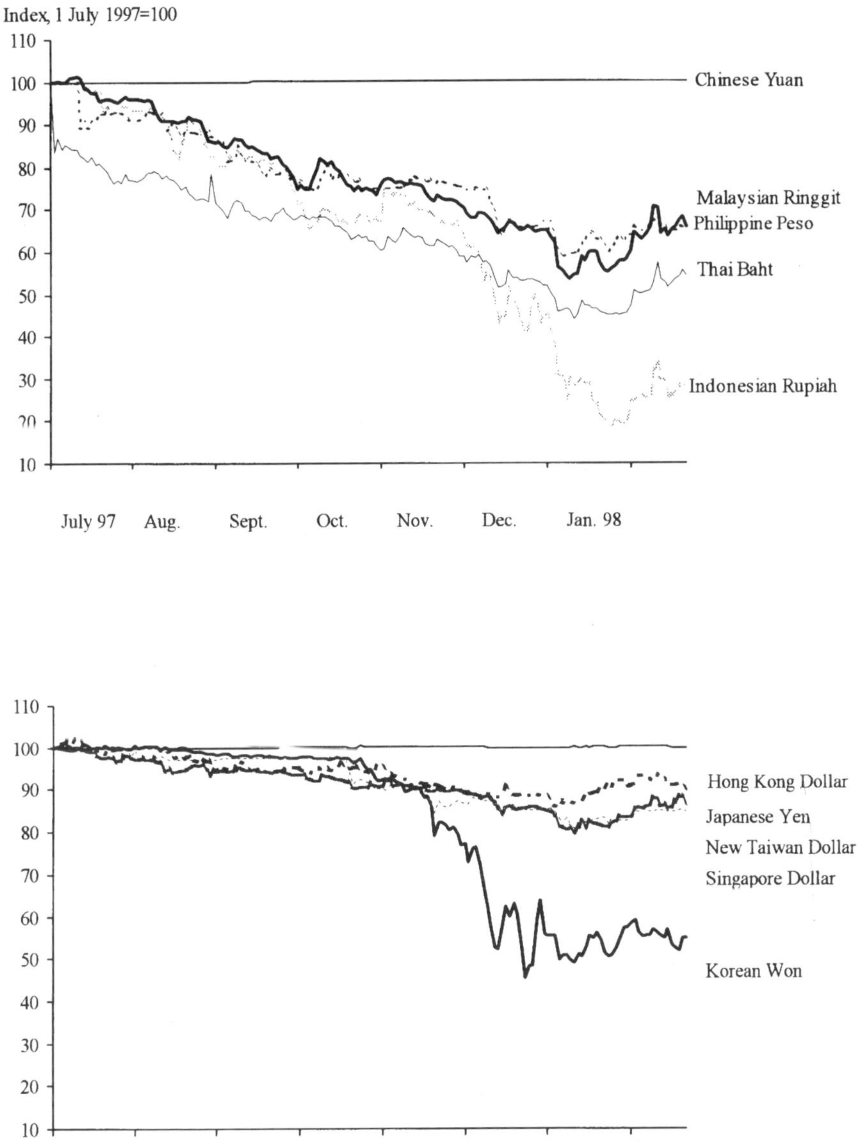

Source: Nomura Research Institute, from Bloomberg data.

The Domino Effect

Following the flotation and sharp depreciation of the baht, Thailand sought assistance from the International Monetary Fund (IMF), receiving standby support from the IMF and international financial institutions in mid-August. Domestic political and financial uncertainties delayed substantive measures until mid-October 1997, when Thailand adopted a comprehensive financial restructuring package. The steady implementation of corrective measures seems to have restored a degree of market confidence.

As the pressure on exchange rates began to spread, on 11 July 1997 the Philippines abolished its exchange rate band (+/–1.5 percent) and quickly accepted financial support from the IMF. Under the IMF package the Philippine economy weathered the crisis relatively smoothly, although its currency was buffeted somewhat by the same instability as others in the region.

Also on 11 July 1997 Indonesia widened its exchange rate band from 4 to 6 percent and finally abolished it on 14 August. Despite announcements of reductions in public works and relaxation of controls on foreign direct investment, Indonesia was forced to turn to the IMF, Japan, Singapore, and the United States for financial support in late October. Then, the rupiah fell dramatically as the markets reacted harshly to the announcement of an expansionary budget on 6 January 1998. Subsequent anti-government demonstrations led to the resignation of President Suharto on 21 May.

The Malaysian central bank quickly intervened to defend the ringgit during early July 1997, but then ceased intervention on 14 July leaving the currency to float freely. Political and regulatory measures to control or punish speculators made the markets wary of Malaysia through the end of 1997. The government of Malaysia also undertook such substantive steps as the deferral of proposed "mega projects," reductions in government spending, and adoption of other stringent fiscal measures. These calmed the market somewhat. The central bank also resumed intervention to support the ringgit on 7 January 1998.

In South Korea the bankruptcy of several major corporations during 1997 worsened the bad debt problem that had been plaguing financial institutions. The contagion effect of the financial crisis in Asia combined with uncertainty about the viability of domestic conglomerates (*chaebol*) and financial institutions made it difficult for Korea to refinance its short-term, foreign currency-denominated debt and led to a sharp fall of the won in November 1997. On 19 November the government introduced an emergency stabilization package while at the same time widening the daily band for the won against the U.S. dollar from 2.25 percent to 10 percent on both sides of the central rate. Because these efforts did not ease the pressure on the won, in late November, South Korea turned to the IMF and other official sources. This international support under very strict conditionality that included monetary and fiscal tightening, restructuring of financial institutions, better exposure of companies, and market opening, relieved the pressure on South Korea. By the end of January 1998 the authorities had been able to work out an agreement with private bankers to restore short-term liquidity to the Korean economy.

The ASEAN countries and South Korea tried very hard to stop their currencies from depreciating further, some more successfully than others. Because currency depreciation would increase the volume of bad debts, allowing exchange rates to fall in order to stimulate exports is simply not a viable option for them.

Will China Join in a Competitive Devaluation?

The sharp fall in the currencies of the ASEAN countries after early July 1997 is expected to improve their export competitiveness against other Asian countries, some of which have also allowed their currencies to depreciate. How China responds to this challenge, in general, and whether it joins this process of competitive devaluation, in particular, will be an important factor determining the short-term economic outlook of the region. In addition to keener competition with other Asian countries, weakening domestic demand and inventory accumulation may tempt China to devalue the yuan to stimulate exports and to reduce imports.

So far, the yuan has stayed firm despite the intense speculation on other Asian currencies. Although the Chinese currency has become convertible for current account transactions, very tight controls on capital flows have helped shelter the Chinese currency from speculation. Indeed, after witnessing the recent turmoil in neighboring countries, China should be in no hurry to liberalize capital account transactions.

China has been reluctant to devalue the yuan because: its external balance is in good shape; it now runs a trade surplus with the United States as large as Japan does, and a devaluation of the yuan would aggravate trade friction with the United States; and a devaluation of the yuan might spark another round of speculation on those Asian currencies that are still under devaluation pressure, including the Hong Kong dollar.

The possibility of a devaluation of the yuan, however, will increase as the deceleration in Chinese exports becomes more apparent. Unlike Hong

Kong, China is already under a managed floating system and has no obligation to peg to the dollar. Instead of a one-off devaluation, China may pursue a crawling peg policy and allow the yuan to depreciate at a gradual and steady pace.

In lieu of immediate devaluation to bolster exports, China has sought to improve its investment environment for foreign companies. In a sharp reversal of the policy of the last few years, for example, in January 1998 China removed tariffs charged on imported machinery when foreign companies set up operation in China. Larger inflows of foreign direct investment should help reduce downward pressure on the yuan by boosting China's export capacity and productivity growth. In addition, there is further room for China to stimulate domestic demand by reducing interest rates and increasing public spending, thanks to the very low domestic inflation rate.

Hong Kong Determined to Defend the Dollar Peg

Thailand's shift to a managed floating system, which triggered the latest currency crisis in Asia, happened to take place one day after the return of Hong Kong to Chinese rule. Financial markets in Hong Kong at first were immune from the crisis and the boom in the stock market continued, but speculation on the Hong Kong dollar escalated in late October. Interest rates surged (the overnight rate in the interbank market reached 300 percent on October 23) and stock prices plummeted, but the Hong Kong dollar has remained firm against the U.S. dollar. This episode confirmed the authorities' determination and ability to defend the dollar peg.[4] Hong Kong authorities have openly stated that the primary objective of monetary policy is to maintain the official parity rate and they have successfully maintained the peg through such shocks as Black Monday in October 1987, the Tiananmen Incident in June 1989, and the Mexican Crisis in late 1994 and early 1995.

To cope with possible attacks on the Hong Kong dollar, the authorities had accumulated foreign exchange reserves reaching US$92.8 billion at the end of 1997, equivalent to 7.8 times the amount of Hong Kong dollars outstanding. In addition to the official backing for currency issued, these reserves include the fiscal surplus, the foreign assets of the Land Fund, and the return on investment accumulated so far. China has also committed to using its own foreign exchange reserves to defend the Hong Kong dollar.

Whether Hong Kong can maintain the dollar peg is widely viewed as a litmus test of whether the transition to Chinese sovereignty has been a success. Leaders in both Hong Kong and China are thus extremely unwilling to change the current tough stance on the exchange rate. The IMF and the U.S. monetary authorities have also openly expressed support of Hong Kong's current system of pegging to the U.S. dollar, partly for fear that if Hong Kong fails to defend the peg, other currencies of developing countries linked to the dollar may also become vulnerable to speculation.

In addition to political considerations, the authorities are determined to defend the Hong Kong dollar because the costs of a devaluation would also be immense. Devaluation would invite further speculation on the Hong Kong dollar as well as other Asian currencies. The argument that a major devaluation of the Hong Kong dollar could allow domestic interest rates (which have remained substantially higher than those in the United States) to decline has become unconvincing, given the recent experience of the ASEAN countries.

Should Hong Kong give up the dollar peg, the right timing would be when the Hong Kong dollar is under pressure to re-value after the crisis in Asia is over. The shock that would force the Hong Kong dollar to devalue is more likely to come from Beijing than from Bangkok or New York, because only such a shock would be accompanied by massive capital flight from Hong Kong.

With asset prices staying in the doldrums and exports losing competitiveness to Asian neighbors whose currencies have depreciated sharply against the U.S. dollar, the Hong Kong economy is under strong deflationary pressure. This would imply a decline in Hong Kong's nominal economic growth rate. Fortunately, this is likely to take the form of a decline in inflation (price adjustment) rather than a decline in real economic growth because Hong Kong has a very flexible labor market where wages adjust swiftly to ensure full employment.

Taiwan and Singapore Manage Controlled Depreciation

Singapore and Taiwan comprise the third group: countries which have allowed exchange rates to depreciate to stimulate exports. So far the depreciation of their currencies has been relatively moderate and controlled. Both are net creditor countries and have maintained surpluses in their current accounts.

Recent depreciation of the NT dollar, for example, can be interpreted as an attempt by the Taiwan government to retain export competitiveness in the face of weakening ASEAN currencies, the Korean won, and the Japanese yen. Taiwan has little foreign debt and immense foreign assets.

Depreciation of the local currency will therefore have little impact on the soundness of the country's financial system. In addition, Taiwan still maintains strict controls on capital flows and the central bank has foreign exchange reserves amounting to nearly US$90 billion (ten months' import coverage) available to defend the NT dollar.

Singapore and Taiwan have always focused more on price stability than external balance as the objective of macroeconomic policy, in general, and exchange rate policy, in particular. However, the moderate depreciation of the Singapore dollar and NT dollar is not likely to lead to a surge of inflation in these two countries because the currencies of other Asian countries, including Japan, have also depreciated against the U.S. dollar.

IMPACT ON THE REGIONAL ECONOMY

The Asian economies are decelerating on the back of weakening domestic demand. Their prospects of recovery hinge on whether they can cut the vicious circle of currency depreciation and the accumulation of bad debt. Should turmoil in the Asian economies continue, the deflationary effect will sooner or later be transmitted to the major industrial countries. While the short-term outlook for the regional economy is at best "cautiously pessimistic," supply-side factors suggest a more optimistic picture in the longer term.

Impact on the Thai Economy

Mexico's path towards recovery from a similar crisis in late 1994 and early 1995 may serve as a benchmark for predicting the short-term outlook of the Thai economy (Figure 2.6). In 1995, Mexico enjoyed a rebound in exports which contrasted with the sharp drop in real retail sales. It took about a year until the year-on-year growth of manufacturing output turned positive again. As in the case of Mexico, in Thailand net exports are expected to do better than domestic demand. Nevertheless, Thailand's recovery may take longer, given the more serious bad debt problem plaguing Thai financial institutions.

Companies in Thailand (including financial institutions) with liabilities denominated in foreign currencies have found the repayment burden in terms of the local currency rising in proportion to the scale of the devaluation. Of these, companies (including foreign companies) serving the local Thai market have been most adversely affected. Foreign banks lending to Thailand in foreign currencies (dollars and yen, for example) have not

FIGURE 2.6
Mexico's Path to Recovery

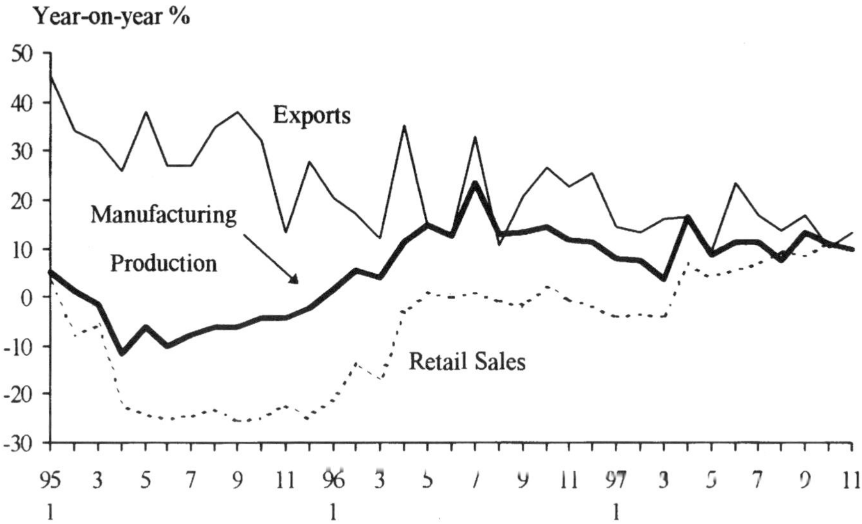

Source: Nomura Research Institute, from official statistics.

suffered direct capital losses resulting from the devaluation, but the default risk on their outstanding loans has increased as the debt burden of the borrowers (in baht terms) has risen. The devaluation has therefore aggravated the bad debt situation that already weakened Thailand's financial institutions. Concern about the health of financial institutions in turn adds new downward pressure on the exchange rate.

Domestic demand has been adversely affected by the compounding problems of bad debt and currency depreciation, which have resulted in a credit crunch situation. Thai companies find it difficult to raise funds either domestically or from overseas sources. In addition, domestic demand has been further constrained by higher interest rates needed to support the exchange rate, the negative asset effect on consumption resulting from the sharp declines in stock and property prices, and the fiscal austerity conditions imposed by the IMF.

Although a weaker baht should boost exports and suppress imports, the contribution of exports to economic growth is expected to be much lower than it was in Mexico in 1995 for the following reasons. First, currency depreciation in neighboring countries has partly offset the gain in export competitiveness resulting from the baht's devaluation. Second, many manufacturers have difficulty obtaining funding from banks to finance the import of intermediate goods. Third, the prolonged recession in Japan, Thailand's second largest export market, will also constrain exports. This contrasts sharply with Mexico's situation in 1995, when the economic recovery was led by exports to the United States to take advantage of opportunities arising from the newly-formed NAFTA. Indeed, the improvement in the current account balance so far has reflected a sharp fall in imports rather than stronger exports.

A precondition for a full-fledged recovery in Thailand is severing the link between currency depreciation and additional bad debts. This will require raising further funds from overseas, in addition to the $17.2 billion committed by the IMF and other official sources so far.

The situation in other ASEAN countries suffering sharp currency depreciation, notably Indonesia, and in South Korea is similar to that in Thailand. Again, the recovery of exports will not be enough to compensate for the sharp decline in domestic demand so that economic growth in these countries should stay in the doldrums in 1998 and 1999.

Rising Risk of Global Deflation

The currency crisis in Asia not only dealt a heavy blow to the regional economy but also may mark the beginning of a global recession. This is clear if we consider the outlook for the U.S. economy in the context of the global economy. On the one hand, the dollar has strengthened substantially against the yen and European currencies since 1995 and against most Asian currencies since the summer of 1997. On the other hand, the stark contrast between robust economic growth in the United States and the recession in Asia including Japan has continued into 1998. As a result, U.S. exports are expected to slow down sharply while imports should remain strong, leading to a deterioration of the U.S. current account balance. The decline in net exports should also put a drag on U.S. economic growth, and it could become more and more difficult for the United States to continue to play the role of locomotive for the global economy.

Despite the rising trade imbalance with Japan, so far the United States has not pressed for a stronger yen, largely reflecting the confidence of the U.S. authorities in the strength of the U.S. economy. However, if domestic economic growth starts to show clear signs of deceleration, the United States is likely to put more pressure on Japan. This may initiate a trade war among the economic powers involving competitive devaluation and rising protectionism, and the possibility that the global economy may plunge into a recession will increase as a result. Instead of pursuing such a beggar-thy-neighbor policy, the major economic powers should seek to sustain economic growth by stimulating domestic demand.

End of the Asian Miracle?

Some commentators have argued that the latest currency crisis in Asia may mark the end of the Asian miracle, as "predicted" by Professor Paul Krugman in 1994 (Krugman, 1994). However, there are good reasons to remain optimistic about the future of the Asian economies. While short-term economic growth largely depends on demand-side factors, long-term growth is determined mainly by supply-side considerations. Although a period of adjustment is inevitable following the crisis, if Asian governments take the appropriate steps to address the problems mentioned earlier, high economic growth can still be achieved in the longer term. This is because the basic factors contributing to the Asian miracle—high savings rates, heavy investment in human resources, and a market-friendly stance towards economic policy—are not likely to change with the latest shock.

For example, Thailand's savings rate averaged 34.9 percent of GDP between 1991 and 1996, twice as high as that of Mexico (Table 2.1). An additional net inflow of funds equivalent to 7.7 percent of GDP boosted gross capital formation (investment) to 42.6 percent of GDP and allowed Thailand to achieve a growth rate of 8.2 percent a year in the same period. If the relation between the investment ratio and GDP growth (that is, the incremental capital output ratio, or ICOR) remains unchanged at this level of 5.2 (42.6/8.2), domestic savings alone should still be able to sustain economic growth at about 6.7 percent.[5]

IMPACT ON THE JAPANESE ECONOMY

The Japanese economy, which has developed close ties with the rest of Asia in recent years through foreign direct investment, trade, and bank lending, is deemed to be adversely affected by the latest currency crisis in the region.

Japanese Investment in Asia at the Crossroads

The crisis that began in the summer of 1997 aggravated the slowdown in Japanese foreign direct investment in Asia that has accompanied the yen's

TABLE 2.1
Estimated Growth of Asian Countries in the Absence of Capital Inflows
1991–96

	Savings S (% of GDP)	Capital Inflow F (% of GDP)	Investment I = S + F (% of GDP)	GDP Growth G (%)	Incremental Capital-Output Ratio ICOR = I/G	GDP Growth without Capital Inflows G' = S/ICOR (%)
ASEAN						
Thailand	34.9	7.7	42.6	8.2	5.2	6.7
Malaysia	35.0	6.5	41.5	9.0	4.6	7.5
Indonesia	32.1	2.6	34.7	7.8	4.4	7.2
Philippines	19.0	3.2	22.2	2.8	8.1	2.4
South Korea	35.4	1.5	36.9	7.4	5.0	7.1
China	40.1	–1.0	39.2	11.5	3.4	11.7

Source: Nomura Research Institute, from *Asian Development Outlook* (Asian Development Bank 1997 and 1998).

depreciation since the summer of 1995. To cope with this new environment, Japanese companies have become more cautious when considering investment in Asia. The ASEAN countries are likely to gain at the expense of China in receiving direct investment from Japan, particularly for investors taking advantage of the region as an export base.

The most important factor determining Japanese direct investment in the rest of Asia is the yen-dollar rate. As most Asian currencies have been pegged to the U.S. dollar, production costs in the rest of Asia relative to Japan tend to decline as the yen appreciates and to rise as the yen depreciates. The depreciation of the yen since mid-1995 has helped to improve the profitability of Japanese exporting companies, making it less attractive for them to invest in Asia. According to the Ministry of Finance, Japan's investment in Asia dropped by 7.2 percent in fiscal 1996 to $11 billion, marking the first negative growth since 1991 (Table 2.2). In the case of manufacturing, Japan's investment in Asia, which surpassed its investment in the United States in fiscal 1994 and 1995, fell back below the latter in fiscal 1996.

Simultaneous currency depreciation in the ASEAN countries since July 1997 has dealt a heavy blow to Japanese companies serving local markets in the region. Many subsidiaries of Japanese manufacturers located in ASEAN countries (notably Toyota Motors) have been forced to curtail production by suspending operations. These companies, which raise funds primarily from abroad in foreign currencies and rely heavily on parts and components imported from Japan, are being exposed to higher production

TABLE 2.2
Japan's Direct Investment in Other Asian Countries, Amount and Share, 1989–97
US$ millions

	Fiscal Year								1997	
	1989	1990	1991	1992	1993	1994	1995	1996	1st half	YoY%
Asian NIEs	4,900	3,355	2,203	1,922	2,419	2,865	3,236	3,540	1,500	–21.6
	7.3%	5.9%	5.3%	5.6%	6.7%	7.0%	6.3%	7.4%	6.4%	
South Korea	606	284	260	225	245	400	449	416	129	–53.8
	0.9%	0.5%	0.6%	0.7%	0.7%	1.0%	0.9%	0.9%	0.5%	
Taiwan	494	446	405	292	292	278	455	521	277	0.0
	0.7%	0.8%	1.0%	0.9%	0.8%	0.7%	0.9%	1.1%	1.2%	
Hong Kong	1,898	1,785	925	735	1,238	1,133	1,147	1,488	394	–51.2
	2.8%	3.1%	2.2%	2.2%	3.4%	2.8%	2.2%	3.1%	1.7%	
Singapore	1,902	840	613	670	644	1,054	1,185	1,115	700	27.6
	2.8%	1.5%	1.5%	2.0%	1.8%	2.6%	2.3%	2.3%	3.0%	
ASEAN	2,782	3,242	3,083	3,197	2,398	3,888	4,138	4,951	3,409	62.4
	4.1%	5.7%	7.4%	9.4%	6.7%	9.5%	8.1%	10.3%	14.5%	
Indonesia	631	1,105	1,193	1,676	813	1,759	1,605	2,416	1,677	58.1
	0.9%	1.9%	2.9%	4.9%	2.3%	4.3%	3.1%	5.0%	7.1%	
Malaysia	673	725	880	704	800	742	575	572	307	86.4
	1.0%	1.3%	2.1%	2.1%	2.2%	1.8%	1.1%	1.2%	1.3%	
Philippines	202	258	203	160	207	668	717	560	293	18.4
	0.3%	0.5%	0.5%	0.5%	0.6%	1.6%	1.4%	1.2%	1.2%	
Thailand	1,276	1,154	807	657	578	719	1,240	1,404	1,133	80.6
	1.9%	2.0%	1.9%	1.9%	1.6%	1.8%	2.4%	2.9%	4.8%	
China	438	349	579	1,070	1,691	2,565	4,478	2,512	1,158	–19.1
	0.6%	0.6%	1.4%	3.1%	4.7%	6.2%	8.7%	5.2%	4.9%	
Asia	8,120	6,946	5,865	6,189	6,508	9,318	11,852	11,003	6,067	11.5
	12.0%	12.2%	14.1%	18.1%	18.1%	22.7%	23.1%	22.9%	25.8%	
U.S.	32,540	26,128	18,026	13,819	14,725	17,331	22,649	22,015	8,925	–25.7
	48.2%	45.9%	43.3%	40.5%	40.9%	42.2%	44.1%	45.8%	38.0%	
Europe	14,808	14,294	9,371	7,076	7,940	6,230	8,586	7,376	3,248	–9.9
	21.9%	25.1%	22.5%	20.7%	22.0%	15.2%	16.7%	15.4%	13.8%	
World Total	67,540	56,911	41,584	34,138	36,025	41,051	51,392	48,041	23,501	–4.4
	100.0%	100.0%	100.0%	100.0%	100.0%	100.0%	100.0%	100.0%	100.0%	

Note: Figures do not include reinvestment.
Source: Japanese Ministry of Finance.

costs and a heavier debt burden (in terms of the local currency). At the same time, they are also suffering from declining sales as demand in Asia slows down. By contrast, Japanese companies exporting from Thailand and other ASEAN countries are benefiting from lower production costs (in terms of foreign currencies) and improved export competitiveness.

Between 1992 and 1995, Japanese investment in the rest of Asia, especially in new projects targeting local markets, tended to concentrate on China, but lower-than-expected earnings there have sapped Japanese investors' enthusiasm. Japanese investment in China tumbled by 43.9

percent to $2.5 billion in fiscal 1996. China's tightening of its policy toward foreign capital, along with the yen's depreciation, has accelerated the decline in Japanese investment in China. Removal of tax exemptions for imported equipment and cuts in the reimbursement rate for value-added taxes on export products (from 17 percent of export value previously to 14 percent in July 1995 and 9 percent in January 1996) have also increased foreign companies' production costs, depriving China of its attractiveness as an export base.

The present changes in the Asian business environment are prompting Japanese companies to shift their focus from China to the ASEAN countries to take advantage of lower production costs to expand exports. Since the recent currency crisis has driven the ASEAN countries into a recession, Japanese companies investing in this region are likely to aim at increasing exports more than local sales.

Further Deceleration of Exports to Asia Inevitable

Japan's exports to Asian countries have been stagnating since 1996 despite the yen's sharp depreciation. Normally a lower yen would increase the international competitiveness of Japanese goods and expand exports of those goods. However, this simple economic principle applies only to Japanese exports to the United States and Europe but not to exports to Asia, because the weaker yen also causes Asian economies to slow down as discussed earlier. Reflecting this asymmetric relation, Asia's share of Japanese exports increases when the yen appreciates and decreases as the yen depreciates (Figure 2.7). Japan's exports to Asia thus had been slowing down even before the currency crisis in Asia because of, rather than despite, the yen's depreciation. This fact, combined with the deepening recession affecting ASEAN economies due to the simultaneous depreciation of their currencies since early July 1997, is likely to hold down Japan's exports to Asia for some time. With Asia absorbing over 40 percent of total Japanese exports, the negative impact on the profitability of Japanese exporters is expected to be large.

With no signs of domestic economic recovery, there has been growing pressure for further depreciation of the yen as a way to stimulate Japanese exports. However, this strategy would probably lead to a further deceleration of exports to Asia, forcing Japan to turn to the American and European markets. As a result, Japan's trade surplus with the United States would increase sharply, eventually intensifying Japan-U.S. trade friction and putting upward pressure on the yen rate against the dollar.

FIGURE 2.7
Asia as a Built-in Stabilizer for Japanese Exports

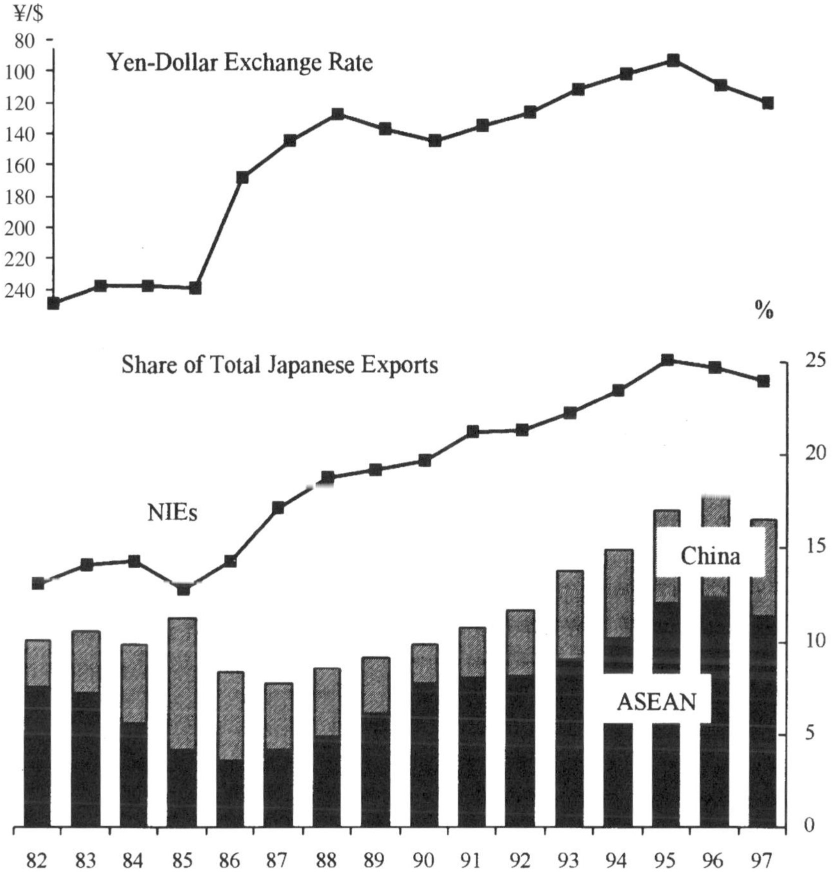

Source: Nomura Research Institute, from Japanese trade statistics.

Rising Default Risks of Lending to Asia

Japanese lending to Asia amounted to $271.3 billion at the end of June 1997, accounting for 34.3 percent of total lending to the region by BIS reporting banks (Table 2.3). Besides Hong Kong and Singapore, which function as regional financial centers, there is a tendency for Japanese lending to be concentrated in Thailand, Indonesia, and South Korea, the three countries that have been most adversely affected by the Asian crisis.

TABLE 2.3
Positions of BIS Reporting Banks on Asian Countries
US$ millions

	Lenders					
	Total	**Japan**	**U.S.**	**Germany**	**U.K.**	**France**
Thailand	69.4	37.7	4.0	7.6	2.8	5.1
Indonesia	58.7	23.2	4.6	5.6	4.3	4.8
Malaysia	28.8	10.5	2.4	5.7	2.0	2.9
China	57.9	18.7	2.9	7.3	6.9	7.3
South Korea	103.4	23.7	10.0	10.8	6.1	10.0
Taiwan	25.2	3.0	2.5	3.0	3.2	5.2
Philippines	14.1	2.1	2.8	2.0	1.1	1.7
Hong Kong	222.3	87.4	8.08	32.2	30.1	12.8
Singapore	211.2	65.0	5.2	38.4	25.2	15.4
Asia Total	791.0	271.3	43.2	112.6	81.7	65.2
Share of Asia Total	100.0%	34.3%	5.5%	14.2%	10.3%	8.2%

Source: Compiled by Nomura Research Institute based on BIS "The Maturity, Sectoral, and Nationality Distribution of International Bank Lending", first half 1997.

Lending to these countries by Japanese banks is usually denominated in foreign currencies such as dollars or yen so that devaluation of local currencies does not directly imply a capital loss for them. However, the default risk of loans outstanding has increased accordingly, as borrowers have seen their debt burden in local currency terms increase sharply as a result of currency depreciation and at the same time have faced a shrinking market at home.

The bulk of lending by Japanese banks in the rest of Asia has been concentrated in subsidiaries of Japanese companies, but the share of large local companies has been increasing. The default risk is low for lending to Japanese subsidiaries because they usually have support from their headquarters. However, the shocks have been so great that local blue chip companies borrowing from Japanese banks (or finance companies formed as joint ventures with local banks) may have problems to repay as scheduled.

With Asia now plunging into recession and the default risk on outstanding bank loans rising, Japanese banks have become more and more cautious about expanding loans to the region and in some cases even about rolling over short-term loans. There is now growing concern that this "credit crunch" situation might aggravate the financial crisis in Asia, which in turn would boomerang on Japanese banks as their profits suffer.

Hedging against the Risks of Fluctuations in Asian Currencies

The exchange risks faced by Japanese companies investing in the rest of Asia can conceptually be grouped into those relating to changes in the yen-dollar rate and those stemming from changes in local currency-dollar rates. The perception that Asia belongs to a de facto dollar bloc has caused Japanese companies to underestimate the exchange risks of local currencies against the dollar, and to focus on hedging against changes in the yen-dollar rate.

This strategy fails to consider the possibility that the exchange rates of Asian currencies may fluctuate against the dollar on a scale such as experienced over the last few months. The sharp devaluation of ASEAN currencies has thus exposed Japanese companies to substantial exchange losses. The impact has been especially heavy on the companies that procure funds and intermediate goods in foreign currencies and sell their products in local markets. It is not clear yet whether ASEAN countries will return to an adjustable system of pegging their currencies to the dollar or shift to a more flexible exchange system. In any case, it will be necessary for Japanese companies doing business in Asia to pay greater attention to the exchange risks associated with local currencies in the future.

It has also become apparent that local production does not necessarily help to reduce exchange risks. Typical strategies of Japanese companies, based on siting factories close to the market while relying on overseas sources for funds and for intermediate goods, are now resulting in exposure to high exchange rate risk. If Asian countries loosen the link between their currencies and the dollar, Japanese companies exporting from production bases in Asia to the United States will also need to prepare themselves for higher exchange rate risk.

Japan's Expected Role

With its ties with the rest of Asia strengthening in recent years, Japan's economic fortunes hinge more and more on the future of the region. Some commentators have argued that rapid growth in Asia would be a threat to Japan, but the latest crisis clearly shows that it is more in Japan's own interest to be surrounded by prosperous and stable nations than by poor and unstable ones.

To overcome the current crisis, Asian countries are expecting Japan to play a leading role. On the one hand, Japan should provide financial support in concert with the IMF. On the other hand, it should boost domestic demand, prevent the yen from depreciating, and rebuild confidence in its own financial system.

LESSONS FROM THE ASIAN CURRENCY CRISIS

To achieve economic stability, Asian countries should give up the traditional exchange rate policy of pegging to the dollar and seek closer ties to the yen, while at the same time strengthening macroeconomic control and their domestic financial sectors. Further cooperation among monetary authorities will be required to cope with currency crises that become contagious across national borders.

Pegging Closer to the Yen

The latest currency crisis, which occurred against a background of massive capital flows and a highly volatile yen-dollar rate, has raised doubts over whether the Asian countries should continue to stick to their traditional exchange rate policy of pegging loosely to the dollar.

Given the very large impact of the fluctuations in the yen-dollar rate on economic growth, stability of the yen-dollar rate is crucial for stability in the regional economy. Since the yen-dollar rate is beyond the control of Asia's developing countries (or even of the major industrial powers, including Japan and the United States), as a second-best solution, these countries should seek to stabilize their exchange rates not only against the dollar but also against the yen. So long as the yen-dollar rate fluctuates, however, it is impossible for an Asian currency to achieve stability against both the dollar and the yen at the same time. One way to compromise would be to peg to a basket of currencies in which the yen carried substantial weight. The higher the weight assigned to the yen, the stronger the synchronization between the host country's currency and the yen. For example, if the yen carried 50 percent weight in Korea's reference basket, the won would be allowed to appreciate by 5 percent when the yen strengthened 10 percent against the U.S. dollar (or to depreciate by 5 percent when the yen weakened 10 percent against the dollar).

The "optimal" weight to be assigned to the yen in this currency basket should differ from one country to another, depending largely on how much the host country competes with Japan. Higher income countries are more likely than lower income countries to compete with Japan (Figure 2.8). Thus South Korea, for example, should peg closer to the yen than Thailand, which in turn should assign a higher weight to the yen in its reference basket than Indonesia, for example.[6]

FIGURE 2.8
Trade Structure Correlation between Japan and Other Asian Countries, 1993

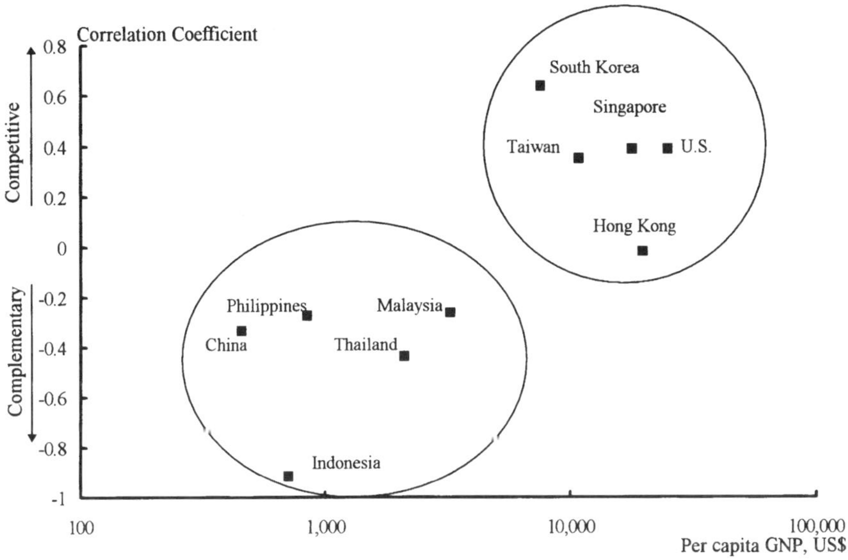

Note: Trade composition is based on 3-category classification (primary commodities, machinery, and other manufactures) for both exports and imports (a total of 6 categories).
Source: Compiled by Nomura Research Institute based on World Bank, *World Development Report*, 1995.

Judging by this criterion, the weight assigned to the yen in Thailand's reference currency basket (estimated at 10 percent) before the change to managed floating in mid-1997 was too low (and the weight assigned to the U.S. dollar was too high). Had the yen carried a higher weight in that basket, the baht would have depreciated more sharply over the last two years as the yen depreciated. This, in turn, would have moderated the appreciation of the baht in real effective terms and helped sustain Thai export growth. It would also have avoided the abrupt devaluation.

Preconditions for Liberalization of Capital Account Transactions

The experience of the ASEAN countries shows the difficulty of macroeconomic management in an environment of high capital mobility.

Although many Asian countries achieved high economic growth with the support of foreign capital, the turmoil of 1997 and 1998 can be traced at least in part to the aftermath of the capital inflows.

A developing country should not liberalize capital account transactions at too early a stage when banks' risk appraisal is inadequate and monetary control is difficult. Put the other way round, a sound banking system and ability to control the money supply are the two preconditions that should be met before opening up.

Capital inflows promote economic growth only if they are channeled into productive instead of speculative activities. Developing countries should therefore rely more on foreign direct investment than on short-term capital flows as a source of external finance. Capital inflow could weaken the export competitiveness of the host country by pushing up its real exchange rate through either an appreciation of the nominal exchange rate or higher inflation. This is analogous to the so-called 'Dutch disease.'[7] In particular, an inflow of short-term funds, by lowering interest rates and boosting the money supply, usually leads to rising stock and property prices, which in turn raise consumption at the expense of domestic savings. In this case, by crowding out domestic savings, an inflow of short-term funds may not contribute to higher total investment and thus to economic growth. In contrast, an inflow of foreign direct investment, by increasing production capacity and productivity, reduces inflationary pressure and helps maintain export competitiveness. In addition, foreign direct investment is usually undertaken with a long time horizon and is therefore less volatile than portfolio flows, which respond sensitively to changes in interest rate differentials and exchange rate expectations. No wonder that the countries suffering most during the latest currency crisis in Asia (Thailand, Indonesia, and Korea) are those with very high ratios of short-term debt.

These concerns have given rise to proposals that capital flows should be regulated and not left totally to the free market. For example, Professor James Tobin of Yale University challenges the claims that liberalization and globalization of financial markets are the path to prosperity and progress and reiterates his proposal to impose a tax (the so-called 'Tobin Tax') on currency transactions (Tobin 1997). Given imperfect financial markets at home, perfect capital mobility may lead to market failures, and some form of government intervention would provide a second-best solution. Along this line, Malaysian Prime Minister Mahathir's criticism of speculators can be justified by the economic reasoning that attacks on national currencies involve externality and abuse of monopoly power.

Coping with Capital Outflow

An economy highly dependent on foreign capital is constantly subject to the risk of capital outflow, which may be prompted by a deterioration in domestic economic fundamentals or by spillovers from overseas developments.

An outflow of funds can be countered by such measures as imposing restrictions on capital outflows, monetary tightening, and intervention (by selling foreign currencies to buy local currency). Each of these options has its own demerits. First, ad hoc measures to restrict capital outflow hurt not only speculators but also genuine investors and should therefore be reserved as a last resort. Second, if the scale of the outflow is large, monetary restraint will drive up interest rates, which in turn will have a major deflationary effect and deal a heavy blow to the banking sector. Third, the scale of intervention is limited by the level of the central bank's foreign currency reserves, forcing the monetary authorities to devalue their currencies, with adverse effects on price stability and confidence among overseas investors.

With international capital movement becoming more and more active, foreign currency reserves now play an important role as a buffer for maintaining stable exchange rates. During the latest currency crisis, countries with abundant foreign exchange reserves such as Taiwan, Hong Kong, Singapore, and China have been much less adversely affected than Thailand, Indonesia, Malaysia, the Philippines, and South Korea, which were forced to allow their currencies to plummet in the foreign exchange markets.

Following the Mexican debt crisis in late 1994, there has been growing recognition that coping with similar crises in Asia requires reinforcing cooperative relationships among monetary authorities within the region. Such efforts, including commitments made to lend to each other using U.S. treasury bonds as collateral (so-called 'repo agreements'), proved helpless in coping with, let alone preventing, the current Asian crisis. Additional coordinated efforts will be needed to prepare for a similar crisis in the region in the future. Coordinated efforts should also be devoted to preventing a "competition" among the Asian countries to devalue their currencies to stimulate exports.

Discussion among international financial institutions and monetary authorities in Asia and the United States to further regional financial cooperation led to the Manila Framework reached in November 1997, which presented the following four initiatives: 1) a mechanism for regional surveillance to complement global surveillance by the IMF, 2) agreement to enhance economic and technical cooperation particularly in strengthening domestic financial systems and regulatory capacities, 3) measures to strengthen the IMF's capacity to respond to financial crises (quota increases and the New Arrangement to Borrow), and 4) a cooperative financial arrangement that would supplement IMF resources.

So far the IMF has played a pivotal role in this process. Notwithstanding the massive financial support received from the IMF and other official sources, market confidence in the ability of Thailand, Indonesia, and South Korea to overcome the crisis has remained weak. This has raised doubts over whether the conditionality imposed on these countries by the IMF based on fiscal and monetary austerity as well as financial liberalization is the right therapy for the current situation in Asia. Further research needs to be done to explore alternatives to cope with the kind of financial crisis that hit Asia in the summer of 1997.

Notes

1 In contrast, the Asian NIEs and Japan, which are at much higher levels of economic development, have trade structures complementary to that of China. These countries should find China an attractive destination for their exports and direct investment. Complementary relations can be characterized as a win-win game in which both sides can benefit through trade and investment.

2 China had a dual exchange rate system comprising an official rate and a market-based swap center rate until January 1994, when the two rates were unified. This was achieved by adjusting the official rate to the market rate, leading to a devaluation of the official rate from US$1 = 5.76 yuan to US$1 = 8.7 yuan. Since the swap center rate already applied to about 80 percent of China's exports before devaluation, the impact on China's export competitiveness should be much smaller than the magnitude of the devaluation suggested.

3 The primary aim of BIBF was to promote Bangkok as an offshore financial center serving Indochina. Since 1993, however, improving relations with the United States have allowed Vietnam to set up direct relations with established international financial centers without going through Bangkok. From the very beginning, BIBF has been engaged primarily in out-in transactions (in which funds raised from nonresidents are loaned to residents), in sharp contrast to out-out transactions among nonresidents in conventional offshore markets.

4 Hong Kong's dollar peg and currency board system are described in Chapter 6.

5 In a more rigorous analysis, possible shifts in the savings rate and ICOR should be taken into consideration. Paradoxically, the savings rate may actually increase as falling asset prices suppress consumption. The ICOR may either rise or fall depending on the relative strength of the following two factors. On the one hand, if inflows in the past have been dominated by investment in bubble-type projects, the ICOR should decline (that is, capital efficiency should improve) with the bursting of the bubble. On the other hand, if inflows have taken the form of direct investment accompanied by technology transfer, lower capital inflows from now on would imply a higher ICOR (that is lower capital efficiency). The same logic suggests that lower-income countries that compete with China (such as Thailand and Indonesia) should assign a high weight to the yuan in their currency baskets.

6 The same logic suggests that lower-income countries that compete with China (such as Thailand and Indonesia) should assign a high weight to the yuan in their currency baskets.

7 The Dutch disease, in which the discovery of some natural resource, such as oil, tends to drive up the real exchange rate and shrink the domestic manufacturing sector, is discussed in the Appendix to Chapter 1.

References

Kwan, C. H. 1994. *Economic Interdependence in the Asia-Pacific Region.* London and New York: Routledge.

Krugman, P. 1994. "The Myth of Asia's Miracle". *Foreign Affairs.* November/December.

Tobin, J. 1997. "Why We Need Sand in the Market's Gears". *Washington Post*, 21 December .

3

Banking on Contagion: The Southeast Asian Currency Crisis

Manuel F. Montes

INTRODUCTION

The Southeast Asian currency crisis began on 2 July 1997 when Thai monetary authorities abandoned the baht peg to a basket of currencies with very heavy weight for the U.S. dollar. By the end of January 1998, the baht had subsequently lost 55 percent of its value in terms of the U.S. dollar. Other currencies in the region also suffered drastic declines in a rout—or perhaps in recrimination—as non-resident portfolios retreated from investments in economies that seemed to be similar to Thailand's. From July 1997 to January 1998 the Malaysian ringgit lost 44.9 percent of its value against the dollar, the Philippine peso lost 39.4 percent and the Singapore dollar lost 18.8 percent. The Indonesian rupiah suffered the heaviest loss of all; at an exchange rate of 14,800 rupiah to the dollar, its value had fallen 83.6 percent.

The Thai baht crisis and the subsequent Indonesian rupiah crisis are the latest in a series of crises in developing countries in which a currency attack is brought on (or is justified) by an unhealthy domestic banking system following a 3- to 5-year period of swelling capital inflows. The currency attack itself further weakens the domestic banking system by multiplying the number of projects that are no longer viable under the post-attack exchange rate, and hence it magnifies the financial crisis.

Understanding these crises is important because their social costs are not insignificant. In the past, these types of crisis have tended to be resolved by using taxpayer resources and through higher unemployment and lower growth, so that the costs have been borne mostly by those whose incomes are not based on asset holding. The cost of rescues in previous crises has been as low as 8 percent and as high as half of GDP (Table 3.1). In the case of Thailand, the extent of non-performing loans is estimated to

TABLE 3.1
Costs of Some Systemic Banking Crises with Heavy Capital Flows

Country	Scope of crisis	Cost of rescuing banks (% of GDP)
Argentina 1980–82	16% of assets of commercial banks; 35% of total assets of finance companies	55.3
Chile 1981–83	45% of total assets	41.2
Israel 1977–83	Entire banking sector	30.0
Finland 1991–93	Savings banks affected	8.2
Mexico 1995–?	Commercial banks past due to gross loan ratio reaches 9.3% in February 1995	12–15

Source: Reisen 1997, Table 7.

be as much as $40 billion, which is equivalent to about 15 percent of Thai GDP.

As a result of the internationalization of investment funds (pension funds, mutual funds, country funds), this type of crisis—beginning with the 1994–95 Mexican crisis—has tended to involve many countries. The 1997–98 crisis in Southeast Asia shares many features of the earlier crises in developing countries but it has a distinct character of its own as well.

BANKING CRISIS AS THE SPARK FOR A CURRENCY CRISIS

The Southeast Asian currency crisis came in the wake of the "twin liberalizations." Countries in the region had recently undertaken both the liberalization of their domestic financial systems and the opening of their capital accounts. In Thailand, these liberalization efforts began in 1990 and included foreign exchange decontrol, removal of all interest rate restrictions, encouragement of nonbank capital markets, and adoption of the capital adequacy standard for bank supervision. Indonesia's capital account had been open since 1972 but liberalization of the domestic banking system began in 1988 when domestic banks and Indonesian corporations were given much more freedom in their methods of raising financing.

The first liberalization had far-reaching consequences on domestic financial systems. For example, financial liberalization in Thailand reduced the dependence of domestic financial units on lending to the government and created the need for banks and domestic financial firms to evaluate the credit-worthiness of projects. Financial liberalization inaugurated intense competition in the Thai domestic financial system. Eventual financial dominance depended on the outcome of the race to expand lending portfolios, generate off-balance sheet transactions (less subject to prudential supervision), and create quasi-banking operations. With the encouragement of nonbank sources of capital funding, Thai companies became less dependent on banks for resources and the shift to the capital adequacy approach to bank supervision increased domestic banks' independence in lending activities.

In Indonesia, the banking reforms of October 1988 permitted new entry into the banking system (entry had been closed since the beginning of the 1970s) and removed the legal restrictions which forced banks to specialize in specific areas. The number of banks increased from 111 in 1988 to 240 by March 1994 (Nasution 1996); these were the same 240 banks that met the currency crisis in July 1997. Each of Indonesia's large business conglomerates was forced, by competitive pressure, to own at least one bank. Many pension funds of state-owned enterprises established their own banks, opting to manage their financial resources themselves. Twenty Indonesian foreign exchange banks also opened branches in 14 countries; all of these had offshore banking units in Cayman and Cook Islands most "probably to launder obscure and illegitimate transactions of their customers at home" (Nasution 1996, p. 9). The increasing incidence of assistance to major banks since 1993 indicates that competition for market share led to lowering of credit standards in the banks (Nasution 1996); credit risks were not properly priced and scant attention was paid to interest risks.

The second liberalization effort consisted of opening the capital account. Most developing countries in Asia (except Korea) have encouraged the inflow of foreign investment and their economies have been open to incoming capital for a long time. Thus, liberalizing the capital account effectively consisted of (1) providing guarantees to non-residents that they could withdraw their investment effortlessly, and (2) easing outward investment restrictions on and limitations to foreign asset holdings by nationals, given that a significant proportion of non-residents could actually be nationals of the country. (This action was especially significant in such places as Mexico and Hong Kong.) Opening the capital account, along with the removal of interest ceilings gave Thailand's financial units and corporations access to offshore funds. As a consequence of Indonesia's open capital account, domestic investment became heavily dependent on external finance. There was a distinct surge in external borrowing by private Indonesian corporate groups. Demand for bonds and securities of Indonesian companies increased, so that the corporate sector became especially vulnerable when the rupiah began to devalue in late 1997.

When developing countries, including those in Southeast Asia, move to open the capital account, it is important that they dismantle the subsidies that they had put in place to encourage capital inflows (Williamson 1993). However, because these implicit subsidies are often provided through a myriad of investment incentive programs it is difficult to remove them completely. Moreover, the nature of the capital account liberalization process does not make countries eager to change their stance of encouraging inflows. Liberalizing countries are usually still capital-short and the inflows provide additional financing. But more important, the availability of external funds means that the problems of distribution between gainers and losers in the liberalization process can be avoided. New entrants can compete with old established banking institutions based on their wits and tolerance for risk (as long as government regulators do not get in the way).

Because international interest rates are generally lower than domestic interest rates in developing countries, opening the capital account has given the domestic financial systems of the developing countries access to lower cost funds with which to fuel intermediation and stimulated domestic rivalry between financial groups. It has permitted the rapid flourishing of offshore banking operations as the convenient conduit for private domestic borrowing from private external sources. Opening the capital account in the manner defined also has provided foreign fund managers access to the domestic stock and bond markets of the developing countries. In this way, the short-term and liquid liabilities of developing economies have been diversified way beyond the trade credits (deposits) that had comprised their short maturity exposures in times past. As a result, if these liabilities had to be called in a crisis, a country would have to use its international reserves. Mexico's short-term foreign currency-denominated liabilities were estimated to have exceeded its reserves by five times before the crisis there in 1995 (Calvo and Mendoza 1996).

In terms of the statistics normally used to analyse the success of liberalization programs, the Thai financial and capital account liberalization proceeded extremely well. For the main deposit money banks, lending to the government declined from 2.6 percent of GDP in 1990 to 0.6 percent in 1995 and lending to government enterprises declined from 5.1 percent to 2.6 percent of GDP. At the same time, lending to the private sector increased dramatically from 64.3 percent of GDP in 1990 to 99.8 percent by 1995. It seemed that the affliction of financial repression had been banished from the Thai economy at minimal political cost. It also appeared that the process of financial intermediation had taken off. For the whole financial industry, lending to the private sector dramatically increased from 71.9 percent of GDP in 1990 to 142 percent in 1995, a signal success.

In Indonesia, the liberalization process also appeared to be quite successful. The M1/GDP ratio started at 10 percent in 1988 and had increased to 41 percent in 1994; for M2/GDP, the increase was from 81 percent in 1988 to 101 percent in 1994. The stock market valuation to GDP ratio increased from 0.3 percent in 1988 to 7.1 percent by 1994 (Nasution 1996, p. 15). The number of bond issues increased from 6 in 1988 (with a value of 0.9 trillion rupiah) to 31 in 1994 (with a value of 2.9 trillion rupiah). Ending the exclusive access of state-owned banks to government deposits along with the removal of restrictions on credit ceilings and selective credit policy increased market competition. The share of state-owned banks in total deposits dropped significantly from 58.8 percent in 1988 to 38.6 percent in 1994.

The twin liberalizations created the conditions for a banking crisis in some countries and that banking crisis eventually culminated in the region-wide currency crisis. Throughout Southeast Asia, the post-liberalization boom in private sector lending supported dramatic increases in property lending, nourished by rising property and stock prices. In Thailand property companies were able to borrow money from banks to start up projects. Either these projects would be sold to prospective buyers or they would be floated in an initial public offering (IPO). Rising asset prices permitted banks and the original investors to recover their exposure quickly and often with handsome capital gains. Property lending booms occurred to a smaller extent, in Singapore, Malaysia, and the Philippines, all of which had also been deregulating their financial markets albeit at different speeds and from different starting points. The boom was particularly strong in Singapore with its already highly developed financial and real property markets. Informal estimates suggest that about one-fourth of the financial system's outstanding loans in Malaysia were in real estate although asset prices did not rise as steeply there as in Thailand.

Seeking to restrain the boom, in 1996, Singapore imposed heavy charges on the re-sale of property within three years of purchase. Later in the same year, Indonesia and the Philippines imposed limits on bank exposure to property lending. This latter measure conflicted with the objective of financial liberalization to remove all restrictions on private sector credit allocation.

Along with the Philippines and, of course, Singapore, Malaysia exercised active and rather effective prudential supervision over its financial system. The expansion in the financial systems of the Philippines and Malaysia before the currency crisis appears distinctly modest when compared with that in Thailand. For example, the capital adequacy ratio of Malaysia's banks stood at over 10 percent before the crisis, 2 percent above the BIS benchmark minimum.

In contrast to the situation in the three other Southeast Asian countries, over-expansion in the property sector and supervisory weaknesses became critical problems for the banking systems in Indonesia and Thailand. In fact, Indonesia had already experienced some bank failures before the 1997-98 currency crisis. The problem of non-performing loans is particularly critical for Indonesia since recent estimates suggest they comprise about 9 percent of Indonesia's portfolios, approaching the 10 percent that is presumed to prevail in Thailand (these numbers are rough estimates).

WHY THE CRISIS BECAME SO DEEP: THE LAWSON DOCTRINE AND OTHER SUPERSTITIONS

The Thai financial meltdown and the subsequent Indonesian episode resulted from a credit boom that got out of hand. Just as in the 1981 Chilean crisis, all parties (domestic public authorities, international financial institution staff, and private international investors) paid insufficient attention to the mounting consequences of the lending boom. The failure of public authorities to act and the failure of private lenders to curb their behaviour were both due to unrealistic perceptions, expectations, or superstitions.

Public Sector Misperceptions

The volume of capital flowing into Southeast Asia was enormous. In the case of Thailand, capital flows consistently exceeded 8 percent of GDP after 1993, peaking at 12.8 percent in 1995. For Indonesia, net capital inflows averaged 3.9 percent of GDP between 1990 and 1996, hitting a high of 5 percent in 1991 and 1996. Most of the Indonesian flows were financial flows since direct foreign investment accounted for an average of 1.4 percent of GDP during that period. Malaysia stands in stark contrast to Thailand and Indonesia. Malaysian authorities were particularly successful in resisting the entry of short-term capital immediately before the crisis. Capital inflows into Malaysia peaked in 1993 at a fantastic 22.5 percent of GDP, with 14 percent of GDP estimated to be short-term flows, another fantastic amount. Through a combination of policies, net inflows subsided between 1994 and 1996, when short-term flows actually turned negative.

When capital began surging into Thailand, the excess of investment over savings in the private sector was the decided cause of the country's current account deficit. The public sector savings rate was consistently positive during this period and was quite high for a developing country (Figure 3.1). The hesitation of Thai authorities to prick the boom can be traced to two attitudes which proved to be self-defeating: that it was inappropriate for public authorities to worry about purely private-sector driven current account deficits and that imposing a heavy regulatory hand would unnecessarily stifle the financial sector development program.

The Thai authorities' stance on current account deficits has precedents, notably in the "Lawson doctrine" named for UK Chancellor of the Exchequer Nigel Lawson. In September 1988 (before the UK's output crisis of 1989) Lawson proclaimed: "We are prisoners of the past, when UK current account deficits were almost invariably associated with large budget deficits, poor economic performance, low reserves and exiguous net overseas assets. The present position could not be more different." Corden (1994) expresses the "what-me-worry" attitude toward privately determined current account deficits in more formal economic terms:[2]

FIGURE 3.1
Thai Current Account Deficit and Excess Savings in the Public and Private Sectors

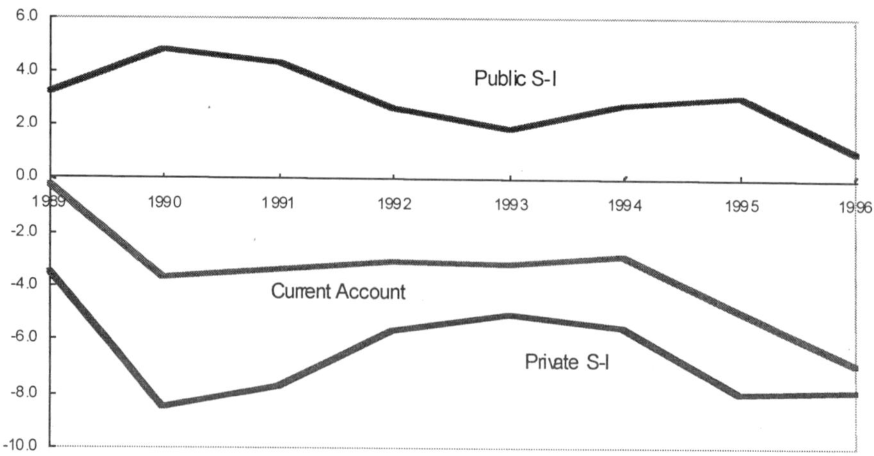

> The current account is the net result of savings and investment, private and public. Decentralized optimal decisions on private saving and investment will lead to a net balance—the current account—which will also be optimal. There is no reason to presume that governments or outside observers know better how much private agents should invest and save than these agents themselves, unless there are government-imposed distortions. It follows that an increase in a current account deficit that results from a shift in private sector behaviour should not be a matter of concern at all.

The central bank of Mexico held a similar attitude before the 1994 crisis there, as Reisen (1997, p. 1) relates:

> In January 1994, the Governor of the Banco de Mexico told *The Economist* that the current account deficit was not a problem because it was associated with the inflow of foreign funds, rather than expansionary fiscal or monetary policy. A year later, foreign and domestic investors forced Mexico to reduce the deficit on her current account from almost 8 percent of GDP in 1994 to about zero.

Thai public authorities' efforts at macroeconomic management between 1990 and 1995 might be described as a gallant rear guard action in the face of enormous offers of portfolio financing seeking to participate in Thailand's development. Despite the large volume of capital inflows, Thailand managed to maintain the real baht exchange rate remarkably close to its 1990 level (Bond 1997, p. 8). Thai inflation rates were also low during the period. This achievement must have entailed enormous leaning against wind by the Bank of Thailand. First, as already discussed, the public sector was generating surpluses that offset the demand effects of the capital inflow. Second, there would have been substantial sterilization operations at significant cost in terms of quasi-public deficits. Thailand engaged in periodic and significant sterilization operations in defence of its real exchange rate, that is, against its appreciation. It has been suggested that the baht should have been depreciated earlier, but this would have required accepting higher public deficits from an even greater measure of sterilization. Sterilization, of course, exerts upward pressure on domestic interest rates, widening the differential between domestic and foreign interest rates and provoking further capital inflows. Thailand's exchange rate peg and sterilization operations kept domestic interest rates high and meant that differentials increased, especially when international rates began to fall after 1992. Bond (1997) estimates that increased differentials account for 26.5 percent of Thailand's accumulation of reserves over the period 1988–95.

Interest rate differentials do not tell the whole story. Korea (which had not undertaken the twin liberalizations to the same extent (Griffith-Jones, Montes and Nasution 1997)), and the Philippines actually had higher interest rate differentials than Thailand. In Thailand, the differential increased in 1995, when the largest capital inflow (and presumably the most sterilization activity) occurred. The differential fell in the middle of 1996 and then started to rise, preparatory to the baht crisis. The same pattern holds for Indonesia. The differential peaked in 1991 when the largest volume (measured as a proportion of GDP) in external financial inflows was recorded. It declined until 1994, when it began to rise steadily, preparatory to the 1997 crisis.

The major failure of Thai authorities appears to have been in neglecting the long-term viability of the banking system through prudential regulation. In hindsight, given the unprecedented scale of capital inflows, they should have abandoned the objective of rapidly increasing financial intermediation, if such intermediation principally entailed unsustainable portfolio build-up in property development, in order to abide by their charge of prudential regulation. A slowdown that might have been too destabilizing and fiscally costly to engineer through a devaluation might have been accomplished by requiring the financial system to meet prudent standards. By 1996 after the first cases of financial failure emerged, Thai authorities faced the dilemma that macroeconomic policies directed at lowering the interest differential and devaluing the currency would have increased the number of financial failures. In any case, even a controlled devaluation would have been too blunt an instrument to force the banking sector to implement a pause in its growth and to recognize the increasing proportion of its portfolio as uncollectable. In the end, the Thai authorities began the adjustment by attempting a controlled devaluation which was eventually overtaken by market forces, in much the same way that Mexico's widening of its exchange rate band in December 1994 led to the "tequila crisis."

Indonesia's current account deficits, while still at restrained levels during the period, exhibited a distinct increasing trend in 1995 and 1996. Since the early 1970s, Indonesia has operated a "balanced budget" system in which it annually negotiated with official donors the level at which its investment budget would be financed externally. In a situation where only the government had effective access to international funding, the level of external financing for the government investment budget was practically equivalent to the level of the current account deficit. With a liberalized financial system and capital account, however, the private sector could now obtain external financing on its own account and became the dominant influence in setting the current account deficit. The Indonesian government budget system thus constituted the purest form of the Lawson doctrine and the government needed to utilize additional tools to obtain sustainable current account deficits. In late 1996 and 1997, the Indonesian government had just begun to use some of these tools (such as raising reserve requirements) when it found itself swept into the region's currency crisis.

During the capital surge of the 1990s public authorities in Southeast Asian countries might have permitted their currencies to appreciate. Had they adopted fully flexible exchange rate regimes, for example, appreciation would have kept interest rates constant and confined interest differentials within a narrow range and would have limited, if not completely eliminated, the fund injections into the domestic banking sector which fuelled the lending booms. There would have been no need to sterilize and accumulate reserves. However, the passions and pressures are quite different in export-oriented Southeast Asia than in other climes where the public and the business sector tend to applaud currency appreciation and lower-cost imports. For Southeast Asian countries to adopt fully market-determined exchange rates in the era of capital inflows would have been equivalent to their abandoning the region's export-oriented development model. To the extent that the capital flows were judged to be permanent, some currency appreciation would have been justified and it would have reduced the opportunity cost inherent in higher domestic interest rates and in reserve accumulation. Even so, Singapore and Malaysia which did undertake controlled appreciation did not escape the rigors of the currency market during the crisis in Southeast Asia.

Private Behavior and the Three Guarantees

Public authorities share the blame with private investors. If private agents in capital importing countries such as Thailand had behaved according to economic models of inter-temporal optimization, the outcome would have been very different (Glick and Rogoff 1995 and Razin 1995). When international interest rates temporarily fell the private sector would have increased its savings rate in order to smooth its consumption over time, and the current account deficit would have declined accordingly. If this had been the case, the domestic financial systems should have strengthened during periods of portfolio inflows instead of weakening. However, for various reasons the private sector does not always behave in economically rational ways (Griffith-Jones, Montes, and Nasution 1997). Some of the increased spending in the early 1990s might have been justified by the increase in "permanent income" in the Southeast Asian economies. However, it is doubtful that international investors had this concept in mind when they increased their exposure to the Southeast Asian economies. Rather, it is likely that they were more motivated by the perceived benefits of their private decisions.

In theory the private sector will internalize the costs of its own behaviour. This would mean, for example, that private lenders (domestic and international) to Thai finance companies would carefully consider the rising risk of their increasing exposure. They would be cognizant of the susceptibility of property markets to speculative bubbles. However, as the current and previous crises demonstrate, reality is often quite different from theory. One reason for the discrepancy is that private lending decisions often are made on the basis of certain implicit guarantees that limit risk. Three such guarantees can be seen to have encouraged private investors to over-invest in Southeast Asia, contributing to the crisis.

The first guarantee is the fact that public authorities stand behind the viability of a domestic financial system. This is not a market distortion; it is a feature of a capitalist economy in which markets for financial assets are indispensable. Financial assets constitute an uncertain contract for delivery of resources at a future date and entail substantial risks of asymmetric information, moral hazard, and contractual enforcement (Stiglitz 1994). At least implicitly, if not explicitly, a monetary authority extends the guarantee to foreign investors by standing by the foreign liabilities that are under its direct supervision.

Recently, as the sources and destinations of lending to non-supervised financial activities have expanded as the result of financial liberalization, the guarantee has been extended to the non-supervised portion as well. For example, during the 1984 financial crisis in Chile, foreign lenders forced the government to absorb their liabilities despite the fact that the government had explicitly announced—in line with its free-market philosophy—that the state would not guarantee foreign borrowing. The extent of the guarantee to foreign lenders was one of the stickiest issues in formulating the current IMF rescue package for Thailand.

Dooley (1996) identifies two other guarantees that help to explain the private basis of the banking-cum-exchange crisis in Southeast Asia: (1)

the commitment to an open capital account, and (2) the adoption of a fixed exchange rate (or a regime with limited flexibility). In combination, these two guarantees effectively subsidize private short-term external financing. They have a minor effect on direct foreign investment, but they represent significant support for non-resident equity investments and offshore banking facilities.

These two guarantees, plus the standard guarantee to the domestic financial system, remove the incentive for international investors to monitor the use of their lent resources and provide enormous incentive for them to lend more. Dooley (1996, p. 200) draws a provocative parallel between external financing in developing countries and the U.S. savings and loan crisis of the 1980s: ". . . depositors did not care if the savings and loan bought a junk bond (international reserves), a shopping centre (domestic investment), or a new car for the bank president (imports of consumer goods)." Thailand's fixed exchange rate regime offered a particularly beguiling guarantee to international investors in the form of a guarantee against currency-risk. Because the baht was closely pegged to the U.S. dollar, as the dollar appreciated in 1996, yen investors into baht were conferred, at the minimum, unrealized exchange gains.

CONTAGION: FUNDAMENTALS AND "SENTIMENTALS"

This paper suggests that contagion played a significant role in the Southeast Asian currency crisis, but in a specific way. The Thai financial crisis quickly spread a haze of uncertainty over the sustainability of both macroeconomic performance and the health of domestic financial systems throughout the region. Based on the situation before the crisis, only the domestic financial systems should have been at stake, although international investors might take a short while to distinguish between the two. Nevertheless, even with financial systems that were significantly more healthy than those in Thailand and Indonesia the currencies of Malaysia, Singapore, and the Philippines also came under attack. This is the special aspect of the contagion in Southeast Asia. It was based on "sentimentals" not fundamentals.

International funds had once expressed frustration over the heavier regulation and stodgy attitude toward entry and flotation of new instruments in these three other ASEAN economies. But then these funds retreated from the more staid economies at the same time that they fled from their more flamboyant neighbors. Malaysia, Singapore, and the Philippines in turn remain relatively healthy precisely because they depended less on—or were less successful in obtaining—such international financing. Clearly "punishment" and "discipline" are inappropriate words to explain the impact of financial markets on real economies.

Rather than locate the source of the contagion in the ardour of speculation, as public authorities are roused to do, it is more fruitful to attribute it to incomplete information. Data on economic fundamentals in Southeast Asia—current account deficits, savings rates, public sector deficits—are readily available and they support the contention that there should have been no generalized currency crisis. Information about the health of domestic financial systems is less readily available, however. Even in industrial economies publicly available quantitative data for evaluating the health of financial intermediaries are scarce and the supervisory reputation of the authorities generally substitutes for such information. The Southeast Asian economies had been undertaking to raise the quality of their accounting information and modernizing their bankruptcy procedures to Western standards. The crisis has overtaken these efforts. In the future, after the crisis has passed, it would be valuable for the larger financial institutions in the region to be rated by international commercial rating agencies. Heretofore, the informational value of these ratings has been rather limited because the variance in ratings among the few rated institutions was narrow and tended to hew closely to the rating of externally traded public sector bonds of their country of origin.

Projecting the image of a solid supervisory reputation and forthrightness in reducing current account deficits has become imperative for all the economies of the region. But, if their fundamentals are basically sound why should these countries try to build an image and risk another round of unsustainable currency appreciation as a result of the re-flow of external voluntary financing? The answer is that there is a real threat that further currency declines will exacerbate domestic banking difficulties so that the currency markets create a second round of crisis.

With weaker currencies more domestic income has to be devoted to servicing the same amount of external debt. This situation by itself weakens bank portfolios. Calls to set up a $100 billion Asian fund to respond to potential crises of this sort became a prominent non-agenda item at the annual joint meeting of the World Bank and the International Monetary Fund in Hong Kong in September 1997. These calls should be understood in the context of heading off a second round of domestic banking crisis, such as could be sparked precisely by over-adjustment of currency values.

Such a currency stabilization fund would have been inappropriate for the initial Thai crisis, because stabilizing the baht would have squandered resources to sustain an unsound financial system. In the Thai case, only a direct reform program would have justified the use of such a fund. In fact, Thailand itself drew down its own reserves and borrowed heavily in a futile attempt initially to defend the baht.

The contribution of asset prices to real recovery in Southeast Asia will be limited. For both Thailand and Indonesia, restoration of liquidity is the key and it has less to do with the recovery of asset prices and more to do with the workouts of non-performing loans. For Indonesia, identifying a program for servicing the external liabilities of the corporate sector is proving to be even more critical than a macroeconomic adjustment program. If panic and contagion in asset markets can be halted, the recovery of the Asian economies will depend on their fundamentals. The key fundamentals in regard to the Southeast Asian currency crisis are:

Viability of Domestic Financial Systems

One fundamental that must be faced in the current crisis is the resolution of bad debt in the banking system. Thailand's problem is particularly acute. The resolution of these problems is critical to re-start investment, but it raises complex political problems of assigning the burden of the write-off. Even Japan has not fully resolved this problem created by the bursting of its own property price bubble. Putting the burden on taxpayers (including those in source countries through an IMF package) would be the fastest way to resolve the issue. However, like the Mexican bailout and the earlier bailout in connection with the international debt crisis of the 1980s, this approach raises issues of moral hazard and does not help in preventing similar crises.

Just as in the period of capital inflow, the "sentimentals" have an enormous capacity to influence the health of the domestic financial system, regardless of the fundamentals. If intense sentiment drives the value of Southeast Asian currencies down too far, bank portfolios will face an increasing proportion of projects that are not viable at the new exchange rate. This situation could provoke a second round of domestic banking crises.

Responsiveness of Exports and Domestic Output to Nominal Devaluations

In 1996, key Asian economies suffered an export slowdown. The recovery of the Thai economy and the continued health of the other Southeast Asian economies depend on the impact of the recent currency changes on their real sectors. This impact hinges on two factors: (1) the ability of nominal currency changes to bring about real devaluations and (2) the responsiveness of the tradable goods and export sectors to a real devaluation.

The highly urbanized Latin American economies have not been able to engineer real devaluations, because real wages have tended to adjust rapidly to the internal inflation provoked by a nominal devaluation. In contrast, Thailand, Indonesia, Malaysia, and the Philippines, where rural areas have a larger weight in the economy, have in the past managed to carry out real devaluations from nominal changes in currency value. The success of these countries in achieving a real devaluation will depend on inflation rates; to date, inflation continues to be moderate in all the Southeast Asian countries.

In regard to the second factor, the Southeast Asian economies have robust export sectors that are not hobbled by supply-side rigidities in responding to real devaluations. Thailand is doubly blessed in having an export-oriented agricultural sector, so that a devaluation can actually improve rural incomes, alleviating the normal adverse distributional implications of the fall in average real wages necessary for a real devaluation.

Indeed, the actual impact on the real sector from the recent asset price crises in Southeast Asia raises questions about the "social" or "real" role of currency, equity, and portfolio markets in the development process. (See FitzGerald 1997 for a discussion of the different channels by which these markets might affect real economic performance.) Consider this question: if prices in Southeast Asian asset markets were to bounce back from their overshot levels in the next three months, would there be a significant impact on real economic performance? There would be some easing of credit constraints, but not much, since sterilization activities in each of the countries had already driven interest rates to historical highs for long stretches even before the crisis. Savings rates are still at historically high levels in all of the Southeast Asian economies except the Philippines, and fiscal revenues are quite healthy. These factors—interest rates, savings rates, and fiscal revenues—more than price declines in asset markets, provide the domestic resources to complete current investment projects. Quite uncontroversially, Malaysia forecasts a reduction of only one percentage point in its economic growth rate for the whole of 1997.

Even in the industrial economies, stock markets have functioned less as institutions in which to raise financing and more as venues for risk-sharing among asset owners—as "respectable casinos" (Stiglitz 1994). In recent years, the Southeast Asian economies have been Latinized to the extent that liberalization (such as the establishment of the BIBF in Thailand) has created asset markets whose influence on the exchange rate, arguably the most important single price in an open economy, far exceeds their social contribution to real investment. These asset markets have of course provided another arena for Asian banks and financial institutions to play in (and in which perhaps to learn Western methods of risk-sharing) and they have created new-found excitement in initial public offerings (IPOs).

The "sentimentals" can also adversely affect the output and export response if (1) a high level of uncertainty over future currency values disrupts trade credit to the region and (2) changes in currency values spawn political consequences. Disruption of trade credit is not likely, but political instability is a greater possibility. Even the most egregious governments and political systems stake a significant part of their reputation on a stable currency. Drastic changes in government can lead to further policy uncertainty, if not policy reversals, that could undermine the output response.

Sustainability of Current Account Deficits

Current account deficits measure the extent of total external financing provided to an economy. In the 1990s, equity and portfolio investments began to overtake direct investment, loans, and trade credit as the main forms of external financing in Southeast Asia. *Ex post,* a large current account deficit signifies both a high rate of external borrowing and a strong willingness on the part of non-residents to lend to the country. Given that private actors have not proven trustworthy in generating current account deficits that are consistent through time (based on intertemporal optimization), how should public authorities judge when deficits are "excessive" and therefore when to put a brake on external borrowing by residents?

Reisen (1997) suggests that offers of financing by non-residents should be resisted when they cause unsustainable currency appreciation, excessive risk-taking in the banking system, and a sharp drop in private savings, all of which raise sore points in terms of the fundamentals-sentimentals dichotomy. The strength of the Southeast Asian currencies prior to the 1997 crisis, while for the most part gallantly resisted by public authorities, undermined the region's international competitiveness and now necessitates a search from sentimentals to fundamentals for the "proper" exchange level between these currencies and the international economy and the proper relationship among the Southeast currencies themselves. In a world driven by market sentiment, on the other hand, just as currencies can be made "too strong" when offers of financing are abundant, they can be made "too weak" in episodes of capital withdrawal. Currencies that are "too weak" would help current account recovery in the Southeast Asian economies but they may at the same time seriously erode the health of domestic financial systems.

High Savings Rates and Robust Public Finances

During the 1990s Singapore's gross national savings rate hovered at 49 percent of GDP, Thailand's and Malaysia's at 35 to 38 percent, and Indonesia's at over 30 percent (Table 3.2). Even the 20 percent savings rate of the Philippines is considered respectable among developing economies.

In the years before the crisis, the public finances of Southeast Asian economies were extremely healthy. Troubled Thailand ran eight consecutive years of government surpluses, on the order of 2 to 3 percent of GDP, except during the export slump in 1996 when the surplus fell to 1 percent of GDP (Table 3.2). The Philippines had been strengthening its fiscal sector, and had basically balanced budgets in the last three years. The robustness of savings rates and of fiscal finances in the region means that these economies have more-than-normal domestic resources to address weaknesses in their financial systems, barring further gratuitous depredations from private currency markets.

In order to maintain the confidence of currency markets, Southeast Asian governments are delaying or cutting back on investment projects, implicitly aiming at current account deficits below 3 percent of GDP, a benchmark for developing countries. These cutbacks are a macroeconomic tragedy because the region's established export industries, its higher-than-average productivity growth, and its relative success in attracting more stable inflows of foreign direct investment would sustain current account deficits above this level (Reisen 1997).

WHAT IS TO BE DONE? INTERVENTION, POLICY, AND CO-ORDINATION

Does policy matter in managing short-term capital flows in a context of capital account liberalization, domestic financial market liberalization, and the influence of external arbitrage markets on exchange rates?

TABLE 3.2
Key Macroeconomic Data of Southeast Asian Economies

	1991	1992	1993	1994	1995	1996
			GDP Growth Rate (% per year)			
Indonesia	7.6	7.0	4.1	4.0	7.6	6.0
Malaysia	8.7	8.0	9.0	9.1	10.1	8.8
Philippines	–0.6	0.3	2.1	4.4	4.4	5.5
Singapore	7.3	6.2	10.4	10.5	8.8	7.0
Thailand	8.5	8.1	8.3	8.9	8.7	6.7
			Gross National Saving Rates (% of GNP)			
Indonesia	30.4	32.3	32.8	31.9	31.4	33.7
Malaysia	29.9	34.1	35.3	35.5	36.4	38.8
Philippines	18.2	19.4	18.1	19.0	19.0	20.5
Singapore	45.8	46.5	45.9	49.2	49.9	49.7
Thailand	35.4	34.5	34.2	35.2	35.0	35.3
			Change in Consumer Prices (% per year)			
Indonesia	9.4	7.6	9.6	8.5	9.4	7.9
Malaysia	4.4	4.7	3.6	3.7	3.4	3.5
Philippines	10.7	8.9	7.6	9.0	8.1	8.4
Singapore	3.4	2.3	2.3	3.1	1.7	1.4
Thailand	5.7	4.1	3.4	5.1	5.8	5.9
			Current Account Balances (% of GNP)			
Indonesia	–3.5	–2.1	–1.4	–1.6	–3.6	–4.1
Malaysia	–9.2	–3.9	–4.6	–6.0	–9.0	–6.3
Philippines	–2.2	–1.8	–5.5	–4.5	–3.3	–4.1
Singapore	11.1	11.1	7.3	15.9	17.6	15.3
Thailand	–7.8	–5.8	–5.2	–5.8	–8.3	–8.1
			Central Government Budget Surpluses (% of GNP)			
Indonesia	–0.7	–0.4	–0.4	0.2	–0.2	—
Malaysia	–2.0	–0.8	0.2	2.3	0.9	0.6
Philippines	–2.1	–1.2	–1.5	1.0	0.6	0.3
Singapore	4.7	5.4	4.6	3.4	7.4	5.4
Thailand	4.3	2.6	1.9	2.7	3.0	0.9

Source: Asia Development Bank 1997.

The Scope for Independent Policy Making

There is a limited but still significant scope for monetary independence in the countries of Southeast Asia because the types of financial assets traded domestically are not complete substitutes for external assets (Montes 1997b). Public authorities would do well not to let the ideology of liberalization obstruct the objectives of sound development of the financial system and more productive investment. Public authorities in Chile had their sights on these specific objectives when they asserted that because they took a longer term perspective than the market, they were justified to intervene in setting the exchange rate and in slowing down speculative activity (Agosin and Ffrench-Davis 1995).

During periods of external speculation in favor of a developing economy, authorities have significant capacity to intervene to prevent unsustainable currency appreciation, the weakening of the domestic banking system, or a decline in the domestic savings rate (Montes 1997b). Public monetary and fiscal authorities should be sceptical of economists' market fatalism because they do have significant contingent liabilities when financial systems fail, as was proven in other earlier episodes and once again in the Thai case. The scope for monetary independence depends on the soundness of macroeconomic management and on the willingness of authorities to take discretionary action. "Moral suasion" used to be listed as one instrument of monetary policy. Unfortunately, it becomes an awkward instrument to use when authorities also seek to develop the financial system through the private sector.

Stricter supervision of the banking system at a time when capital account liberalization has expanded banks' sources of funds is not only prudent but is also a means to counter the overheating of the economy (Montes 1996). Through stricter banking supervision some of the burden of fighting overheating is lifted from the shoulders of public authorities. In practice, this requires considerable sophistication since it is also important not to constrain the financial development that is the rationale for liberalization. For example, imposing limits on consumer and property lending immediately contradicts the intent of removing credit ceilings as part of the financial liberalization process.

Every economy has its own capacity and characteristics for monitoring, regulation, and supervision. Regulatory procedures should not be dismantled in the interest of completing the twin liberalizations just because they are regulatory or just because they are financially repressive. The U.S. financial system, after all, has prospered for decades under Regulation Q restrictions. In many cases, previously dismantled policies and regulations have to be reinstated. In 1996 Indonesia began using reserve requirements as an instrument of policy after they had been dramatically lowered in order to minimize financial repression. Financial repression is often the consequence of retaining tools with which to supervise the domestic financial system. The cost of financial repression, estimated at around 2 percent of GDP, is far lower than the cost of rescuing a banking system, on the order of 8 percent of GDP (Table 3.1) and this figure ignores the loss of investment confidence, unemployment, and other social costs imposed by a system-wide banking failure. Moreover, having to re-instate restrictions that have been dismantled can be destabilizing, as Malaysia learned in early August 1997 when it tried to reinstate some Regulation Q-type ceilings.

Implications for Policy in Developing Countries

This analysis of the Southeast Asian currency crisis has at least three broad implications for developing countries. First, weakening the implied guarantees on the open capital account and stabilizing the exchange rate (either by floating the currency or by having a wide band) are critical to ensure that private actors internalize the risks of holding portfolio positions in emerging markets, even though these steps may reduce the confidence of international investors.

This means in part that exchange rates have to be more flexible. In Chile, where the volume of inflows has been significant over a long period of time, authorities have had to resort to discrete nominal appreciations followed by a series of depreciations to return the currency to a value that they consider consistent with the development objective of expanding and diversifying exports (Agosin and Ffrench-Davis 1995). Thailand's situation underscores the perils of pegging too closely to a currency that is appreciating, even though the pegged regime was successful in achieving a real depreciation.

A second broad implication is that during periods of currency attack, capital controls and other efforts to prop up a currency are ineffective and actually subsidize further speculation. Krugman's (1979) model of a currency attack has three key features: (1) countries have finite reserves and when the reserves run out, speculators' bets are rewarded with significant gains; (2) raising domestic interest rates can hurt both the domestic financial system and the tradable goods sector, undermining external performance; and (3) investing additional resources to prop up the currency only provides additional subsidy for speculative activity.

Developments since July 1997 confirm the proposition that controls are ineffective in episodes of capital outflows and that investing more resources to defend the currency only subsidizes speculative activity further. Moreover, the difficulties of the ringgit, which have been interpreted as market reaction to Malaysia's policy responses, appear to have affected the other Southeast Asian currencies.

These events suggest the indispensability of closer consultation among ASEAN countries. International co-operation and co-ordination are the best response to these episodes. One of the institutional realities of today's international financial markets is their tendency to view all projects in a single country or even in a single region with one eye. For this reason, it is critical that central banks in the region give each other prior private notice of intended drastic changes in policy. More frequent meetings among central bank and treasury officials will create the mutual confidence to underpin these prior notice arrangements.

Moreover, it is particularly important for the ASEAN countries to avoid the exigency of competitive devaluations, both for game-theoretic reasons (the number of rounds of devaluation could be quite high) and because recent experience proves the power of international markets to force a certain relationship among the ASEAN currencies.

Co-ordinated actions in the currency markets apparently helped to defend the baht in May 1997. Nevertheless, no amount of co-ordinated action could have avoided the drastic Thai adjustment later in 1997, because Thailand's weakened banking system required radical policy attention. Had these financial system difficulties been faced earlier they would have remained a totally domestic problem. This situation illustrates one of the sticky points of international co-operation, where to draw the line between external co-operation and purely national responsibility (Montes 1997*a*).

Each individual country should have the primary responsibility for prudent development of its financial system while other countries in the region should have the ability to comment—in private—on financial sector trends they perceive to be unhealthy in neighbouring countries. Standard IMF surveillance procedures should have been and should continue to be the first approach. But, as the 1980s debt crisis indicated and as was proven again in this episode, Bretton Woods staff may not sound the alarm bells until too late because they are too deep in the throes of their own liberalization ideology. Individual countries themselves and countries that might be affected by policy failures in neighbouring countries have to take more responsibility. Efforts to increase information-sharing among prudential and regulatory authorities in the region, particularly in order to minimize regulatory evasion need to be supported. These efforts at prudential and regulatory co-operation should also involve the source countries—Japan and the United States in particular.

Countries such as the Philippines should be encouraged to build up their international reserve balances to levels at least comparable to the level of short-term government liabilities. Bringing reserves up to such levels improves a country's ability to withstand speculative attacks and furthermore reduces the risk to the system as a whole. Beyond their April 1996 agreement, Asian countries might consider standing ready as an initial position to match a certain proportion of the reserves of a country whose currency comes under speculative attack (Montes 1997*a*).

The third broad conclusion of this analysis is that for developing countries the approach to domestic financial liberalization is critical both to the effectiveness of short-term macroeconomic policy and to the sustainable use of incoming capital funds. As suggested above, the crisis in the Thai financial system and weaknesses in the financial systems in other Southeast Asian economies are the only real and fundamental feature of the current crisis. These kinds of weaknesses are endemic, even in industrial economies. In Southeast Asia, the enormous availability of short-term foreign funds, as a result of the "three guarantees," exacerbated this weakness and created a large asset price bubble in Thailand. The role of short term foreign funds in the current crisis should not be exaggerated and should not misdirect attention away from the kind of adjustment that is required to restore the region to financial stability.

In the longer term, there are justifications for isolating domestic banking systems from short-term volatility through regulatory measures and capital controls (Kaminsky and Reinhart 1996). There is also a need to strengthen bank regulation and to devote increased attention to consumer and property lending during periods of capital inflows. More sophisticated understanding on the part of the international private asset managers is called for in this regard; because developing countries have more limited policy handles, their authorities often must resort to blunt and abrupt policy actions to stop consumer and property lending. Such actions are appropriate in a period of capital inflows but can be counter-productive in an episode of capital withdrawal.

Prudence suggests that in developing countries the bias should be in the direction of stricter regulation (especially in regard to the introduction of new financial instruments). When public authorities' capacity for financial regulation does not match that in industrial economies, there is strong justification for imposing capital adequacy requirements higher than the 8 percent minimum under the Basle rules (which were originally suggested for financial institutions in advanced industrial economies). Authorities in developing countries are particularly hobbled by their weaker capacity to monitor international transactions and by inexperience in evaluating new financial instruments. (Even multinational corporations have suffered large losses as a result of taking positions in derivatives.) Monetary and fiscal authorities have to increase the capability of their human resources to monitor the activities of financial companies and to provide prudential supervision.

Nevertheless, while monitoring and supervision of domestic financial systems are primarily the responsibility of domestic authorities, there is an enormous scope for international co-operation to reduce the mischief of "policy arbitrage." Policy arbitrage occurs when countries are forced to relax regulatory standards in order to compete with the standards in nearby economies. For example, lower capital adequacy requirements in some countries create pressure for other countries to reduce their capital requirements in order to attract financial companies.

Notes

1 In the case of Thailand, the introduction of the Bangkok International Banking Facilities (BIBF) in March 1993 was a key strategy for internationalizing the financial market. The Thai effort sought to integrate more closely with international financial markets and to provide a market in which the other countries in mainland Southeast Asia could raise their capital requirements. Under a BIBF license, a company not only received tax and regulatory incentives competitive with other offshore centers, it was also allowed to operate practically all the standard international banking activities. In particular, the offshore facility permitted onshore lending, as a means to introduce new foreign financial institutions to the domestic financial market. In fact, BIBF licensees were permitted to open two branches outside of Bangkok. By March 1995, BIBF accumulated inflow into the Thai economy stood at US$12.5 billion; the corresponding amount that came into the facility and was lent out of Thailand was US$0.6 billion (Nijathaworn 1995). The BIBF evolved into a vigorous source of short-term funds for Thai banking operations.

2 In fact, under Ricardian equivalence even publicly dominated current account deficits are not a policy problem because households are expected to automatically increase their savings in response to public deficits in anticipation of higher tax liabilities in the future.

3 The classic treatment of this problem was made by Diaz-Alejandro (1985) in response to the Southern Cone financial crises in the early 1980s.

References

Agosin, Manuel R. and Ricardo Ffrench-Davis. 1995. "Managing Capital Inflows in Latin America". Manuscript. Universidad de Chile, 28 November.

Bond, Timothy James. 1997. "Capital Flows to Asia: The Role of Monetary Policy". Paper presented at the IIASA Conference on Financial Flows to Transition Economies, Laxenburg, Austria, 9–10 May.

Calvo, Guillermo and Enrique G. Mendoza. 1996. "Petty Crime and Cruel Punishment: Lessons from the Mexican Debacle". AEA *Papers and Proceedings*, May, pp.170–73.

Corden, W.M. 1994. *Economic Policy, Exchange Rates and the International System*. Oxford: Clarendon Press.

Dooley, Michael P. 1996. "Capital Controls and Emerging Markets". *International Journal of Finance and Economics*, 1, pp. 197–206.

Diaz-Alejandro, Carlos. 1985. "Good-bye Financial Repression, Hello Financial Crash". *Journal of Development Economics*.

Fischer, Bernhard and Helmut Reisen. 1993. *Liberalizing Capital Flows in Developing Countries: Pitfalls, Perquisites and Perspectives*. Paris: OECD Development Centre Studies.

FitzGerald, E.V.K. 1997. "Short-Term Capital Flows and the 'Real Economy' in Developing Countries". Manuscript. United Nations University/World Institute for Development Economics Research (UNU/WIDER), Helsinki, July.

Krugman, Paul. 1979. "A Model of Balance of Payments Crises". *Journal of Credit, Money, and Banking*, 11 (August), pp. 311–25.

Glick, R. and Rogoff, K. 1995. "Global versus Country-Specific Productivity Shocks and the Current Account". *Journal of Monetary Economics*, May.

Griffith-Jones, Stephany, Manuel F. Montes and Anwar Nasution. 1997. "A Latin American and Asian Perspective on Managing Capital Surges". Manuscript. University/World Institute for Development Economics Research (UNU/WIDER), Helsinki, June.

Harberger, A. 1985. "Lessons for Debtor-Country Managers and Policymakers". In *International Debt and the Developing Countries*, edited by G.W. Smith and J.T. Cuddington, pp. 236–57. Washington, D.C.: The World Bank.

Kaminsky, G. and Reinhart, C.M. 1996. "The Twin Crises: The Causes of Banking and Balance-of-Payments Problems". Working Paper No. 17, University of Maryland at College Park: Center for International Economics.

Montes, Manuel F. 1996. "Country Responses to Massive Capital Flows". United Nations University/World Institute for Development Economics Research (UNU/WIDER) Working Paper No. 121, Helsinki, September.

______. 1997*a*. "Private Deficits and Public Responsibilities: Philippine Responses to Capital Inflows". In *Papers and Proceedings of the International Symposium on Macroeconomic Interdependence in the Asia-Pacific Region*. Tokyo: Economic Research Institute, Economic Planning Agency, Government of Japan, March, pp. 409–60.

______. 1997*b*. "Public Responses to Private Capital Flows: Why, If, and How?" Manuscript. United Nations University/World Institute for Development Economics Research (UNU/WIDER), Helsinki, June.

______. 1997*c*. *The Currency Crisis in Southeast Asia*. Singapore: Institute of Southeast Asian Studies.

Nasution, Anwar. 1996. "The Banking System and Monetary Aggregates Following Financial Sector Reforms: Lessons from Indonesia". *Research for Action* Series No. 27, September.

Nijathaworn, Bandid. 1995. "Central Banking Policies in Thailand in the 1990s". Paper presented at the First International Conference on Forecasting the Singapore Economy and Annual Review of Central Banking Policies in the Asia-Pacific Basin, Singapore, 10–11 August.

Razin, A. 1995. "The Dynamic-Optimizing Approach to Current Account". In *Understanding Interdependence: The Macroeconomics of the Open Economy*, edited by P. Kenen Princeton: Princeton University Press.

Reisen, Helmut. 1997. "Sustainable and Excessive Current Account Deficits". United Nations University/World Institute for Development Economics Research (UNU/WIDER) Working Paper No. 151, Helsinki, May.

Stiglitz, Joseph. 1994. "The Role of the State in Financial Markets". *Proceedings of the World Bank Annual Conference on Development Economics 1993*. Washington D.C.: The World Bank, pp. 19–52.

Williamson, John. 1993. "A Cost-Benefit Analysis of Capital Account Liberalization". In *Financial Opening: Policy Issues and Experiences in Developing Countries*, edited by H. Reisen and B. Fischer. Paris: Organisation for Economic Co-operation and Development, pp. 25–34.

4

Coping with Capital Flows and Monetary Policy Framework: The Case of Korea[1]

Dongchul Cho

INTRODUCTION

Economic liberalization and deregulation have become a general trend in the era of globalization. The Korean economy is no exception to this trend. Despite the miraculous performance under a government-led growth strategy, Korea began to relax some of its regulatory policies in the 1980s, and it accelerated the liberalization process in the 1990s. With respect to external sectors of the economy, the Korean government introduced a market-based exchange rate system in 1990, and began to open the official capital markets in 1992 by allowing foreigners to invest more directly in the Korean stock market. Since then, capital market deregulation has become an irreversible trend. The only remaining matter seems to be how fast the liberalization process will, or should, be carried out.

With the current interest rate differentials between Korea and the developed economies, drastic, full-scale liberalization would certainly induce a large influx of capital and appreciate the Korean won. This would hurt the price competitiveness of Korean products in international markets, which could bring about significant instability in Korea's export-oriented economy. An urgent question among Korean policy-makers is whether there exists any policy combination that could minimize the macroeconomic instability associated with the inevitable trend of capital market liberalization.

CAPITAL FLOWS AND RELATED MACROECONOMIC VARIABLES IN KOREA

Exchange Rate System

With the abandonment of the fixed exchange rate system in 1980, Korea let the exchange rate float by pegging it to a basket of foreign currencies. Nevertheless, the government continued to exercise great discretionary power over the exchange rate in the name of "policy considerations," the most important of which seemed to be maintenance of a healthy current account balance.[2]

It was recognized, however, that it was no longer possible to operate the exchange rate as an independent policy tool since Korea's capital markets were no longer insulated from the world capital market. To prepare for the forthcoming capital account liberalization process, the Multiple Basket Peg System was finally replaced in March 1990 with the Market Average Exchange Rate System. Under the new system, the exchange rate is determined by demand for and supply of the Korean won *vis-à-vis* foreign currencies, and the government can affect the exchange rate only indirectly through the market. Although the Korean government still appears to be a major player in the market for the Korean won, its relative market power will certainly diminish as Korea's capital market becomes integrated with the international market.

Exchange Rate Fluctuations and the Current Account Balance

In an economy like Korea's that relies heavily on international trade, the importance of maintaining a stable real effective exchange rate (REER) has long been recognized as a necessary condition for the stability of the macroeconomy.[3] In the second half of the 1980s, the REER experienced a swing of more than 25 percent (Figure 4.1). The main reason was the time lag between a change in the yen/dollar rate and the adjustment of the won/dollar rate. In 1985 after the Plaza Accord the yen/dollar rate appreciated sharply, but the won/dollar rate depreciated in 1985 and only started to appreciate after 1986. Under the new exchange rate system in the 1990s, the REER has been fairly stable, fluctuating within a 10 percent range.

Most impressive, however, is the close correlation between the REER and the current account balance (as a percentage of GDP). The effects of the REER on the current account appear with a substantial time lag—a stylized fact that is known as the J-curve effect. This time lag is most prominent around the second half of the 1980s (Figure 4.1). The surge in

FIGURE 4.1
Real Effective Exchange Rate (REER) and Ratio of Current Account Balance to GDP, 1982–96

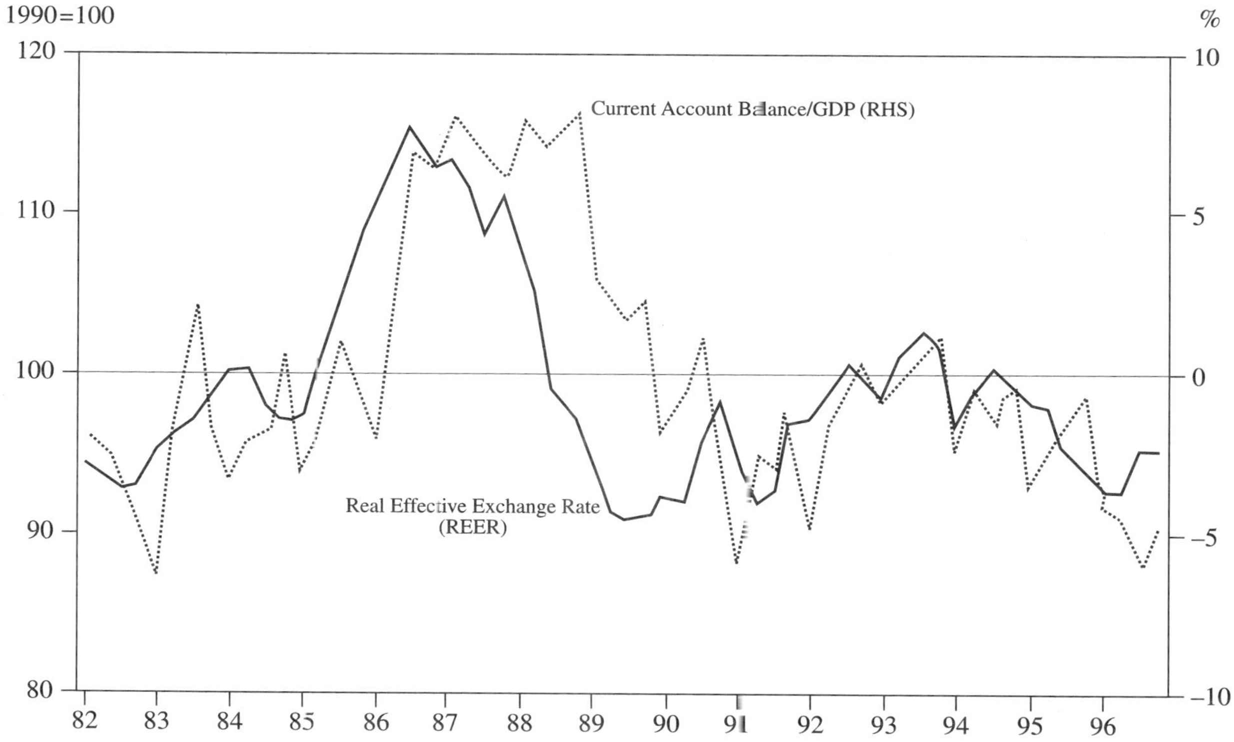

the REER from 1985 was reflected in a huge current account surplus only after 1986, and the drastic reversion of the REER in 1988 was finally transformed into the current account balance in 1989.

A direct measure of the time lag is the correlation coefficient between the current account surplus as a percentage of GDP and the lagged values of the REER. The correlation coefficient reaches a maximum of more than 0.8 at a lag of 4 quarters.[4] This high correlation shows clearly how sensitive Korea's external transactions are to the exchange rate and how important exchange rate policy is in Korea.

So far, we have focused on the relationship between the exchange rate and the current account in Korea because the capital account, the other important driving force of external transactions, has passively adjusted to the other macroeconomic variables. As Korea liberalizes capital account transactions, however, the interactions between the current account and capital account along with the exchange rate determination process change substantially.

Capital Market Liberalization to Date

In Korea, capital market liberalization has proceeded gradually, taking into account such factors as the current account balance, the money supply, and the exchange rate. For example, when the current account showed large deficits in the first half of the 1980s (Figure 4.2), capital outflows were strictly limited to slow down the pace of foreign debt accumulation. This situation was completely reversed in the latter half of the 1980s. A current account surplus reaching 7.8 percent of GDP in 1988 forced the Korean government to decontrol capital outflows. As a result, the net level of foreign debt plunged from 37.7 percent of GDP in 1985 to 1.4 percent in 1989. But the increased capital outflows were insufficient to contain the growth of reserve money (Figure 4.3). Hence, private credit was restricted, and massive sterilization was conducted through monetary stabilization bonds (MSBs).[5]

Controls on capital flows became increasingly difficult as the Korean economy became more integrated into the global economy. Foreign investors, as well as domestic companies, constantly demanded further opening of Korean markets to exploit the wide interest differential with overseas markets. To meet their demands to a certain degree, a capital account liberalization plan was finally announced in 1993. This plan was superseded by the Foreign Exchange Reform Plan in 1994, which in turn was revised in late 1995. Further liberalization was recently announced in April, 1996 (Table 4.1).[6]

FIGURE 4.2
External Balances as a Percentage of GDP, 1980–95

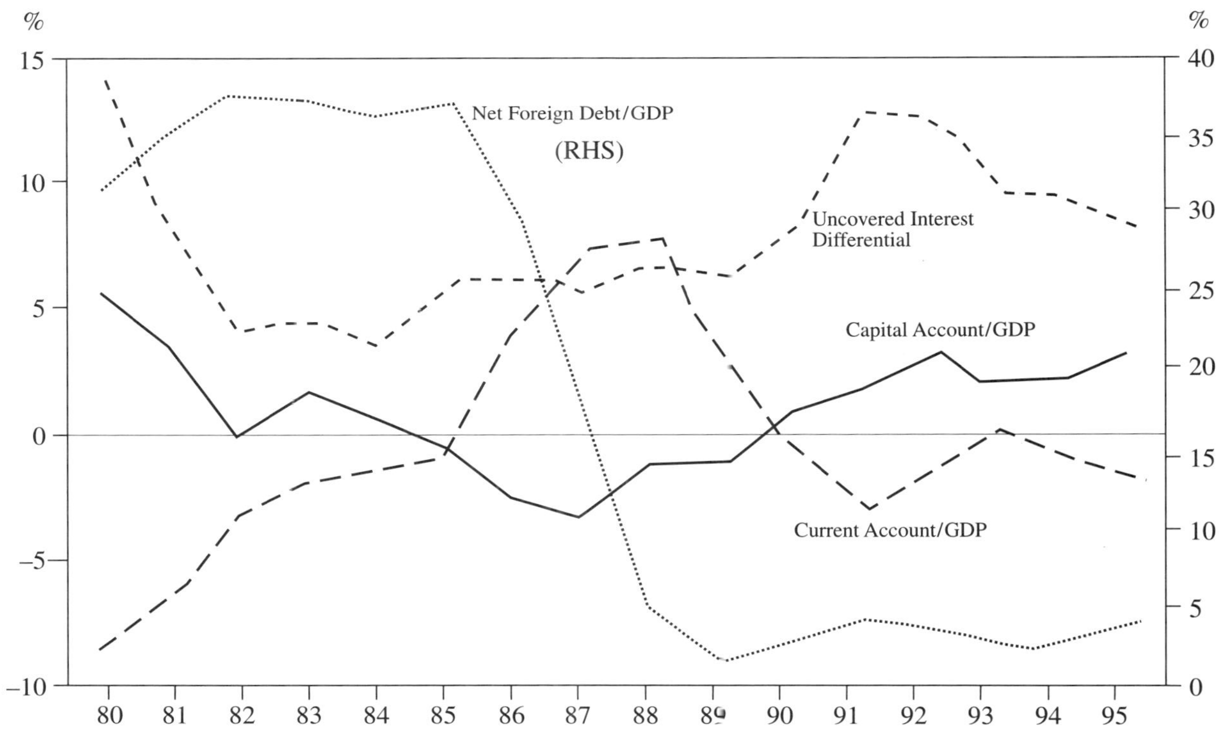

FIGURE 4.3
Annual Growth Rate of Monetary Aggregates, Monetary Stabilization Bonds, and CPI, 1980–95

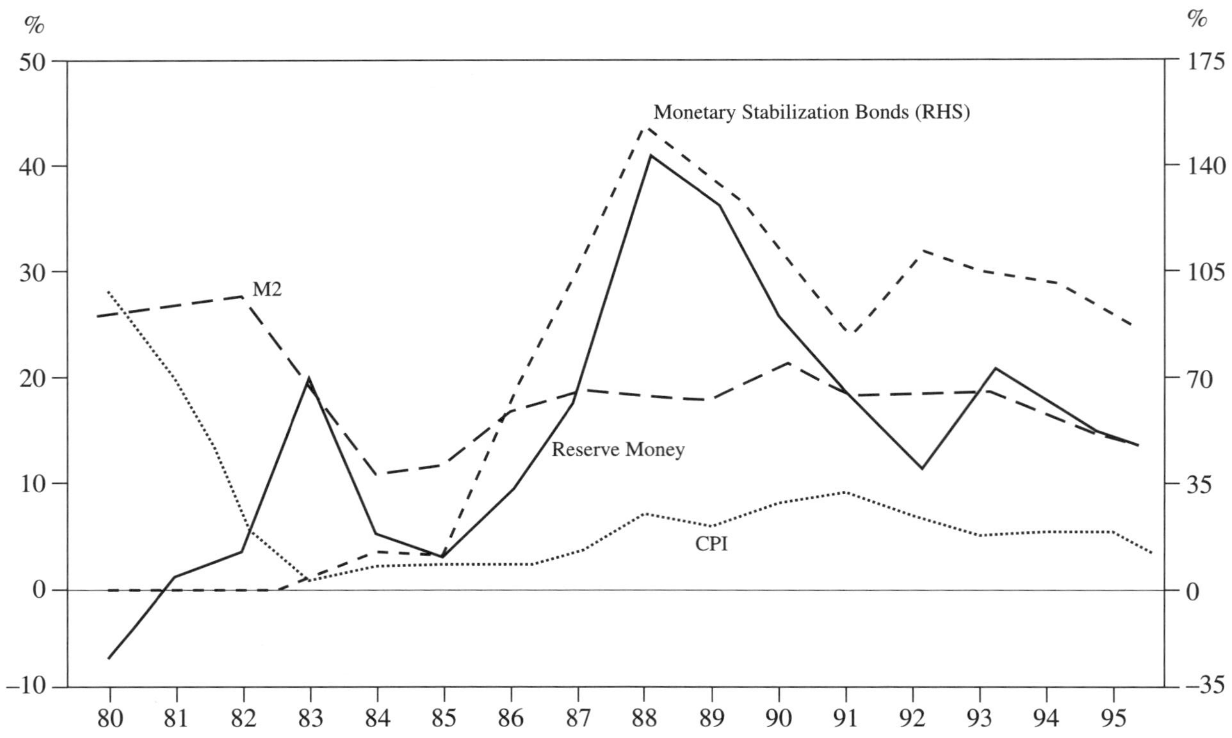

TABLE 4.1
Korea's Capital Account Liberalization Plan

		Long-Term Capital Flows
1993	Portfolio	Outward limits raised for institutional investors. Public allowed to purchase foreign stocks through trusts. Limits on inward investment in 5 percent foreign-owned businesses reduced
	Borrowing	Notification of foreign corporate borrowing. Deferred payment period for imports of raw materials for export extended. Foreign high-tech enterprises allowed to borrow short-term.
1994–95	Portfolio	Inward stock ownership limits raised. Definition of non-resident narrowed.
	Borrowing	International organizations allowed to issue won-denominated bonds in domestic market. Non-residents allowed to purchase convertible bonds of small and medium-sized enterprises and government or public bonds in the primary market.
1996–97	Portfolio	Inward stock ownership limits raised.
	Borrowing	Direct inward purchase of non-guaranteed long bonds floated by small businesses. Commercial borrowing allowed (if interest rates are comparable). Deferred payment for imports.

		Short-Term Capital Flows
1993	Exchange rate	Fluctuation margin widened to ±1.0 percent.
	Position limits	Limits equalized between banks based on equity capital.
	Documentation	No longer required for transactions under $300 million. Third currency forward contracts freed. Limit increased for forward won transactions.
	Forward transactions	After-the-event documentation.
	Non-resident won	Non-interest-bearing transferable accounts permitted, won settlement of trade transactions up to $100,000.
1994–95	Exchange rate	Fluctuation margin widened again.
	Non-resident won	Settlement limit raised.
1996–97	Exchange rate	Floating rate introduced.
	Position limits	Focus shifted to prudential control of banks' exposure.
	Documentation	Normal transactions completely exempted from underlying documentation requirements, but the principle of real demand maintained.
	Non-resident won	Invisible transactions partly settled in won.

Source: Ministry of Finance and Economy.

Korean residents now have a great deal of freedom as far as capital outflows are concerned. Individuals, as well as institutional investors, can make unlimited investments in overseas securities. Institutional investors can hold deposits in foreign banks up to 100 million U.S. dollars, while lower limits apply to legal entities and individuals. Outward foreign direct investment (FDI) is going to be completely liberalized soon.

In contrast, considerable restrictions still remain on capital inflows: a maximum of 23 to 26 percent of the outstanding shares of a company can be held by non-residents and a maximum of 5 percent can be held by a single non-resident; direct holding of bonds by non-residents is allowed only for convertible bonds issued by small and medium enterprises; bond-holding by non-residents is allowed indirectly through the Korea Trust and Country Fund; domestic companies can use foreign commercial loans within certain limits only for the import of capital goods and for FDI; delayed payment for imports is currently permitted for up to 120 days. Some of these restrictions are expected to be removed or loosened in the near future, but complete liberalization of critical markets (e.g., bond markets) will not be allowed until the interest rate differential narrows substantially.

The major components of capital inflows to Korea since 1990 are private loans and portfolio investment. The share of public loans has been shrinking continuously and FDI has fallen to less than one-fifth of portfolio investment. The gross amount of foreign debt is estimated to be slightly over US$100 billion (around 22 percent of GDP) by the end of 1996, while accumulated net foreign loans reached US$33.4 billion (6.9 percent of GDP).

Capital Flows and the Interest Rate Differential

Since external capital flows were tightly controlled in Korea, the capital account balance was extremely insensitive to the uncovered interest differential.[7] This can be confirmed by regressing the capital account balance on the interest rate differential adjusted for expected depreciation (Table 4.2).[8] If capital were perfectly mobile across national borders, if domestic and foreign assets were perfect substitutes, and if there were no uncertainty, then the coefficient on the interest rate differential variable would approach infinity, so that only the exchange rate adjusts to restore equilibrium. In the regression results, the uncovered interest rate differential shows a small, but significantly positive correlation with the short-term capital account (skb_t) while the correlation with the long-term capital account balance (lkb_t) is negative and significant.[9]

TABLE 4.2
Regression of Capital Flows on Uncovered Interest Rate Differential

	Short-term Balance (skb_t)		Long-term Balance (lkb_t)		Overall Balance (kb_t)	
Constant ($x10^{-2}$)	−0.03 (0.13)	−0.13 (0.54)	1.26 (2.83)	0.88 (2.15)	1.23 (2.38)	0.76 (1.63)
Uncovered Interest Rate Differential, $i_t - i_t^f - \log(e_{t+1}/e_t)$	0.04 (1.81)	0.09 (2.45)	−0.11 (2.63)	0.09 (1.33)	−0.07 (1.47)	0.18 (2.39)
Time trend (t-1995)		0.01 (1.69)		0.04 (3.76)		0.04 (4.14)
R^2	0.06	0.11	0.12	0.32	0.04	0.29

Notes: Capital account balances, skb_t, lkb_t, and kb_t, are normalized by potential GDP. The uncovered interest rate differential is calculated from the domestic interest rate i_t (yield on 3-year corporate bonds), the foreign interest rate i_t^f (3-month eurodollar rate), and the won/dollar exchange rate e_t. The linear time trend, t-1995, is normalized so that t=1995 yields 0. The sample period is Q1 1983 to Q4 1995, and numbers in parentheses are t-statistics.

Although the correlation between Korea's capital account balances and the uncovered interest rate differential is not strong, it seems clear that the capital account has become more responsive to the interest rate differential with Korea's financial market deregulation. In a second set of regressions a linear time trend is significant for both short- and long-term capital account balances.[10] In addition, the estimates for the overall capital account balance regression imply that the coefficient became positive in 1991, approximately the same time that the stock market began to open to foreign investors.

Secular Trend in the Interest Rate

The annual yield rate on three-year corporate bonds in Korea is still around 12 percent, which implies a real interest rate of approximately 7 percent, given the roughly 5 percent annual inflation. This relatively high interest rate makes Korea an attractive market for foreign investors that has not yet been sufficiently explored. The most relevant questions to our analysis are what maintains the high (real) interest rate in Korea and how will it evolve over time.

Severe government controls kept official interest rates on bank loans as well as corporate bonds at levels far below the market rate in Korea until the first half of the 1980s. Although the gap between the official rates and the curb market rate substantially narrowed as a result of the continuous financial deregulation in the 1980s, the curb market rate seemed to be a better measure for the market rate at least until the first half of the 1980s. The curb market rate has been in a downward secular trend from over 20 percent in the early 1970s to around 7 percent in 1995 (Figure 4.4).[11] The corporate bond rate, which is widely used in the 1990s as the representative market rate, has followed a similar downward trend if the sample is restricted to the recent period, say, 1983–1995.

This downward trend of the real interest rate is in accordance with the transitional dynamics of the neo-classical growth model. In a stylized neo-classical growth model, employing the Cobb-Douglas production function, $Y_t = A_t K_t^{\alpha} L_t^{1-\alpha}$ (where Y denotes potential output, A the level of technology, K capital stock, and L the labour supply) the interest rate is equated to the marginal productivity of capital, $\alpha Y_t/K_t$, less the depreciation rate, δ. In an economy with an initial capital-labour ratio (K/L) below the steady state level, the marginal productivity of capital (hence interest rate) declines over time to converge to the steady state level (say, the world level of the interest rate).

A plot of rough estimates of $\alpha Y_t/K_t - \delta$ using $\alpha = 1/3$ and $\delta = 0.066$ per year closely approximates the trend of the curb rate and supports the assertion that transitional dynamics is a plausible description for the secular trend of the Korean interest rate (Figure 4.4). The average growth rate of investment has been far greater than the average growth rate of GDP in Korea since the 1960s.[12] This was the main cause of the declining trend of Y_t/K_t, and it seems unlikely that the trend will suddenly reverse direction.

In relation to potential capital inflows, the implication of the downward trend of real interest rates (or marginal productivity of capital) is clear; the pressures of capital inflow will diminish over time. This expectation justifies the gradual liberalization by the Korean government which wishes to minimize the macroeconomic impacts of capital inflows.

SIMULATION RESULTS OF A BIG BANG VERSUS GRADUAL LIBERALIZATION

The main question is how fast Korea's liberalization should proceed. Cho and Koh (1996) simulated a model of the Korean economy to compare the paths of macroeconomic variables if liberalization took place as a Big

FIGURE 4.4
Real Interest Rate Trend, 1972–95

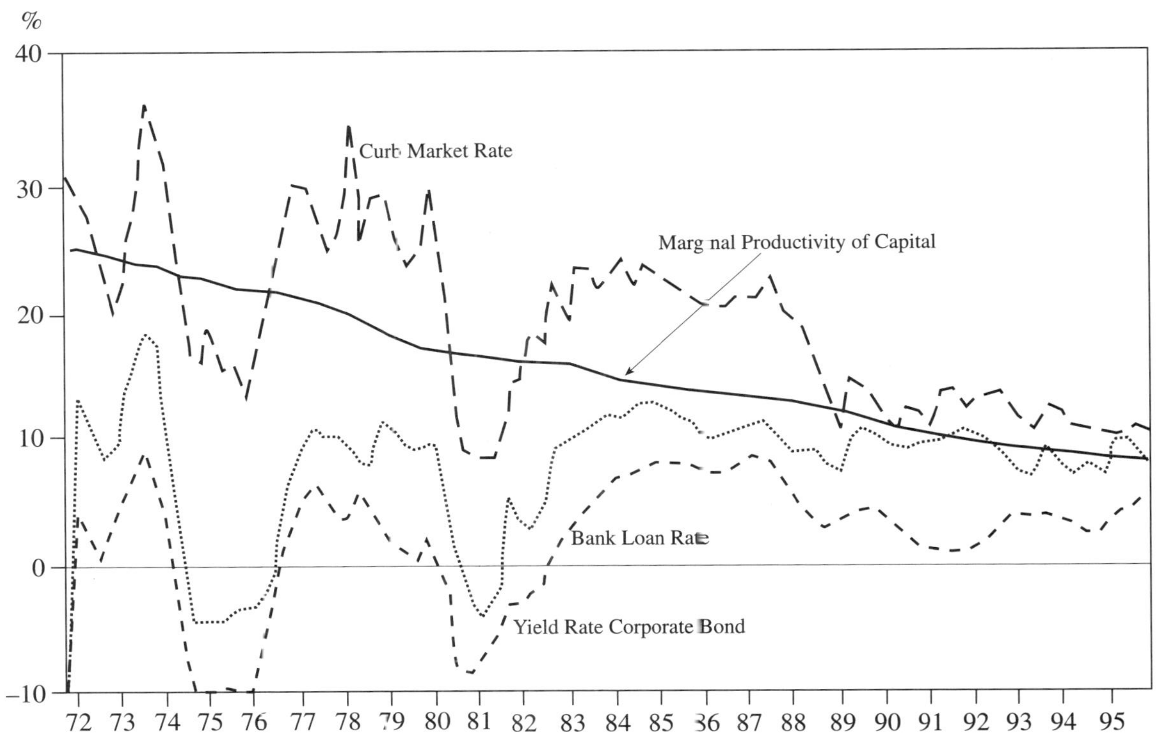

Bang or more gradually. The model is neo-classical in the long-run, but Keynesian in the short run. All the real variables are determined by the supply side in the long run, but demand shocks matter in the short run. The capital account balance is largely determined by the interest rate differential adjusted for the rate of expected depreciation (that is, $i_t - i_t^f - \log(e_{t+1}/e_t)$, where i_t is the domestic interest rate at time t, i_t^f is the foreign interest rate at time t, and e_t is the exchange rate at time t). For the Big Bang case, uncovered interest parity abruptly replaces the exchange rate determination process in 1996.[13] For the two gradual liberalization cases, the elasticity of the capital account balance with respect to the interest rate differential gradually increases to infinity over time (Figures 4.5a through 4.5h).

Following the Big Bang, the exchange rate initially appreciates by approximately 15 percent from its long-run equilibrium level and then gradually depreciates by the interest differential until it converges to the PPP rate at around the year 2005. This is the path that a typical sticky-price monetary model would predict (Dornbusch 1976). The (real) interest rate declines faster in the Big Bang scenario than when liberalization occurs gradually because of more active investment and the resulting capital accumulation (Figure 4.5b). Potential output also increases fast with a Big Bang, but the economy goes through a recession for the first two to three years due to the contraction of foreign demand (Figures 4.5c and 4.5d). Prices, particularly the Producer Price Index (PPI), which is far more affected by import prices than the Consumer Price Index (CPI), become very stable (Figures 4.5e and 4.5f). But the current account deficit reaches almost 5 percent of GDP in 1997 and then approaches balance (Figure 4.5g), rapidly accumulating (net) foreign debt to 15 percent in 1999 (Figure 4.5h).

The only sustainable exchange rate policy in this Big Bang case is exchange rate overshooting. Targeting the nominal exchange rate at the level consistent with the current account balance in 1996 would bring on hyperinflation. Since interest parity should hold, the only way to support nominal exchange rate stability ($e_{t+1} = e_t$ for all t) is to equate the domestic interest rate to the foreign rate ($i_t = i_t^f$ for all t). The initial monetary expansion that sets i_t equal to i_t^f brings about inflation. Hence, i_t begins to rise, requiring accelerating monetary expansion to keep i_t equal to i_t^f.[14]

With gradual rather than Big Bang liberalization, fluctuation of the economy depends on the pace of capital market opening. If the exchange rate is left to adjust, the results are basically the same, except in magnitude, as the Big Bang case (Gradualism-e case in Figure 4.5). The exchange rate initially appreciates to a relatively mild extent and then depreciates over time until it reaches the PPP rate. The direction of all the other results is the same as the Big Bang case, but the magnitudes are smaller.

A more interesting case of gradual liberalization is one in which monetary policy to fix the nominal exchange rate is sustainable (Gradualism-M case in Figure 4.5). When the capital account balance is not only finite but also rather insensitive to the interest rate differential, the monetary authority has much greater policy-making leeway. When the nominal exchange rate is fixed at the level consistent with the current account balance in 1996, then the money supply expands almost as much as the capital account surplus, unless the government sterilizes the increased liquidity. The resulting inflation has two opposing effects on the money supply. On the one hand, it raises the nominal interest rate and thus induces capital inflows which increase the money supply. On the other hand, the inflation causes appreciation of the real exchange rate and the current account balance goes into deficit, which decreases the money supply. The relative size of the opposing changes in the money supply depends on the speed of liberalization.

With very gradual liberalization, the real exchange rate effect of inflation could dominate and the money supply contract. The monetary contraction worsens the recession that emerges in 1999 following the boom generated by the initial monetary expansion (Figure 4.5c). The deep recession eventually decreases the rate of inflation (Figure 4.5e), and the nominal interest rate finally drops below the world rate in 2001, bringing about capital flight along with a current account surplus after the year 2002 (Figure 4.5g). In this case, there is a smaller accumulation of foreign debt than in the case of a Big Bang liberalization with exchange rate overshooting (Figure 4.5h), but potential output is smaller (Figure 4.5d), and the economy goes through a similar degree of macro-instability in the opposite direction (Figure 4.5c).

Under this second gradual liberalization scenario and given the expected downward trend of the interest rate, a government policy of sterilized intervention appears to be sustainable for exchange rate stability as well as sensible for macro-stability. In order to avoid the initial recession and current account deficit, however, the government should bear the burden of the public debt. In other words, the external debt that would otherwise accumulate should be replaced by the internal debt of the government (at the cost of higher interest rates). The benefit of this policy is macroeconomic stability, while its cost is the lost opportunity to exploit foreign savings to augment the productive capacity of the economy.

FIGURE 4.5
Simulations of Big Bang and Gradual Scenarios for Capital Liberalization, 1995–2005*

4.5a
Real Exchange Rate Adjustment

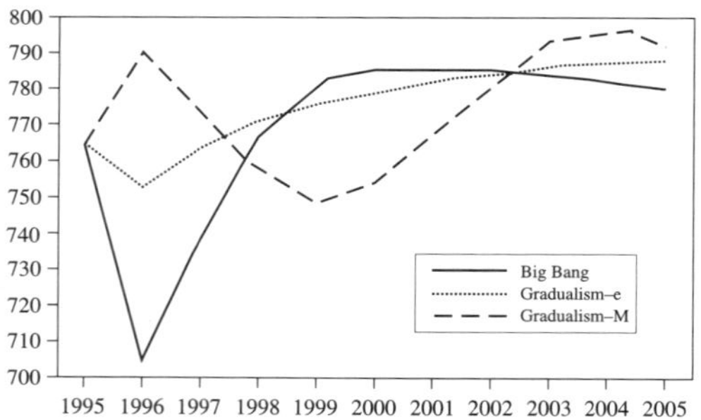

Note: 1990 is used as the base year.

4.5b
Real Interest Rate Adjustment

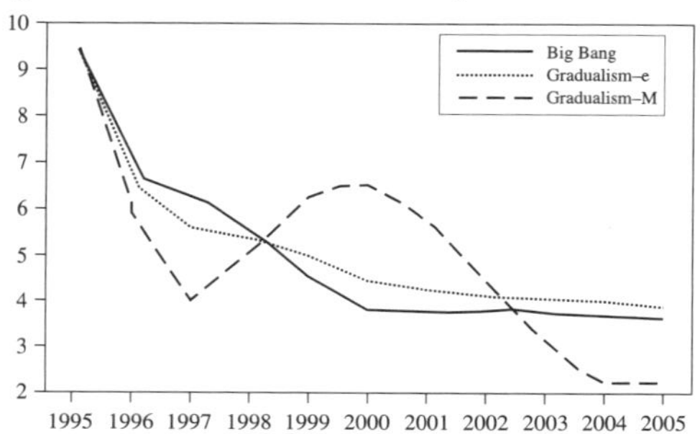

4.5e
Consumer Price Adjustment

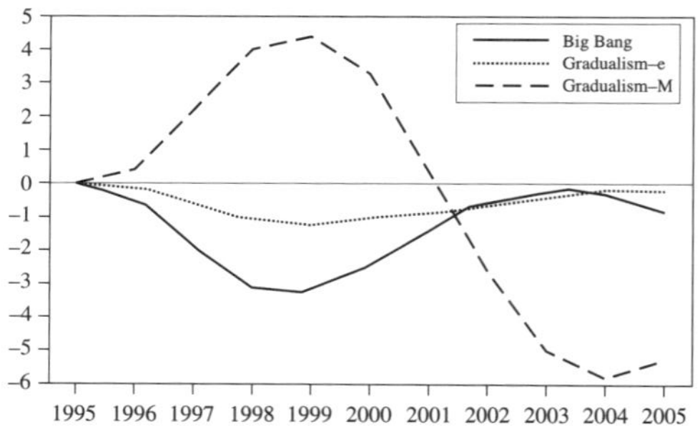

Note: Graph plots percent deviation of consumer price index (CPI) for each scenario from benchmark scenario.

4.5f
Producer Price Adjustment

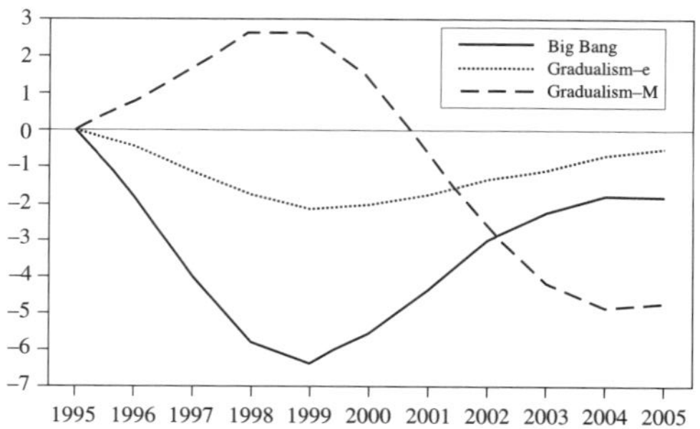

Note: Graph plots percent deviation of producer price index (PPI) for each scenario from benchmark scenario.

4.5c
GDP Adjustment

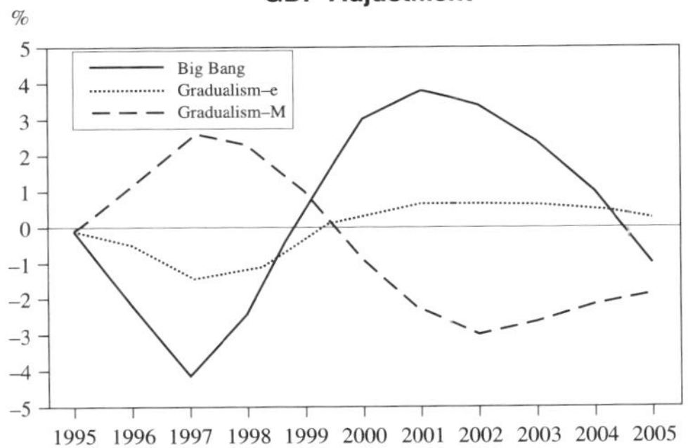

Note: Graph plots percent deviation of GDP for each scenario from benchmark scenario.

4.5g
Adjustment of Ratio of Current Account Balance to GDP

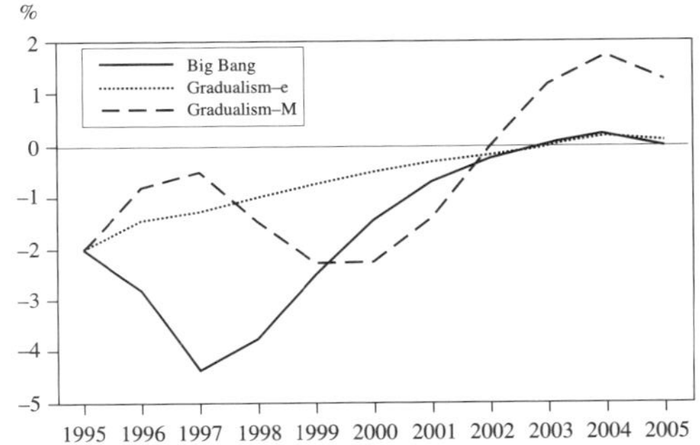

4.5d
Potential Output Adjustment

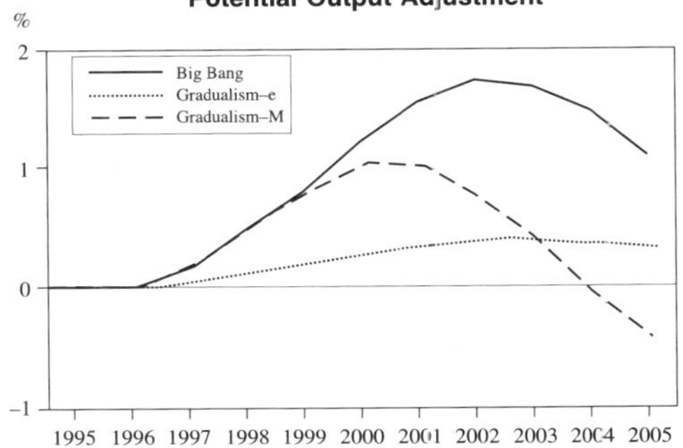

Note: Graph plots percent deviation of potential output for each scenario from benchmark scenario.

4.5h
Adjustment of Ratio of Net Foreign Debt to GDP

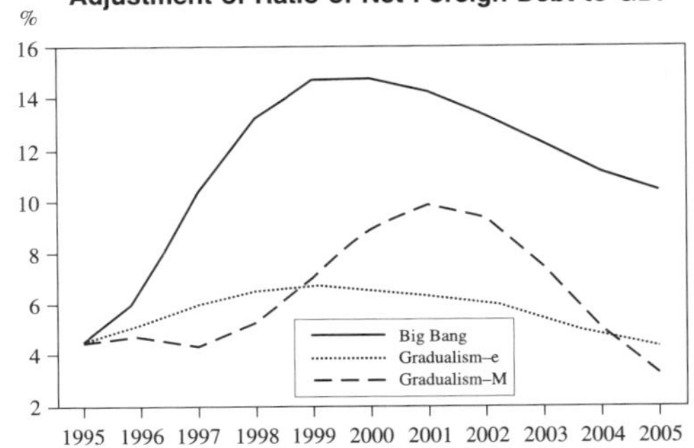

Notes: Gradualism-e denotes the gradual liberalization scenario in which the exchange rate adjusts; gradualism-M denotes the scenario in which monetary policy is used to fix the nominal exchange rate.

All in all, liberalization of the capital account in Korea will inevitably put the current account in deficit (Figure 4.5g). As far as there exists a substantial gap between domestic and foreign *real* interest rates (or, equivalently, marginal returns to capital), government policies that change nominal variables, such as money supply or the nominal exchange rate, will not have much effect on real variables in the long run. Controlling the pace of liberalization may be the only policy measure that will change real variables in the long run. Even so, the rapid development of financial instruments that enable investors to evade capital controls creates some doubt about the sustainability of a gradual approach.

Notes

1 Many parts of this chapter are based on my papers with Dr. Bongsung Oum (1995) and Youngsun Koh (1996).

2 For details of Korea's exchange rate movements, see Oum and Cho (1995).

3 Formally stated,
$REER_t = NEER_t/(P_t/P)$, $NEER_t = e_t/e$, $e = -i_1 e_{i,t}^{w(i,t)}$, and $P =- -i_1 P_{i,t}^{w(i,t)}$,
where e_t is the won/dollar exchange rate, P_t is the domestic price level, $e_{i,t}$ is the exchange rate of country *i*'s currency against the dollar, $P_{i,t}$ is the price level of country *i*, *n* is the number of countries considered, and $w(i,t)$ is the weight of country *i* at time *t* that satisfies $-i_1 w(i,t) = 1$ for all *t*.

4 The correlation increases gradually from 0.70 with no time lag to 0.84 at a 4-quarter lag and then slowly dies out.

5 Outstanding MSBs amounted to 88 percent of reserve money at the end of 1995.

6 For a survey of Korea's liberalization process, see Park (1995).

7 Since futures or forward markets are not yet established in Korea, we could not test covered interest parity.

8 The actual rate of won/dollar depreciation can be used as a proxy variable for the expected rate of change, $\log(e_{t+1}/e_t)$

9 Considering the forecast error about e_{t+1} at time *t*, there must be measurement errors in the expected appreciation rate, hence a downward bias in the regression coefficient. Nevertheless, there seems to be no reason to expect that this bias would change the sign of the coefficient estimate, and the increase in the coefficient estimate over time seems to indicate that the capital flows are getting more sensitive to the uncovered interest differential.

[10] The results for several other specifications of the coefficient were not very different from the linear time trend.

[11] Figure 4.4 plots three series of interest rates: the official bank loan rate, the yield rate on 3-year corporate bonds, and the curb market rate, all of which are converted into real terms by subtracting the actual inflation rates.

[12] Estimates of labour's income share, 1-α, in Korea range from 60 to 70 percent (see Table 2.2 in Hong 1994) and the depreciation rate of capital, δ, is estimated by Park (1992) to be 6.6 percent per year. The average annual growth rate of investment during the period 1970–95 in Korea is approximately 12 percent, while that of GDP is around 8 percent.

[13] Specifically, the elasticity of the capital account balance (kb_t) with respect to the interest rate differential adjusted for expected depreciation suddenly becomes infinity.

[14] It could be argued that another way to lower i_t may be to run an extremely large budget surplus. However, numerous regressions of the interest rate on public bonds yielded an extremely small and statistically insignificant elasticity. Even using the largest estimated elasticity, the reduction in outstanding bonds required to equate i_t to i_t^f would be 30 to 50 percent of GDP, or 2 times the current level of total government expenditure. Such an expenditure level would be impossible to achieve.

References

Barro, Robert and Xavier Sala-i-Martin. 1990. "World Real Interest Rates". In *NBER Macroeconomics Annual*, edited by O.J. Blanchard and S. Fischer. Cambridge: MIT Press.

Blanchard, Olivier and Stanley Fischer. 1989. *Lectures on Macroeconomics*. Cambridge: MIT Press.

Cho, Dongchul and Youngsun Koh. 1996. *Liberalization of Capital Flows in Korea: Big-bang or Gradualism.* NBER Working Paper No. 5824.

Dornbusch, Rudiger. 1976. "Expectations and Exchange Rate Dynamics". *Journal of Political Economy* December: 1161–76.

Hong, Sung-Duk. 1994. An Analysis of the Factors for Korean Growth: 1963–92 (in Korean). *Korea Development Review* Fall: 147–78.

Jwa, Sung-Hee. 1992. *Capital Mobility in Korea Since the Early 1980s: Comparison with Japan and Taiwan.* Korea Development Institute Working Paper No.9216.

Oum, Bong-Sung and Dongchul Cho. 1995. "Korea's Exchange Rate Movements in the 1990s: Evaluations and Policy Implications". Paper presented at the Korea Development Institute Symposium on Prospects of Yen-Dollar Exchange Rates and Korea's Exchange Rate Policy, 12 December, Seoul.

Park, Woo-Kyu. 1992. Research on Macro-Policy in Korea (in Korean). Korea Development Institute Research Paper Series 92–01.

Taylor, Mark P. 1995. "The Economics of Exchange Rates". *Journal of Economic Literature* March: 13–47.

UPDATE

THE KOREAN ECONOMY AT THE CROSSROADS

The Korean economy is currently undergoing its most severe crisis since the economy took off thirty years ago. In the midst of a financial and foreign exchange crisis, the Korean government finally signed an IMF (International Monetary Fund) rescue plan on 3 December 1997. Nevertheless, financial markets are still unstable. Since November 1997 the exchange rate has skyrocketed from 900 to 1,800 won per dollar, the stock market index has collapsed from 600 to 350, and the annualized yield rate on three-year corporate bonds has soared from 13 to 30 percent. The crisis has not been not limited to financial markets. Numerous firms have gone bankrupt in the drastic credit crunch, domestic demand has frozen with the loss of consumer confidence, and even foreign demand has become sluggish under the turmoil of the East Asian crisis.

The Korean economy stands at a critical crossroads for its future. If it can utilize this crisis as an opportunity to implement necessary structural reforms, it will eventually overcome the crisis and become even stronger. This essay reviews the current situation and describes the direction in which where the Korean economy ought to head.

WHAT HAS BEEN HAPPENING TO THE KOREAN ECONOMY?

For the last three decades, Korea has achieved remarkably fast economic growth; the average annual GDP growth rate has been over 8 percent. The Korean economy has expanded in size and experienced a drastic structural change as well. Between 1965 and 1995, the share of agriculture in GDP decreased from 38 percent to less than 7 percent, exports exploded from less than $2 billion to over $120 billion, and the major export items rapidly shifted from light industrial to heavy industrial and chemical products.

The recent macroeconomic performance of the Korean economy has been rather impressive (Table U4.1). During the boom period of 1994–95, the GDP growth rate was over 8 percent, the rate of inflation was around 5 percent, and the current account deficit remained within 2 percent of GDP. Although the economy began to slow down from 1996, the current account deficit appeared to be a problem at almost 5 percent of GDP, but it declined very rapidly from 1997.

TABLE U4.1
Macroeconomic Performance of the Korean Economy, 1994–97

	1994	1995	1996	1997
GDP Growth Rate (%)	8.6	8.9	7.1	5.9[1]
Unemployment Rate (%)	2.4	2.0	2.0	2.6[2]
CPI Inflation (%)	6.2	4.5	4.9	4.4
Current Account (US$ billions)	–4.5	–8.9	–23.7	–8.8
Foreign Debt (US$ billions)	56	78	105	153[3]
Won/Dollar Exchange Rate	789	775	844	1,696[4]
Exchange Rate Appreciation (%)	2.4	1.8	–8.2	–50.2
Yield on Corporate Bonds (%)	12.9	13.8	11.9	29.0[4]
Ordinary Income to Equity Ratio (%)	11.5	12.4	4.6	n.a.
Ordinary Income to Sales Ratio (%)	2.6	2.7	1.0	1.4[5]

Notes: 1) KDI forecast.
2) The unemployment rate is the average from January to November 1997.
3) Foreign debt is as of December 20, 1997.
4) The exchange rate and yield rate on corporate bond are as of 31 December 1997.
5) The ordinary income to sales ratio is for the first half of 1997.

Unlike the fairly stable performance of the macro-economy, however, the profitability of the corporate sector was volatile. The ratio of ordinary income to equity fluctuated around 11 to 13 percent during the boom period of 1994–95, but it dropped drastically to 4.6 percent in 1996 (Table U4.1). This profit squeeze in the corporate sector was greatly affected by the collapse of export prices in international markets, particularly the prices of semi-conductors, the biggest single Korean export item.

During 1996, the unit price of semi-conductors fell by more than 70 percent. A rough estimate suggests that this fall in semi-conductor prices alone decreased the value of exports by more than $10 billion (over 2 percent of GDP). In addition, international prices of many of Korea's other export items, such as steel and chemical products, also fell in 1996. As a result, the terms of trade deteriorated by more than 20 percent in 1996 to their worst since 1974, the first oil-shock period (Figure U4.1). The decline in export prices and the resulting profit squeeze were accompanied by the bankruptcy of many conglomerates, which greatly exacerbated market instability given the over-leveraged financial structure of the Korean economy.

Following July 1997, tension rose in Korea, while the currency turmoil spread from Thailand to Indonesia, Malaysia, and the Philippines. In September, Hong Kong, the financial center of the region, was finally attacked by speculators. Although Hong Kong succeeded in defending its

FIGURE U4.1
Korea's Terms of Trade, 1974–97

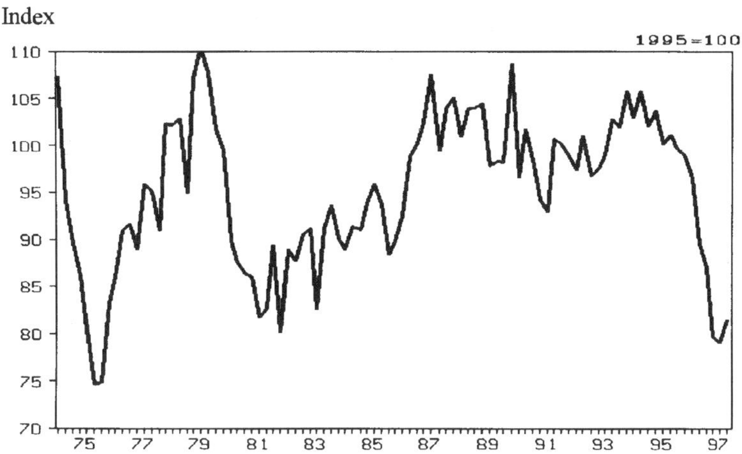

Note: terms of trade = unit value of exports / unit value of imports

currency by raising the interbank interest rate to some one-hundred percent, it paid the price in the form of a stock market collapse. At the same time, Japan, the biggest creditor to the region, was suffering from its own financial market troubles, and the Japanese yen had further depreciated against the U.S. dollar. Investors became scared by the Asian market and rapidly withdrew from the region, particularly from Korea where the financial market appeared to be shaky and the political situation unstable with an upcoming presidential election.

The Korean won faced severe depreciation pressures from September, but the government made an attempt to defend the currency against the international capital market. Most investors knew that the government would not succeed and many domestic as well as foreign speculators began to sell off Korean won. The stock market began to collapse, and foreign investors swiftly fled from the Korean market. The Korean government finally gave up defending the currency and widened the one-day fluctuation band from 2.25 to 10 percent in November, but the action appeared too late. International capital markets had completely lost confidence in the Korean market by then.

On 21 November the government announced that Korea had applied for an IMF financial aid package. However, when it was made public that the country's available foreign reserves were below $10 billion at the end of November, the exchange rate depreciated yet again. The declaration by some presidential candidates that they would re-negotiate the "too strict" agreements with the IMF weakened the currency even further. In addition, the two leading credit rating companies, Moody's and S&P, competitively downgraded the Korean market from A1 and AA- to Baa2 and BBB- within a period of one and a half months (from 28 November to 11 December for Moody's and from 24 October to 11 December for S&P). As a result, the spread on bonds issued by the Korean Development Bank (KDB) in international capital markets shot well above the spread on bonds issued by Thailand at the end of 1997 (Figure U4.2).

The Korean currency stabilized only after president-elect Kim Dae Jung publicly re-committed to complying with the IMF reform program, and G7 countries expressed their support for Korea on Christmas Eve 1997. Nevertheless, the credit crunch induced by the foreign capital outflow and the contractionary monetary policy imposed by the IMF raised the interest rate to 30 percent from a normal range of 12-14 percent. Many more companies went bankrupt under the credit squeeze, and financial market instability continued. Figure U4.3 gives some sense of how the main indicators of the financial market had changed in 1997. In the first month of 1998, stock prices have been rising and interest rates have been stabilized, but the general consensus is that it will take a long time until Korean financial markets completely settle down.

FIGURE U4.2
Spreads on Bonds Issued by KDB, China, and Thailand, 1997

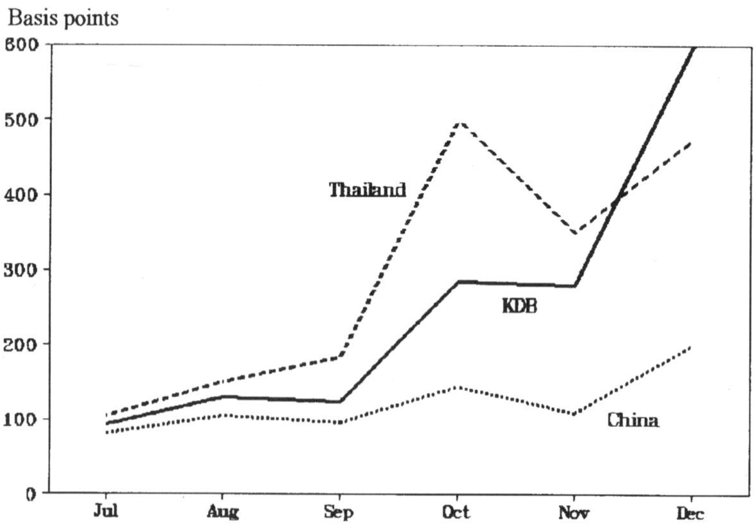

FIGURE U4.3
Main Indicators of the Korean Financial Market in 1997

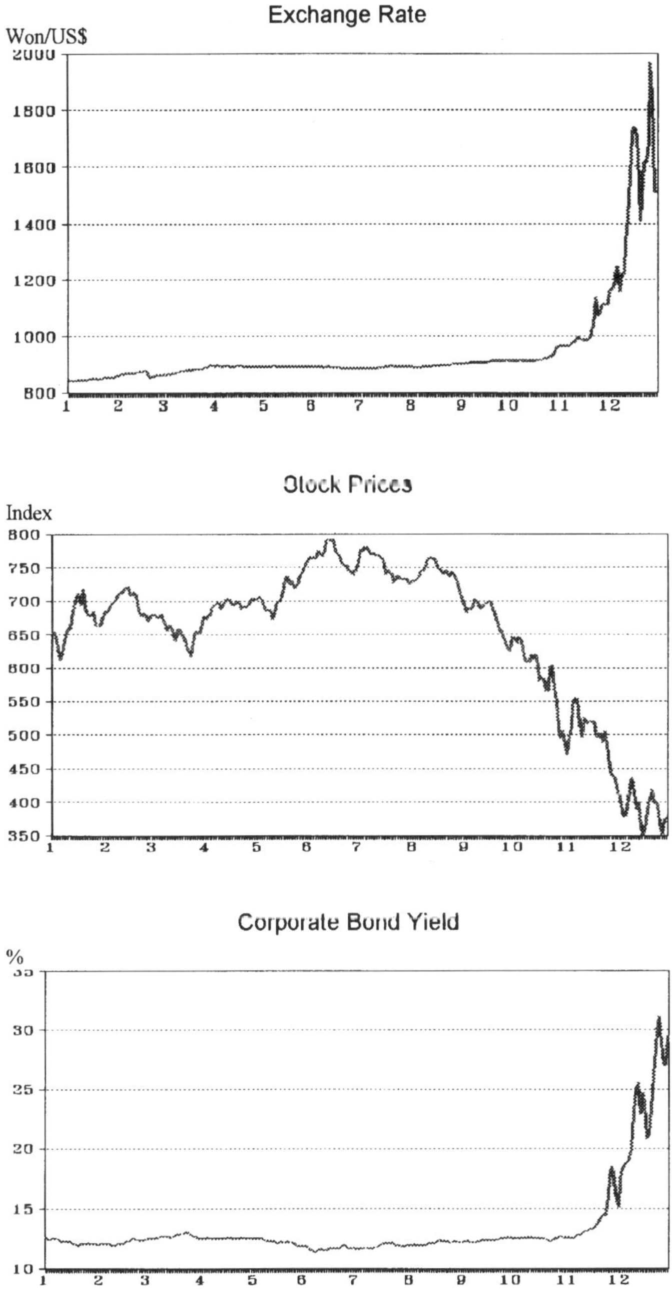

WHAT CAUSED KOREA'S ECONOMIC CRISIS?

Korea's current crisis was triggered by the collapse of major export prices and by the resulting profit squeeze in the business sector. This business crisis escalated the financial crisis which finally exploded into a currency crisis. Once the currency crisis materialized, it drastically exacerbated the business crisis by sharply increasing the burden of foreign debt and by raising interest rates. Additional business failures now further threaten financial market stability, generating a vicious circle of crisis. This section examines the causes of each component of the crisis—the business crisis, the financial crisis, and the currency crisis. At the end of the section, I will add some remarks about what I believe is the primary cause of the whole crisis—the leadership crisis.

The Business Crisis: Lack of Market Discipline

There is a unique characteristic in the business sector of Korea: thirty years' experience of government bail-out policies created the expectation that big conglomerates would never be allowed to fail. With this expectation, therefore, Korean conglomerates had strong incentives to keep expanding without careful consideration of the attendant risks and returns. As a result, a few conglomerates grew to command huge portions of the country's resources and thus became too big to fail. They expanded via subsidiary companies from heavy and chemical industries to various service industries, many of which were not profitable at all.

In 1994–95 when the world market was booming, these conglomerates made substantial profits which were used to expand still further into the such industries as automobiles, semi-conductors, and steel. When the world market began to stumble in 1996, they found themselves competing against each other in the same businesses and their profitability was further squeezed.

This business crisis was aggravated by the inflexibility of Korea's factor markets. Since 1987, under the atmosphere of democratization, wages had been rising rapidly at an average annual rate of 15 percent, but it was very hard to adjust employment. In fact, companies were not permitted to layoff redundant workers without going to court to justify the action. Moreover, high interest rates, ranging from 12 to 14 percent per year, squeezed the profitability of the business sector. The fact that interest rates remained high despite declining profit margins might reflect the excessive demand for funds by Korea's conglomerates.

The Financial Crisis: Moral Hazard under Government Guarantees

A major instrument of Korea's development strategy was government control over financial resources. Although the government had gradually liberalized financial markets from the 1980's, the legacy of control was not easily eliminated. The government still exercised strong discretionary power in allocating large loans, and most economic agents took the government role for granted. In conjunction with continued bail-outs of large conglomerates, government intervention in financial markets generated a serious moral hazard problem. Because financial institutions tended to believe that there were implicit government guarantees on the liabilities of the conglomerates they had little incentive to scrutinize the financial soundness of these businesses. That is how Korean *chaebol* were created. Furthermore, in return for their compliance with government directions, major financial intermediaries also had been bailed out whenever they got into trouble. Consequently, under the government-led development strategy there emerged a strong symbiosis among the government, financial institutions, and the *chaebol*.

In this environment, the *chaebol* made aggressive investments through profligate borrowings from financial institutions, and quite often they financed long-term investments from short-term capital markets without worrying seriously about consequences. Loans from the financial sector were heavily concentrated in the 30 biggest *chaebol*, whose average debt ratio was over 350 percent. These activities created a financial structure that made the whole economy vulnerable to adverse shocks.

The failure of Hanbo in early 1997 revealed that many large-scale lending decisions had been made under the influence of politicians or government discretion. From this time, foreign lenders began to lose confidence in a Korean capital market that did not function by market principles. In addition to the structural moral hazard itself, apprehension grew concerning the volume of non-performing loans in the financial market that had explosively accumulated with the bankruptcies of several *chaebol*. By the end of September 1997 when Kia (the eighth largest *chaebol* in Korea) failed, the volume of loans more than three months in arrears was estimated to exceed 30 trillion won (approximately 8 percent of GDP). This amount may have been large enough to scare off investors, but even more worrying was the risk that the whole financial system could collapse with the next failure of a major *chaebol*.

The Currency Crisis: Attempt to Defend the Currency Value

The cause of the currency crisis was no different in Korea than in other countries. Always and everywhere, the most direct cause is an attempt to defend the currency value against the market. The market perceived the Korean won to be over-valued from the second quarter of 1996 when the price of semi-conductors collapsed. The current account deficit increased sharply, but the Korean government attempted to ease the depreciation pressure by intervening in the foreign exchange market. When the Hanbo scandal was publicized and foreign investors began to lose confidence, in March 1997 the Korean government again intervened to defend the currency. Through these two interventions, the government wasted more than $7 billion of official foreign reserves, which declined from $37 billion at the end of June 1996 to $29 billion at the end of March 1997 (Figure U4.4).

FIGURE U4.4
Korea's Official Foreign Reserves, 1996–97

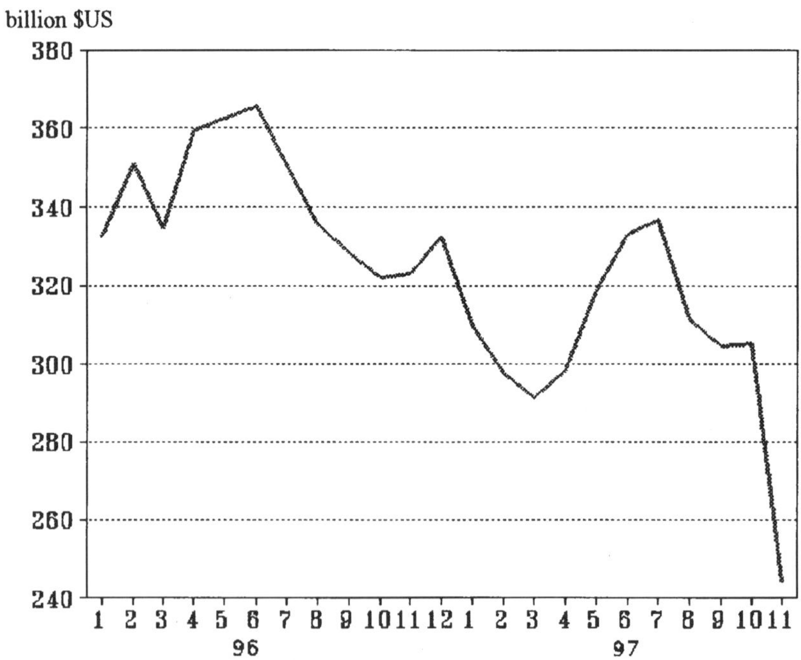

After three months of peace, the foreign exchange market began to tremble again when the Southeast Asian crisis was triggered in July 1997. Under these circumstances, the government's decision to "nationalize" Kia in September was interpreted by international capital markets as a message that the Korean government had neither the intention nor the courage to correct the structural problems. Foreign investors completely lost confidence and rapidly withdrew short-term debt from Korea. Severe depreciation pressure accumulated, but the futile attempt to defend the currency continued, only to deplete foreign reserves and thereby aggravate the market's fears. Even worse, the government repeatedly declared itself ready to defend the exchange rate at a particular level only to retreat several days later, making the market scorn the promises of the Korean government. Later, it was made public that approximately $15 billion of foreign reserves had been lost in the month of November 1997 alone.

Figure U4.5 compares the exchange rate in on-shore markets, which were heavily influenced by the government, with the rate in the off-shore market (Non-Deliverable Forward market in Hong Kong for one-month maturity: NDF), which was largely immune to the Korean government's influence. The difference between the two rates widened in early 1997 with the Hanbo scandal, but the crucial difference was observed after September.

Together with defence of the exchange rate, lack of transparency is a typical ingredient for a currency crisis. Compared to international standards, the accounting system in Korea is loose and unorganized. The coverage of official data is also limited and many figures are not even made publicly available. For example, despite the fact that rumors about some merchant banking corporations having trouble financing abroad had been running throughout the market since early 1997, it was not until October that the Ministry of Finance and Economy finally opened their balance sheets to the public.

Most notorious in this respect was the government's statement that foreign reserves at the end of October were $35 billion, $1 billion *more* than at the end of September. Given the public knowledge of the heavy government intervention in the exchange market, this statement did not make sense at all. This incident decisively destroyed the credibility of the Korean government, and foreign investors began to distrust even official statistics unless they were endorsed by the IMF.

If there is any peculiar cause of Korea's currency crisis, it may be that the term structure of Korea's foreign debt is overly skewed toward the short term. At the end of November 1997, short-term debt comprised almost 60 percent of the approximately $110 billion total foreign debt. It

FIGURE U4.5
On-shore and Off-shore Won Exchange Rates

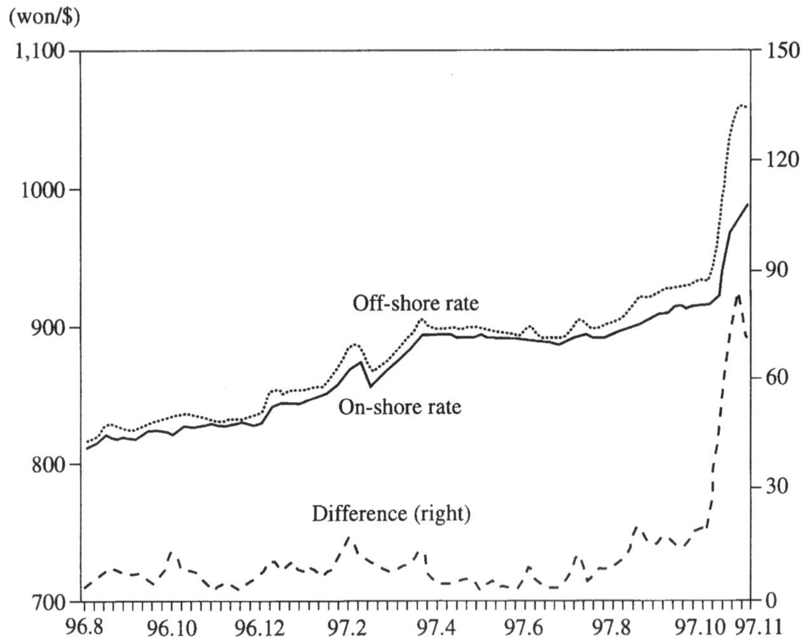

was asserted that Korea was protected from "hot money" because liquid asset markets were not open to foreigners, but once the country's credibility was lost, short-term debt became virtually "hot money".

In a sense, however, the term structure problem is simply a result of the lack of prudential regulations on the financial sector, another familiar cause of currency and financial crises. The most serious mismatch in term structure was found among Korea's merchant banking corporations which were the most loosely regulated of the country's financial institutions.

The Leadership Crisis: Failure to Overcome Conflict of Interest

The structural problems described above have long been recognized by Korean economists. They have argued that as the economy grows and the world economy becomes more integrated, the old paradigm of government-led development will no longer work as efficiently as a free market system. However, their efforts to establish a new order inevitably confronted resistance from interest groups and Korean "leaders" failed to lead the society to a new paradigm.

This leadership crisis culminated around the time of the presidential election in December 1997. A leading example was the conflict between the Ministry of Finance and Economy (MOFE) and the Bank of Korea (BOK) regarding where to affiliate the Consolidated Financial Supervision Agency (CFSA). The National Assembly kept delaying a decision on a proposal submitted by the Presidential Commission for Financial Reform (PCFR), and MOFE and BOK, which were supposed to be coping with the financial unrest, were lobbying to acquire hegemony over CFMA until the last moment when the currency crisis broke out in November. In December 1997 under IMF pressure, the National Assembly promptly passed a financial market reform package that was almost identical to the original proposal submitted by the PCFR. Korean leaders could not overcome the conflict of interest to implement necessary reforms. In this sense, lack of leadership may be pointed out as the primary factor that invited external shocks.

WHAT SHOULD KOREA DO?

Answers to a normative question like "What should Korea do?" can be rather unscientific and subjective. By now, the consensus seems to be that the most urgently needed reform is to restructure the financial market to restore market confidence. However, given the causes of the crisis as described in the previous section, I believe that the Korean economy needs revolutionary, across-the-board structural reforms, and for this purpose it needs strong leadership now more than ever.

Restoration of Confidence

Mutual confidence is the basic element of financial transactions. Given the fact that the current crisis exhibits most severely in financial markets, it is natural to list restoration of confidence as the top priority. To reduce uncertainty and help re-build market confidence, a prompt distinction between reliable and unreliable financial institutions is necessary. The first step toward this goal should be opening balance sheets to the public so that unreliable institutions can be naturally selected by the market. Once unreliable institutions are identified, the government should apply decisive prescriptions to prevent them from generating further moral hazard problems.

A more serious challenge, however, is to restore the confidence of foreign investors. A slight increase in foreign reserves or a limited range of financial market restructuring will not be sufficient. Only consistent and continuing efforts to implement comprehensive structural reforms will resolve the problems at the roots.

Structural Reforms

It is far beyond the scope of this paper to detail all the necessary reforms. Generally speaking, however, since the core legacy of the government-led development era is the symbiosis among *chaebol*, financial institutions, and the government, then the key reforms should be focused on exposing these institutions to market discipline. That is, the goal of the structural reforms should be to establish a new market order in which only market forces, as opposed to informal relationships with the government or political power, determine the survival of economic agents.

A full-scale introduction of M&A markets could awaken *chaebol* to the importance of profitability and market pressure over size and political power. Regulations against mutual loan guarantees among subsidiary companies can help prevent *chaebol* from becoming too-big-to-fail in the first place. In addition, forcing the release of transparent balance sheets to the market can reduce the degree of financial resource concentration in *chaebol*.

Restructuring of financial institutions is already proceeding in this direction. Two major banks are about to be sold in the open market and many ailing merchant banking corporations will soon be closed. Considering that no major financial institution has failed in Korea's history, the current situation may well be called a "Big Bang". However, in order to completely segregate *chaebol* from implicit government protection, the full independence of the central bank as well as prudent supervision according to transparent standards should be institutionally ensured.

Perhaps the most difficult reform lies in the government sector, which is invulnerable by nature. However, the invulnerability of the government does not require the invulnerability of bureaucrats. It is necessary to design reforms that can systematically weed out uncompetitive bureaucrats. In particular, guaranteed life-time employment of bureaucrats should be re-considered so that more competent policy makers can be recruited through open competition.

As far as invulnerability is concerned, private-sector workers in Korea are little different from government bureaucrats. Social and institutional changes should be made to allow flexible employment adjustments not only to permit firms to adjust rapidly to the world economic trends, but also to give workers incentives to enhance their own economic value.

Strong Leadership

The common goal of all the reforms is to establish a new order ruled by free market principles in place of the legacies of the thirty years of government-led development that have permeated individuals. In order to effectively accomplish this change, Korea needs strong leaders who can overcome their conflict of interest. In other words, the leaders should be able to present a clear vision for the future to persuade the people who will have to go through a painful adjustment process.

PROSPECTS FOR THE KOREAN ECONOMY

IMF's Macroeconomic Policy

In addition to rapid structural reforms in the financial sector, the IMF imposed a typical combination of tight fiscal and monetary policies. Tight fiscal policy is necessary to mobilize the huge resources needed to recapitalize the financial sector and to resolve non-performing loans promptly. On the revenue side, the government will widen the tax base by curtailing or abolishing tax exemptions or reductions. On the expenditure side, the 1998 budget will be trimmed by about 10 trillion won (2 to 3 percent of GDP).

The IMF's imposition of extremely tight monetary policy, on the other hand, is not an appropriate prescription for the Korean economy, in my opinion. Excess aggregate demand has died away over the past two years of economic slow-down and the current account has moved into surplus. The justification for the tight monetary policy may be to stabilize the exchange rate by raising interest rates. However, it is unlikely that high interest rates can successfully attract foreign capital to stabilize the exchange rate under Korea's current situation. Since the instability of the won/dollar exchange rate was initially caused by financial system risk rather than by low interest rates, monetary policy to stabilize the exchange rate seems to be focused on reducing the systemic risk rather than on raising interest rates.

Prospects for the Korean Economy in 1988

Like it or not, however, the IMF's tight policies are likely to continue throughout the year and they are expected to plunge the Korean economy further into a recession. Under the current restrictive monetary conditions in which interest rates fluctuate at 25 to 30 percent, one cannot exclude the possibility of a negative GDP growth rate. Private consumption will be likely to fall short of last year's level and fixed capital formation will decline by more than 15 percent from 1997. Only export demand will increase by approximately 10 percent (in volume) due to exchange rate depreciation and the current account is expected to record about a $10 billion surplus (approximately 3 percent of GDP). At the same time, the exchange rate depreciation will push the rate of inflation up to almost 10 percent in spite of extremely low domestic demand and stagnating wages.

Medium-Term Prospects

It may sound awkward to mention the medium-term prospects at the moment when even tomorrow's economic situation is unclear. Nevertheless, because the ultimate driving force of an economy is such underlying fundamentals as the quality of its human capital and its savings rate, it can be expected that Korea can eventually recover to a potential growth rate of around 6 percent. However, the speed of recovery will depend critically upon how soon confidence from abroad is restored, which in turn depends upon the leadership of the new president who will have to weather possible social unrest during a period of drastic, comprehensive reform. If Korea successfully accomplishes the reforms necessary to establish solid market principles, it would not be too optimistic to expect that the Korean economy can get back on a normal track by the year 2000.

CONCLUSION

The Korean economy is paying the price for its complacency with past success that has delayed painful but necessary reforms. If Korea were somehow unable to initiate reforms by itself, external forces may have been indispensable for its take-off to the next step. The external forces that led to the current crisis finally triggered structural reforms, and all Koreans now understand that these painful reforms cannot be avoided. There are some positive symptoms that Koreans can wisely utilize the current crisis as an opportunity to strengthen the economy, but it is premature to judge whether the Korean economy has taken the right track completely.

January 1998

5

Monetary Policy and Capital Flows in Taiwan during the 1980s and 1990s

Ya-Hwei Yang

INTRODUCTION

Monetary policy includes interacting policies to control the money supply, interest rates, and foreign exchange. For a small open economy like Taiwan, the external and internal sectors are closely related. To achieve macroeconomic stability, the Taiwan government has adopted numerous financial restrictions, including interest rate regulation, foreign exchange rate regulation, and capital controls, particularly in the economy's early stage of development.

Taiwan had experienced a stable price level and stable monetary environment for decades. Then, in the 1980s, due to a large trade surplus, it accumulated substantial foreign reserves which resulted in dramatic money supply growth. In addition, due to pressure from the United States, the government implemented a policy of gradual exchange rate appreciation. Both measures attracted foreign capital to Taiwan, flooding the stock and real estate markets. The central bank adopted a contractionary monetary policy which stopped the cresting of the stock market. In the 1990s, the growth rate of the money supply fell below the floor of the official money growth target due to weak economic growth and low demand for money. In addition, from the late 1980s to the early 1990s, Taiwan experienced a net outflow of long term capital due to outward investment of traditional labour-intensive industries.

Since the late 1980s, the Taiwan government has adopted several financial deregulation measures, including interest rate deregulation and bank privatization. Taiwan changed from a fixed foreign exchange rate policy to a managed exchange rate policy in 1978, and then to a flexible exchange rate policy in 1989. Several financial crises in the 1990s raised the problem of how to balance the pursuit of financial efficiency and the maintenance of financial stability in the process of financial reform. Although the government has initiated financial liberalization and financial internationalization, many deregulation measures remain to be taken before Taiwan can be considered a regional financial centre. Furthermore, monetary policy instruments must be improved to simultaneously pursue financial efficiency and financial stability.

Several studies have dealt with monetary issues in Taiwan. Yang and Shea (1996) analysed the price determination equation in the 1980s. Liang (1984) set up an econometric model to study the relations between money supply, prices, and balance of payments, and Lee (1990) broadly discussed financial policies and the financial sector prior to the 1980s. Although these papers have examined certain aspects of the monetary problems of Taiwan, there as yet exists no comprehensive survey of Taiwan's monetary environment and monetary policy, especially since the 1980s. This chapter fills that gap.

THE MONETARY ENVIRONMENT IN TAIWAN IN THE 1980S AND 1990S

Taiwan's savings rate, which has been high for decades, had a significant influence on the monetary environment of the 1980s and 1990s. The savings rate averaged 33.2 percent during the 1980s and, although it has been declining since the early 1990s, it is not low by international standards (Table 5.1). Savings are a source of funds for investment. When savings exceed investment, the excess savings add liquidity to the loanable funds market and create a loose monetary environment. Taiwan's savings amounted to 31.3 percent of GNP in 1981, falling to 25.3 percent in 1985 (Table 5.1).

According to the GNP identity, excess saving (S-I) is equivalent to the trade surplus (X-M), where S stands for savings, I for investment, X for exports, and M for imports:[1]

$$S - I = X - M$$

Taiwan has experienced a trade surplus since the mid-1970s and the excess savings ratio has followed a similar trend to that of the trade surplus ratio (Table 5.1). Taiwan's large trade surplus resulted from the long run under-valuation of the NT dollar. The record level trade surpluses of 1985 to 1987 had two consequences. First, although the central bank sterilized the foreign currency accumulation through open market operations, the growth rate of the money supply rose dramatically. Second, the trade surplus brought strong pressure from the United States government for appreciation of the NT dollar against the U.S. dollar. Complying with U.S. wishes, the central bank adopted a gradual appreciation policy in 1986 (Table 5.1).

In contrast to the current account surplus, Taiwan has experienced a net outflow of capital for most of the last decade or longer. Net flows of long-term capital have been negative in every year since 1984, while there have been a few years of net short-term capital inflows, particularly 1986 and 1987 (Table 5.2). The outflow of long-term capital was mostly in the form of outward direct investment which increased as Taiwan's domestic investment environment worsened since the late 1980s. Rising wages, land

TABLE 5.1
Excess Savings, Trade Surplus, and Exchange Rate,1966–95

Year	Savings Share of GNP %	Excess Savings (S-I) Share of GNP, %	Net Exports (X-M) Share of GNP %	Exchange Rate NT$/US$
1966–70	23.41	–0.81	–2.87	40.05
1971–75	30.71	0.57	0.34	38.87
1976–80	32.99	2.19	3.36	36.99
1981–85	32.18	1.68	9.92	39.09
1986–90	34.38	13.21	12.64	30.29
1991–95	27.39	3.60	4.15	26.26
1981	31.34	1.31	2.90	36.84
1982	30.07	4.84	6.75	39.12
1983	32.13	8.70	9.11	40.07
1984	33.80	11.87	14.09	39.60
1985	33.57	14.83	16.75	39.83
1986	38.46	21.35	20.17	37.84
1987	38.52	18.33	17.98	31.74
1988	34.48	11.39	8.55	28.59
1989	31.10	8.18	8.99	26.41
1990	29.33	6.80	7.50	26.89
1991	29.40	6.66	7.10	26.81
1992	28.29	3.86	4.24	25.16
1993	27.79	3.03	3.42	26.39
1994	26.11	2.53	3.01	26.46
1995	25.34	1.94	2.97	26.48

Source: *Statistical Abstract of National Income in Taiwan Area, R.O.C.; Monthly Statistics of Exports and Imports, Taiwan Area, R.O.C.;* and *Financial Statistics Monthly, Taiwan District, R.O.C.*

TABLE 5.2
Capital Flows, 1984–95
US$ millions

	1984	1985	1986	1987	1988	1989	1990	1991	1992	1993	1994	1995
Long-term Capital	–1,124	–1,020	–1,583	–2,585	–6,273	–7,761	–6,601	–2,827	–3,458	–2,600	–1,960	–1,227
Direct Investment	131	260	260	11	–3,161	–5,347	–3,913	–583	–990	–1,534	–1,085	–1,119
Portfolio Investment	–50	-46	69	–371	–1,711	–902	–1,006	45	445	1,067	905	493
Other Long-term Capital	–1,205	–1,234	–1,912	–2,225	–1,402	–1,512	–1,682	–2,289	–2,913	–2,133	–1,780	–601
Short-term Capital	–1,470	–2,143	8,521	12,983	–5,182	–4,369	–8,549	600	–3,450	–2,062	563	–6,963
Resident Official Sector	1	1	1	1	0	0	0	0	0	0	0	0
Deposit Money Banks	–1,381	–2,427	7,100	8,970	–3,701	–3,552	–4,399	2,684	1,430	233	796	–2,156
Other Sectors	–90	283	1,420	4,013	–1,481	–817	–4,150	–2,084	–4,880	–2,295	–233	–4,807
Total	–2,594	–3,163	6,938	10,398	–11,455	–12,130	–15,150	–2,227	–6,908	–4,662	–1,397	– 8,190

Source: Central Bank of China. 1996. *Balance of Payments, Taiwan District, R.O.C.* December.

cost, and social demands for pollution prevention have made Taiwanese businessmen reluctant to invest at home. On the other hand, the fluctuation in short-term capital flows into Taiwan can be explained by the country's foreign exchange policy. The announcement in 1986 that the government would permit gradual appreciation of the NT dollar had a tremendous impact on capital inflows. Capital was attracted to Taiwan to take advantage of expected profits in currency exchange. Short-term capital inflows hit a peak in 1986 and 1987 (Figure 5.1). Short-term capital movements include activity in both the banking (including the central bank) and private sectors, but because of capital controls on the private sector, most of Taiwan's total short-term capital flows took place in the banking sector. (Figure 5.1).

The flows of short-term capital into Taiwan were reflected in the growth rate of the money supply and, with a lag, in fluctuations in the stock price index (Figure 5.2). The influx of short-term capital in 1986 and 1987 contributed to a surge in the money supply. In 1986, M1A grew 16.1 percent, M1B grew 51.4 percent, and M2 grew 25.3 percent (Table 5.3). Money supply growth rates declined somewhat in 1988, but still remained high. The short term capital inflows also quickly entered the stock and real estate markets.

FIGURE 5.1
Net Flows of Short-term Capital, 1974–95

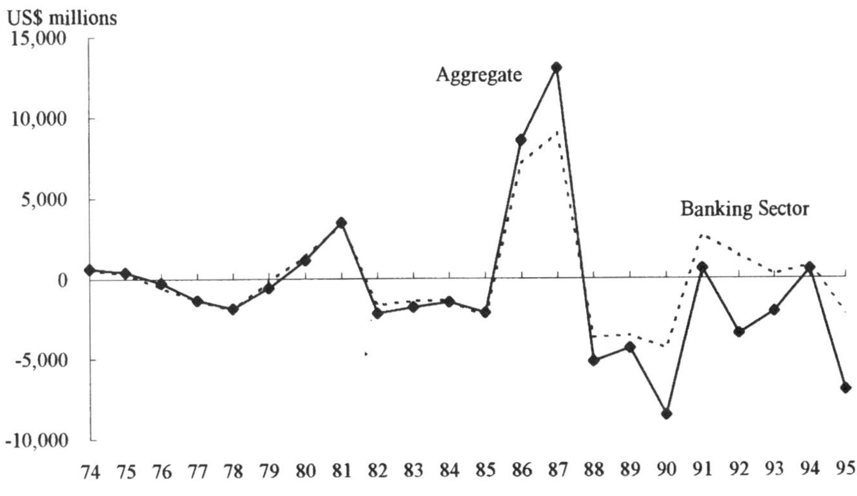

Source: Central Bank of China. *Balance of Payments, Taiwan District, R.O.C.*.

Reacting to the loose money environment caused by the trade surplus and the inflow of short-term capital, the central bank adopted a contractionary monetary policy in 1987. Required reserve ratios were raised substantially, forcing up interest rates. By 1990 the money growth rate dropped to –1.5 percent for M1A, to –3.3 percent for M1B, and to 11.0 percent for M2. The stock price index dropped sharply from a peak of 12,495 in 1989 to 2,560 in 1990. For most years from then until 1996, the stock price index has fluctuated between 3,000 and 7,000.

From the late 1980s to the early 1990s, the Taiwan government eased capital controls, privatized banking, deregulated interest rates, and implemented a flexible exchange rate system (Figure 5.3). Since the 1990s, financial liberalization and financial internationalization have speeded up. At the same time, new policy issues have arisen in the 1990s. Financial crises have occurred more often than in the past. Scandals involving several local financial institutions and a large bills finance company resulted in financial chaos. In addition, sluggish economic growth and the consequent low demand for money have brought a stop to the rapid increase in the money supply. The money growth rate has fallen, sometimes below the floor of the government's target rate.

FIGURE 5.2
Capital Flows, Stock Price Index, and Growth Rate of the Money Supply

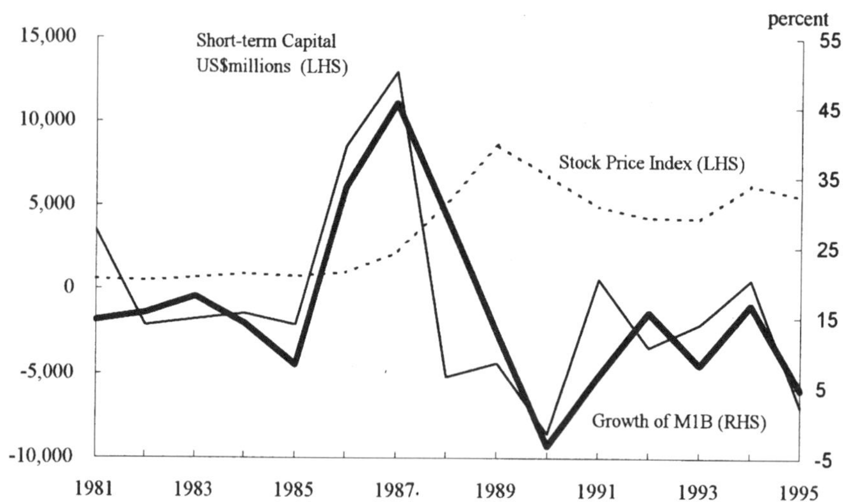

Source: Central Bank of China. *Balance of Payments, Taiwan District, R.O.C. Financial Statistics Monthly, Taiwan District, R.O.C.*

FIGURE 5.3
Summary of Monetary Policy Changes, 1979–95

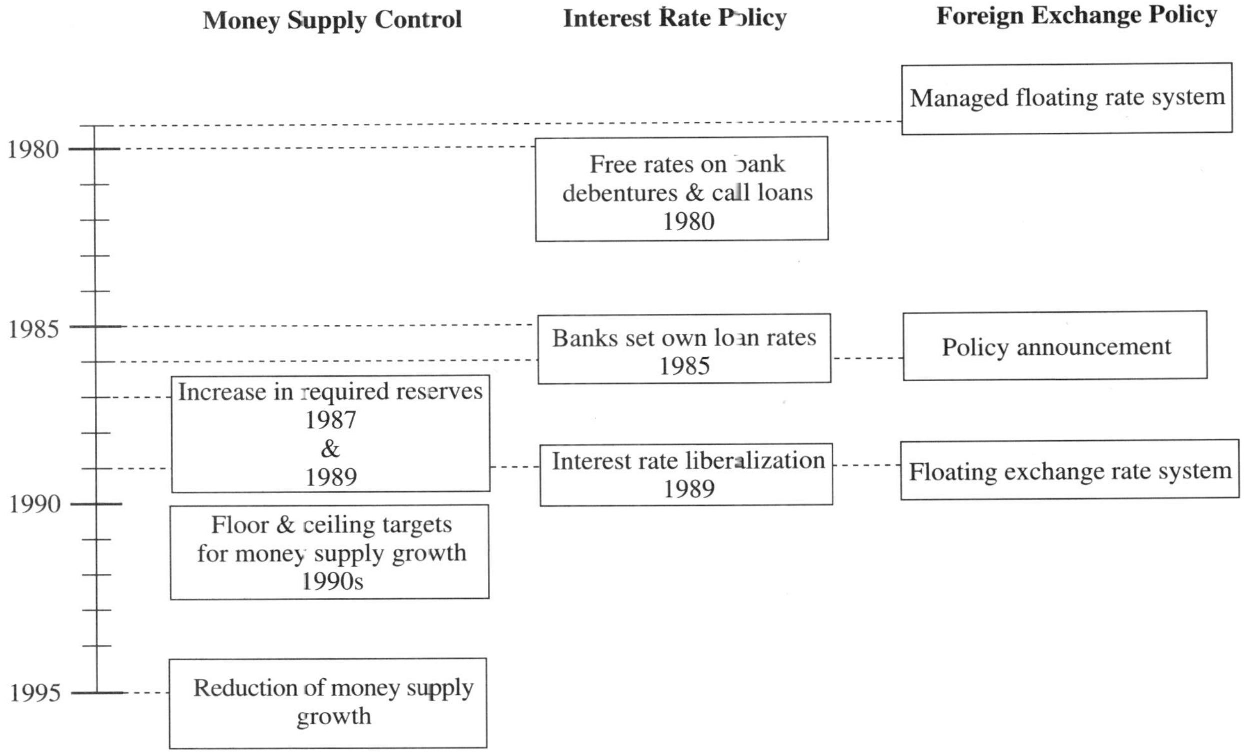

EVALUATION OF MONETARY POLICIES DURING THE 1980 AND 1990S

Money Supply Control

During the 1980s Taiwan experienced simultaneously a rapidly expanding money supply and a low inflation rate. The combination was not new to Taiwan. Over the whole period from 1966 to 1995, while the average growth rate of M2 surged between 15 and 30 percent, the average growth rate of the GDP deflator fluctuated between 2 and 12 percent (Table 5.3).

Because traditional money demand theory cannot explain this phenomenon, Yang and Shea (1996) developed a theoretical model that included stock trading and import prices to explain the relationship between the money supply and the GDP deflator.[2] Their empirical results show that the decrease in import prices (due to NT dollar appreciation and import decontrol) helped stabilize domestic prices when money supply growth was surging. They also found that, to a certain extent, stock trading absorbed the influence of the expanding money supply on prices during the period 1986 to 1991.[3]

Emery (1984 and 1987) examined how Taiwan used monetary policy to deal with the impact of the oil shocks and the surge in foreign exchange. According to Emery's analysis, the central bank's efforts to reduce the inflationary pressure from the two oil shocks by changing the rediscount rate were too small and too late to prevent large initial rises in consumer prices in 1974 and 1980. Also, Emery found that the central bank has relied almost exclusively on open market operations to control the impact of the accumulation of foreign exchange reserves. It has engaged in a massive sterilization operation, selling primarily central bank certificates of deposit to neutralize the potential inflationary impact from the increase in the money supply. However, he found that open market operations have not been a particularly important instrument of monetary policy, although they could play a larger role in the years ahead. On the other hand, the reserve requirement weapon, is more useful at times. In addition, the most important instrument has been interest rate policy, especially in the 1950s when high nominal interest rates did absorb lots of liquidity.

These studies suggest that NT dollar appreciation, import decontrol, stock market price increases, and various monetary policy tools for money supply control together helped to stabilize domestic prices during the late 1980s. Reserve policy has been the most powerful among the various monetary control tools. The money supply growth rate dropped dramatically after the central bank raised the required reserve ratio in 1988. The required reserve ratios went from 23 to 25 percent for checking accounts, from 21 to 23 percent for passbook savings deposits, from 8 to 9 percent for time savings deposits, and from 10 to 11 percent for time deposits. Required reserve ratios were raised further in 1989. The money supply growth rate fell, and the stock price index also declined as a result (Table 5.3).

In the 1990s, the money supply has been under much stricter control than it was in the 1980s. The central bank has set ceiling and floor targets for money supply growth. The target range in the early 1990s was 10 to 15 percent and it was adjusted to 9 to 14 percent at the end of 1995. In most months from late 1995 to the end of 1996, the money growth rate did

TABLE 5.3
Stock Price Index, Annual Growth Rate of Prices, and Money Supply

	Growth Rate of Prices			Growth Rate of Money Supply			
	GDP Deflator	CPI	WPI	M_{1A}	M_{1B}	M_2	Stock Price Index
1966–70	4.76	4.39	1.88	15.10	16.83	18.90	119.27
1971–75	11.69	13.33	12.57	28.13	30.16	29.52	296.31
1976–80	8.94	8.81	8.89	22.61	25.20	23.87	591.15
1981–85	3.78	4.09	0.83	9.33	14.04	22.56	659.69
1986–90	2.38	2.21	–1.83	23.17	23.62	19.95	4,734.69
1991–95	3.03	3.76	1.71	5.89	10.41	15.60	5,042.40
1981	12.07	16.33	7.63	11.03	14.50	18.89	548.84
1982	3.42	2.96	–0.19	8.48	15.53	23.03	477.20
1983	1.92	1.37	–1.17	11.13	17.92	26.25	654.28
1984	0.89	–0.03	0.46	11.75	14.07	23.33	872.51
1985	0.59	–0.16	–2.59	4.28	8.19	21.29	745.62
1986	3.39	0.70	–3.34	28.57	33.55	23.31	944.74
1987	0.56	0.52	–3.26	40.32	45.66	26.57	2,135.03
1988	0.92	1.29	–1.56	26.31	29.45	22.06	5,202.21
1989	3.29	4.40	–0.37	22.16	12.75	16.83	8,616.14
1990	3.75	4.13	–0.61	–1.50	–3.31	10.96	6,775.32
1991	3.85	3.62	0.16	1.25	6.62	16.03	4,928.83
1992	3.93	4.47	–3.67	8.96	15.70	19.89	4,271.63
1993	3.51	2.94	2.51	6.10	8.24	16.17	4,214.78
1994	1.89	4.09	2.17	12.26	16.79	15.02	6,252.99
1995	1.94	3.68	7.37	0.86	4..70	10.90	5,543.75

Notes: Growth rates are percentage change from previous year. M_{1A}, M_{1B}, M_2 are end-of-year data.

Source: *Statistical Abstract of National Income in Taiwan Area, R.O.C. Commodity-Price Statistics Monthly in Taiwan Area; Financial Statistics Monthly, Taiwan District, R.O.C.*

not even reach the floor of the target range. There are two reasons for this phenomenon. One is that sluggish economic growth led to a low demand for money. The other is that the central bank misjudged when it determined the monetary targets.

As a result of the cautious control of the money supply by the central bank and the combined effect of rising stock prices and decreasing import prices in the 1980s, Taiwan has not faced a serious threat of inflation in the past 20 years, except during the two oil crises. However with the opening and deregulation of Taiwan's financial system, the central bank will find the job of controlling the money supply more and more difficult.

Interest Rate Policy

At the beginning stage of economic development governments regulate interest rates in order to provide low cost capital to entrepreneurs. Once the economy has developed to some extent, they may allow more liberal interest rate determination in order to improve the allocational efficiency of the financial market.

The government in Taiwan controlled bank interest rates for a long time, setting uniform interest rates for loans and deposits until 1975. Interest rates have been liberalized very gradually since 1975 when the Central Bank of China was charged with setting uniform deposit rates and the Interest Rate Recommendation Committee of the Banks Association was to fix the ceiling and floor for bank loan rates, subject to the approval of the central bank. Subsequently, the range between the ceiling and floor interest rates for bank loans was gradually enlarged. Beginning in 1980 interest rates for bank debentures and negotiable call loans were allowed to fluctuate freely. In 1985, banks were permitted to set their own interest rates on loans (prime rate) within prescribed limits. In 1986, the ceiling on loan rates was abolished although the floor was retained.

Interest rate liberalization was finally completed with the promulgation of the new Banking Law on 19 July 1989 when all limits for deposit and loan rates were abolished. At the same time the Interest Rate Recommendation Committee was dissolved. Although banks were technically free to decide their own rates, interest rates remained stable for a period of time before the privatization of commercial banking in 1991. The three major commercial banks had similar cost of capital so that their interest rate structures were also similar. After the 1989 interest rate liberalization, these three banks acted as price leaders for a while, typically maintaining identical interest rates. In effect, they colluded to monopolize the market.

Since late 1991 when private banks began to be established, the variance of the prime rate has widened, almost doubling from 0.24 percent before August 1991 to over 0.45 percent after September 1991.

Prior to interest rate liberalization, Taiwan's banks adopted a variety of approaches to avoid rate-limiting regulations. For example, they required compensating balances and they tied loans to agreements to use fee-based bank services. During periods of tight money, instead of lending money directly, banks would guarantee bankers' acceptances and then buy them back from the borrower in the money market at a discount. This practice gave the bank a higher interest rate and meant that the actual cost of a loan was higher than the loan rate.

The deregulation of banking and interest rates was undertaken to make Taiwan's financial market more efficient. The success of this policy should be reflected in changes in the spread between loan and deposit rates, between the bank interest rate and the money market rate, and between domestic interest rates and international interest rates. All three indexes should narrow following Taiwan's banking privatization and interest rate liberalization.

As a rule of thumb, the smaller the spread between loan and deposit rates, the more competitive is the financial market. During the period of controlled rates, the Taiwan government announced only the floor and ceiling for interest rates, never the actual spread. In the period of interest rate regulation, the actual loan rates mostly apply to the ceiling of secured loans. We weighted rates for different kinds of loans according to the volume of each type of loan and compared the average with the rate on time savings deposits. The overall trend in the spread has been downward since 1970, although it increased in 1984 and it has shown ups and downs in the short run (Figure 5.4).

The difference between the bank interest rate and the money market rate is a measure of the deviation of bank rates from the equilibrium rate and can be used to identify the adjustment speed and flexibility of bank interest rates. The closer the bank rate is to the market rate, the greater the degree of financial liberalization. Taiwan established a money market, a market for exchange of short-term bills, in 1976. Interest rates in this market are flexible—not under the control of the government—so changes in the bill rate can quickly reflect the demand and supply of loanable funds. This money market interest rate is usually taken as a proxy for the equilibrium market rate. Figure 5.5 shows the spread between the money market and bank rates. In the tight money period of the early 1980s, money market rates were as much as 3 percentage points higher than bank

FIGURE 5.4
Spread between Loan and Deposit Rates, 1970–95

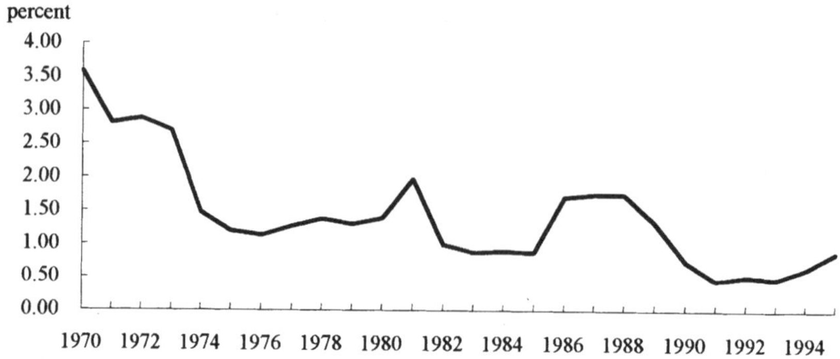

Note: Spread is calculated as the weighted average of various loan rates minus the rate on time savings deposits.
Source: Calculated from Central Bank of China. *Financial Statistics Monthly, Taiwan District, R.O.C.*

FIGURE 5.5
Spread between Money Market and Bank Loan Rates, 1982–95

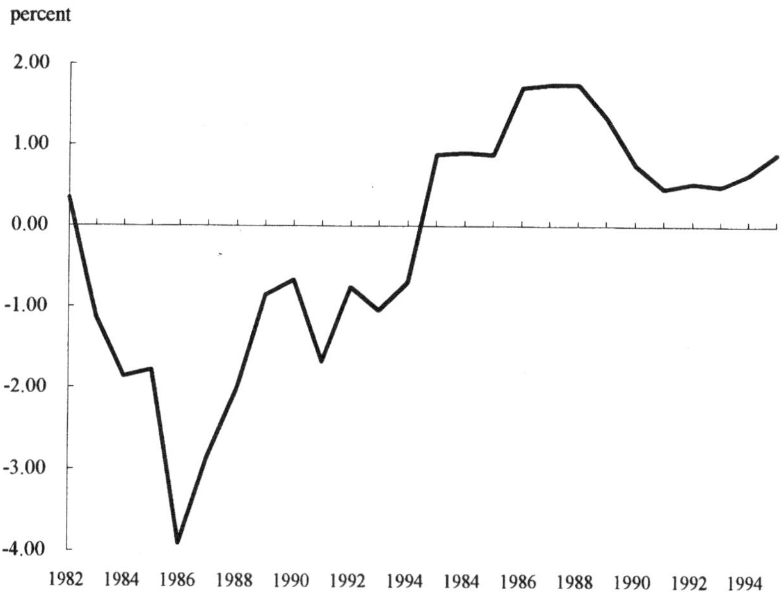

Note: Spread is calculated as the money market rate minus a weighted average of bank loan rates.
Source: Calculated from Central Bank of China. *Financial Statistics Monthly, Taiwan District, R.O.C.*

rates. In the loose monetary environment of the mid-1980s, money market rates fell below bank rates by as much as 4 percentage points. Since 1988 the spread narrowed and since 1992 it has approached zero.

The difference between the domestic interest rate and the international rate should diminish with financial liberalization. International comparisons should be based on real interest rates after deducting inflation rates. Making this adjustment, Taiwan's domestic interest rates appear to be approaching international levels. The difference between real interest levels in Taiwan and levels in both the United States and Japan has narrowed significantly since the early 1980s (Figure 5.6).

Cunningham and Cunningham (1991) studied interest rate linkage between the United States and Taiwan. Hwang (1996) modified their approach to investigate *ex ante* the real interest rate linkage between Taiwan and the United States from September 1982 to May 1995. He found a positive but relatively low correlation between movements of real rates in Taiwan and those in the United States, so that it is still possible for monetary policy in Taiwan to affect domestic rates and hence domestic economic activity. Chinn and Frankel (1995) investigated the relative influence of U.S. and Japanese real interest rates on local Pacific Rim rates. They defined influence as the presence of common stochastic trends and they examined the degree to which long run real interest parity holds. Their results indicate that Taiwan as well as Hong Kong and Malaysia are linked with both the United States and Japan, while only Singapore is linked solely with the United States. On the other hand, Korea, and perhaps Indonesia and Thailand, appear to be more closely linked with Japan. According to their findings real interest parity only holds for the following interest rate pairs: U.S.-Taiwan, Japan-Taiwan, and U.S.-Singapore.

Financial interdependence is deepening among Taiwan and other countries, such as the United States, Japan, and the ASEAN countries. Therefore, real interest rates in Taiwan should move more and more together with real rates in these countries.

Exchange Rate Policy

In February 1979, Taiwan officially converted from a fixed rate system to a managed floating foreign exchange rate regime. Under the new rules, exchange rates were to be limited to a very small margin on either side of a central rate, which was to be set daily by a group of five major commercial banks together with the central bank. The intervention band was

FIGURE 5.6
Spread between Domestic and Foreign Interest Rates,1971–95

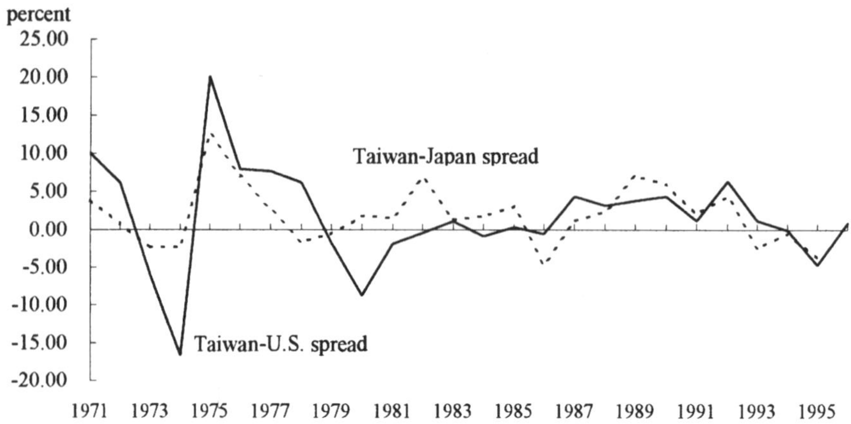

Notes: Taiwan-U.S. spread denotes real interest rate in Taiwan minus real interest rate in the United States. Taiwan-Japan spread denotes real interest rate in Taiwan minus real interest rate in Japan. Real interest rates are calculated as prime rate minus rate of growth of wholesale price index for each country.
Source: IMF, *International Financial Statistics.* Central Bank of China. *Financial Statistics Monthly, Taiwan District, R.O.C.* Directorate-General of Budget, Accounting and Statistics R.O.C. *Commodity-Price Statistics Monthly in Taiwan Area of R.O.C.*

initially limited to 0.5 percent. Subsequently, the central bank withdrew from participation in rate-setting and the limit on the day-to-day fluctuation was widened to 2.25 percent. The heavily managed float kept the NT dollar undervalued at a stable level from 1981 to 1985. As a result, the current account balance in Taiwan increased drastically in 1985. Due to the limitation of sterilization operations and persistent pressure from the U.S. government, the monetary authorities finally let the currency start appreciating at the beginning of 1986. From 1986 to 1988 the Taiwan currency appreciated by 40 percent relative to the U.S. dollar.

In 1989, the central bank announced a flexible exchange rate system. Since then, the exchange rate has been determined by the market. However, the central bank continues to intervene to stabilize fluctuation of the foreign exchange rate through open market operations.

Moreno (1989) examined the extent to which exchange rate movements explain improvements in competitiveness and rising rate surpluses in Taiwan and Korea in the 1980s. He found that exchange rate movements improved competitiveness and thus contributed directly to trade imbalances for Korea, but not for Taiwan. Moreno and Yin (1992) showed how the credibility of Taiwan's unsterilized intervention policy may have affected its pattern of adjustment in the exchange rate, velocity, and asset prices during the second half of the 1980s. When the outcome of unsterilized intervention is credible, any degree of exchange rate stability can be achieved at the cost of a sufficiently large, one-time change in the money supply. When the outcome of intervention is not credible, intervention can lead to persistent, and possibly accelerating, changes in exchange rates, money supply, velocity, and asset prices. Under certain conditions, intervention may even amplify the cumulative change in the exchange rate, rather than reduce it. Sato and Lii (1994) found that the foreign exchange market is stable in the short run as well as in the long run in both Japan and Taiwan and that the J-curve effect is present in Japan but absent in Taiwan.

Generally speaking, it can be concluded that the policy to keep the NT dollar undervalued contributed to Taiwan's phenomenal export performance which stimulated economic growth to a great degree. The gradual implementation of the exchange rate appreciation had two opposing results. The good point was that it dampened the harmful impact on export firms by giving them a chance to adjust. The bad point was that it provided room for hot money to enter the domestic stock and real estate markets, bringing the dangers of a bubble economy. If the government had adjusted the exchange rate system earlier, pressure from the United States might have been avoided, and the negative influence on the domestic economy might have been smaller.

POLICY OBJECTIVES

The central bank has been the major government agency executing monetary policy in Taiwan. The central bank reacts to changes in the economy, such as fluctuations in the GNP growth rate or price level, employing a mix of tools to adjust the domestic monetary environment to meet its policy objectives. Maintaining a low inflation rate and stimulating economic growth are the usual objectives. The reaction function of the central bank indicates specifically how it adjusts domestic credit to changes in income, prices, interest rates, and foreign reserves.

Central Bank Reaction Function

We set up a simplified model for the money market as follows:

(1) $L / P = k(Y, i, P)$,
$k_Y = \delta Y / \delta k > 0$, $k_i = \delta Y / \delta i < 0$, and $k_P = \delta Y / \delta P < 0$

(2) $M = h(F + D)$

(3) $M = L$

(4) $Pk(Y, i, P) = h(F + D)$

where:

L	=	money demand
P	=	price level
k	=	real balance ratio
Y	=	real income
i	=	nominal interest rate
M	=	money supply
h	=	money multiplier
F	=	foreign assets
D	=	domestic credit

Equation (1) is a real money demand function, showing that income and price have a positive influence and the interest rate has a negative impact on money demand. The price level has a negative impact on real money demand. Equation (2) is a money supply identity. The money supply is equal to the product of the sum of domestic credit and foreign assets multiplied by the money multiplier. Equation (3) is the money market equilibrium. Money supply is equal to money demand. Equation (4) can be derived by combining equations (1), (2), and (3).

Rearranging equation (4) gives the expression for domestic credit:

(5) $D = D(Y, P, i, F)$ $\qquad \delta D / \delta Y > 0$, $\delta D / \delta i > 0$,
$\delta D / \delta F < 0$, $\delta D / \delta P >< 0$

The derivatives of this equation with respect to Y, P, i, and F indicate how the level of domestic credit changes in response to changes in the other economic variables. Since the level of domestic credit is largely controlled by the central bank, these derivatives indicate how the central bank adjusts credit in response to the other economic variables.

We estimated this equation on annual data for Taiwan for the years 1977 to 1995 in order to understand the government's policy objective in terms of income growth and price stability and to determine its reaction to the monetary environment, including the interest rate level and foreign asset accumulation. The ordinary least squares (OLS) estimates are given below, where Y represents real GDP, P represents the GDP deflator, i represents the loan rate, F is foreign assets in total money reserves, and D is domestic credit in total money reserves:

$$\Delta D = \underset{(1.861)}{198968.62} - \underset{(-2.074)^{*}}{926408.64\ \Delta \ln P} + \underset{(0.047)}{34438.161\ \Delta \ln Y}$$

$$+ \underset{(2.094)^{*}}{25002.259\ \Delta \ln i} \quad \underset{(-14.860)^{**}}{-0.938\ \Delta F}$$

$R^2 = 0.946$
DW = 2.045

This regression has satisfactory fitness with an R-squared of 0.95 and the Durbin-Watson statistic indicates that there is no serial correlation. The coefficient estimates indicate that:

- When the price level rises, the central bank reduces domestic credit.
- Although the central bank increases domestic credit when income rises, this positive reaction is not statistically significant.
- When the interest rate rises and the monetary environment becomes tighter, the central bank reacts by increasing domestic credit.
- The accumulation of foreign assets causes the central bank to reduce domestic credit (The coefficient of F can also be called the offset coefficient.)

In summary, Taiwan's central bank clearly reacts to changes in prices, interest rates, and accumulation of foreign assets, while its reaction to economic growth is insignificant.

Financial Liberalization and Internationalization

Financial policy in Taiwan lacks efficiency but provides a high degree of financial stability. In recent years, Taiwan has implemented financial liberalization and internationalization in order to improve financial efficiency. It is difficult to achieve financial efficiency and financial stability simultaneously. A great deal depends on the policy mix. This section summarizes the liberalization measures adopted since the 1980s and evaluates their effect on financial stability.

Deregulation of Private Banks

The government prefers government-owned financial institutions to private banks in order to completely secure the stability of financial markets and control the flow of funds. However, government banks are much less efficient than private banks (Yang 1994). Consequently, when the economy develops to a certain extent financial liberalization becomes a trend.

Banking privatization has been one of the most significant reforms in Taiwan's financial history. Private banks were first allowed by the Banking Law of 1989. In June of 1991, 15 new banks were authorized. By the end of 1996, 18 new banks were in operation, improving service and competition in the whole banking industry.

Relaxing Restrictions on Foreign Banks

Local branches of foreign banks were welcomed in order to attract foreign capital, but for decades they were usually subject to some restrictions in order not to put too much pressure on domestic financial institutions. Despite these restrictions, foreign banks did create some competition for local banks. Going along with the tide of financial liberalization and internationalization, Taiwan gradually reduced its regulation of foreign banks.

Limits on the number of local branches was one aspect of restriction of foreign banks. Before 1986, foreign banks were allowed to open just one branch. In 1987, a second branch was first approved. In 1991, a third branch was approved. Since 1994, restrictions on the number of branches have been removed if the capital transmitted from the head office is over NT$150 million for the first branch or over NT$1.2 million after the first branch in Taiwan.

Broadening Bank Activities

Approved activities for banks have been gradually broadened. For example, bills transactions, which in the past were allowed to be conducted only by bills finance companies, were opened to some private banks in 1992. The Ministry of Finance seems to be planning to develop the banking industry into a universal banking system, which would allow traditional banking activities and bills transactions to be conducted at one bank.

Deregulation of the money market. The interbank call market for foreign reserves was opened in 1989; eight new bills finance companies had opened by the end of 1996 joining the three old companies. The scale of the money market has grown quickly in the 1990s as well.

Relaxation of capital controls. Government limits on capital outflows have been relaxed gradually over the past five years. By the beginning of 1996, the ceiling on annual capital inflow and outflow had been raised to US$5 million per individual and to US$20 million per company.

Establishing Taipei as an Asian Financial Centre

The government of Taiwan wants to follow Singapore, Tokyo, and Hong Kong to become one of the Asian financial centres. Taiwan boasts abundant savings, plentiful foreign reserves, and highly-educated human resources. However, it needs to increase freedom of capital movement, revise the preferential tax system, improve information systems, and introduce internationally accommodating financial regulations and affiliated financial services. It will take time for Taipei to make these changes and to reach necessary standards.

Financial Efficiency and Financial Stability

Some conflict exists among Taiwan's financial policies. Reforms intended to increase financial efficiency create strong competition which may put fragile financial institutions in danger of bankruptcy when the economy goes into recession. Taiwan experienced several serious financial crises in the early 1980s, and in the slow economic growth period of 1995–96 it witnessed more financial crises, particularly involving local financial institutions. This experience has led Taiwan to consider how to make the goal of financial efficiency consistent with the goal of financial stability. Another problem is the conflict between price stability and market efficiency. If the central bank wants to stabilize the foreign exchange rate, maybe it will have to sacrifice control of the money supply. Although the central bank has tried to sterilize surplus money, there is a limit to its influence.

Financial policy can be modified to suit different stages of economic development. For example, Taiwan's preferential low interest rates for exports and its under-valued NT dollar policy stimulated exports in the early stage of development, but those policies do not need to remain for all time. Exports lost their place as the only policy target in the 1980s. Letting the financial market operate freely seems more suitable to Taiwan's current stage of development. It is believed that a liberalized financial system is the most efficient. This is a long-run goal and the pace of financial liberalization is quickening now. Nevertheless, when market failure occurs, private financial institutions and the interest rate mechanism cannot meet the demands of industry. Special financial institutions such as specialized banks and guarantee systems can be designed to address these problems. A sound supervisory system and a well-designed sequence of financial liberalization are essential to avoid financial instability. These require time to put in place.

In order to pursue financial efficiency and financial stability simultaneously, the government should make efforts to search for an optimal policy. The active role of the Taiwanese government has diminished over time with the progress of economic development. In the 1950s, the government adopted a high interest rate policy in order to curb inflation and in the 1960s it maintained an undervalued currency and offered preferential interest rates to support its export-oriented strategy. However, in the 1990s, the need for an efficient market system is urgent and inappropriate government intervention is not welcome.

Taiwan's central bank has a good record of maintaining low inflation. Financial stability also helps economic growth. All of these achievements should not be neglected. In the process of financial reform, setting up a self-stabilizing mechanism in the financial system, such as a good financial supervision system and a sound deposit insurance system, is very important.

Notes

[1] Because the government sector is usually in fiscal balance, we ignore it here.

[2] They tested their model using a two-stage least squares analysis of quarterly data from the first quarter of 1978 to the second quarter of 1993 and employing the unit-root test and co-integration test.

[3] Yang and Shea's model forecasts better than does the traditional model without stock and import variables.

References

Chinn, Meazie D. and Jeffrey A. Frankel. 1995. "Who Drives Real Interest Rates around the Pacific Rim: the U.S. or Japan". *Journal of International Money and Finance* 14(6): 801–21.

Cunningham, T.J. and R.T. Cunningham. 1991. "The Behavior of Real Rates of Interest in a Small, Opening Economy". *Journal of Economic Development* 16: 191–202.

Emery, Robert F. 1984. "Postwar Financial Policies in Taiwan". Federal Reserve Board International Finance Discussion Paper, 252, December.

______. 1987. Monetary Policy in Taiwan, China. Board of Governors of the Federal Reserve System International Finance Discussion Paper, 313, November.

Hwang, Jyh Dean. 1996. The International Linkage of Real Interest Rates: The Case for the U.S. and Taiwan. Conference for Economic Structural Adjustment of International Regional Integration, 15 March, Academia Sinica.

Lee, Sheng-Yi. 1990. *Money and Finance in the Economic Development of Taiwan.* London: Macmillan Press Ltd.

Liang, Fa-Chin. 1983. "The Money Supply, Price and Balance of Payments". In *Collected Essays on Money and Finance in Honour of Professor Lin Hsir Fan at Age 81*(in Chinese).

______. 1989. "Exchange Rate and Trade Adjustment in Taiwan and Korea". Federal Reserve Bank of San Francisco *Economic Review* Spring: 30–48.

Moreno, Ramon and Norman Yin. 1992. "Exchange Rate Policy and Shocks to Asset Markets: The Case of Taiwan in the 1980s". Federal Reserve Bank of San Francisco *Economic Review* No. 1: 14–34.

Sato, Kazuo and Sheng-Yann Lii. 1994. "Exchange Rate Dynamics in Japan and Taiwan". *Journal of Asian Economics* 5(1):43–63.

Yang, Ya-Hwei. 1994. "Taiwan: Development and Structural Change of the Banking System". In *The Financial Development of Japan, Korea, and Taiwan : Growth, Repression, and Liberalization*, edited by Hugh Patrick and Yang-Chul Park. New York: Oxford University Press.

______ and Jia-Dong Shea. 1996. "Money and Prices in Taiwan in the 1980s". In *Financial Deregulation and Integration in East Asia*, edited by Takatoshi Ito and Anne O. Krueger. Chicago: University of Chicago Press.

UPDATE

THE FINANCIAL CRISIS OF 1997 IN TAIWAN

The financial turmoil in Southeast Asia in 1997 has had an impact on financial markets in Taiwan, especially the foreign exchange and stock markets. The impact was not as severe as in most Southeast Asian countries, but up until the end of 1997, the situation in Taiwan was more serious than in Hong Kong or Singapore.

THE ECONOMY BEFORE JUNE 1997

Stable prices and a high economic growth rate have supported Taiwan's good economic performance. Taiwan has enjoyed a trade surplus for years. Although heavy overseas investment led to capital outflows after the late 1980s, the outflow was largely long-term rather than short-term capital.

The Stock Market

The Taiwan stock market grew abnormally for several months before the shock wave of the financial turmoil hit (Table U5.1). From a level of 6,881.57 at the end of 1996 the stock market soared in the first half of 1997 to reach 9,890.34 by the end of August. This surge in stock prices set the market up to take a dive.

The Foreign Exchange Market

Under the floating exchange rate system adopted in the late 1980s Taiwan's central bank does not impose any restrictions on the determination of the exchange rate, but it may intervene in the foreign exchange market once in a while if necessary. From the end of 1996 until July 1997, the exchange rate remained between 27.0 and 28.0 NT (New Taiwan) dollars per U.S. dollar. The local foreign exchange market was considered stable.

TABLE U5.1
Taiwan Stock Market Index, Dec. 1996 to Nov. 1997
1966 average = 100

1996 Dec.	1997 Jan.	Feb.	Mar.	Apr.	May	June	July	Aug.	Sept.	Oct.	Nov.
6,881.57	7,135.16	7,642.26	8,166.46	8,505.78	8,146.61	8,604.60	9,553.26	9,890.34	9,111.67	7,983.28	7,731.90

Source: Taiwan Stock Exchange, *TSE Monthly Review*, No.427.

FINANCIAL TURMOIL FROM JULY TO THE END OF 1997

The financial crisis that originated in Southeast Asia in 1997 has spilled over into many neighboring countries, including Taiwan. After its half-year surge the Taiwan stock market collapsed in August 1997. The stock price index reached a stable level by the end of November. At 7,731.90 it was down more than 20 percent from its August peak.

As other Asian currencies depreciated against the U.S. dollar, Taiwan also felt strong pressure to depreciate the NT dollar. However, the central bank has shown a determined attitude in supporting the value of the currency since July 1997, fighting the continually increasing pressure by absorbing NT dollars and selling U.S. dollars. Although the NT dollar moved out of the 27.0 to 28.0 range for a few days at the end of July, the central bank pegged the exchange rate at a level between 28.6 and 28.7 until the end of September. In October, the central bank even tried to reverse the depreciation pressure and force the NT dollar to appreciate, selling a large amount of foreign currency reserves.

In order to loosen the tight credit environment, the central bank announced reductions in the required reserve ratio and initiated other expansionary policies. However, this did not give any significant stimulus to the stock market. The contractionary effect of the exchange rate stabilization measures made the domestic credit environment tighten further. Despite the determined countermeasures of the central bank, pressure from abroad, from local branches of foreign banks, and from domestic citizens continued to build up. Finally, on 17 October 1997 the central bank abandoned its defense policy and allowed the market to seek its own equilibrium. The NT dollar depreciated day by day immediately after the policy announcement (Figure U5.1) and the stock market price index also slid downward. A mood of instability prevailed for several days, forcing the government and the public to confront the problem. Fortunately, both markets found equilibrium points after about one week.

FIGURE U5.1
Spot Exchange Rate for the NT Dollar, 1 July to 30 October 1997

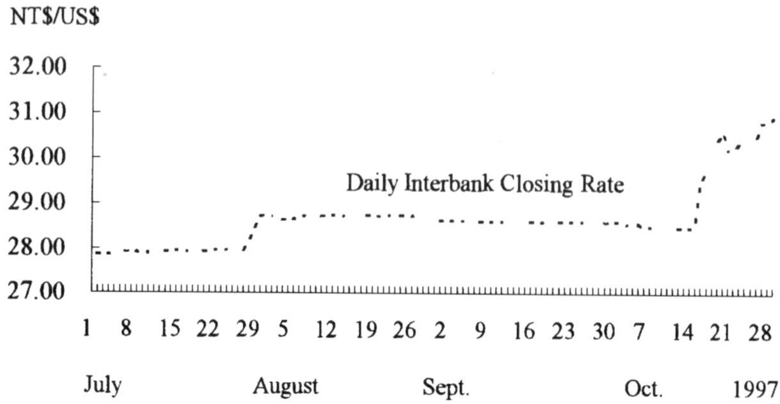

Source: Central Bank of China *Financial Statistics Monthly*, Taiwan District, ROC.

During the process of the stock market collapse in October 1997 the Ministry of Finance also proposed several measures to boost confidence in the local stock market. One such measure was to relax the margin for stock purchases.

RELATED ISSUES OF MONETARY POLICY

Although Taiwan's economy and financial system are not as fragile as those of other Southeast Asian countries, the financial turmoil in the region have raised many questions about monetary policy in Taiwan. The role of the central bank has been strongly questioned, regarding, for example, whether or not it should intervene in the foreign exchange market.

If the central bank can really handle the pressure of international financial speculation, then intervention by the central bank has a function. However, a rigid exchange rate policy is apt to collapse when foreign speculative pressure is too strong. Intervention does not help stabilize the foreign exchange rate. On the other hand, the stock market exerts pressure on the central bank and the Ministry of Finance to help maintain the stock price index. Whether the government should play such a role or not is also a subject of discussion and a challenge for monetary authorities.

The solid foundation of the manufacturing sector in Taiwan helped dampen the impact of the financial turmoil. Up to the end of 1997, Taiwan's financial system and economic performance were in a better state of health than those of most Asian countries such as Thailand, Malaysia, Philippines, Indonesia, and South Korea. However, the financial crisis continues to influence worldwide financial developments and economic growth. We should pay more attention to this phenomenon. More importantly, we should learn some lessons from the crisis. In particular the experience has shown that too early deregulation is not good for an economy. We need to learn how to find the optimum trade-off between stability and efficiency of the financial system.

January 1998

6

The Role of Monetary Policy under a Linked Exchange Rate Regime: The Case Of Hong Kong

Raymond Ng and Edward Chen

Over the past decade Hong Kong made a deliberate effort to reform its monetary management mechanism in order to strengthen its ability to maintain a stable exchange rate and to facilitate the development of the financial market. In principle, the linked exchange rate regime, which has been in place since 1983, is self-maintaining through arbitrage. However, in view of the increase in adverse capital flows and the more frequent speculative attacks, the Hong Kong government saw the need to gain more effective control over interbank interest rates to defend the exchange rate when necessary. Equally important in reshaping the monetary management environment was the fact that Hong Kong has been facing increasing competition from financial centres in the neighbouring region. Despite Hong Kong's place as an international financial centre, the Hong Kong dollar debt market was rather inactive and under-developed. These factors, combined with the increasing sophistication of financial products and growing demand for long term debt instruments, led the government to take steps to expand and upgrade the financial market infrastructure and boost the debt market in Hong Kong.

HONG KONG'S MONETARY MANAGEMENT MECHANISM

Hong Kong has always been a small and open economy with a free capital account. As an international financial centre in an increasingly integrated global capital market, Hong Kong is particularly subject to massive cross-boarder capital flows. The increasing size, strength, and volatility of institutional and portfolio capital in the financial market have posed another challenge to Hong Kong's exchange rate policy. More importantly, since the exchange rate was linked to the U.S. dollar in 1983, monetary policy has been devoted primarily to maintaining the stability of the external value of the Hong Kong currency.

Until the more recent reforms of the monetary management framework in the late 1980s and early 1990s, the Exchange Fund lacked (effective) control over the level of liquidity in the interbank market and was not the last-resort-lender of bank reserves. The monetary authority's ability to alter the interbank interest rate in order to defend the peg was weak. In addition, the lack of a deep and active money market limited the extent of open market operations to achieve monetary and exchange rate targets.

The Linked Exchange Rate Regime (a Currency Board System)

The Exchange Fund is Hong Kong's version of a currency board. A currency board is essentially a monetary institution which issues and redeems domestic currency on demand against international reserves at a fixed rate and maintains 100-percent international reserves against the currency issued (Hong Kong Monetary Authority 1995*c* and Ow 1986). It has no other monetary role but to maintain the external value of the domestic currency. A currency board is in general unable and/or unwilling to vary domestic credit and hence monetary aggregates which are determined by balance of payments conditions. The 100-percent reserve requirement also demands that, unlike a central bank, a currency board holds only foreign and not domestic assets, such as government debt (Ow 1986 and Williamson 1995). There is, however, no explicit restriction on the way net foreign reserves should be handled.

The Exchange Fund was established in 1935, when Hong Kong abandoned the silver standard, to regulate the exchange rate of the Hong Kong currency, to issue and redeem Hong Kong currency against foreign reserve currency, and to serve as the custodian of Hong Kong's foreign exchange reserves. Unlike a typical currency board, the Exchange Fund did not issue domestic currency to be circulated in the economy, but instead issued Certificates of Indebtedness (CIs) against sterling to three British "exchange" banks, (the Hongkong and Shanghai Banking Corporation, the Standard Chartered Bank, and the Mercantile Bank). The Hong Kong dollar was floated from November 1974 until October 1983. At that time it was again pegged to the U.S. dollar at HK$7.8 parity in an attempt to check the sudden, rapid depreciation caused by uncertainties arising from Sino-British negotiations on Hong Kong's future (Nugee 1995 and Ow 1986). Essentially, the exchange rate was fixed for the issue and redemption of CIs to be held by banks to cover their note-issuing, but the exchange rate in the foreign exchange market continued to be determined by market forces.

The linked exchange rate is maintained through two types of arbitrage. First, "cash arbitrage" occurs when individuals and institutions take advantage of the differential between the free market exchange rate and the official parity. This helps to contain the market exchange rate within a narrow range around the linked level. Second, "interest rate arbitrage" happens when interest rate differentials cause capital to move to a country with higher rates. For example, when capital outflows put pressure on the Hong Kong dollar, the interbank market strains and the interest rate rises relative to U.S. dollar interest rates. The higher rates attract capital inflows, mitigating the initial devaluation pressure.

Although Hong Kong's linked exchange rate regime is usually referred to as a fixed rate system, in fact, it differs from a fixed rate system in several notable ways. First, the currency board predetermines the rate of exchange for the issue and redemption of Hong Kong currency, rather than for the foreign exchange market. Under a true fixed exchange rate system the central bank commits to maintaining the predetermined rate of exchange (within upper and lower limits) by buying and selling foreign currency in the foreign exchange market (Kreinin 1991). Under the currency board system, intrinsic cash and interest arbitrage mechanisms, rather than explicit central bank operations, maintain the stability of the exchange rate.

Second, under a true fixed exchange rate regime the central bank can also influence the monetary base and money supply by buying or selling domestic assets. A currency board has no such discretion. It increases the monetary base when the private sector wants to sell foreign exchange and reduces the monetary base when the private sector wishes to sell cash and purchase foreign exchange, perhaps to finance a balance of payments deficit (Williamson 1995 and Asian Monetary Monitor 1995).

The cash arbitrage mechanism that helps maintain the linked exchange rate is complicated by Hong Kong's note-issuing procedure. For banks, cash and deposits denominated in Hong Kong dollars are not convertible at exactly a one-to-one rate. This is not much of a problem as long as the market rate for the Hong Kong dollar stays either very close to the fixed rate or fluctuates evenly on either side. However, since the early 1990s the market rate for the Hong Kong dollar has been persistently on the strong side. With the market rate consistently above parity, note-issuing banks could gain by selling Hong Kong dollar notes to the public and buying cheaper notes from the Exchange Fund, whereas note-receiving banks would lose if their main source of funds was cash deposits of Hong Kong dollars. To resolve this problem, in February 1994 the Hong Kong Monetary Authority decided to supply non-note-issuing banks with Hong Kong dollars against their clearing balances at note-issuing banks, *at the market rate*. This way, the note-issuing banks would still benefit when the exchange rate stayed on the strong side, but they would lose out if the exchange rate moved to the weak side. These banks had an incentive to keep the exchange rate on the strong side of parity, rather than closing the gap (Asian Monetary Monitor 1993).

It is widely agreed that the strength of a linked system depends on the size of the country's foreign reserves and on its internal economic fundamentals. However, from an operational point of view, monetary management also plays a crucial role in maintaining the exchange rate. Proper monetary management can minimize and shorten the instability in the exchange rate that is a particular concern in the face of speculative attacks. The government's major monetary policy options to support the linked rate include operations to influence interbank liquidity and short-term interest rates and direct intervention in the foreign exchange markets. In the first few years of the linked system, the government lacked control over interbank liquidity and had to intervene directly in the foreign exchange markets. For instance, the Exchange Fund purchased US$2.7 billion gross in 1987 and US$3.1 billion gross in 1988 (Nugee 1995).

Monetary policy is generally defined as a set of measures by which the monetary authority attempts to affect the level of liquidity, interbank interest rates, and the availability of credit in the economy to achieve macroeconomic objectives. In the case of Hong Kong, the primary objective of monetary policy, as frequently stressed, is to maintain the stability of the Hong Kong dollar exchange rate. A stable exchange rate is of particular importance to Hong Kong which has an extremely outward oriented economy and is a leading international financial centre.[1] Excessive fluctuation of the exchange rate would create uncertainty that would harm the economy. Moreover, because Hong Kong also depends heavily on imports for domestic consumption and investment, adverse movements in the exchange rate, and hence import prices, would cause domestic price instability.

With capital flows into Hong Kong, the first-round expansionary effect on the clearing balances of the banking system from the sale of U.S. dollars to the Exchange Fund is generally sterilized. This can be achieved by funding the purchase of U.S. dollars from money in the banking system, for instance by the sale of Exchange Fund papers, or by reducing deposits with banks, or even by straight borrowing from banks. Nonetheless, capital inflows still lead to an increase in bank deposits and thereby money supply (Lau, Hawkins, and Chan 1994). Hence, sterilization is mainly adopted to restore equilibrium in the interbank liquidity market to achieve interest rate stability but not to control total money supply growth.

Reforms to Enhance the Monetary Management Mechanism

The weakening of the U.S. dollar in 1986–87 triggered repeated speculation that the Hong Kong dollar would revalue, putting upward pressure on the market exchange rate. These speculative attacks failed in the face of the government's strong determination to maintain the link. Nevertheless they raised concern that sustained speculative pressure could disrupt the exchange rate as well as the economy as a whole. The Hong Kong government saw the need to improve its monetary management capacity in order to defend the linked exchange rate effectively and tackle speculative activities promptly. It introduced a number of monetary management reforms in the late 1980s and early 1990s. These reforms were a deliberate effort to establish a more market-based mechanism of (indirect) monetary management by enhancing the control of the monetary authority over interbank liquidity and interbank interest rates.

Establishment of the Hong Kong Monetary Authority (HKMA)

One of these steps was the establishment of the HKMA on 1 April 1993, by merging the office of the Exchange Fund (in charge of maintaining exchange rate stability and managing foreign reserves) with the office of the Commissioner of Banking (in charge of supervising the banking system) (Figure 6.1). The major functions of the HKMA are: (1) to exercise monetary policy to regulate the exchange rate (to maintain the 7.8 parity), issue and redeem CIs from note-issuing banks, manage foreign reserves, conduct open market operations, and operate the Liquidity Adjustment Facility; (2) to maintain the stability and integrity of the monetary and financial systems by supervising financial institutions and regulating financial markets, and providing emergency support for banks if necessary when the system is under pressure; (3) to act as banker to the government

FIGURE 6.1
Comparison of the Monetary Framework of Hong Kong before and after Establishment of the Hong Kong Monetary Authority

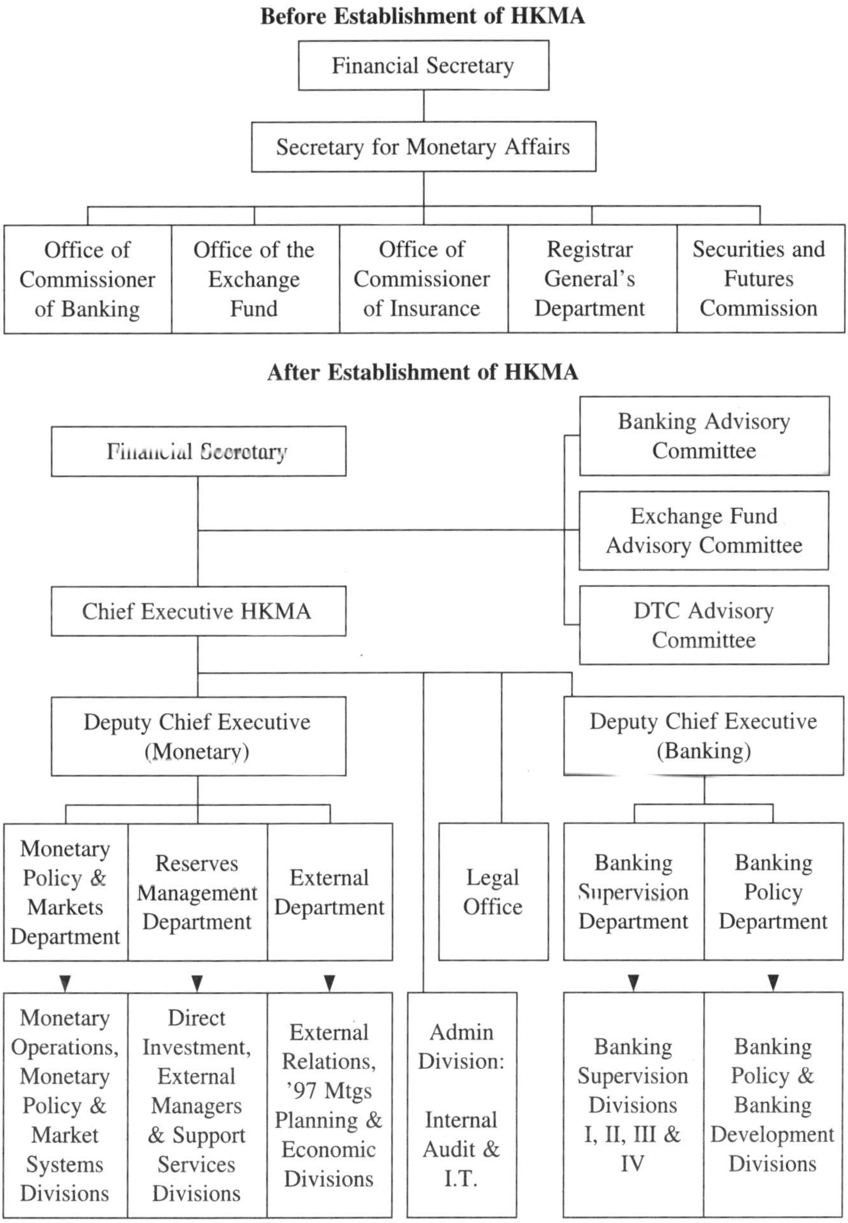

Source: B. J. Beecham. 1996. *Monetary and Financial System in Hong Kong*. Hong Kong: Hong Kong Institute of Bankers, p.52.

by managing the fiscal reserves and advising on major government policy issues that involve financial considerations; and (4) to act as banker to the banking system by being lender of last resort on interbank liquidity. Clearing for the banking system continues to be performed by the Hongkong and Shanghai Banking Corporation Limited (HSBC), the management bank of the Clearing House of the Hong Kong Association of Banks, and by 10 settlement banks. The issue of bank notes is performed by the HSBC, the Standard Chartered Bank, and more recently the Bank of China Group. The only currency issued by the HKMA is coins (see Yam 1994 for details).

In comparison with Hong Kong's system, the monetary system of Singapore consists of a separate currency board and a central bank, the Monetary Authority of Singapore (MAS). The MAS performs all the functions of a typical central bank *except* note-issuing, which is left to the Board of Commissioners of Currency. The MAS requires banks to maintain current balances to satisfy the statutory reserve requirement (6 percent of total deposits) and plays the role of clearing house for the banking sector (see Tan 1989 for details).

Special Rate Rule and Deposit Charges

Other reforms addressed the need to increase the monetary authority's control over interest rates so that it could more effectively defend the Hong Kong dollar against speculation. In December 1987, the government introduced the Special Rate Rule to allow the authority under exceptional circumstances to impose a punitive interest rate on excessive Hong Kong dollar balances in the clearing accounts of banks. In addition, the government introduced legislative amendments to remove the 60-percent statutory ceiling on interest rates as required by the Money Lender Ordinance and to provide the mechanism to charge negative interest rates. If necessary, upon consultation with the Financial Secretary, the Hong Kong Association of Banks may require banks to levy charges on credit balances over HK$1 million with a maturity of less than 3 months (Nugee 1995 and Beecham 1996).

The Accounting Arrangements

The Accounting Arrangements were introduced in July 1988 to enhance control over interbank liquidity and interbank interest rates. Prior to this, the effectiveness of the Exchange Fund's money market operations had been reduced or offset by ability of the HSBC to influence liquidity in the banking system.[2] Under the Accounting Arrangements, the HSBC was required to open an account with the Exchange Fund. The balance in the account represents the net liquidity in the interbank market and it can only be altered by the Exchange Fund. Any liquidity in excess of this balance is charged a penalty rate of interest. With this arrangement, the Exchange Fund became the ultimate provider of liquidity to the banking system (i.e., the lender of last resort) and the effectiveness of its monetary management was greatly improved. For instance, when capital inflows put upward pressure on the exchange rate, the Exchange Fund can now raise the level of interbank liquidity to lower the interbank interest rate by buying U.S. dollars and other assets with Hong Kong dollars, lending Hong Kong dollars to banks, transferring deposits back to the General Revenue accounts with banks, or buying back Exchange Fund Bills and Notes.

Liquidity Adjustment Facility (LAF)

The introduction of the LAF in 1992 gave the government even more control over liquidity and short-term interest rates. The discount and deposit facilities of LAF provide another channel through which the monetary authority can supply extra liquidity to or absorb excess liquidity from the banking system. With the introduction of the LAF, banks can now adjust their clearing accounts after the close of the interbank market by seeking funds overnight at the offer rate (in the form of repurchase agreements with eligible securities), and placing funds with the Exchange Fund at the bid rate. The LAF bid and offer rates fix the floor and ceiling for the Hong Kong interbank offer rate (HIBOR). By varying the bid and offer rates, the Exchange Fund can directly affect the short-term interest rate. In fact, this "discount rate" facility can also be used to signal a change in monetary policy and influence money market conditions.

Development of the Money Market

As monetary policies are generally effected through changes in money market liquidity, it is important that the money market responds rapidly to the monetary authority's actions. In this respect, Hong Kong's interbank market needs to be further strengthened and integrated. The HKMA is taking steps to increase suitable money market instruments for open market operations and develop the financial infrastructure such as the payment and settlement system.

Exchange Fund Bills and Notes Programme

The development of the money market has improved the conduct and effectiveness of monetary management, but Hong Kong's money market remained rather shallow and inadequate. Indeed, prior to March 1990 there were no official money market instruments or debt securities available for open market operations as the government persistently ran a fiscal surplus. Attempting to provide the banking system with highly liquid assets, the government introduced a programme of Exchange Fund Bills (from March 1990) and Notes (from May 1993) which allows the Exchange Fund to influence the interbank interest rate by buying and selling Bills and Notes directly in the money market.

At the primary level, the Exchange Fund tenders Bills and Notes on a weekly basis (Asian Monetary Monitor November-December 1991). When recognized dealers (banks) settle their accounts with the Exchange Fund, the HSBC debits the clearing accounts of the banks involved. The Exchange Fund then decides on the amount of liquidity to recycle into the interbank market. For instance, when the foreign exchange rate is falling or the interbank rate is easing, the Exchange Fund may decide to recycle less liquidity, reducing the "balance" to the level needed to ensure exchange rate stability. More importantly, with frequent operations of the Bills and Notes, the Exchange Fund now has greater scope for fine-tuning the balance of the banking system.

On the other hand, the Exchange Fund has also deliberately promoted secondary market activities in the trading of Bills and Notes. It has appointed market makers from among Recognized Dealers and the monetary authority purchases and sells Bills and Notes only through these market makers. In fact, the secondary market has picked up significantly since June 1990, due at least in part to the market-making system and the quoting of two-way prices. The active trading of Bills and Notes of different maturities helps also to reveal the market expectations of interest rate movements (Lau 1996).

Another advantage of the Bills and Notes Programme is that it is a cost-effective way to tighten conditions in the interbank market. Since the interest income on Bills is exempt from the profits tax, their interest cost is lower than the interbank interest rate. On the other hand, borrowing Hong Kong dollars from or selling U.S. dollars to the money market incurs borrowing costs or loss of interest income on the U.S. dollar assets. From the Exchange Fund's point of view, the Bills are highly liquid and almost risk-free compared to U.S. dollar and other assets. Consequently, they are highly attractive when it needs to inject liquidity into the money market.

Payment and Settlement System

The speed and effectiveness of monetary management operations also depend, to a large extent, on the money market institutions. In particular, an efficient clearing and settlement system, coupled with reserve requirements and discount policies will improve the nature of the money market as a vehicle for trading and obtaining settlement balances.

In theory, the size and variability of payment float are an important determinant of the demand for bank reserves, of the central bank's overdraft, and, above all, of the central bank's ability to implement monetary policy by altering reserve money (Balino, Dhawan, and Sundararajan 1994).[3] Large and variable payments float, which results from the time lag between crediting and debiting of accounts, could create a bottleneck to the development of the money market. The holding of a large amount of excess reserves by banks as a buffer against unexpected payments settlement would constrain their demand for money market instruments, e.g., Exchange Fund Bills and Notes and commercial paper. This would hinder the development of an active interbank market. Also, large and variable payments float makes it difficult to avoid excessive volatility in liquidity or short-term interest rates, putting unnecessary pressure on the exchange rate.

Hong Kong's introduction of a gross settlement arrangement (in particular for large-value transactions that require finality, security, and same-day settlement) in addition to net settlement arrangements through clearing houses for small payments was a major step to encourage the development of money market infrastructure to enhance the transmission mechanism for monetary management. The HKMA has built a Real Time Gross Settlement (RTGS) system jointly with the Hong Kong Association of Banks and established Hong Kong Interbank Clearing Limited to operate it and provide interbank clearing in place of the Clearing House Management by the HSBC. The new system which was fully implemented in December 1996 is essentially a single tier system in which all licensed banks have clearing accounts directly with the HKMA and banks are able to obtain intra-day liquidity through repurchase agreements with the HKMA (for example, using Exchange Fund Bills and Notes).[4] Overnight and intra-day repo facilities are handled by a collateral system operated by the Central Moneymarkets Unit Service (CMU), an electronic computer book-entry clearing and settlement system for Exchange Fund Bills and Notes and other private sector debt issues. The new system marks a major development of the central banking role of the Exchange Fund and makes the interbank payments system more secure and robust. Above all, the

RTGS makes the monetary authority's money market operations more effective as it is more efficient in transmitting the impact of monetary operations. The HKMA has become the regulator of the payment system and the lender of last resort (HKMA 1995*a*).

Co-operation among Asian Monetary Authorities

The speculative attacks on the Hong Kong dollar and several other Asian currencies in January 1995 following the Mexican crisis raised the issue of increasing co-operation among monetary authorities to maintain currency stability and improve the integrity and stability of the financial system in the Asia region. One important development in this area is the repurchase agreements (repos) reached by regional monetary authorities. These greatly enhance the liquidity of money market paper, including U.S. government securities, and thereby the liquidity of the central banks' foreign exchange reserves. By the end of 1996, Hong Kong had signed bilateral repurchase agreements with the central banks of Australia, China, Indonesia, Japan Malaysia, the Philippines, Singapore, and Thailand (HKMA 1996*d*). Such bilateral agreements strengthen regional co-operation at the operational level, enhancing the ability of central banks to maintain stable exchange rates in the face of speculative attacks.

Effectiveness of Monetary Management Reform

The reforms undertaken by the HKMA have improved not only the soundness of exchange rate policy in Hong Kong, but also the efficiency and robustness of money market management. With the strengthened mechanism, monetary management can now be further refined to target interbank interest rates rather than only interbank liquidity. Interbank liquidity has been adjusted more frequently in response to fluctuations in the demand for settlement balances arising from seasonal factors or, at times, public offerings of equity and sales of real property. The primary objective now is to keep overnight HIBOR within the LAF bid and offer rates. So far, this policy has proved successful with very few exceptions in avoiding unnecessary volatility in the interbank market.

The strengthened monetary management mechanism enabled Hong Kong to successfully defend its linked exchange rate against speculative attacks several times during 1995. In early 1995, the HKMA responded quickly to the speculative attacks spawned by the Mexican crisis, supplementing foreign exchange market intervention with money market operations. It did not immediately recycle to the interbank market the liquidity withdrawn by the purchase of Hong Kong dollars. The resultant shortage pushed HIBOR up from 6 percent to 12 percent. The exchange rate then began to rebound and returned to its pre-attack level. The Hong Kong dollar fluctuated by less than 0.4 percent which was considerably less than the fluctuation of other Asian currencies that faced similar attacks at the time (HKMA, 1995a).

Two other speculative incidents happened in 1995—one in late April (caused by unfounded rumours on the health of Deng Xiaoping) and one in August (caused by Moody's sceptical comment on the Hong Kong economy, the political tension across the Taiwan Straits, and the adjustment in the local stock market). Again, similar open market operations by the HKMA halted the weakening of the exchange rate which soon returned to a normal level (HKMA 1995*a*).

Speculative attacks usually take the form of either forward contracts to sell Hong Kong dollars or sales in the foreign exchange market of Hong Kong dollars borrowed from the banking sector. As the interest cost and the actual rate of depreciation of the Hong Kong dollar are the main considerations for speculators, the HKMA can intervene to sell its U.S. dollar reserves in the market, thereby draining interbank liquidity and pushing up the interbank interest rate. This would at the least put off speculators and might attract portfolio capital inflows as well.

The successful defence of a linked exchange rate regime depends to a large extent on the authority's strength and its policy determination. Hong Kong's massive foreign reserves, its strengthened monetary management mechanism, and its repurchase agreements with other central banks in the region, make a formidable target for currency speculation.[5] Furthermore, as a stable exchange rate means almost everything to Hong Kong, the monetary authority is more determined than ever to defend the system. Equally important, the Chinese government also recognizes the importance of the stability of Hong Kong's financial system and is committed in the Basic Law to maintain independent monetary and financial policies to safeguard the financial sector and the linked exchange rate regime. In fact, the authority's effort to maintain the stability of the linked exchange rate has been well-perceived by the market as the Hong Kong dollar has, for some time now, been trading against the U.S. dollar on the stronger side of its pegged level and the yield curve of short-term Hong Kong dollar debt papers tracks closely that of U.S. dollar debt papers. There is no indication of a risk premium for holding Hong Kong dollar-denominated assets.

The currency board-linked exchange rate system, with its built-in self-defence mechanism and the prudent management of the HKMA have functioned remarkably well over the past 13 years. For instance, the linked exchange rate system was well-tested in June 1989 following the 4 June Tianamen incident in China. The exchange rate softened daily from 7.775/ US$ on 1 June 1989 to a low of 7.803 on 7 June and then stabilized close to, but on the stronger side of, the 7.8 parity throughout the rest of the month. Between July 1989 and March 1990, the exchange rate stayed very close to the peg, though on the weaker side, and the highest was 7.813 in November 1989. Since April 1990, the exchange rate has shifted back and stayed persistently on the stronger side of the peg. At present, Hong Kong's linked exchange rate, tough monetary management, and accumulation of huge foreign reserves (US$67.6 billion by the end of June 1997, Land Fund not included) should certainly keep foreign, as well as local, investors' confidence in the exchange rate system.

There are two main areas of concern about Hong Kong's exchange rate. The first is the possibility of capital outflows from Hong Kong. In the case of slow or moderate outflows of capital, the market rate will weaken and the constrained interbank liquidity will push up the short-term interbank interest rate. Normally, the higher rate would attract arbitrage capital inflows that would help offset the initial capital outflows. However, large volume, rapid outflows of capital, which could be triggered by a sudden loss of confidence in the exchange rate regime or in the economy as a whole or by some kind of political consideration, could still threaten the exchange rate. Such a situation would probably involve portfolio capital outflows and the collapse of the stock and real property markets. The market rate would depreciate quickly and the Exchange Fund would intervene by selling U.S. dollars for Hong Kong dollars in the foreign exchange market. The interbank interest rate would rise drastically and whether this would help to check capital outflows depends on whether the market perceived the resulting interest rate differentials to be adequate to compensate for the risk of holding Hong Kong dollar assets. When Hong Kong's foreign reserves were used up, the authority would have no other option but to devalue the exchange rate or abandon the linked exchange rate regime. The linked exchange rate, even when properly managed, is not entirely foolproof.

But, is Hong Kong likely to experience a massive, rapid outflow of capital? Hong Kong has so far not experienced the kind of fiscal and external trade deficits, adverse monetary policy, and mounting inflation that signal reversal of capital flows. One cannot rule out the possibility of capital outflows, but the increasing investment opportunities both in Hong Kong proper and in China ensure that capital will continue to flow into Hong Kong. China's rapidly growing economy coupled with its liberalization of trade and investment, have already made it one of the most popular destinations for foreign investment. Many Hong Kong companies, particularly listed companies, have already actively invested in China. According to China's official statistics, cumulative foreign direct investment from Hong had surpassed US$100 billion by 1996, accounting for 60 percent of the total inflow into China (People's Republic of China 1997). Hong Kong is playing an increasing role as fund raiser for China. On the other hand, twenty-one companies from the mainland have already been listed on the Hong Kong stock exchange (Chen 1996). It is expected that more companies from the mainland will make use of the Hong Kong financial market to tap global capital either by having their equity listed or by issuing debt paper in the money market. Hong Kong will still be the gateway for investment in China and foreign capital will continue to flow in.

The second concern is that currency substitution away from the Hong Kong dollar to foreign currency caused by a complete loss of confidence in the linked exchange rate or the economy could exhaust Hong Kong's foreign reserves. However, as argued by Jao (1996), as long as the Hong Kong dollar remains the legal currency of Hong Kong, there will always be demand for Hong Kong dollars, both transactional and speculative—for the settlement of payments for goods, services, and wages and for active trading in the stock and real property markets. Hence, complete substitution away from the Hong Kong dollar is almost impossible.

Are Hong Kong's reserves sufficient to cope with a loss of confidence and a major substitution away from the Hong Kong dollar? It is possible to judge by looking at the composition of the money supply. The ratio of Hong Kong dollar-denominated-M3 (HK$M3) to total M3 increases with confidence in the economy and falls when lack of confidence causes substitution away from the Hong Kong dollar. The ratio followed a continuous downward trend after the adoption of the linked exchange rate system in October 1983, falling from about 55 percent in 1983–84 to 41 percent in 1989 and 39 percent in 1990 after the Tianamen incident in China. Since then, the ratio has increased steadily, standing at 57 percent in May 1997. Now, if confidence in Hong Kong suddenly waned, people would want to hold fewer Hong Kong dollars and the share of HK$M3 in total M3 would fall. Taking the level of the ratio in 1990 as the worst-case scenario, we can assume that the ratio would fall by 18 percentage points from its current level of 57 to 39 percent. The level of foreign currency assets at the Exchange Fund (32 percent of HK$M3 in May 1997) implies that foreign reserves comprise 18.6 percent of total M3, an amount sufficient to cover the capital outflows caused by a loss of confidence (18 percent of M3). Furthermore, since there is a multiplier relation between HK$M3 and the legal currency, an outflow of capital would result in even faster contraction of HK$M3, leading to an even higher ratio of foreign currency reserves to HK$M3 (Jao 1996). Capital outflows would also strain interbank liquidity, pushing the interbank interest rate and hence attracting capital inflows.

Monetary Management and Economic Stability

Under a fixed exchange rate regime, in particular, under a currency board, the monetary authority has no independent monetary policy or control over the growth in money supply, which is determined by overall balance of payments conditions (Lau, Hawkins, and Chan 1994). With the exchange rate as the nominal anchor for the system, Hong Kong depends on the domestic economy to adjust to economic shocks. Also, the linked exchange rate regime does not allow using interest rates as a tool to fight inflation because the local interest rate must follow closely rates in the U.S. (rather than adjust to the state of the Hong Kong economy).

However, with a free capital account and highly mobile capital, raising interest rates alone may not be adequate to control inflation because capital inflows could offset the initial contractionary impact of a tight monetary policy. In the case of a floating regime, this could lead to overvaluation (and to the persistent Dutch disease).[6] This would hurt the international competitiveness of domestic manufacturing exports leading to de-industrialization in the exporting sector (Sheng 1995). Besides, whether the interest rate is an effective tool (i.e., whether aggregate demand is sensitive to changes in interest rates) and whether inflation is demand-pulled remain empirically controversial.

Table 6.1 compares statistics on three macroeconomic aggregates under the floating rate regime (1974–83) and the linked rate system (1984–95). Interestingly, the figures indicate that the Hong Kong economy has been more stable under the linked rate regime. For instance, the rate of inflation averaged 7.75 percent from 1984 to 1995, below the 8.67 percent average during 1974–83. As measured by the standard deviation of inflation the variability of inflation under the linked rate system was slightly more than half that under the floating rate system (2.8 vs. 5.27). Furthermore, there was only a 9 percentage point difference between the highest and lowest rates of inflation under the linked rate regime, while the range was 16 percentage points under the floating system. This seems to suggest that inflation has been less volatile under the linked rate system. Similar

TABLE 6.1
Comparison of Macro-aggregates under Floating and Linked Exchange Rate Regimes

Macro-aggregate	Floating Rate 1974–1983	Linked Rate 1984–1995
Percent growth in HK$M3		
Mean	19.70	18.17
Standard	10.53	5.65
Range	5–40	12–27
Inflation		
Mean	8.67	7.75
Standard deviation	5.27	2.8
Range	0–16	3–12
Real GDP Growth (%)		
Mean	8.24	6.31
Standard deviation	4.93	3.62
Range	0.3–16.2	0.4–13

Notes: Statistics for HK$M3 are not available before 1978. Because bank deposits from and advances to deposit-taking companies are included in bank deposits from and advances to the public respectively, HK$M2 is used as a proxy for HK$M3 for the years 1974–77. Range indicates the minimum and maximum values.
Inflation is measured as percent growth in the Consumer Price Index.
Sources: Hong Kong Census and Statistics Department, *Annual Digest of Statistics*, various issues.

conclusions can be drawn for growth in HK$M3 and for real GDP growth rates. The exception is that the average real GDP growth rate has been lower under the linked rate regime (6.31 percent) than during 1974–1983. It is not surprising that the rate of economic growth has slowed down as the economy has become increasingly developed and has been transforming from a manufacturing base to a service base.

In brief, Hong Kong's experience suggests that a currency board system suits a small open economy. At least it imposes strict discipline on monetary and fiscal policy. However, since with a currency board system and linked exchange rate, money supply, and interest rates are no longer available as instruments to influence aggregate demand, macroeconomic stability can only be achieved through other means, such as supply-side policy. For this reason it is important for Hong Kong to increase its investment in infrastructure, in more advanced equipment and machinery, and, of course, in human capital that could help to enhance production capacity and efficiency.

HONG KONG'S POSITION AS AN INTERNATIONAL FINANCIAL CENTRE

Hong Kong has long been known as a leading international financial centre. According to a survey conducted by the HKMA in March/April 1995, Hong Kong is the fifth largest foreign exchange trading centre and the seventh largest trading centre for foreign exchange and interest rate derivatives in the world. On the other hand, Hong Kong ranks fifth in terms of foreign exchange turnover and the volume of banks' external assets and eighth in terms of stock capitalization. Hong Kong also has the third largest representation of foreign banks in the world including 85 out of the world's top 100 banks (Lau 1996 and Carse 1996*c*).

The success of Hong Kong's finance industry is attributed to a combination of factors ranging from strategic location as a gateway to China and in a time zone that complements London and New York, stable currency with no exchange controls, free, open markets, excellent transportation and telecommunication connections with the outside world, political stability, and a well-educated work force (Yam 1995*a*). However, the factors that used to put Hong Kong's financial market in a favourable position are no longer adequate sustain its leading status. The financial world is so dynamic and financial activities, particularly derivatives trading, are changing so quickly that the finance business is becoming more complicated and sophisticated than ever. More importantly, along with Singapore, Hong Kong is facing increasing competition from other emerging financial centres in neighbouring economies such as Sydney, Taipei, Bangkok, and Kuala Lumpur. Financial market liberalization together with increasing profit prospects fuelled by rapid income growth in these nearby economies have given rise to attractive investment opportunities that present Hong Kong with keen competition for foreign capital.

The obvious way for Hong Kong's finance industry to proceed is to specialize and expand its capacity in areas with market potential and comparative advantage. To this end, the development of Hong Kong's financial market infrastructure and technological platform is particularly crucial. A competitive international financial market depends on a robust technological platform consisting of an efficient telecommunications network with powerful financial computing technology. As the global capital market becomes more integrated and competitive, in order to attract foreign investors to keep investing in its financial markets, it is important that Hong Kong further reduce its transactions and time costs and lower risk. It is also crucial that the domestic financial market is fully integrated with the world capital market so that global financial products can be traded, cleared, and settled in Hong Kong with the same efficiency.

This approach is consistent with Hong Kong's overall development strategy particularly as the domestic economy has become increasingly service-oriented.[7] As suggested by the conventional production function, the ultimate constraint to further economic development is the stock of capital and state of technology. Hence, it is crucial that Hong Kong invest in the required financial infrastructure and advanced technology to further enhance its comparative advantage in the service industry. Recent changes in monetary management, in general, and in the role of the HKMA, in particular, have supported the development of Hong Kong's finance industry.

Improving Financial Market Infrastructure

The government introduced the CMU (Central Moneymarkets Unit) service to lower settlement risk and facilitate secondary market trading. Initially limited to Exchange Fund Bills and Notes, in early 1994 the CMU was extended to cover other private sector Hong Kong dollar commercial paper, essentially serving as the central custodian and clearing agent for Hong Kong dollar debt instruments. The new payment and settlement technology enabled Hong Kong to link with other international systems, greatly facilitating the trading of debt paper across borders, for instance, with the Euroclear and Cedel (Yam 1995*a*). In December 1995, CMU service was strengthened by introducing end-of-day Delivery vs. Payment (DvP) facility for CMU instruments. It is estimated that more than 70 active market participants have signed up for the DvP facility, about 80 percent of the daily turnover in CMU instruments (HKMA 1995*a*).

The CMU was integrated into the RTGS (Real Time Gross Settlement) system in December 1996. When fully operational it will be able to link with global financial networks, e.g., the securities Central Clearing and Settlement System (CCASS) and other domestic and international payment systems, to provide DvP and Payment versus Payment (PvP) services. PvP service is of particular significance to active foreign exchange trading in Hong Kong as it helps to reduce transaction risk arising from differences in the timing of final settlement. For instance, HKMA has reached an agreement in principle with the People's Bank of China to establish a PvP link between the Hong Kong dollar payment system and China's National Automated Payment System (CNAPS). The connection with other international payment and settlement systems can also create all sorts of new business opportunities. For instance, it makes possible trading in U.S. Treasury instruments in the Asian time zone and trading of the Hong Kong dollar and other Asian currency financial instruments during European and U.S. trading hours.

Strengthening the Supervisory Framework

The highly complex risk structure of new financial products and their associated trading require a more sophisticated supervisory framework and measures. The monetary authority has devoted itself to maintaining a sound and prudent supervisory framework in order to ensure banking and monetary stability in Hong Kong.

Bank supervision is intended to ensure that banks are prudently and honestly managed and that the interests of depositors are properly safeguarded. Hong Kong continues to strengthen and update its regulations and supervision to meet international standards, such as the CAMEL rating system and the risk-based Basle capital adequacy ratio. More importantly, the Banking (Amendment) Ordinance was modified in June 1995 to give HKMA responsibility for supervision of all authorized institutions in Hong Kong. The HKMA took steps in 1995 to enhance the transparency of bank operations by requiring banks to increase their financial disclosure and publish more information about their profitability and balance sheet, e.g., accumulated inner reserves (HKMA 1995*d*). More importantly, the HKMA has formed a working group to prepare a Code of Banking Practices aimed to promote good and fair banking conduct.

In view of the increasing bank involvement in derivatives trading, coupled with the complexity of the instruments and their ability to quickly change a bank's risk profile, there is a need for banks to manage their own risk more prudently and systematically. Banks need to develop an effective mechanism for identifying, measuring, monitoring, and controlling various types of risk associated with derivatives trading. Recent incidents, such as the demise of Barings, have highlighted the danger of financial crises caused by a lack of internal controls and over-trading of derivatives. HKMA has decided to impose the Basle capital adequacy framework for market risk. In March 1996 it circulated to all authorized institutions in Hong Kong a guideline on risk management of derivatives and other related instruments. In September 1996 it required banks on a quarterly basis beginning 31 December 1996 to report a data on market risk exposure based on the standardized methodology in the Basle proposal. Other measures include forming a specialist team within the HKMA to check on banks' quality of control, requesting internal or external auditing reports from banks, and issuing a new guideline on risk management of derivatives (Carse 1996*a* and Yam 1996*b*).

Development of the Hong Kong Debt Market

The debt market in Hong Kong is widely viewed as having much unrealized potential, in part due to the mounting demand for long-term finance to fund domestic and regional investment in infrastructure, housing, and high-technology industry and at the same time the mounting supply of long-term funds fuelled by surging savings and the booming insurance industry. As a regional financial centre and gateway to China, Hong Kong is well positioned to benefit from these trends and develop itself further as the fund-raising centre for the region. In contrast with other finance business, such as stock and foreign exchange trading, the debt market of Hong Kong is rather small and underdeveloped. Its size is equivalent to about 17 percent of GDP. The reasons for such slow development are thought to be primarily the lack of a benchmark yield curve and the strong fiscal discipline of the Hong Kong government which makes it unnecessary to issue government debt for financing expenditure (Lau 1996).

Benchmarks are essential to facilitate the pricing of debt issue in both primary and secondary markets, and can be obtained mainly by a well-structured government debt programme with a full range of maturities. For a benchmark to be reliable and indicative, it has to be determined in a free market. Essentially, Hong Kong's debt market gained its momentum with the introduction of the Exchange Fund Bills and Notes Programme which, as discussed previously, was aimed at creating additional instruments for market operations and managing interbank liquidity (Yam 1995*b*). More importantly, the programme broadened and deepened the debt market through provision of a benchmark yield curve by issuing Exchange Fund paper of various maturities. The benchmark yield curve was later extended by issuing 7-year Exchange Fund Notes in November 1995 and more recently 10-year Notes in October 1996.

Another important step taken by the HKMA to boost the debt market is to widen the scope of repo securities eligible for discounting under the Liquidity Adjustment Facility, such as other high quality and marketable Hong Kong dollar-denominated commercial papers. These debt papers would naturally become useful instruments for banks to manage their liquidity position, thereby enhancing the demand for such papers. The market-making programme in relation to the LAF (i.e., the repo agreement), discussed in the previous section, has also greatly promoted the secondary market trading for debt papers. From September 1994, private sector debt papers which are lodged with the CMU and meet, for instance, the issue size, marketability, and rating requirements are accepted as eligible instruments for repo arrangement. By end 1995, a total of 14 private debt issues amounting to HK$26.3 billion were accepted for this purpose, including the Hongkong and Shanghai Banking Corporation Limited (HK$3.2 billion) and Wharf Treasury Limited (HK$2.3 billion) (HKMA 1995*a*).

The significance of the CMU and the RTGS systems to the development of the debt market, by providing an efficient system of payment and settlement, has already been discussed. Of the HK$59.9 billion new issue of private sector debt papers in 1995, roughly three-quarters were lodged and cleared through CMU. In addition, the HKMA has taken other measures to attract overseas debt issuers to the Hong Kong debt market. For instance, last year the Council of Europe Social Development Fund was added to the list of multilateral agencies exempt from profits tax. In 1995 13 medium- to long-term Hong Kong dollar papers were issued by multilateral agencies, with the issue size ranging from HK$100 to HK$500 million. Total outstanding paper issued by multilateral agencies increased 36 percent to HK$19 billion by end 1996 (HKMA 1996*d*).

Establishment of a Mortgage Corporation

More recently, the government has taken steps to further broaden the scope of the local debt market by introducing a programme to promote mortgage-backed securities. Following a study in July 1995 by the Informal Group on the Secondary Mortgage Market, the government decided to set up a mortgage corporation to develop the secondary mortgage market. A mortgage corporation can also facilitate the intermediation of longer term funds and a deep liquid secondary mortgage market would help to promote home ownership.

Mortgage loans have grown rapidly from HK$11.7 billion in 1980 to HK$421 billion in 1996, an increase of 35 times. They have become increasingly important to the banking sector as the ratio of outstanding residential mortgage loans to GDP and total domestic loans have risen from 8.3 percent and 9.9 percent in 1980 to 35.2 percent and 24 percent in 1996 respectively. Although residential mortgage loans in Hong Kong are of high credit quality, they still carry the funding risk arising from maturity mismatch, as mortgage loans on average have a contractual life much longer than the maturity of bank deposit funding. A mortgage corporation provides an effective option for banks to unload their mortgage loans when needed, thereby lowering the funding/liquidity risk. A mortgage corporation can also help to reduce the sectoral risk arising from banks' over dependence on income from mortgage lending, which makes bank performance particularly vulnerable to adverse economic conditions (HKMA, May 1996).

As mentioned previously, volatility in capital flows under the linked exchange rate system might occasionally give rise to adverse interest rate fluctuations. This would have disturbing impacts on the economy particularly when about 40 percent of private residential units have outstanding mortgages and 96 percent of residential mortgages are on a floating rate basis (HKMA, May 1996*b*).[8] A mortgage corporation can encourage the initiation of fixed-rate mortgage loans by using fixed-rate funds borrowed from the debt market to purchase fixed-rate mortgage loans from authorized institutions. Hence, borrowers of fixed-rate loans can be cushioned from short-term interest rate volatility.

Prospects for Further Development of Hong Kong's Financial Market

In view of the improved market conditions for the Hong Kong dollar debt market, together with the rising supply and demand for longer term funds in Asia, Hong Kong's debt market is expected to grow rapidly over the next few years. Over the past decade, the Asian region has accumulated remarkable wealth, as real GDP growth rates averaged 6 to 10 percent per annum and domestic saving ratios were generally higher than 30 percent, resulting in strong demand for quality financial assets (Yam 1995*b*). The long-awaited mandatory provident fund and the booming insurance industry in Hong Kong (which face longer term liability obligations) are another source of demand for longer term fixed-income securities. A considerable part of the investment by the provident fund would be required in Hong Kong dollar denominated assets, which would certainly boost the local currency debt market.

At the same time, according to the World Bank Report, cumulative infrastructure investment in East Asia between 1994 and 2004 will reach US$1.4 trillion and the demand for housing finance in 2004 will reach US$160 billion (Yam 1995*b*). As for Hong Kong, there will also be great demand for long-term funds to finance infrastructure and housing projects. The growth in savings and huge infrastructure needs in the region will mean the business of intermediation of long-term funds will be in great demand. The improved payments and settlement system, coupled with increasingly active market participation, will reduce the cost and risk associated with debt financing, helping to make Hong Kong the preferred source of financing.

Furthermore, Hong Kong's financial market will be fuelled by the rapid economic growth and the liberalization of the external trade and foreign exchange regimes in China. It was estimated that China will need about US$500 billion for infrastructure projects over the next decade, a considerable part of which would be raised in overseas capital markets. Hong Kong is expected to play an important intermediation role and to obtain a major share of the business. Moreover, as a result of the convertibility of the Chinese yuan for current account transactions and the move to full capital account convertibility, trading in yuan is bound to increase with the growth in external trade and capital flows. Hong Kong would be able to benefit by serving as a bridge between the nascent foreign exchange market in China and the international markets (Chen 1995). Currently, HKMA is working toward connecting its RTGS system with China's RTGS-based system, CNAPS, which is expected to be completed in 1997. When it is fully operational this connection will greatly enhance clearing and settlement between Hong Kong dollar and renminbi transactions (Carse 1996*b*).

The other concern is the likely competition from Shanghai's rapidly growing financial market. Undoubtedly Shanghai (with its developed infrastructure, economic strength, and government-led opening of the banking and finance sector to foreign investors) has every potential to become a major financial centre. However, Shanghai cannot become a truly international financial centre or take the place of Hong Kong before the yuan becomes fully convertible and China has a free capital account. What is likely to happen is that Shanghai will develop into a domestic financial centre specializing in channelling domestic financial resources whereas Hong Kong will become a fund-raising centre for China and will act as China's bridge to global capital markets. China's economic and financial development will therefore be a key factor in the future of Hong Kong's debt and foreign exchange market as well as its finance industry overall (Chen 1995).

CONCLUDING REMARKS

Hong Kong is an example of a successful linked exchange rate regime in a small economy with a perfectly mobile capital account. Market stability and confidence are particularly important to Hong Kong which is an international financial centre with massive capital flows across border and an extremely open economy. A linked exchange rate regime is perhaps most appropriate to reduce uncertainties and maintain market confidence and, above all, to discipline the authorities to commit to consistent and prudent monetary and fiscal policies. The linked exchange rate was introduced at a time when government control over interbank liquidity and thus interest rates was inadequate. This seriously undermined the monetary authority's ability to defend the linked rate (and left most intervention to foreign exchange market operations). In view of increasing portfolio investment flows, which could be huge and adverse at times, and of increasing speculative attacks world-wide, the government saw the need to strengthen its monetary management framework so that it could maintain exchange rate stability effectively and efficiently.

With the introduction of the Accounting Arrangements, the Liquidity Adjustment Facility, and the Exchange Fund Bills and Notes Programme, together with the upgraded payment and settlement system, the monetary authority has strengthened (or, more exactly, gained) control over interbank liquidity and interbank interest rates. The HKMA can now fine-tune interbank liquidity to determine interbank interest rates in line with those of the United States.

Under the linked exchange rate system with the currency board, capital inflows will cause foreign reserves to accumulate and the money supply to expand unless the flows are properly sterilized. The HKMA's Bills and Notes Programme and the deepening of Hong Kong's debt market have greatly enhanced the monetary authority's capacity to sterilize the impact of capital inflows. However, as the primary purpose of monetary management is to maintain a stable exchange rate, the authority has chosen to sterilize only the first round effects of capital inflows on the interbank market to avoid unnecessary pressure on the interbank interest rate, rather than the overall money supply.

At the same time, the monetary authority has also devoted much effort to upgrading and expanding the financial infrastructure and increasing its connection with other international payment systems. This effort greatly enhances the feasibility of trading and clearing global financial products in Hong Kong. The deliberate effort to deepen and broaden the Hong Kong debt market will help Hong Kong to develop as a fund-raising centre for the region and also facilitate the intermediation of longer term funds and the likely initiation of fixed-rate debt and mortgage rate. The latter can help to cushion the economy from short-term interest rate volatility caused by the authority's intervention in the interbank market. It is equally important for Hong Kong to further strengthen its competitiveness in the service industry, as Hong Kong will need a surplus in service trade to compensate for its visible trade deficit if it is to avoid an overall balance of trade deficit which if sustained could be harmful to the linked exchange rate.

Notes

1. In 1995 Hong Kong's ratios of total exports and total trade volume to GDP reached 147 percent and almost 300 percent respectively.
2. Prior to July 1988, as the Management Bank of the clearing mechanism, the HSBC did not itself have a clearing account. It settled Hong Kong dollar transactions with other banks by crediting or debiting the clearing accounts maintained by these banks through the two-tier system with the HSBC
3. Payment float is the amount credited (debited) to (from) a payee's (payer's) account before the corresponding debit (credit) entry has been made in a payer's (payee's) account.
4. Hong Kong had a two-tier bank clearing system, with the HSBC as the management bank and 10 settlement banks in the first tier and over 160 sub-settlement banks in the second tier.
5. The management of the Land Fund was transferred to the HKMA with the handover on 1 July 1997.
6. See the appendix to chapter 1 for an explanation of the Dutch disease.
7. See Chen and Li 1997.
8. Mortgage loans have become the largest liability for average households in Hong Kong.

References

Alexander, W. E., T. J. T. Balino, and C. Enoch. 1996. "Adopting Indirect Instruments of Monetary Policy". *Finance and Development* March.

Asian Monetary Monitor. 1993. "Hong Kong: Ten Years of the Linked Rate System". *Asian Monetary Monitor* 17, no.6 (November-December).

______. 1995. "Hong Kong: The Debate on the Optimum Monetary System". *Asian Monetary Monitor* 19, no.2 (March-April).

Balino, T. J. T., J. Dhawan, and V. Sundararajan. 1994. "Payments System Reforms and Monetary Policy in Emerging Market Economies in Central and Eastern Europe". *IMF Staff Paper* 41, no. 3.

Balino, T. J. T., O. E. G. Johnson, and V. Sundararajan. 1996. "Payment System Reforms and Monetary Policy". *Finance and Development* March.

Beecham, B. J. 1996. *Monetary and Financial System in Hong Kong*. Hong Kong: Hong Kong Institute of Bankers.

Bennett A. G. G. 1995. "Currency Boards: Issues and Experiences". *Finance and Development*, September.

Carse, D. 1996*a*. "The Evolving Supervisory Approach Towards Risk Management". Hong Kong Monetary Authority *Quarterly Bulletin*, no. 6 (February).

______ 1996*b* "Banking and Monetary Links between China and Hong Kong". Hong Kong Monetary Authority *Quarterly Bulletin*, no. 6 (February).

______ 1996*c*. "The Framework of Banking Supervision: the Hong Kong Perspective". Hong Kong Monetary Authority *Quarterly Bulletin*, no. 7 (May).

Chen, Edward and Kui-wai Li. 1997. "Industrial Policy in a Laissez-Faire Economy: The Case of Hong Kong". In *Industrial Policies in East Asia*, edited by S. Masuyama et al. Singapore: Nomura Research Institute and Institute of Southeast Asian Studies.

Chen, Y. 1995. "Financial Relations between Hong Kong and the Mainland". In *Money and Banking in Hong Kong*. Hong Kong: Hong Kong Monetary Authority.

______. 1996*a*. "Prospects for the Financial Relationship Between Mainland China and Hong Kong After 1997". Hong Kong Monetary Authority *Quarterly Bulletin* no. 6 (February).

______. 1996*b*. In *Hong Kong Economic Journal* (newspaper), 11 September.

Dadush, U. and M. Brahmbhatt. 1995. "Anticipating Capital Flow Reversals". *Finance and Development*, December.

Glick, R. and R. Moreno. 1994. "Capital Flows and Monetary Policy in East Asia". In *Monetary and Exchange Rate Management with International Capital Mobility*. Hong Kong: Hong Kong Monetary Authority.

Hong Kong Census and Statistics Department, *Annual Digest of Statistics*, various issues.

Hong Kong Monetary Authority (HKMA). 1994. *The Practice of Central Banking in Hong Kong*. Hong Kong: Hong Kong Monetary Authority.

______. 1995*a*. *Annual Report*.

______. 1995*b*. "Hong Kong's Payment System". In *Money and Banking in Hong Kong*. Hong Kong: Hong Kong Monetary Authority.

______. 1995*c*. "Hong Kong's Currency Board Arrangements". Hong Kong Monetary Authority *Quarterly Bulletin* no. 3 (May).

______. 1995*d*. "Financial Disclosure by Authorised Institutions". Hong Kong Monetary Authority *Quarterly Bulletin* no. 4 (August).

______. 1995*e*. "Hong Kong Bond Market: World Bank Study". Hong Kong Monetary Authority *Quarterly Bulletin* no. 4 (August).

______. 1996*a*. "Banking Survey of Hong Kong 1981–1995". Hong Kong Monetary Authority *Quarterly Bulletin* no. 7 (May).

______. 1996*b*. "Mortgage Corporation Proposal". Hong Kong Monetary Authority *Quarterly Bulletin* no. 7 (May).

______. 1996*c*. "Operation of Monetary Policy". *Hong Kong Monetary Authority, Quarterly Bulletin* no. 7 (May).

______. 1996*d*. *Annual Report*.

______. *Monthly Statistical Bulletin*, various issues.

Jao, Y. C. 1991. "On Central Banking in Hong Kong". In *Monetary Management in Hong Kong: The Changing Role of the Exchange Fund*. Hong Kong: The Chartered Institute of Bankers.

______. 1996. *Hong Kong Economic Journal* (newspaper). 5 and 6 September.

Kreinin, M. E. 1991. *International Economics: A Policy Approach* (sixth ed.). San Diego: Harcourt Brace Jovanovich.

Lau, J. H, Jr. 1996. "Development of Hong Kong's Debt Market". Hong Kong Monetary Authority *Quarterly Bulletin* no. 6 (February).

Lau, J. H, Jr, J. Hawkins, and B. Chan. 1994. "Monetary and Exchange Rate Management with International Capital Mobility: The Case of Hong Kong". In *Monetary and Exchange Rate Management with International Capital Mobility*. Hong Kong: Hong Kong Monetary Authority.

Lee, S. Y. 1986. *The Monetary and Banking Development of Singapore and Malaysia* (2 ed.). Singapore: Singapore University Press.

Moreno, R. 1996. "Models of Currency Speculation: Implications and East Asian Experience". Federal Reserve Bank of San Francisco *Economic Letter*, no. 96 (13 April).

Nugee, John. 1995. "A Brief History of the Exchange Fund". Hong Kong Monetary Authority *Quarterly Bulletin* no. 3 (May).

Ow, C. H. 1986. *The Currency Board Monetary System — The Case of Singapore and Hong Kong*. UMI Dissertation Information Service.

People's Republic of China. 1997. *Statistical Survey of China 1997*. China Statistical Publishing House.

Sheng, Andrew. 1994. "The Tools of Monetary Management". In *The Practice of Central Banking in Hong Kong*. Hong Kong: Hong Kong Monetary Authority.

______. 1995. "The Linked Exchange Rate System: Review and Prospects". In *Money and Banking in Hong Kong*. Hong Kong: Hong Kong Monetary Authority.

______. 1996. "Managing the Risks of Growth: Hard Money and Resilient Financial Systems". Hong Kong Monetary Authority *Quarterly Bulletin* no. 7 May.

Tan, C. H. 1989. *Financial Markets and Institutions in Singapore* (sixth ed.). Singapore: Singapore University Press.

Williamson, John. 1995. *What Role for Currency Boards?* Washington, D. C.: Institute for International Economics.

Yam, J. 1991. "The Development of Monetary Policy in Hong Kong". In *Monetary Management in Hong Kong: The Changing Role of the Exchange Fund.* Hong Kong: The Chartered Institute of Bankers Hong Kong Centre.

______. 1994. "Central Banking and Monetary Policy in Hong Kong". In *The Practice of Central Banking in Hong Kong.* Hong Kong: Hong Kong Monetary Authority.

______. 1995*a*. "Hong Kong as an International Financial Centre". *Hong Kong Monetary Authority, Quarterly Bulletin* no. 4 (August).

______. 1995*b*. "Asian Bond Markets". *Hong Kong Monetary Authority, Quarterly Bulletin* no. 4 (August).

______ 1996*a*. "The New Asian Drama: Monetary Co-operation in Asia". *Hong Kong Monetary Authority, Quarterly Bulletin* no. 6 (February).

______. 1996*b*. "Regulatory Aspects of Product Innovation in Banking — The Hong Kong Perspective" Hong Kong Monetary Authority *Quarterly Bulletin* no. 6 (February).

UPDATE

HONG KONG AND THE ASIAN CRISIS

The speculative attacks on Asian currencies that started in Thailand in the second half of 1997 and the subsequent currency depreciation and financial turmoil have focused concern on the aggressive and destabilizing nature of excessive adverse (portfolio) capital flows. They have also stirred debate over the most desirable exchange rate regime for emerging economies and the need to reform monetary management in the face of rapid capital flows. While most high-performing Asian economies have failed to defend their pegs and let their currencies depreciate, Hong Kong has so far at least been able to maintain its peg of HK$7.8 per U.S. dollar. This update examines the apparent success of the Hong Kong Monetary Authority (HKMA) in coping with the speculative attacks on the Hong Kong currency. Particular attention is given to the need for the authority to modify the existing monetary management framework and strategy in order to reduce the authority's disruption of the financial market in the course of defending the pegged rate regime.

The recent currency crisis in Asia reemphasized how important it is that the exchange rate of an economy be in line with its competitiveness and economic strength, regardless of the exchange rate regime the economy has adopted. An economy's exchange rate will eventually adjust downward when it experiences persistent current account deficits, mounting fiscal and external debts, and surging inflation but shows no signs of improvement or adjustment in the domestic sector. Market pressures, including speculation, will force such an adjustment to take place.

Prudent fiscal and monetary discipline, sound macroeconomic fundamentals, and market flexibility are prerequisites for the regime to be maintained, particularly in the case of a linked exchange rate. The rapid capital inflows experienced by most emerging Asian economies since the 1990s caused rapid expansion in their money supplies which helped to fuel booms in stock and real property markets. These in turn brought about asset inflation which pushed up factor prices, causing real exchange rates to revalue and weakening the price competitiveness of these economies. Without prudent regulation and supervision of the financial sector, banks' over-lending to the finance and real property industries would greatly increase their risk exposures. In addition, when faced with an abundant supply of cheap credit, many companies tended to over borrow and expand too fast. This heavy indebtedness raised the likelihood of insolvency and financial crisis during economic downturn as the reduced earnings would make it difficult for troubled firms to meet their debt service. The accumulation of non-performing bank loans could also bring difficulties to financial institutions.

The Asian currency attacks also revealed the increasing integration and interdependence of the global capital market and the contagious nature of speculative attacks on currencies with a similar exchange rate system. Although the Asian currency speculation was initially targeted at Thailand, which was long troubled by its deteriorating current account deficits and mounting external debt, Hong Kong with strong foreign reserves and sound economic fundamentals was not immune to speculative attacks.

There were several attacks on the Hong Kong currency in the latter half of 1997 each of which was triggered in large part by the failure of other Asian countries to maintain their exchange rates. So far, HKMA has managed to defend the pegged exchange rate. The successful defense of the peg was attributed in large measure to Hong Kong's recently strengthened monetary management (e.g., the Accounting Arrangements and the development of the money market and the liquidity adjustment facility (LAF)) which enabled the HKMA to influence interbank liquidity and interest rates more efficiently and quickly, helping to prevent speculators from selling short in the foreign exchange market with borrowed Hong Kong dollars. Another factor in the defense was the strong foreign reserve backing of the Hong Kong dollar. By the end of September 1997, Hong Kong had US$88.1 billion in foreign exchange reserves (including the Land Fund), the third largest foreign reserve in the world. In addition, China with its US$126 billion in foreign reserves has stressed repeatedly that it will support the Hong Kong currency when requested in the event of a currency crisis (Jao 1997).

Despite this backing, during the recent turmoil, the HKMA departed from orthodox reliance on the built-in stabilizing mechanism of the currency board and adopted a more interventionist approach using discretionary power to influence interbank interest rates. Most notably, on 17 October when the Hong Kong dollar was under severe attack following Taiwan's move to let its currency depreciate, the HKMA withdrew liquidity from the interbank market and at the same time attempted to impose punitive interest rates on banks involved in currency speculation. As a result, the three-month Hong Kong dollar lending rate soared to 50 percent and the overnight lending rate to a record high of 300 percent. The prime lending rate also increased 3/4 of a percentage point to 9.5 percent. These high interest rates caused the stock market to tumble and the Hang Seng Index fell to as low as 8,775 on 28 October 1997, compared with almost 16,000 points in August. The Hong Kong dollar forward rate was also weakened, in part due to the interest rate differentials which widened the forward premium, although the spot exchange rate stayed below HK$7.75. The weakening of the forward rate could also have been due to the increase in hedging activities of local companies in the forward market against a possible fall in the Hong Kong dollar. The resultant increase in the forward premium would in turn put upward pressure on interbank interest rates. (*Asian Wall Street Journal*, 20 November 1997).

In implementing this intervention the HKMA failed to clearly define which "repeated borrowers" were subject to punitive interest charges on liquidity provided by the LAF. This ambiguity fueled market chaos, causing interest rates to surge further. In a bid to bring down interbank interest rates and to avoid further upward pressure on the prime lending rate, on 12 November 1997, the HKMA clarified the definition. Only licensed banks that had borrowed through the LAF more than eight times over a 25-day period or on more than four consecutive days would be defined as "repeated users" who would need to provide satisfactory explanations for their transactions or face the penalty interest rates. Following this statement, Hong Kong dollar interbank interest rates declined, with the three-month rate falling to 11.5 percent and the one-month rate easing four percentage points to about 11 percent. (South China *Morning Post* 19 November 1997). As this experience showed, because the LAF is the liquidity provider of last resort, particularly for banks that need to but cannot obtain funds from the interbank market to cover their positions, the policy governing the use of the facility must be well-defined and consistent.

Although the HKMA's activism demonstrated its determination and ability to defend the pegged exchange rate, it also obstructed the automatic functioning of a currency board, thereby making the defense more disruptive than necessary (Stein 1997). Such intervention could also cause interest rate uncertainty which would in turn further destabilize the equity and real property markets. With the increasing sophistication of financial markets (e.g., derivatives trading) and the growing involvement of relatively mobile foreign portfolio capital in local financial markets, the authority should be more circumspect in using high interest rates to defend the peg. Disruption of the financial market could cause portfolio managers to shift their capital out of Hong Kong which would put further downward pressure on the exchange rate, in a vicious circle. Speculators could also gain from going short on the equity market or using the Hong Kong dollar forward market in addition to speculating in the spot currency market.

There is clearly a need for the authority to refine its monetary management framework and clarify its role in order to reduce uncertainty and the adverse effects of speculative attacks on financial markets. One suggestion is to introduce an LAF denominated in U.S. dollars through which banks could borrow U.S. dollars with U.S. Treasury bills as collateral and then sell them for Hong Kong dollars to cover their liquidity positions. Importantly, banks would be allowed to repay the loan in either U.S. or Hong Kong dollars, which could indicate the commitment of the authority to maintain the pegged exchange rate. Particularly when the Hong Kong dollar is under speculative pressure—when interbank liquidity normally decreases and interest rates increase and the authority is reluctant to supply liquidity to the interbank market—a U.S. dollar-denominated LAF could not only supply liquidity to banks but also support the pegged rate as banks could sell borrowed U.S. dollars for Hong Kong dollars. This would also encourage interest rate arbitrage activities as banks could borrow in U.S. dollars and lend in Hong Kong dollars, helping to bring the Hong Kong-dollar interbank interest rates close to U.S.-dollar interest rates. The main weakness of this system is perhaps that the HKMA would need to bear the risk of fluctuations in the price of U.S. Treasury bills (Hong Kong *Economic Journal*, 18, 19 November 1997).

Though theoretically sound, the operation of a U.S.-dollar LAF requires extreme caution. In particular, effort should be made to ensure that the increased liquidity in the interbank market will not be used by banks involved in currency speculation. Besides, interbank interest rates may not come down in a period of currency speculation when higher local interest rates reflect expected rate of depreciation (foreign exchange risk) or forward premium. If this is the case, the U.S. dollar-LAF may provide banks with additional funds to earn the interest differential which might sustain, without bearing the supposed foreign exchange risk. It should be stressed that if risk-adjusted interest rates are attractive enough, there should naturally be inflows of arbitrage capital seeking the higher rates. There should be no need for another (artificial) interest arbitrage force which might cause further complication and confusion in the foreign exchange market.

Another suggestion is to strengthen the supposedly built-in "cash arbitrage" mechanism of Hong Kong's currency board. The cash arbitrage mechanism cannot function fully because Hong Kong currency is issued not by the currency board directly (i.e., the Exchange Fund), but through three note-issuing banks (NIBs). Since the February 1994 reform that allowed non-note issuing banks to obtain bank notes from NIBs at the market exchange rate instead of at the pegged rate, direct cash arbitrage has been restricted to NIBs. In addition, holding only 5 percent of their deposits in cash under Hong Kong's fractional reserve system, banks are unlikely to engage in active cash arbitrage because it would flood or drain their cash holdings. As a solution, the authority might consider a "convertible-reserves" currency board arrangement such as was adopted in Argentina, Estonia, and Lithuania in 1991, 1992, and 1994 respectively. Under a convertible reserves currency board, currency arbitrage can be carried out without using cash. Banks maintain two kinds of reserves with the central bank as a certain proportion of their total deposits, one in the reserve currency (i.e., U.S. dollars) and the other in any currency. The HKMA would guarantee the exchange of the other currency to U.S. dollars at the linked rate of HK$7.8 per U.S. dollar. When the market exchange rate of the Hong Kong dollar moved away from the pegged level, banks could conduct currency arbitrage through these clearing accounts with the central bank, with no cash involved (Tsang 1997). Such a strengthened currency arbitrage mechanism would help reduce the reliance on the interest rate as the main instrument to defend the pegged exchange rate.

On the other hand, it has been argued that the recent speculative attacks on the Hong Kong dollar were caused in part by the HKMA's behaving more like a central bank than an orthodox currency board system. Doubting the commitment of the HKMA to the currency board system, it is said, speculators may have tested whether the HKMA, like a typical central bank, would abandon the pegged exchange rate, particularly as defending the peg could be costly (e.g., in terms of damaging volatility in stock and real property markets) and as depreciation of other Asian currencies would hurt Hong Kong's relative competitiveness. With strong foreign reserves and sound economic fundamentals such as Hong Kong has, a currency board should be capable of defending the linked exchange rate and hence the authority should let the self-restoring mechanism work automatically. In this regard, the authority could separate the foreign reserves that back the issue of Hong Kong dollars from the other assets of the HKMA and establish a separate, orthodox currency board. This would alleviate the confusion between the currency board of Hong Kong and central banking and hence reduce speculative attacks. Furthermore, as Hong Kong has more than enough foreign reserves to cover the supply of Hong Kong-dollar M1 (about 3.4 times by September 1997) at the pegged rate, the authority could "dollarize" the economy (Schuler 1997).

It should be stressed that for a small and open economy such as Hong Kong, a pegged exchange rate regime encourages trade and foreign investment by reducing exchange rate volatility and the uncertainty caused by adverse portfolio capital movements. A currency board also requires prudent monetary and fiscal discipline which is a precondition for maintaining any exchange rate regime. Moreover, a flexible exchange rate regime would not be perfect either. For instance, persistent (portfolio) capital inflows could cause overvaluation of the Hong Kong dollar, reducing the competitiveness of the economy and perhaps resulting in deterioration of the current account balance. In addition, under a flexible exchange rate regime with free capital movements, the ability of the authority to conduct independent monetary policy would be seriously reduced. An interest rate increase, caused for instance by the authority's effort to cool down an overheated economy by reducing the money supply, would attract capital inflows that would offset the initial reduction in money supply.

Perhaps the most widely mentioned weakness of Hong Kong's pegged exchange rate regime is its contribution to the asset inflation, fueled by capital inflows and the subsequent rise in money supply, that caused the real exchange rate to appreciate and hurt the economy's competitiveness. However, Hong Kong has experienced a rapid relocation of its manufacturing industry to Mainland China and a dramatic structural change towards a highly service-oriented economy. Whereas rising labour and other factor prices could be more or less justified by an increase in labour and other factor productivity, the present exchange rate does not appear overvalued if one looks at the prices of Hong Kong's traded goods, which have increased by a moderate 2.1 percent per annum on average since 1984 (*The Economist*, 23 August 1997, p. 57). In addition, Hong Kong has not experienced a persistent current account deficit which is the usual result of real exchange rate appreciation and weakened international competitiveness. Therefore, it is important for the HKMA to defend the peg against speculative attacks with the view to maintaining investors' confidence in the Hong Kong dollar. Loss of confidence could cause investors in deposits or assets denominated in Hong Kong dollars to switch to foreign currency deposits or assets. This could also cause panic selling and boost the disruption initiated by currency speculation.

This far into the Asian currency crisis that began in 1997, Hong Kong has been successful in defending the peg. Among other factors, the reform of the monetary management framework which gave the HKMA effective control over interbank liquidity and hence interest rates played an important role. However, despite the intrinsic self-restoring mechanism of a currency board, the HKMA seemed to rely more on intervention to tackle the speculative attacks by attempting to impose punitive interest rates on speculators. The subsequent upsurge in interbank interest rates apparently caused more disruption than otherwise would have occurred in the financial and property markets. As frequently stressed in the media by government officials, the authority has clearly shown to the market its determination and ability to maintain the linked exchange rate. What the HKMA needs to do now is to modify the existing monetary management framework to reduce disruption of the financial markets and of the economy as a whole.

January 1998

References

Economic Report (in Chinese). 1997. No. 2545 (10 November): 6–7.

Jao, Y.C. 1997. "Of Pegs and Boards". Hong Kong Monetary Authority, *Quarterly Bulletin*, no. 13 (November): 70–72.

Schuler, Kurt. 1997. "Tighten the Dollar Link". *Asian Wall Street Journal*, 6 November.

Stein, Peter. 1997. "Korea sets Hong Kong Investors on Edge". *Asian Wall Street Journal*, 20 November.

Tsang, Shu-ki. "The Linked Rate System: Through 1997 and into the 21st Century". *The Other Hong Kong Report 1996*. Hong Kong: The Chinese University Press, pp. 221–48.

7

Capital Flows and Macroeconomic Stabilization in Singapore

Amina Tyabji

INTRODUCTION

Whether capital inflows are a bane or a boon to an economy depends on its institutional and policy setting, including the initial conditions and policy mix. This is demonstrated by the differing experiences of countries that have surges of capital inflow. A decade or more ago the impact of capital inflows was by and large country-specific, but today the increased integration of financial markets poses another threat, that of systemic risk. This contagion implies that country-specific policies, while necessary, may be insufficient to cope with spillovers, which may demand international co-operation in varying degrees.

The next section of this chapter describes the initial conditions and policy setting that have affected Singapore's policy stance and the outcome of macroeconomic policies with respect to capital inflows. The subsequent section discusses Singapore's policy response to the surge of capital inflows that began in the late 1960s, and a final section provides concluding remarks.

INSTITUTIONAL AND POLICY SETTING

Economic Fundamentals

Singapore's economy grew rapidly and on a sustained basis over the last three decades, with 9 percent annual average growth in real GDP. Over the same period, gross fixed capital formation grew at 11 percent, to reach 33 percent of GDP by 1995. From 11 percent of GNP in 1965, gross national savings hit 50 percent in 1995. Singapore has been a net exporter of capital since 1986. Exports and foreign investment are the main engines of growth.

During the last decade the unemployment rate was above 4 percent only in the recession and recovery years 1985–87, and it has averaged 2.4 percent during the 1990s. Guest workers comprise around 15 percent of the labour force. The tight labour market generates cost-push pressures which are ameliorated partly by the entry of foreign workers and by the low inflation level which moderates wage demands.

Inflation in Singapore, as measured by the CPI, has been very moderate, except for the oil crisis years. Since 1987, the CPI has changed by only between 0.5 and 3.4 percent (Table 7.1). During the last 15 years, domestic factors have been the predominant source of price changes. Imported inflation has been dampened by the strong Singapore dollar. The domestic sources of inflation emanate from the non-tradable sector, mainly services, with its higher labour and lower import content, and to some extent from the asset market. Asset inflation is fuelled by economic growth and also by the liberalization of the uses to which compulsory savings may be put. (Details of this scheme are discussed subsequently.) These domestic sources of inflation cannot be addressed by the exchange rate policy.

Singapore's balance of payments has been in surplus since 1968. The government's budget has also been in surplus since 1968 except for a

TABLE 7.1
Change in the Consumer Price Index, 1970–95

Year	% Change	Year	% Change
1970	0.4	1983	1.2
1971	1.8	1984	2.6
1972	2.2	1985	0.5
1973	19.6	1986	–1.4
1974	22.3	1987	0.5
1975	2.6	1988	1.5
1976	–1.9	1989	2.4
1977	3.2	1990	3.4
1978	4.8	1991	3.4
1979	4.0	1992	2.3
1980	8.5	1993	2.3
1981	8.2	1994	3.1
1982	3.9	1995	1.7

Source: Department of Statistics, *Yearbook of Statistics, Singapore*, various years.

couple of years in the mid-1980s. (These two conditions are examined in greater detail below.)

While Singapore's strong fundamentals are the result of sound macroeconomic policies, they simultaneously maintain investor confidence and allow the economy to fend off speculative attacks fairly quickly.

The Financial Setting

There are three aspects of Singapore's financial setting that affect the impact of capital inflows. They are: financial liberalization, the mode of currency issue, and the compulsory savings scheme.

Financial Liberalization

Singapore adopted a number of major financial liberalization policies in the 1970s, earlier than many developed countries. These policies decontrolled prices (exchange and interest rates) and opened the country's capital account. Specifically they included:

- Abolishing the cartel system of foreign exchange rate quotation by commercial banks in 1972. This was followed by the floating of the Singapore dollar, on a managed basis, in June 1973 after the breakdown of the Smithsonian Agreement.
- Introducing competitive interest-rate setting by abolishing the cartel system of rate-setting by commercial banks in July 1975. This was preceded by the issue of Singapore dollar-negotiable certificates of deposit (S$NCD) in May 1975.
- Lifting the remaining exchange controls in June 1978. This allowed residents to borrow and lend in all currencies, including participation in Singapore's offshore market, the Asian dollar market. Merchant banks became free to engage in foreign exchange transactions and offshore banks, which had been restricted to dealing with banks and approved financial institutions, could now deal with resident non-bank customers. The lifting of exchange controls also encouraged non-residents to hold Singapore dollar denominated assets since it permitted freer dividend and interest payments.

The financial liberalization boosted foreign exchange, money, and capital market transactions. Capital mobility has thus become almost perfect.

The main limitation on capital mobility is that bank lending of Singapore dollars to non-residents and to residents who use the funds outside

Singapore has been restricted and strongly discouraged. This limitation has been imposed in order to prevent internationalization of the Singapore dollar and the resultant potentially destabilizing speculation. Such an outcome could lead to destabilizing capital movements, making exchange rate management more difficult, although given its large holding of foreign exchange reserves, the Monetary Authority of Singapore (MAS) is better positioned than others to deal with short-term speculative pressures.

Recent official announcements suggest however that gradual internationalization is now envisioned for the Singapore dollar. In particular, the Finance Minister announced on 15 October 1996 that the forty foreign currency-denominated stocks quoted on the Stock Exchange of Singapore could apply to have their shares converted to Singapore dollars if they met certain criteria.[1] This policy change, which is intended to develop the capital market, can be viewed as a response to the liberalization and deregulatory measures taken in other regional financial markets which portend intensified competition.

Singapore has long subscribed to an open trading regime. Since 1968 import protection measures have been repeatedly reduced and removed. Today, 95 percent of Singapore's imports are duty free. There are no taxes on exports. This open trading regime was strengthened by the lifting of exchange controls in 1978.

Apart from the above major liberalization measures, Singapore has undergone other changes in policy, both official and market driven, that have increased competition and contributed to lower transactions costs, in turn facilitating financial intermediation. These include the lowering of brokerage and other fees and the reduction and removal of stamp duties. Various facets of the electronics funds transfer system that have been introduced, including ATMs, shared ATMs, automated cheque clearing, interbank GIRO, and EFTPOS, are a case in point. Arguably the rapid movement towards cashlessness has been driven by the visible hand of government, particularly through financial institutions where it has a large stake, to promote efficiency.

Similar changes may be observed in Singapore's capital markets, viz., scripless trading, listing eligible foreign companies on the stock exchange, permitting foreign share holdings in stock exchange member firms. In the words of the Monetary Authority, Singapore has a "... degree of foreign participation that is probably unsurpassed in the world financial sector" (MAS 1995/96, p. 54).

The financial liberalization measures outlined above would be expected to increase the interdependence of Singapore's financial markets with those in the rest of the world. This expectation is confirmed by various empirical studies, including Glick and Hutchinson (1990), Frenkel (1991), Faruquee (1992), Ariff, Kapur, and Tyabji (1995), Ouliaris (1995), and Tan and Tse (1996). The most obvious measure of interdependence is the convergence of interest rates in Singapore with those of the United State, for example. Tan and Tse's (1996) findings suggest that both the band and the variability of the deviations from covered and uncovered interest differentials have been declining over time (see also Ngiam 1996). This convergence restricts further the possibility of Singapore policy makers' independently affecting domestic real interest rates.

One lesson from the experience of countries that encountered problems as a result of financial liberalization and capital account convertibility is the recognition of the need to strengthen prudential supervision of financial institutions. Simultaneously, steps need to be taken to reduce moral hazard associated with the regulations where they provide a safety net. Singapore is a paragon of such prudence. There is no deposit insurance (except that deposits of the Post Office Savings Bank are guaranteed by the government); prudential regulations and supervision are tight; reserve requirements have been at 6 percent since 1975; liquid asset requirements are 18 and 10 percent for commercial banks and finance companies respectively. As liberalization has proceeded, prudential regulations have been strengthened to raise the standards of financial and corporate governance.

Singapore's financial system is generally sound and efficient. This makes it possible for it to intermediate large capital inflows and to respond to exogenous shocks quickly.

Currency Issue

Singapore's currency is backed 100-percent by foreign reserves. It is issued and redeemed on demand by a currency board that has no regulatory functions. Regulation is the responsibility of the Monetary Authority of Singapore (MAS) which performs all central banking functions except currency issue.

Capital inflows expand the issue of currency and subsequently the money supply. Many analysts regard Singapore's currency board system as anachronistic. Still, since there is no fiduciary issue, it imposes a certain fiscal discipline. Perhaps this affects the government's budgetary philosophy.

Compulsory Savings

The main vehicle for social security (primarily for retirement) is Singapore's compulsory savings scheme, operated by the Central Provident Fund (CPF). Employees and employers contribute stipulated sums monthly into individual accounts maintained with the CPF. The present rate of contribution by both employers and employees is set at 20 percent of salary. As the scheme is fully funded, it is not redistributive. Before retirement, people may only use their accumulated savings for approved purposes such as the purchase of housing or financial assets and medical expenses.

Two consequences of the compulsory savings system are relevant for the present purpose. First, the high rate of contribution to the savings scheme is responsible for Singapore's low aggregate consumption, or high aggregate savings, noted earlier. Second, given the present demographic structure, contributions to the fund generally exceed withdrawals. The law requires contributions to be invested in government securities. Since, as will be seen subsequently, the government's budget is almost invariably in surplus, these CPF funds are often invested overseas. This capital outflow tightens liquidity in the economy and, together with the surplus in the government and public sector budgets, dampens the growth of money supply (Table 7.2).

TABLE 7.2
Determinants of the Money Supply
S$ millions

Year	M1	Government	Private Sector	External Sector	Other
1985	–81.3	–3,083.1	–919.2	3,106.4	814.3
1986	1,036.3	1640.9	–3,074.3	4,480.4	–2,010.7
1987	1,209.2	849.4	–2,716.9	2,755.3	321.4
1988	927.2	–4651.1	24.0	3,624.1	1,930.2
1989	1,786.9	–6,159.4	296.3	5,600.5	2,079.5
1990	1,516.3	–2,504.9	–1,742.7	4,753.8	1,010.1
1991	1,169.1	–1,191.8	400.1	6,733.1	–4,772.3
1992	2,085.6	–3,554.2	2,023.7	8,686.9	–5,070.8
1993	4,366.6	–4,473.0	8,397.1	5,382.3	–4,939.8
1994	529.3	–4,978.0	772.6	4,153.0	581.7
1995	1,937.7	–7,570.7	12,461.5	1,798.1	–4,751.2

Source: Monetary Authority of Singapore, *Monthly Statistical Bulletin*, various.

Trends in the Balance of Payments

The key indicators of Singapore's balance of payments portray the changes in capital flows (Table 7.3). At the aggregate level the balance of payments has been positive; between 1970 and 1995, the overall surplus ranged between 3.0 and 14.5 percent of GNP, and during the 1990s it averaged 11.0 percent of GNP. The surpluses in the balance of payments are mirrored by official foreign reserves.

The aggregate picture of balance of payments surplus masks certain underlying circumstances that are worth noting. First, although the merchandise trade balance remains negative, it has declined significantly, especially between 1994 and 1995, as a percentage of GNP, despite the fact that the ratio of imports and exports to GNP has remained more or less the same. Second, in contrast, the balance on services remains positive, averaging around 19 percent of GNP between 1990 and 1995. Third, Singapore's current account surplus has risen sharply since it became a net exporter of capital in 1986.

Fourth, the capital account was positive between 1965 and 1992 (except for 1986) due to the large inflows of foreign direct investment. Significant outflows of non-monetary capital were recorded between 1993 and 1995, partly a reflection of overseas investment by Singapore companies and partly due to short term capital outflow (MAS 1995/96, p. 44). It is useful to reiterate that the large non-monetary inflows during the late 1980s and early 1990s have been directed to *investment*, especially in the manufacturing and financial services sectors. Because both of these sectors are export oriented, the inflows fed back into the current account surplus. In a word, the impact is on tradable goods.

Fifth, the monetary component of the capital account, although smaller in magnitude than the non-monetary component, is highly volatile, as is to be expected given its short-term nature. Monetary inflows were particularly large in 1995, almost S$8 billion, due to the uncertainty in global currency markets in the wake of the Mexican peso crisis and the weakening of the U.S. currency in the first half of that year. The inflow caused appreciation of the Singapore dollar, requiring intervention by the Monetary Authority.

In summary, Singapore's balance of payments position remains strong despite the country's rapid economic growth. The resultant large accumulation of foreign reserves, a measure of the strength of capital inflows, puts pressure on the currency to appreciate. This is seen in Table 7.4. Singapore's nominal exchange rate against the U.S. dollar has appreciated

TABLE 7.3
Key Indicators of the Balance of Payments, 1965–95

	1965	1970	1975	1980	1985	1986	1987	1988	1989	1990	1991	1992	1993	1994	1995
Current A/C															
$bill	–150.1	–1,750.8	–1,385.2	–3,345.6	–7.8	693.7	331.8	3,788.2	5,700.2	5,612.9	8,437.0	9,146.1	6,794.7	17,235.8	21,391.8
% GNP	–4.9	–29.9	–10.2	–13.8	–0.2	1.7	–0.8	7.4	9.5	8.2	11.2	11.1	7.3	15.9	17.6
Merchandise Trade															
$bill	–759.8	–2,619.4	–5,692.7	–8,994.5	–6223.5	–4.497.3	–5,152.0	–2,720.1	–3,707.3	–6,703.3	–4,382.4	6,367.3	–7,980.6	–1,600.6	–1,056.5
% GNP	–24.8	–44.7	–42.0	–37.2	–15.4	–11.2	–11.9	–5.3	–6.2	–9.8	–5.8	–7.7	–8.5	–1.5	–0.9
Services Trade															
$bill	658.6	8,92.2	4,399.8	5,576.5	6,684.7	5,589.4	5,312.4	7,110.5	10,122.1	1,3119.1	13,682.8	1,6391.5	15,744.1	19,958.3	23,707.4
% GNP	21.6	15.2	32.4	24.3	16.6	13.9	12.3	13.8	16.9	19.2	18.2	19.9	16.8	18.4	19.5
Capital A/C															
$bill	104.4	532.6	1,374.4	3388.3	1,536.9	–967.7	989.6	1,987.6	2,438.5	7,154.8	4,051.9	2,920.9	–1,746.0	–13,851.4	9,737.6
% GNP	3.4	9.1	10.1	14.0	3.8	–2.4	2.3	3.9	4.1	10.5	5.4	3.5	–1.9	–12.8	–8.0
Non–Monetary															
$bill	87.1	429.1	1,586.2	3,096.7	2554.8	2,820.8	2,799.8	3,982.9	5,057.1	4,109.7	5,722.7	4,093.6	–6,137.4	–1,558.7	–17,734.8
% GNP	2.9	7.3	11.7	12.8	6.3	7.0	6.5	7.7	8.5	6.0	7.6	5.0	–6.7	–14.4	–14.6
Monetary															
$bill	17.2	103.5	–211.8	291.6	–1,017.9	–3,788.5	–1,810.2	–1,995.3	–2,618.6	3,045.3	–1,670.8	–1,172.7	4,391.4	1,707.3	7,997.2
% GNP	0.6	1.8	–1.6	1.2	2.5	–9.4	–4.2	–3.9	–4.4	4.5	–2.2	–1.4	4.7	1.6	6.6
Errors & Omissions															
$bill	31.6	1783.0	977.2	1376.6	1412.6	1482.6	1670.7	–2432.2	2804.5	–2875.2	–5,226.1	–2,108.0	7,105.0	3,917.3	519.7
% GNP	1.0	30.4	7.2	5.7	3.5	3.7	3.9	–4.7	–4.7	–4.2	–6.9	–2.6	7.6	3.6	0.4
Overall Balance															
$bill	–14.2	564.8	966.4	1433.8	2941.7	1208.6	2328.5	3346.6	5334.2	9892.5	7,262.8	9,959.0	12,153.7	7,301.7	12,173.9
% GNP	–0.5	9.6	7.1	5.9	7.3	3.0	5.4	6.5	8.9	14.5	9.6	12.1	13.0	6.7	10.0
Change in Official Foreign Reserves	14.2	–5,64.8	–966.4	–1,433.8	–2,941.7	–1,208.6	–2,238.5	–3,346.6	–5,334.2	–9,892.5	–7,262.8	–9,959.0	–12,153.7	–7,301.7	–12,173.9

Source: Department of Statistics. *Yearbook of Statistics, Singapore*, various years.

TABLE 7.4
Nominal and Real Effective Exchange Rates, 1981–95

Year	Nominal Exchange Rate S$/US$	Real Effective Exchange Rate 1990 = 100
1981	2.11	104.1
1982	2.14	107.1
1983	2.11	105.3
1984	2.13	104.8
1985	2.00	100.4
1986	2.17	91.5
1987	2.10	90.3
1988	2.01	92.2
1989	2.00	93.0
1990	1.81	100.0
1991	1.73	103.0
1992	1.63	104.4
1993	1.62	102.2
1994	1.52	105.6
1995	1.42	106.9

Source: Asian Development Bank, *Asian Development Outlook* (Manila, various).

steadily since 1981 (except for 1986, the year following the 1985 recession) by around 34 percent. In real effective terms the currency depreciated in the latter half of the 1980s but it has appreciated moderately since then.

POLICY RESPONSE

Financial liberalization and the resulting capital inflows remove some autonomy from domestic stabilization policies. Capital inflows may put pressure on the real exchange rate to appreciate, with adverse consequences on tradable goods. The policy question becomes, What policy mix can avoid or slow down the real appreciation of the currency? Put another way, What are the roles and directions of macro-stabilization policies in the face of capital inflows? We examine individual macro-stabilization policy alternatives, and then consider what can be said about the appropriate mix of policies to deal with capital inflows.

Monetary Policy

Singapore's two-decade experience of full employment underscores the basis of the country's monetary policy, which is to promote sustained economic growth with low inflation.

Monetary policy may target monetary aggregates, interest rates, or exchange rates. The choice of target(s) depends on the structural and other characteristics of the economy. Countries have been known to switch from one target to another as circumstances change. This has been true of monetary policy in Singapore in the past two decades.

During the 1970s monetary policy was conducted using interest rates and money stock as targets. This was largely conditioned by the financial regulatory regime. As explained earlier, interest rates were fixed by a bank cartel until 1975 and capital movements were restricted until 1978.

Inflation emerged as a significant stabilization problem in the 1970s. Singapore's CPI skyrocketed from an average of below 2 percent for the whole of the 1960s, to 19.6 percent in 1973, and to 22.4 percent in 1974 before it eased to 2.5 percent in 1975 (Table 7.1). The global food and energy crises of the early 1970s were one cause of this inflation. The other contributing factor was the large capital inflow into the banking system in the wake of the sterling and U.S. dollar crises and in anticipation of the appreciation of the Singapore dollar.

To cope with these large capital inflows, the Monetary Authority sharply raised reserve requirements for depository institutions and implemented other measures to restrain credit growth. Given the turbulence in international currency markets, the credit-restraining measures were insufficient to curb the capital inflows. The inflows subsided with the floating of the Singapore dollar in 1973 and its subsequent appreciation. It is important to note that fiscal policy was already contractionary during this period.

Since the early 1980s monetary policy has targeted the exchange rate. The shift in the choice of targets was explained by the Monetary Authority of Singapore in its 1981–82 Annual Report:

> As in the past several years, monetary policy in 1981 was affected through the Authority's operations in the money market and foreign exchange market. It differed somewhat in 1981 in that the policy direction was aimed largely at maintaining a strong exchange rate for the Singapore dollar, while ensuring sufficient liquidity to accommodate real economic growth. Underlying this shift in emphasis away from targets for interest rates and money supply growth in the conduct of monetary

> policy is the view that the exchange rate is a relatively more important anti-inflation instrument in the context of the small and open Singapore economy. Price stability then, continues to be the prime objective. The emphasis given to a strong exchange rate policy also facilitates the policy of upgrading and restructuring the domestic economy (MAS 1982, p. 4).

Singapore's exchange rate is managed against a trade-weighted basket of currencies of its major trading partners and competitors. The MAS intervenes whenever market forces threaten to push the exchange rate out of an undisclosed target band. Intervention endogenizes the stock of money and influences the exchange rate. Within the band the exchange rate appears to be determined on a daily basis by market forces (Lim, Tyabji, et al. 1988, p. 302). The policy objective for Singapore's fully employed economy is to achieve a low and stable rate of inflation. To reduce imported inflation in domestic prices the Singapore dollar is allowed to appreciate; the extent of appreciation depends "on prevailing and projected levels of world inflation and domestic sources of inflation" (Teh and Shanmugaratnam 1992, p. 297).

In 1980 and 1981 inflation was relatively high again, due partly to the second oil shock and increases in world commodity prices and partly to domestic wage-push pressures that began in 1979 (Table 7.1). Capital inflows were also particularly high in 1980, adding to the inflationary pressure. The MAS thus allowed a higher appreciation of the currency in order to moderate inflation and keep it below the double-digit levels being experienced in other countries at the time.

With regard to the exchange rate, the authorities are committed to maintain a strong and stable Singapore dollar. The stabilizing effect that any official exchange rate commitment has on expectations depends on its credibility. Lack of credibility will lead to capital flight or currency substitution, either of which will exert downward pressure on the currency. Credibility is affected by policy outcomes. Singapore's exchange rate commitment enjoys strong credibility because policy outcomes have created the generally sound economic environment described earlier.

Another objective of the exchange rate policy is to avoid unnecessary volatility. A recent study examining the volatility of exchange rates in Singapore and some selected countries for the period 1979–92 suggests that possibly because of MAS intervention, nominal exchange rate volatility was lowest in Singapore compared with the United States, United Kingdom, Germany, Japan, and Malaysia (Yip 1996). This stability should also discourage speculation against the Singapore dollar. However, the same study shows that the volatility of the real effective exchange rate has been greater and is observed to have a negative impact on Singapore's domestic exports.

Short-term capital movements could make it necessary for the MAS to intervene to smooth out the exchange rate fluctuations. Such intervention could be at odds with the policy to stabilize monetary growth. This conflict suggests the need for the MAS to develop other instruments for sterilization. The revamping of the government securities market in 1987 which enhanced the scope for open market operations was a step in this direction. Growing volumes of repo transactions are reported in the MAS Annual Reports. However the MAS accounts do not provide data on its holdings of government securities. Thus, it is not possible to judge the importance of such operations. Foreign exchange intervention appears to be the main policy instrument for stabilization.

Fiscal Policy

Singapore's fiscal policy has a number of important features which are relevant to the present discussion. First, the policy is conservative, with large and persistent budget and public sector surpluses. The fiscal surplus is defined to include not only the budget surplus, but also that of major public enterprises for which data are reported and net contributions to the CPF compulsory savings scheme. The available official data on the budget balance are assembled in Table 7.5.[2]

The large surpluses are consistent with the broad budgetary philosophy which is summed up in the following statement:

> The long term objective of budgetary policy is to contain operating and development expenditure at a level that can be financed by *operating revenue*. (emphasis added) (Ministry of Trade and Industry 1992, p. 26)

This philosophy extends to Singapore's public enterprises which are generally expected to cover their operating expenditures from operating receipts.

Second, given the government's development orientation, the focus of Singapore's fiscal policy is on economic growth and efficiency rather than on welfare. Third, and related to the second feature, Singapore's fiscal policy has made widespread use of fiscal incentives to promote the growth of targeted sectors, including Singapore companies operating abroad. In a bid to keep the level of taxation internationally competitive, company and personal income tax rates have been successively reduced during the last decade. And in line with international trends, a 3 percent general sales tax was implemented from April 1994 in order to shift the tax mix towards consumption taxes.

Fourth, in Singapore current expenditure averaged 76 percent of total government expenditure between 1990 and 1993, a significantly lower share than in European countries (Table 7.6). Security, education, and infrastructure including housing account for the bulk of Singapore's public spending; welfare payments are insignificant. Since the share of current spending is relatively low, fiscal policy in Singapore acts not so much through the non-tradable goods sector, but through the tradable goods sector (the importable goods sector, in particular).

Singapore's conservative fiscal stance has a number of implications for macro-stabilization. First, the fiscal surplus has limited the expansion of narrow money and served to counter the strong increase in aggregate demand brought about by capital formation and export growth. This can be observed in Table 7.2 where net claims on the government make significant negative contributions to the growth of narrow money. Second, Singapore's fiscal stance has made it easier for the MAS to set and achieve monetary targets. In contrast to Singapore, countries with large fiscal

TABLE 7.5
Public Sector Budget Balance, 1990–95

	1990	1991	1992	1993	1994	1995
			S$ billions			
Government[1]	1.8	3.5	4.9	7.0	9.2	9.2
Statutory Boards[2]	2.6	2.8	1.7	2.1	2.4	1.4
Central Provident Fund	3.2	3.4	3.6	–0.5	4.0	6.3
Total	7.6	9.7	10.2	8.6	15.6	16.9
			% of GDP			
Government	2.7	4.8	6.1	7.5	8.7	7.8
Statutory Boards	3.8	3.8	2.1	2.3	2.3	1.2
Central Provident Fund	4.7	4.7	4.5	–0.5	3.8	5.3
Total	11.2	13.3	12.7	9.3	14.7	14.2

Notes: 1) The government surplus reported here differs from the official statistics as some inter-fund transfers have been excluded. 2) Data pertain only to the major statutory boards. They exclude grants received from government.

Source: Singapore Ministry of Trade and Industry, *Economic Survey of Singapore*, various issues; Department of Statistics. *Yearbook of Statistics, Singapore,* various issues.

TABLE 7.6
Government Revenue and Expenditure, 1990–95

	1990	1991	1992	1993	1994	1995
			S$ billions			
Operating Revenue[1]	13.1	14.9	17.2	19.5	23.3	24.8
Total Expenditure	11.3	11.3	12.3	12.6	14.1	15.6
Operating Expenditure	7.1	7.8	8.5	9.1	9.7	10.9
Development Expenditure[2]						
Surplus[3]	4.2	3.5	4.9	7.0	9.2	9.2
	1.7	3.5	4.9	7.0	9.2	9.2
			% of GDP			
Operating Revenue	19.4	20.4	21.7	21.0	21.9	20.9
Total Expenditure	16.7	15.5	15.5	13.6	13.3	13.2
Operating Expenditure	10.5	10.7	10.7	9.8	9.1	9.2
Development Expenditure	6.2	4.8	4.8	3.7	4.1	4.0
Surplus	2.7	4.8	6.1	7.5	8.7	7.8

Notes: 1) Comprises tax revenue and fees and charges, but excludes non-tax revenue. 2) Excludes loans to statutory boards, industrial and commercial enterprises. 3) The government surplus reported here differs from the official statistics as some inter-fund transfers are excluded.

Source: *Yearbook of Statistics, Singapore,* various; *Economic Survey of Singapore,* various.

deficits have had greater difficulty coping with financial liberalization and innovation.

Third, under Singapore's managed floating exchange rate regime, exchange rate targeting makes the money stock endogenous which seems to suggest that fiscal policy again comes on its own as an effective stabilization tool.

Fourth, although the conventional wisdom suggests (monetary) sterilization in the face of capital inflows, this is only a short term solution; other means of sterilization appear to be necessary in a situation of sustained capital inflows. In Singapore's case, the contractionary fiscal stance (on a long-term basis) has been an important means of anchoring long-term economic stability (see also Claassen 1992 and Fischer and Reisen 1993).

Finally, the above points emphasize the interdependence among macroeconomic policies. This makes policy co-ordination essential. In Singapore, at least at the administrative level, co-ordination is neatly achieved by fact that the Minister for Finance is also the Chairman of the Monetary Authority of Singapore. While proponents of central bank independence may find this joint responsibility heretical, independence per se does not necessarily result in price stability (low inflation). (See the discussion in, for example, Cukierman 1992 among others.)

CONCLUDING REMARKS

For almost three decades Singapore has a enjoyed healthy balance of payments situation, the result largely of capital account surpluses. Since 1986, the current account has also been positive. Simultaneously inflation has been very low with remarkably stable real effective exchange rates. This situation has been achieved without recourse to capital controls, which were abolished in June 1978; or to raising reserve requirements, which have remained at 6 percent since 1975; or to sterilized (monetary) intervention via the government securities market.

How was liquidity managed in Singapore and why was the economy able to cope with these inflows? Singapore's strong economic fundamentals (the initial conditions) have helped to maintain investor confidence while allowing the economy to fend off speculative attacks. The three important facets of Singapore's policy response to capital inflows have been: the management of the exchange rate, which has contributed to lower inflation; the sound financial system capable of intermediating the inflows; and, last but not least, the restrictive fiscal stance, often referred to as fiscal discipline. Included in the fiscal stance is the country's compulsory savings scheme, which together with the government and public enterprise surpluses, has dampened liquidity.

Another significant aspect of Singapore's experience is that the capital flows have largely taken the form of investment, which has a greater impact on tradable goods, rather than consumption. The economy's high degree of openness, in both real and financial terms, suggests that the inflows are vented again through the tradable sector.

Thus, the generally favourable outcome for Singapore has been a function of the initial conditions, the special features of the economy, and the appropriate mix of policy. It is perhaps necessary to reiterate that the country's restrictive fiscal stance anchors long-term stability.

As systemic risk increases, national (domestic) policies may prove insufficient. The current consensus is towards greater international co-operation, whether at the micro- or macro-level, or bilateral and multilateral. International co-operation may range all the way from setting international standards to swap arrangements between central banks. But such arrangements cannot be regarded as a substitute for sound monetary and fiscal policies.

Notes

[1] *Business Times* (Singapore), 16 October 1996.

[2] Government budgetary data are unconsolidated; that is, they include inter-fund transfers. To some extent therefore, the balance is understated. It is important to note also that this balance includes only the government's operating revenue. According to the IMF, capital receipts between 1990 and 1993 ranged between 14 and 25 percent of total revenue (1995, p. 539). Hence, including capital receipts would make the surplus even larger.

References

Ariff, M., B.K. Kapur, and A. Tyabji. 1995. "Money Markets in Singapore". In *Asian Money Markets*, edited by D.C. Cole et al. New York: Oxford University Press.

Axilrod, S. 1990. *Interdependence of Capital Markets and Policy Implications*. Washington, D.C.: Group of Thirty.

Business Times (Singapore), 14 October 1996.

Claassen, E.M. 1992. *Financial Liberalization and its Impact on Domestic Stabilization: Singapore and Malaysia*. Singapore: Institute for Southeast Asian Studies (ISEAS).

Corbo, V. and L. Hernandez. 1996. "Macroeconomic Adjustment to Capital Inflows: Lessons from Recent Latin American and East Asian Experience". World Bank *Research Observer* 11 no. 1 (February).

Cukierman, A. 1992. *Central Bank Strategy, Credibility and Independence: Theory and Evidence*. Cambridge, MA: MIT Press.

Department of Statistics (DOS). 1996. *Singapore Statistical Highlights*. Singapore: DOS.

______. *Yearbook of Statistics*. Singapore: DOS, various years.

Faruquee, Hamid. 1992. "Dynamic Capital Mobility in Pacific Basin Developing Countries". *IMF Staff Papers* 39.

Fischer, B. and H. Reisen. 1993. *Liberalizing Capital Flows in Developing Countries : Pitfalls, Prerequisites and Perspectives*. Paris: Organisation for Economic Co-operation and Development.

Frankel, J. 1991. "Quantifying International Capital Mobility in the 1980s". In *National Saving and Economic Performance*, edited by D. Bernheim and J. Shoven. Chicago: University of Chicago Press.

Glick, R. and Hutchinson, M. 1990. "Financial Liberalization in the Pacific Basin: Implications for Real Interest Linkages". *Journal of the Japanese and International Economies* 4.

International Monetary Fund (IMF). 1995. *Government Finance Statistics Yearbook 1995*. Washington D.C.: IMF.

Lim, C.Y., A. Tyabji, et al. 1988. *Policy Options for the Singapore Economy*. Singapore: McGraw-Hill.

Monetary Authority of Singapore (MAS). *Annual Report*. Singapore: MAS, various years.

Ministry of Trade and Industry (MTI). *Economic Survey of Singapore*. Singapore: MTI, various years.

Ngiam, K.J. 1996. "Comment" on "Interest Parity and Dynamic Capital Mobility: The Experience of Singapore". In *Financial Deregulation and Integration in East Asia*, edited by T. Ito and A.O. Krueger. Chicago: University of Chicago Press.

Ouliaris, S. 1995. "An Economic Analysis of Asian Money Markets". In *Asian Money Markets*, edited by D.C. Cole et al. N.Y.: Oxford University Press.

Tan, K. S. and Y. K. Tse. 1996. "Interest Parity and Dynamic Capital Mobility: The Experience of Singapore". In *Financial Deregulation and Integration in East Asia*, edited by T. Ito and A.O. Krueger. Chicago: University of Chicago Press.

Teh, K.P. and T. Shanmugaratnam. 1992. "Exchange Rate Policy: Philosophy and Conduct over the Past Decade". In *Public Policies in Singapore*, edited by M. H. Toh and L. Low. Singapore: Times Academic Press.

Yip, P. S. L. 1996. "Exchange Rate Management in Singapore". In *Economic Policy Management in Singapore*, edited by C.Y. Lim. Singapore: Addison-Wesley.

UPDATE

SINGAPORE AND THE REGIONAL FINANCIAL CRISIS

The macroeconomic data in Table U7.1 form the basis of an initial assessment of the impact of the regional financial crisis on the Singapore economy. This assessment is necessarily preliminary because the full impact is yet to be felt.

Real GDP growth has remained strong at 7.5 percent for the first three quarters of 1997. This buoyancy can be attributed to three factors. (1) A large part of Singapore's regional trade comprises intermediate and capital goods (for export industries) and intra-firm trade destined for the growing demand from the United States and the EU. (2) The global electronics recovery boosted the manufacturing sector which has strong sectoral linkages. (3) The volume of stock market transactions was higher than normal due to the regional turmoil and to uncertainty over the merging of the local and foreign transactions of some listed companies. Not unexpectedly, currency turmoil raised transactions on SIMEX as investors attempted to hedge risks. Rising interest rates and volatile equity markets are expected to sustain the stronger volumes on SIMEX into the next year.

Singapore's employment situation remains robust. The seasonally adjusted unemployment rate for September 1997 was 1.8 percent. Productivity improved in line with increased economic activity and improved unit business costs in manufacturing.

Inflation, as measured by the 1.9 percent increase in the CPI, has been slightly higher in 1997 compared to the 1.4 percent increase in 1996.

The overall balance of payments for the first three quarters of 1997 exceeds that for the whole of 1996, with both the current and capital accounts in surplus. At S$4.2 billion in the third quarter capital inflow was higher than the S$1.4 billion during the second quarter. The inflow comprised foreign direct investment and Asian dollar loans. Since the data are reported on a net basis, there is no information on the outflow. Still, the sell down in the equity market could be expected to have led to an outflow given that the Singapore dollar has also depreciated significantly, although not as massively as elsewhere in the region. While foreign (meaning U.S. and European) funds have been widely reported to have quit the local market, regional investors fleeing their own battered markets could be parking their monies in Singapore because of its stronger fundamentals.

TABLE U7.1
Selected Macroeconomic Indicators for Singapore, 1996–97

	1996			1997		
	Q3	Q4	Annual	Q1	Q2	Q3
GDP at 1990 Market Prices			Year on Year % Change			
Total	3.3	5.8	7.0	4.1	8.2	10.1
Manufacturing	–3.9	–07	3.4	–5.5	3.5	9.5
Construction	16.3	13.7	18.4	9.6	11.8	13.4
Commerce	2.1	5.4	6.0	2.9	8.0	8.6
Transportation & Communication	6.2	7.6	8.1	8.1	9.6	10.8
Financial & Business Services	6.4	10.0	8.2	10.5	11.4	11.6
			Thousands			
Net Job Creation	22	40	103	16	37	28
			Year on Year % Change			
Mfg. Unit Business Cost Index	5.6	3.3	2.4	5.6	0.7	–1.4
			S$ billions			
Net Investment Commitments, Mfg.	2.6	1.7	8.1	2.2	2.5	2.2
			Year on Year % Change			
Consumer Price Index	1.4	1.6	1.4	1.7	1.8	2.3
External Trade at Current Prices			Year on Year % Change			
Exports	0.1	1.7	5.2	–2.8	5.9	8.8
Domestic Exports	—	0.4	5.2	–4.1	3.8	7.6
Re-exports	0.4	3.5	5.3	–0.9	9.1	10.5
Imports	–2.4	1.3	5.0	–2.2	4.6	14.6
Balance of Payments			S$ billions			
Current Account Balance	7.3	4.5	19.9	4.2	6.2	5.3
Capital (net)	1.2	0.4	–2.0	–7.0	1.4	4.2
Overall Balance	2.7	3.1	10.4	6.1	1.7	2.9

Source: Ministry of Trade and Industry 1997.

The exchange rate picture is mixed. In the third quarter of 1997, the Singapore dollar depreciated against the U.S. dollar (6.5 percent), the Japanese yen (1 percent), the French franc (5.2 percent), the Deutschemark (4.8 percent), the pound sterling (3.4 percent), the Hong Kong dollar (6.8 percent), the New Taiwan (NT) dollar (3.9 percent), and the Korean won (3.7 percent). However, it strengthened against regional currencies including the Thai baht (32 percent), Indonesian rupiah (26 percent), and Malaysian ringgit (18 percent). The impact of these changes on Singapore's trade in goods and services will also be mixed. For example, Singapore's exports to the United States should increase, given the weaker

Singapore dollar. Since the import content of its manufactures is very high, Singapore's competitiveness will also be affected by the sources of its imports. In the same way, the number of tourists from the region can be expected to decline quite significantly.

Depreciating currencies have prompted central banks elsewhere in the region to raise interest rates or put in place other monetary measures. Under Singapore's open economy and capital account, interest rates are not targeted. However, Singapore's currency is managed to keep it strong and stable with a view to keeping inflation low. The currency's recent slide against the U.S. dollar, for example, does not appear to have prompted intervention, partly to help Singapore's competitiveness and partly because world inflation is low.

As a result of the currency turmoil and the depreciation of the Singapore dollar, interbank rates have risen. Prime lending rates and three-month fixed deposit rates remained firm until the end of the third quarter, but they have since increased.

The strongest impact of the regional financial turmoil has been on stock prices which have been battered with attendant negative wealth effects. Still, Singapore's non-performing loans are reported to be less than three percent, much the lowest in the region (*Business Times*, 21 October 1997).

The Singapore property market has entered a period of glut; prices have softened as have rental rates, and developers are beginning to offer new units at somewhat reduced prices in a bid to reduce inventories. The glut is the result of a number of factors. (1) Beginning in May 1996 the government introduced policies to reduce property speculation, including tighter margin financing. (2) More recently, the appreciation of the Singapore dollar against the ringgit and the rupiah has reduced foreign demand for properties in Singapore. (3) The regional slowdown will impact adversely on Singapore's economic growth and thus reduce housing demand across the board for the foreseeable future.

In early September 1997 the Singapore government announced that it would reduce the sale of land for private housing next year, offering only 5,000 units, compared to 6,000 in 1996 and 7,000 in 1997. Estimates suggest that a total of around 35,000 to 40,000 units will be available in the next 15 months, equivalent to five to seven years' supply of private housing (*Business Times*, 30 September 1997). Since demand is slack, the announced policy cannot make a difference to the present situation.

As this review has indicated, the real economy has not been affected by the regional currency crisis. Thus far, the impact has been on financial variables—the exchange rate, interest rates (only recently), and stock prices.

The Composite Leading index, an indicator of economic activity for about three quarters ahead, rose by 2.1 percent in the third quarter of 1997. The government's survey of business expectations for the third quarter found manufacturing establishments more upbeat than service establishments, particularly those in commerce including tourism and financial services (MTI 1997). For 1997 at least, growth appears to be on track and the year should see around 7 percent growth.

The outlook for 1998 appears less sanguine. With the spread of the crisis to Korea and slower growth expected in Japan, the IMF has lowered its 1998 forecast for world economic growth from 4.3 to 3.5 percent. As one of the most open economies in the world, Singapore cannot escape the consequences of this slowdown. While its economy is diversified, it is still highly dependent on the region; Malaysia, Thailand, and Korea are respectively its second, fifth, and eighth largest trading partners and Indonesia is a significant trading partner, even though trade statistics with Indonesia are not published. Thus, the regional impact on Singapore will depend particularly on how rapidly Malaysia and Indonesia are able to revive their economies. Mexico's recovery from its currency crisis has been described as "V" shaped. Whether Asian economies will bite the bullet in the same way is a difficult question and it is perhaps too soon to ask. Regional recovery is expected to take two years at best. Singapore's official medium term target is 5 to 7 percent growth; achieving this target depends in the main on supply side factors. Singapore's fundamentals have remained in tact despite the regional crisis. In the short term, the demand-side impact may shave growth by around 2.0 percent.

December 1997

References

Business Times (Singapore). Various.

Ministry of Trade and Industry (MTI). 1997. *Economic Survey of Singapore.* Third Quarter 1997. Singapore.

8

Adverse Consequences of Capital Inflows and Thailand's Optimal Policy Mix

Bhanupong Nidhiprabha

INTRODUCTION

Despite a chronic current account deficit, Thailand accumulated international reserves continuously for the decade after 1986, reaching US$39.8 billion in 1996. Capital inflows through direct investment, portfolio investment, and foreign borrowings have produced a surplus in the capital account far exceeding the deficit in the current account. In 1996, Moody's Investors Service downgraded the three top Thai commercial banks from "Prime-1" to "Prime-2" because it felt that escalating short-term foreign currency debt, which outstripped international reserves, made Thailand more vulnerable to financial shocks. Confidence in the economic management of the Thai government was further eroded by the poor performance of the export sector, the accumulation of non-performing bank loans, and the badly damaged real estate sector. It is argued here that the roots of these problems are the mismanagement of capital inflows and unfavourable external factors. Thailand should not continue to pursue the goal of establishing Bangkok as a financial centre in the region, because the country can also obtain cheap funds cheap through international money markets so long as it maintains sound economic fundamentals.

This chapter shows that although capital inflows can bring about economic expansion and reduce the foreign exchange resource constraint for developing countries like Thailand, excessive capital inflows can disrupt the stability of both internal and external balances. An appropriate mix of fiscal and monetary policies can mitigate the adverse impacts of capital flows to some extent, provided that exogenous factors remain favourable to the exchange rate regime.

COMPOSITION, CAUSES, AND CONSEQUENCES OF CAPITAL INFLOWS

The composition of total net private capital flows to Thailand has changed since 1992. The boom in nonbank private sector inflows began in 1988 and reached its peak in 1991 (Figure 8.1). During the same period, commercial bank borrowing started to rise rapidly and surpassed nonbank private borrowings in 1994, before tapering off in 1995. The share of banks in total private capital flows, which averaged a mere 6.5 percent from 1987 to 1991, rose to 55.6 percent during the period 1992–96 (Table 8.1). During this latter period there was a significant decline in the share of nonbank flows, due to the reduction in direct foreign investment and other private loans. The share of foreign direct investment declined to an average of 10.9 percent for 1992–96 from the 22 percent average in the period 1987–91 (Table 8.1). Both portfolio investment and non-resident baht accounts have emerged as significant components in nonbank capital flows (Figure 8.2).

FIGURE 8.1
Bank and Nonbank Net Private Capital Flows, 1988–96

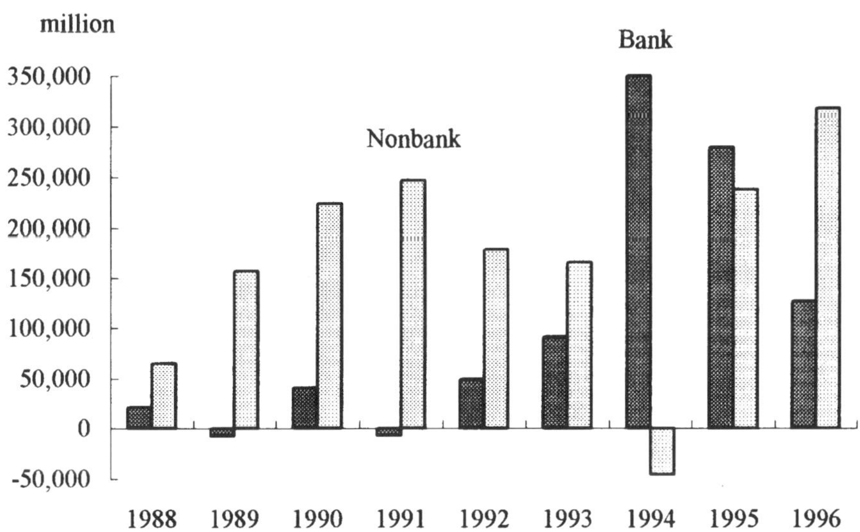

Source: Bank of Thailand.

FIGURE 8.2
Nonbank Private Capital Flows by Type

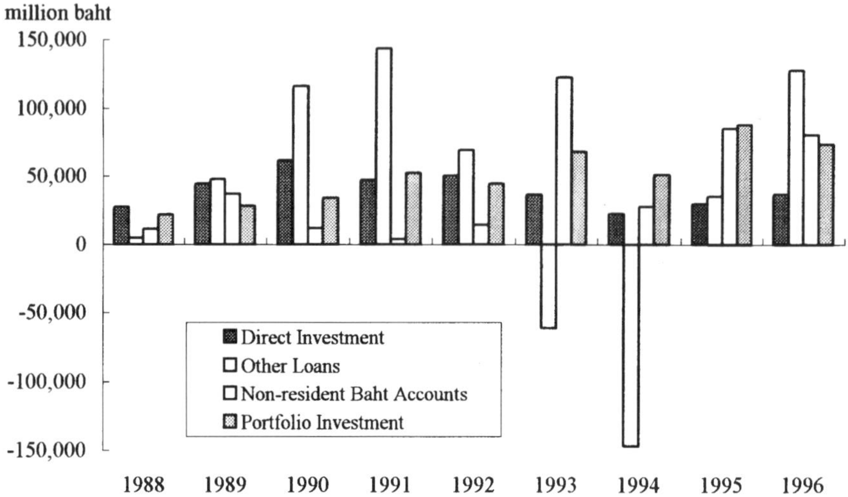

Source: Bank of Thailand.

TABLE 8.1
Composition of Total Net Private Capital Flows, 1987–96
(Percent)

	1987–1991	1992–1996
Bank	6.5	55.6
Nonbank	93.5	44.4
Direct Investment	22.0	10.9
Other Loans	35.2	1.5
Portfolio Investment	9.1	20.4
Non-resident Baht Account	17.5	20.2

Source: Bank of Thailand.

Causes

The government's efforts to liberalize the capital account and in particular the establishment of the Bangkok International Banking Facility (BIBF) in March 1993 contributed to capital inflows. The government's motivation in setting Bangkok up as a regional financial centre was to reduce the cost of funds to local investors to the level in international money markets. Foreign capital was encouraged by the exemption of loans through the

BIBF from the withholding tax on interest. By the end of 1995, the short-term debt through the BIBF amounted to $41 billion, out of a total debt of $80 billion. Although foreign deposits in foreign branches of Thai banks were about 45 billion, the amount of short-term debt seems high relative to the $36 billion level of international reserves in 1995. Through the BIBF some representative offices of foreign banks expanded their lending vigorously to demonstrate their serious involvement in financial activity so that they could qualify for a full banking license in Thailand.

When large portions of capital inflows consist of borrowings by the private sector, changes in interest rate differentials must be an important determinant of capital flows, alongside output growth and inflation differentials. Thailand's prime lending rate, or the Minimum Lending Rate (MLR), has always been higher than foreign interest rates such as the LIBOR, reflecting the shortage of capital in Thailand. The wider the gap between these two rates, the greater incentive for banks to borrow abroad and lend to domestic borrowers who have no access to foreign credit markets. Large private corporations can also access international money markets and substitute foreign debt for domestic bank credit. Commercial banks can substitute foreign debt for local deposits as a source of funds for loan extensions. Because of this substitutability of foreign debt, changes in the gap between the MLR and domestic deposit rates can also influence capital flows to Thailand.

Since 1992 widening differentials between the lending interest rate and the cost of funds led to high profitability of commercial banks in Thailand. Large capital inflows permitted the MLR to decline further in 1993, despite a rising loan-to-deposit ratio. From 1994 to 1995, when the differential between the MLR and Thailand's fixed deposit rate (12 months) narrowed and when the gap between the MLR and the LIBOR grew larger (Table 8.2), Thailand experienced large flows of foreign borrowings by commercial banks. Foreign borrowings by banks relative to the monetary base (FLMB) rose from 22 percent in 1970, to 59 percent in 1990, and to almost triple the size of the monetary base in 1995 (Figure 8.3).

During the period 1994–95, bank credit expanded more than 30 percent on an annual basis. In the late 1980s, credit extensions had expanded rapidly, but deposits also grew and the MLR was on a rising trend. The situation was totally different after 1992 because deposit growth lagged behind credit growth and the MLR was on the decline from 1991 to 1993 (Figure 8.4). Over lending by the banking sector in 1994–95 contributed to the subsequent financial distress and serious imbalances that threatened Thailand's economic stability.

TABLE 8.2
Interest Rate Differentials
Percent

						Differential	
		MLR	LIBOR	Fed Funds Rate	Fixed 12-mo.	MLR - Fixed 12-mo.	MLR - LIBOR
1992	Q1	12.50	4.20	4.00	9.83	2.67	8.30
	Q2	12.00	3.90	3.75	8.67	3.33	8.10
	Q3	12.00	3.10	3.00	9.00	3.00	8.90
	Q4	11.50	3.00	3.00	8.67	2.83	8.50
1993	Q1	11.25	3.10	3.00	8.50	2.75	8.15
	Q2	11.25	3.10	3.00	8.50	2.75	8.15
	Q3	11.25	3.10	3.00	8.50	2.75	8.15
	Q4	10.50	3.00	3.00	7.33	3.17	7.50
1994	Q1	10.00	3.70	3.50	6.67	3.33	6.30
	Q2	11.00	4.60	4.25	7.17	3.83	6.40
	Q3	11.50	5.10	4.75	7.75	3.75	6.40
	Q4	11.75	6.00	5.50	8.17	3.58	5.75
1995	Q1	13.00	6.10	6.00	9.08	3.92	6.90
	Q2	13.50	6.10	6.00	10.25	3.25	7.40
	Q3	13.50	5.90	5.75	10.25	3.25	7.60
	Q4	13.75	5.90	5.50	10.25	3.50	7.85
1996	Q1	13.75	5.38	5.25	10.00	3.75	8.37
	Q2	13.25	5.52	5.25	9.33	3.92	7.73
	Q3	13.25	5.63	5.25	8.81	4.44	7.63
	Q4	13.25	5.50	5.25	8.00	5.25	7.75

Source: Bank of Thailand.

The expansion of bank credit slowed down sharply in 1996 because commercial banks became more cautious about lending as the amount of substandard loans was increasing considerably. Credit expansions declined further in 1997, when lenders were not willing to extend credit due to high default risk, and investors were not willing to borrow due to the gloomy prospects for the Thai economy.

Consequences

Booms in exports, investment, and construction financed by the domestic credit expansion led to economic growth rates above 8 percent from 1987 to 1995. The trend growth path of the Thai economy was around 7.6 percent. Because continued expansion above capacity requires financing from foreign savings, in 1995 the Bank of Thailand (BOT) became more

FIGURE 8.3
Foreign Borrowing by Banks and Relative Prices

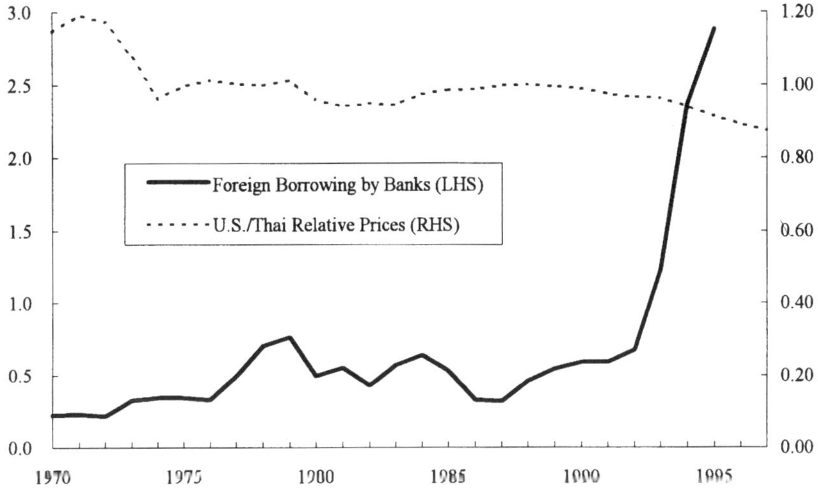

Note: Foreign borrowing by banks is shown relative to the monetary base.
Source: Bank of Thailand.

FIGURE 8.4
Bank Deposit and Loan Growth

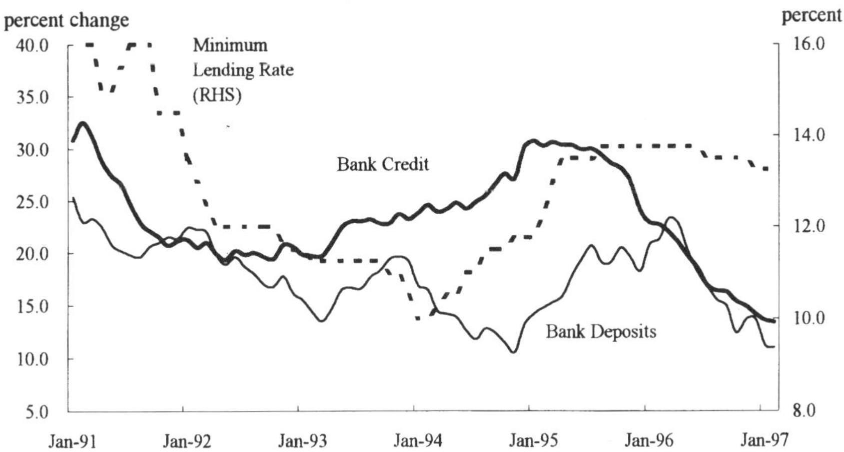

Note: Minimum Lending Rate is percent. Bank Credit and Bank Deposits are percent change from previous year.
Source: Bank of Thailand.

concerned with high inflation and the growing current account deficit. Since 1988 high economic growth in Thailand has been associated with a rising price level and a mounting current account deficit (Figure 8.5). Output expansion affects the inflation rate with a lag of one or two years. The delayed response of inflation precludes a stabilization program from producing immediate results.

There is also a cyclical relationship between economic growth and the current account deficit (as a share of GDP). The current account deficit was relatively small during the boom years (1987–90), but it grew in the later years (1990–91, Figure 8.5). Then the current account balance showed a surprising improvement during the economic downturn in 1991–93. Thus, it appears that expenditure-reduction policy is necessary to reduce the current account deficit. Moreover, a stabilization program does not have any obvious impact within a short period after its implementation. Thailand's current account deficit appears to respond to a reduction in expenditures but not to short run stabilization measures.

FIGURE 8.5
Growth, Inflation, and the Current Account Deficit

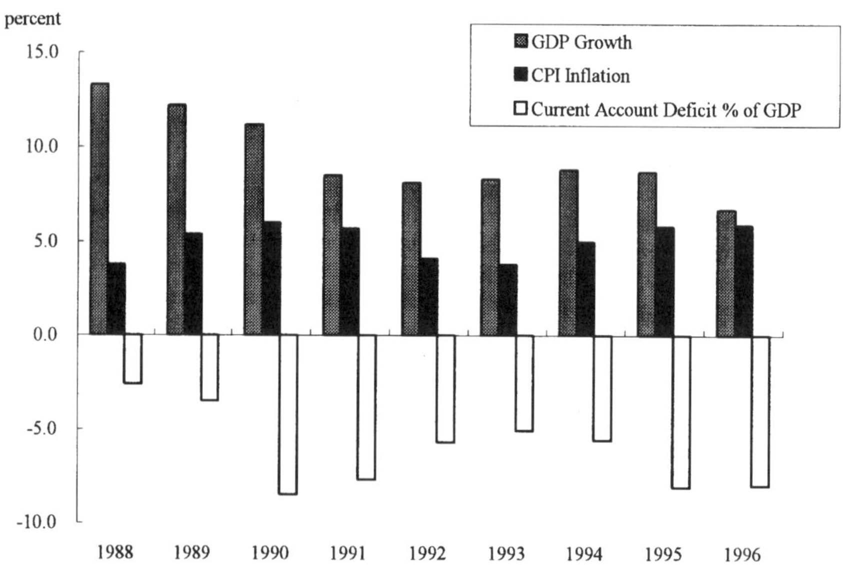

Source: Bank of Thailand.

By the mid 1990s inflation was emerging as a problem in Thailand. The inflation rate measured by the CPI registered 3.8 percent in 1993, but accelerated to 5.9 percent in 1996. By 1995, the Bank of Thailand became concerned with introducing measures to cope with rising capital inflows and inflation. Monetary tightening in 1995 was successful in reducing non-food inflation from 4.3 in 1995 to 3.6 percent in 1996 . The economy slowed down substantially in 1996, when GDP grew only 6.7 percent—the lowest rate in ten years.[1] However, the BOT did not anticipate the slowdown in world trade expansion that occurred in 1996. Thailand's exports actually declined by 0.7 percent that year, as opposed to their hefty 24 percent growth in 1995. The fact that Thai export performance was the worst the region in 1996, while the baht-dollar exchange rate was also the most stable in the region triggered the 1996 speculative attack on the baht.

Since the large capital inflows to Thailand began in 1989, the consumer price level has risen more rapidly in Thailand than in the United States, indicating a decline in Thailand's international competitiveness. Since 1984, the price level of the United States relative to Thailand has been negatively correlated with the level of foreign borrowing (relative to the monetary base) by Thailand's banking sector (Figure 8.3).

Because the U.S. dollar has the greatest weight in Thailand's basket of currencies, the dollar-yen exchange rate dictates movements in the baht-yen exchange rate. Thus, when the dollar strengthens against the yen, the baht also appreciates against the yen. In 1995–96 the real exchange rate of the baht appreciated against the yen by more than the nominal appreciation because inflation in Thailand was higher than in Japan. This situation contrasted with the situation from 1991 to 1994 when the yen appreciated against both the dollar and the baht. In the early 1990s, Thailand could have increased its competitiveness even more if it had been able to keep domestic inflation below the inflation rate in Japan.

From 1984 to 1988 and from 1991 to 1995 the real exchange rate of the baht depreciated against Thailand's six major trading partners (Figure 8.6). Despite huge international reserves, the Bank of Thailand hesitated to let the baht appreciate against the major currencies. Only when the U.S. dollar rose against the yen in 1995 did it permit the effective exchange rate of the baht to appreciate. Because the BOT did not allow the nominal exchange rate to appreciate when the balance of payments was in surplus in 1993–95, the burden of adjustment fell on the price of non-traded goods, which had to rise. As a result, Thailand's traded goods sector lost competitiveness and the current account deteriorated, as the price of non-traded goods rose faster than the price of traded goods, attracting resources to the non-traded goods sector.

FIGURE 8.6
Real Exchange Rate
1990 =100

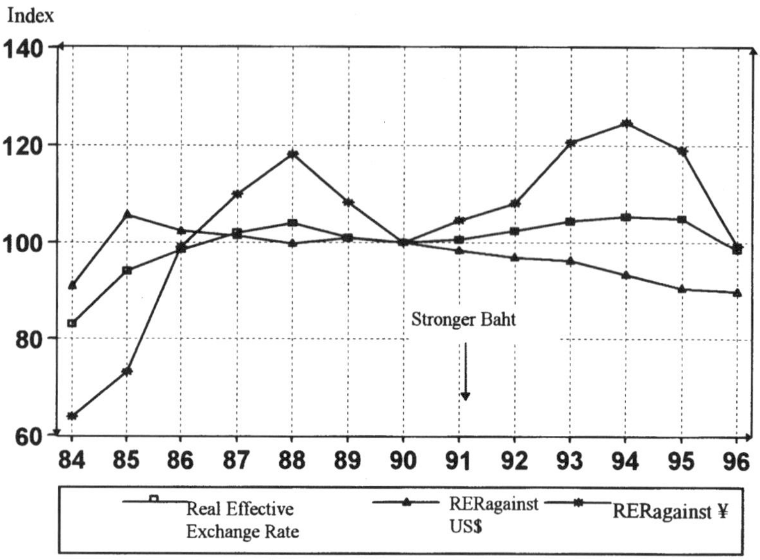

Source: Bank of Thailand.

Interdependence of Capital Flows and Macro Policy Targets

A current account deficit induces capital inflows, but also capital inflows lead to a current account deficit. Liberalization of Thailand's capital account, by permitting the inflow of foreign capital, played a role in the deteriorating current account balance. The newly liberalized inflow of foreign capital reduced liquidity constraints on Thai investors and consumers. Over lending by commercial banks led to over spending and to a fall in household savings. The ratio of household savings to disposable income declined rapidly over the past five years. Although investment remained buoyant, the decline in the private saving ratio caused the investment-savings gap to widen and this gap had to be financed by foreign savings. Thus, because the capital inflows relaxed liquidity constraints they induced a decline in household savings that resulted in the deterioration in the current account balance.

This effect of capital inflows on the current account balance can be identified statistically by means of a Granger Causality Test. A test of the relationships among several macroeconomic variables indicates that economic growth, inflation, and the current account deficit "Granger-cause" capital inflows in Thailand (Table 8.3)[2]. But according to the test, the relationships are bi-directional—that is, capital inflow (CAP) also "Granger-causes" the current account deficit (CA), inflation (CPI), and economic growth (GDP). This means, for example, that the government may be able improve the current account deficit and lower the inflation rate by controlling capital inflows, but it may sacrifice high economic growth. According to Obstfeld (1986), such mutual inconsistency of macroeconomic policy objectives provides a fertile breeding ground for speculative attacks and financial crisis when some economic fundamentals fail to meet expectations.

TABLE 8.3
Granger Causality Test on Capital Flows and Macroeconomic Variables

	Minimum FPE Value	Result
FPE CAP(6)	3.68E+08	FPE CAP(6) > FPE CAP, CA(6,5)
FPE CAP, CA(6,5)	3.07E+08	CA Causes CAP
FPE CA(12)	1.23E+08	FPE CA(12) > FPE CA, CAP(12,12)
FPE CA, CAP(12,12)	9.34E+07	CAP Causes CA
FPE CAP(6)	3.68E+08	FPE CAP(6) > FPE CAP, CPI(6,3)
FPE CAP, CPI(6,3)	3.63E+08	CPI Causes CAP
FPE CPI(16)	6.35E–01	FPE CPI(16) > FPE CPI, CAP(16,6)
FPE CPI, CAP(16,6)	5.28E–01	CAP Causes CPI
FPE CAP(6)	3.68E+08	FPE CAP(6) > FPE CAP, GDP(6,12)
FPE CAP, GDP(6,12)	2.31E+08	GDP Causes CAP
FPE GDP(8)	4.93E+08	FPE GDP(6) > FPE GDP ,CAP(8,14)
FPE GDP, CAP(8,14)	3.40E+08	CAP Causes GDP
FPE CPI(16)	6.35E–01	FPE CPI(16) > FPE CPI,MB(16,12)
FPE CPI,MB(16,12)	3.82E–01	MB Causes CPI
FPE MB(8)	3.77E+07	FPE MB(8) > FPE MB,CPI(8,14)
FPE MB,CPI(8,14)	3.75E+07	CPI Causes MB

Notes: Granger causality test based on FPE criterion. All variables are expressed as logarithmic form of first differences to remove nonstationary components of each series.
CAP = Net Total Private Capital Flows
CA = Current Account
CPI = Consumer Price Index (1990=100)
GDP = Gross Domestic Product
MB = Monetary Base
FPE X (m) = [(T+m+1)/(T-m-1)] * [RSS/T]
FPE X,Y (m,n) = [(T+m+n+1)/(T-m-n-1)] * [RSS/T] where T = Number of observations
RSS = Sum of Square Residuals

The Granger Causality analysis also suggests that the growth rate of the monetary base (MB) and the inflation rate (CPI) are simultaneously determined (Table 8.3). Thus, if capital flows could be controlled effectively, the monetary base might be a good intermediate target for monetary policy, since the monetary base "Granger-causes" inflation. The sources of the monetary base are net foreign assets (which cannot be controlled under the rather fixed exchange rate regime) and central bank claims over the government and financial institutions. Under certain circumstances, the Bank of Thailand could influence the monetary base by altering the credit to government and commercial banks. By restraining the central bank's lending to the private sector, as well as by adopting strict fiscal policy, the government could reduce the adverse impact of capital flows on liquidity.

THAILAND'S OPTIMAL POLICY MIX

Fiscal Policy Response

As long as the nominal exchange rate remains unchanged, conservative fiscal policy plays an important role in relieving the pressure from capital inflows. Fiscal discipline requires that the government budget is balanced on an *ex ante* basis. In addition, institutional factors such as the Budget Law are also important to maintain discipline. The Budget Law states that the government cannot run a budget deficit larger than 20 percent of anticipated revenue. The law effectively sets an upper limit on public spending. While the ratio of public revenues to GDP has been rising over the years because of more effective tax collections and widening tax bases, the share of public spending in GDP has not always moved in a pro-cyclical manner (Figure 8.7).

Thailand's fiscal discipline has been demonstrated by the flexibility of public expenditure. In fact, the 1988 turning point from a deficit to a surplus budget was the result of a cut in military spending and public investment programmes. However, during the ensuing period of economic prosperity and large accumulated cash balances, the government seems to have found it difficult to resist spending requests from the unscrupulous politicians who happened to be in power, and the share of government spending in GDP began rising once again in 1991. It should be noted that although the planned budget must be balanced, the actual budget can be in surplus—because actual tax revenue is pro-cyclical, while actual public spending is always below the planned level. During economic booms, tax

FIGURE 8.7
Trend in Government Revenues and Expenditures as a Share of GDP

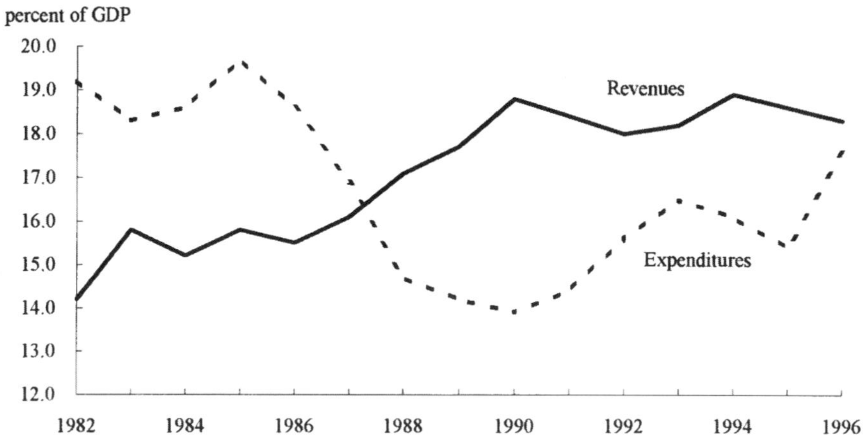

Source: Bank of Thailand, *Monthly Bulletin*.

revenues rise and the budget goes into unplanned surplus, while during economic slumps, tax revenues fall below target producing a larger-than-planned deficit or smaller-than-planned surplus. The importance of this automatic stabilising feature of the Thai fiscal system should not be underestimated (Warr and Nidhiprabha 1996). To some extent, this feature insulates the Thai economy from external shocks.

The 1996 slowdown in economic growth caused a decline in revenues to finance the current budget of 984 billion baht. In January 1997 the government announced budget cuts of 100 billion baht over the next two fiscal years, a reduction of five percent from the planned budget. The budget cuts focused on expenditures with low priority and ones that require substantial foreign borrowing. Large public expenditures for construction of a second international airport were delayed; Thai International Airline's plan for purchasing 21 new aircraft was replaced by a leasing arrangement. This reduction in public spending was intended to reduce the price of non-traded goods relative to traded goods, thereby depreciating the real exchange rate to restore Thailand's international competitiveness.

A surplus in the government budget is one ingredient of an optimal policy package to cope with the impact of the large capital inflows into

Thailand. But depending on the budget surplus is not as feasible during an economic downturn. Since a cut in public spending on productive programmes can be harmful to long-run growth, only unproductive spending should be curtailed. Hence, Thailand cannot rely solely on tight fiscal policy and that is why adjustment in exchange rate policy was also required.

Exchange Rate Policy

The real exchange rate rule suggests that a country should automatically depreciate its currency in line with inflation differentials in order to maintain external competitiveness. As Aghevli al. (1991) pointed out, persistently maintaining a real exchange rate target can be destabilising if the equilibrium real exchange rate is changing. Thailand steadfastly resisted altering the baht-dollar exchange rate from 1987 until 1997. The motivation for this policy of maintaining exchange rate stability was to provide a strong anchor for price stability. Empirical evidence from developing countries supports the hypothesis that exchange rate volatility causes inflation variability (Bahmani-Oskooee 1991). Fluctuations in the inflation rate create risk and uncertainty. Since unanticipated inflation has a social welfare cost, exchange rate stability reduces this cost by reducing the prediction errors of the inflation rate. Furthermore, exchange rate volatility can create uncertainty and have a significant negative impact on exports (Holly 1995). Thus, it is hard to deny the contribution of the stable baht-dollar exchange rate to the favourable trade and investment environment in Thailand over the past decade.

The Bank of Thailand has employed a basket of currencies to set the mid-exchange rate, or the price of the dollar in terms of baht. Since the U.S. dollar carries the greatest weight in the basket, the movement of the baht-dollar rate is negatively related to the strength of the dollar against other major currencies. The appreciation of the yen against the dollar in early 1995 caused appreciation of the baht against the dollar, while the baht also depreciated against the yen, albeit by a smaller percentage than the dollar depreciated against the yen (Figure 8.8). The situation reversed since the summer of 1995 when appreciation of the dollar against the yen induced appreciation of the baht against the yen. The resulting appreciation of the baht's effective exchange rate in part explains the sharp slowdown in export growth that cannot be accounted for by robust economic growth in the industrial countries (Figure 8.9).

Anticipated appreciation of the dollar gave rise to speculation. Since June 1996, several large U.S. banks operating in Singapore took short

FIGURE 8.8
Nominal Exchange Rate

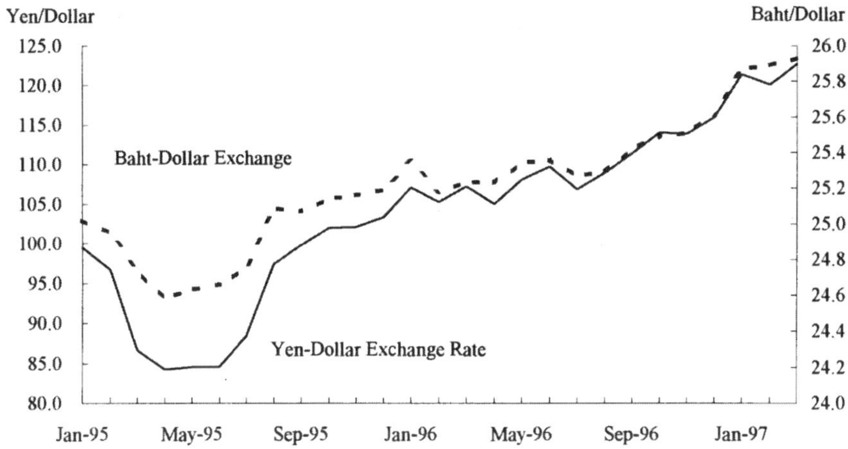

Source: IMF, *International Financial Statistics.*

FIGURE 8.9
Growth of Thailand's Exports and the World Economy

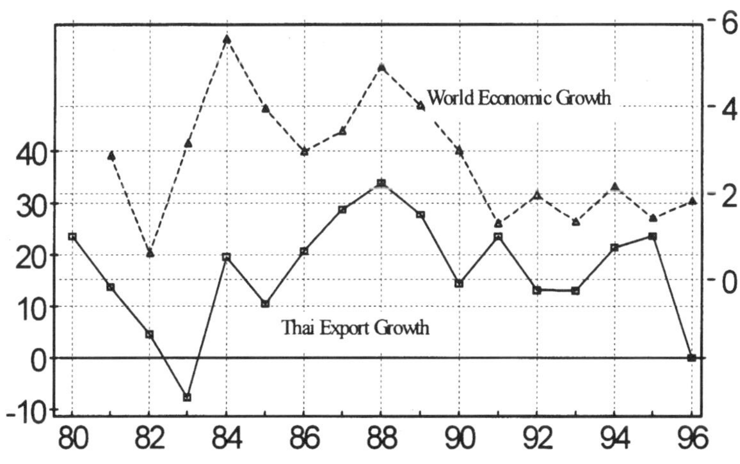

Note: World economic growth is approximated by the average of the growth rates of the United States and Japan.
Source: Bank of Thailand.

positions on the baht, while some Thai large corporations began to keep foreign assets offshore. This speculation and natural hedging pushed the forward premium upward.

A speculative attack on the baht took place on 29 July 1996 following a rumour in Hong Kong's financial markets that the Bank of Thailand was about to devalue the baht. Devaluation was deemed necessary for Thailand to resolve its deteriorating current account deficit and poor export performance. Foreign investors started selling baht for dollars, causing a serious liquidity shortage in the domestic money market. The interbank rate rose to 25 percent (Figure 8.10) as some commercial banks were trying to borrow from the money markets to purchase the dollar. The interbank rate reached its highest level since January 1995. The one-month forward premium went up from 5 satang (5/100 of a baht) per dollar to 18 satang/dollar on 31 July 1996.

To counter the speculators, the Bank of Thailand took the unprecedented step of intervening in Singapore and Hong Kong by selling dollars in the forward markets where some commercial banks were speculating on the baht/dollar exchange rate by dumping baht for dollars. On 1 August

FIGURE 8.10
Interbank Rate and 1-Month Forward Premium

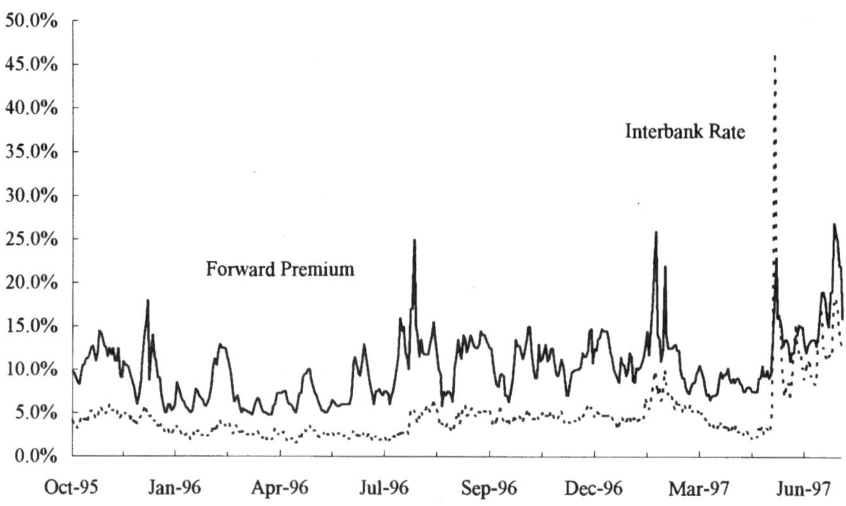

Source: Bank of Thailand.

1996 alone, the BOT is reported to have spent half a billion U.S. dollars from its international reserves to defend the baht. The forward premium declined sharply by 5 satang in one day. Hedge funds and asset allocation managers in Hong Kong suffered substantial losses after the counterattack by the BOT on their home turf. At the same time, the dollar depreciated against the yen and the mark, resulting in the appreciation of the baht against the dollar. In addition, the BOT also intervened in the domestic money market, injecting liquidity by purchasing bonds in the repurchase market to bring down the interbank rate. The intervention seemed to pacify market sentiment. Market participants perceived that if the BOT were planning to devalue the baht it would not favour speculators by cheapening the cost of speculation. Confidence in the baht was restored because of the swift and massive intervention in offshore markets where daily transactions tripled the size of domestic foreign transactions.

At the same time that the BOT was intervening to defend the exchange rate, it also changed the rules determining the target for exchange rate stability. Since the beginning of 1995 the BOT secretly reduced the weight of the dollar in the basket. This move ran counter to the practice following the 1984 devaluation through 1994. According to Warr and Nidhiprabha (1996), the weight of the dollar in the basket increased until the end of 1994, producing the remarkable stability of the baht-dollar exchange rate.

For the sake of international competitiveness, the Bank of Thailand prefers a weak baht-dollar exchange rate, but devaluation is a painful option for Thailand. Notwithstanding the political consequences, devaluation would severely affect Thai corporations with large dollar liabilities. Furthermore, devaluation could trigger another round of financial crisis, since Thai financial institutions have substantial dollar-denominated debt. It appears that the BOT chose to adjust the weight in the basket as an alternative to these consequences of devaluation. Adjustment of the weights has the advantage that, unlike devaluation, it has no announcement effect that might shake public confidence in the value of the baht.

Not every country can be immune to speculation on foreign exchange markets. In an attempt to discourage speculation, the Bank of Thailand prefers to keep the interbank interest rate high during when the dollar is appreciating against the yen. It can refrain from injecting liquidity through the repurchase market when it expects the dollar to appreciate. The interest rate thus bears the burden of adjustment to capital outflows and speculative attacks. Nevertheless, if the BOT kept the interbank rate high over the long run it would find it impossible to stimulate the economy, since the minimum lending rate is also dictated by short-term interest rates.

Monetary Policy Response

Thailand introduced a series of capital control relaxation measures after the establishment of the BIBF in 1993. Individuals were allowed to open foreign exchange accounts up to $500,000 and corporations to open accounts up to $2 million. Gradual steps were made to ease the restrictions on foreign capital outflows such as the elimination of the approval from the Bank of Thailand for repatriation of investment funds. Since then, there has been no other relaxation of capital controls.

In 1995 in response to the rapid accumulation of foreign short-term debt, the Bank of Thailand reintroduced capital controls. Barriers to capital inflows were created by imposing a cost on borrowers. The minimum size for loans made through the BIBF was raised from $500,000 to $2 million in order to exclude small borrowers from overseas borrowing. In August 1995, commercial banks were required to place at the BOT 7 percent of their non-resident baht deposits with maturity of less than one year. In April 1996, finance companies were required to deposit as reserves at the BOT 7 percent of their short-term baht currency borrowings or deposits from non-residents, including promissory notes, bills of exchange and negotiable certificates of deposit (NCDs). In June 1996, commercial banks, finance companies, and the BIBF were required to deposit at the BOT 7 percent of their new short-term foreign borrowings. This series of regulations served as a uniform tax on short-term capital flows to prevent exogenous excess volatility in financial markets. As a result, capital inflows through non-resident baht accounts declined and there was a sign of lengthening in the maturity of BIBF borrowings (Bank of Thailand 1996).

Thai authorities introduced contractionary monetary policy measures in 1995 to cope with the current account deficit and inflation. The maximum rate of bank credit expansion was set at 24 percent in 1995, and, with the aim of slowing down the overheated economy, maximum credit growth was reduced to 21 percent in 1996. A maximum loan-deposit ratio of 117 was also imposed in 1995. Monetary policy medicine must be strong enough to dampen growth and discourage loan demand. The loan-deposit ratio measure was not sufficiently strong. It could only discourage foreign borrowing by banks that were not able to generate domestic deposits to keep up with their loan growth; it could not deter foreign borrowing among those banks that could attract adequate deposits.

In early 1996 to reduce the current account deficit, the central bank regulated commercial banks' issuing of credit cards, imposing the conditions that new applicants must be at least 20 years of age with a minimum monthly income of 20,000 baht. In addition to this credit control, the Bank of Thailand also employed regulatory measures by limiting bank credit to the real estate sector as well as by raising the minimum capital-risk asset ratio according to the BIS standard. This kind of prudent financial policy was essential to prevent a financial crisis during the downturn in the economy, when non-performing loans and bad debts surfaced.

Sterilization through open market operations is not feasible in Thailand because the supply of government bonds is too limited. In about two years' time, all government bonds would disappear from the market when they had been redeemed at maturity. Although the Bank of Thailand issues its own bonds, their amount is insignificant compared to the size of capital inflows. In addition, as argued by Calvo et al. (1996), sterilization is costly if the interest rate on domestic bonds is higher than the rate foreign exchange reserves could earn in the international money market. Sterilization will remain an excessively costly means to insulate the monetary base from capital inflows as long as the 30-year U.S Treasury bond yield is below 7 percent and the interest rate on fixed deposits in Thailand is above 10 percent. Furthermore, sterilization can only work in the short run. In the long run, any remaining interest rate differential would attract additional capital inflows, unless capital controls were completely effective.

The forward premium on foreign exchange can also be an important insulating mechanism against the destabilizing effects of capital inflows. The forward rate adjusts up and down according to news or rumours of baht devaluation, but it also changes in response to changes in interest rate differentials. When the federal funds rate is adjusted downward, enlarging the interest rate gap, the forward premium tends to rise as predicted by the interest rate parity theorem. The rising implied interest rate, or the cost of forward-covered foreign borrowings, helps deter capital inflows, which would be larger in the absence of upward adjustment in the forward premium rate.

Thailand's tight monetary policy and control of capital inflows brought about a slowdown in economic activity in 1996. The growth rate of bank credit declined sharply on a year-over-year basis in both 1995 and 1996 (Figure 8.11). The investment index and the manufacturing production index continued their declining trend into 1997. Judged by the decline in the non-food inflation rate, the policy relieved the pressure from the over heated economy.

FIGURE 8.11
Change in Manufacturing Production, Private Investment, and Bank Credit
Year-over-Year Percent Change

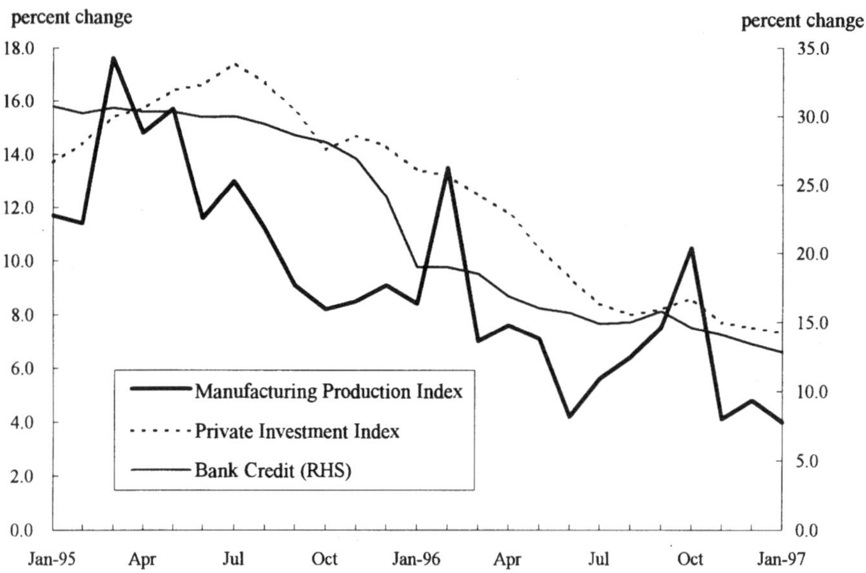

Source: Bank of Thailand.

On the whole, Thailand succeeded in keeping the money supply under control. Capital inflows to Thailand led to accumulation of international reserves, since the Bank of Thailand did not allow the baht to appreciate against the U.S. dollar. The BOT's purchases of dollars to maintain the exchange rate brought about increases in the monetary base. On the other hand, net foreign assets (NFA) of the BOT accumulated over the years as a result of the continued surplus in the balance of payments (Figure 8.12). Nevertheless, the monetary base increased more slowly than international reserves. This is explained by the fact that public debt held by the BOT was declining. The government budget surplus meant that net claims on government (NCG) by the BOT declined, offsetting the rise in NFA, producing a smoother rise in the monetary base. The other source of the monetary base stems from the need for the BOT to provide liquidity to financial institutions. When there is no financial distress, claims on financial institutions (CF) remain stable and do not excessively expand the monetary base.

FIGURE 8.12
Monetary Base and its Components

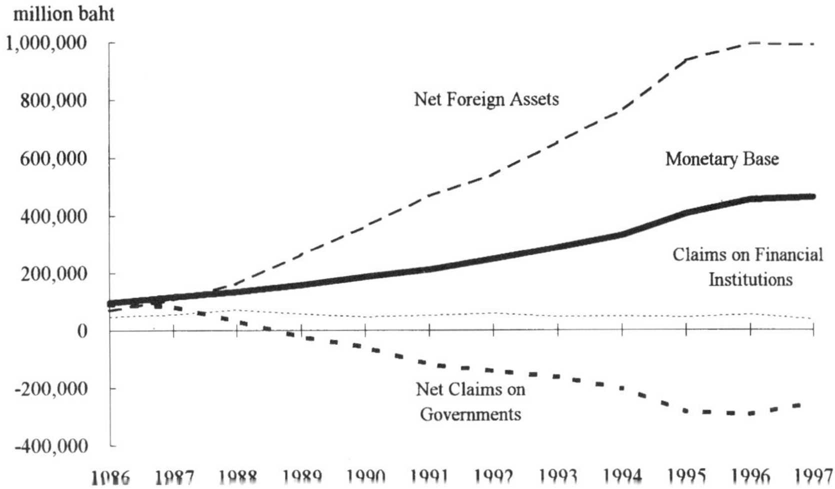

Source: Bank of Thailand, *Monthly Bulletin*.

CONCLUDING REMARKS

A surge in capital inflows into Thailand began in the late 1980s and continued unabated until 1996. The flows brought high economic growth and a surplus in the balance of payments. The rise in capital inflows stemmed from external and internal factors. A decline in world interest rates widened the interest rate differentials, inducing excessive foreign borrowings. Also, domestic financial liberalization increased the sensitivity of capital flows to the interest rate differential. High economic growth in Thailand in the early 1990s also contributed to the surge in capital inflows. Finally, the measures undertaken to establish Thailand as a regional financial centre induced short-term capital flows through offshore borrowings by the nonbank private sector.

The surge in capital inflows caused a Thai case of the so-called "Dutch disease", which results in the appreciation of the real exchange rate and a consequent reduction in external competitiveness. In the Dutch disease, the current account deficit worsens since the price of non-traded goods rises faster than that of traded goods. Moreover, capital inflows relax liquidity constraints and stimulate over lending by commercial banks, resulting in a decline in the private savings rate. Although capital flows contributed to Thailand's high economic growth rate, they also put upward pressure on the domestic price level. Consequently, by 1995 the Thai economy was characterized as overheated.

There was a considerable time lag between the emergence of the need for restrictive policy measures and the recognition of that need on the part of Thai authorities. By 1995 the Bank of Thailand realized the damaging effects of excessive capital flows on macroeconomic stability and responded by introducing capital control measures and by embarking on restrictive monetary policy. However, monetary policy takes time before its impact is transmitted to the real sector. By mid 1996, when the credit crunch had slowed down domestic economic activity, world trade had also declined, resulting in a dismal performance of Thai exports. This export shortfall had not been anticipated by the BOT in 1995 when it formulated the contractionary monetary policy. As a result, the real GDP growth of 6.7 percent for 1996 was far below any expectation.

Thailand's adherence to strict fiscal discipline mitigated the adverse consequences of the surging capital inflows by reducing the growth of the monetary base. Exchange rate stability was maintained to preserve price stability and to uphold confidence in the baht. Since the exchange rate could not be utilized as a policy instrument, the burden of adjustment fell upon capital controls and the mixture of fiscal and monetary policies, which provided a soft-landing in 1996. The slowdown in the Thai economy was hardly anticipated, but it seems that the below-trend real GDP growth path was necessary to bring about stability in the future.

Changing external factors made the management of the stabilization policy more difficult. The slowdown in world trade and poor export performance, the volatility of the yen-dollar exchange rate, the Bank of Thailand's attempt to bail out ailing financial institutions, and the oversupply in the real estate sector were some of the difficulties encountered by Thai economic managers in 1996. Some of these factors remained as a threat in 1997 and they may further complicate the management of capital inflows in the years to come.

Notes

[1] The inflation rate remained high in 1996 despite the sluggish economy largely because of two years of floods. Flood-caused crop damage pushed the food component of the CPI to 8.1 percent in 1995 and to 8.7 percent in 1996. This cost-push inflation intensified the contractionary

effects of monetary policy, leading to a slowdown in private investment and manufacturing production. The low inflation rate in 1993 had been due mainly to weak pressure from food prices which rose only 2.2 percent that year. The weight of food items in the CPI is 39 percent, which explains why exogenous factors such as weather conditions can complicate stabilization policy.

[2] When distributed lag values of certain variable (X) can improve the forecast of another variable (Y) made by its own distributed lag values, that contributing variable (X) is said to "Granger-cause" the variable in question (Y). The Granger causality test does not have the same interpretation as the usual sense of a cause-effect relationship. However, since effects cannot occur before causes, the Granger causality test provides some other seemingly unrelated variables.

References

Aghevli, B.B., M.S. Khan, and P.J. Montiel. 1991. *Exchange rate policy in developing countries: Some analytical issues*. International Monetary Fund Occasional Paper, No. 78 (March).

Bahmani-Oskooee. M. 1991. "Effect of exchange rate variability on inflation variability". *World Development* 19(6).

Bank of Thailand. 1996. "Analysing Thailand's short-term debt. Bank of Thailand". *Economic Focus*.

Calvo, G. A., L. Leiderman and C. M. Reinhart. 1996. "Inflows of capital to developing countries in the 1990s". *Journal of Economic Perspectives* 10(2): 123–39.

Corbo, Vittoro and L. Hernandez. 1996. "Macroeconomic adjustment to capital inflows: Lessons from recent Latin American and East Asian experience". The World Bank *Research Observer* 11(1): 61–85.

Claessens, S., M. P. Doolcy, and A. Warner. 1995. "Portfolio capital flows: Hot or cold?" The World Bank *Economic Review* 9(1): 153–74.

Grilli, Vittorio and Gian Maria Milesi-Ferretti. 1995. "Economic effects and structural determinants of capital controls". International Monetary Fund *Staff Papers* 42(3): 517–551.

Holly, Sean. 1996. "Exchange rate uncertainty and export performance: Supply and demand effects". *Scottish Journal of Political Economy* 42(4): 381–391.

Obstfeld, Maurice. 1986. "Rational and self-fulfilling balance-of-payments crises". *American Economic Review* 76: 72–81.

Spiegel, Mark. M. 1995. "Sterilization of capital flows through the banking sector: Evidence from Asia". Federal Reserve Bank of San Francisco *Economic Review* 5.

Warr, Peter. G. and Bhanupong. Nidhiprabha. 1996. *Thailand's macroeconomic miracle: Stable adjustment and sustained growth.* Washington D.C.: The World Bank and Oxford University Press.

UPDATE

THE 1997 CURRENCY CRISIS IN THAILAND

Since this chapter was written, another round of speculation against the baht occurred in mid May 1997 and the Bank of Thailand (BOT) fought back in both spot and forward markets. The forward premium rate and interbank rate rose sharply (Figure 8.10). In addition, in an effort to prevent further attack from speculators who still held short baht positions, the BOT imposed a ban on offshore baht swap transactions. In effect, it created a two-tier, offshore and onshore, market. On 2 July 1997 because of the excessive cost of defending the existing exchange rate, the BOT finally moved towards a managed float of the baht.

After the de facto floating of the baht, the value of the Thai currency plunged precipitously more than 50 percent. The baht float took place when the credibility of Thai monetary policy was low and the government's economic policy direction seemed to be in disarray. For this reason, the Bank of Thailand had to maintain a high interest rate policy for a considerable period of time to deter currency speculation. In consequence, economic activity slowed substantially, with an enlarging volume of non-performing loans and a concurrent banking crisis. The GDP growth rate declined to 0.6 percent in 1997, a sharp fall from the 6.7 percent registered in 1996. Furthermore, severe contraction in the Thai economy is widely anticipated for 1998. The large amount of foreign private debt and the rising level of non-performing loans of the banking sector have delayed the recovery of the Thai economy. Unless exports respond vigorously to the depreciation, the Thai economy will experience a negative growth rate and rising unemployment for the first time in recent economic history.

In 1997, the unemployment rate was estimated at 3 percent with one million people out of work. The number of unemployed in 1998 is expected to double due to the loss of two million jobs, equivalent to an unemployment rate of 10 percent. It should be recognized that the labor market is quite efficient in terms of the adjustment in real wages, which are declining sharply in all sectors. Real wages have fallen because nominal wages have been cut or frozen, while inflation is expected to be above 10 percent in 1998. The reduction in the real wage rate serves as a correction for the continued rising real wage rate over the last decade, which eroded Thailand's international competitiveness. The reduction in the real wage rate is a key to economic recovery in Thailand.

During the recent bull market, huge inflows of portfolio investment pushed the Thai stock index up by 26 percent in 1992 and by 88 percent in 1993. The continued upward pressure on asset prices in the stock and property markets was sustained by rapid expansion of bank credit and by margin loans made available from financial institutions. When unfavorable news hit the market and rapidly reversed market sentiment, the Thai stock market index declined sharply by 35 percent in 1996 and plunged by a further 56 percent in 1997. As a result, there has been a substantial reduction in the financial wealth of households and corporations. Private consumption spending contracted due to increasing uncertainty and risk as well as the negative wealth effect after the sharp fall in economic activity.

Under the previous exchange rate regime, in which the baht was pegged to a basket of currencies dominated by the U.S. dollar, the Bank of Thailand was unable to employ monetary policy effectively to combat inflation and current account deficits; the capital control liberalization led to large capital inflows and the Bank of Thailand had maintained a rather fixed exchange rate. The extended economic boom in Thailand caused memories of past disastrous over-lending by the banking sector to fade and replaced them with the euphoria of rising per capita income and the strengthening value of the baht. The expectation of extraordinary capital gains from appreciation of asset prices was sustained by excessive credit expansion from the financial sector.

On 21 August 1997 Thailand secured $17.2 billion of rescue funds from the IMF (International Monetary Fund). In return it is obliged to control fiscal spending to produce a budget surplus of at least one percent of GDP for fiscal 1998. The planned 982 billion baht fiscal budget for 1998 has been cut three times, reducing spending to 800 billion baht in order to meet the IMF condition. In addition, the value-added tax rate was increased from 7 to 10 percent in August 1997 to boost tax revenues. Under the IMF-led bailout package, Thailand must maintain a high interest rate policy to curb bank lending. Also, Thailand must overhaul its financial structure by strengthening rules and regulations. Fifty-six ailing finance companies were closed in December 1997 so that there will be no more bailouts of troubled financial institutions.

In the past, the stable exchange rate between the baht and the U.S. dollar kept exchange rate risk low, encouraging both bank and non-bank sectors to borrow from international money markets, especially when excess liquidity brought down world interest rates. Cheap funds obtained in this way were channeled to inefficient industries and speculative ventures. Excess capacity became widespread, particularly in construction-related sectors, which are sensitive to economic cycles. Enormous short-term foreign debts were created by the private sector in Thailand. A large portion of these debts was not covered for foreign exchange risk. The weakening of the baht increased the debt burden of financial institutions as well as corporations. By the end of 1997, the total short-term debt was $39 billion, while total long-term debt amounted to $67.2 billion, including $8.7 billion from the IMF. As of 15 December 1997 Thailand's international reserves registered $26.9 billion, with outstanding forward obligations of $18.7 billion. The forward obligations, undertaken during the defense of the baht before July 1997, last until August 1998. Since Thailand's international reserves were not sufficient to cover its short-term debt, it was imperative that these short-term debts be rolled over to avoid a debt moratorium. Nevertheless, at the end of 1997 international reserves surpassed $23 billion, the target set by the IMF for the release of subsequent loans.

The IMF austerity program failed to restore confidence and induce capital to flow back to Thailand. The value of the currency plunged further during late 1997, increasing the amount of baht needed to repay Thailand's dollar-denominated debt. For every one baht that the exchange rate depreciates Thailand owes an additional one hundred billion baht on its foreign debt. In July, the government had set aside 8.2 billion baht for debt repayment based on the post-float exchange rate of 27 baht to the dollar, but at the year-end exchange rate of 47.5 baht to the dollar the repayment obligation amounted to 14 billion baht. The government can raise some additional revenue by selling its stake in two state enterprises, Thai Airways International and Bangchak Petroleum, which are almost ready for full privatization as required by the IMF. The planned reduction in public spending will not be able to balance the fiscal 1998 budget, since tax revenue shortfalls will occur as a result of the contractionary effect of the budget cuts.

As long as the Asian currency turmoil continues, the contagion effect will produce uncertainty and discourage capital inflows. The Bank of Thailand has admitted that it did not anticipate the slow response of capital inflows after Thailand undertook the IMF stabilization program. Re-capitalization of commercial banks must rely on foreign investors. Several plans for foreign share participation in troubled banks did not materialize due to the continued weakening of the baht. Raising capital in local markets has been even more difficult since liquidity has been declining.

By January 1998, the interbank rate stood at 20 percent, indicating a very severe credit crunch. The Bank of Thailand has taken over some ailing banks after writing off their bad debts. Loans from the Financial Institutions Development Fund to these technically bankrupt institutions were swapped into equity. These banks' problems stemmed from enormous substandard loans and substantial dollar-denominated debts.

Floating the baht during the period of foreign debt overhang compounded Thailand's deflationary problem. Furthermore, large corporations which needed dollars to settle their short-term debts started hoarding dollars in anticipation of further weakening of the baht. As a result, both the spot rate and the forward premium were rising rapidly. The exchange rate passed the 50 baht per dollar level during the won and rupiah crises in late 1997. Because of contagion from these crises, the value of the baht depreciated to 55 baht per dollar at the end of January 1998. Thailand employed a two-tier exchange rate system to make it difficult for offshore currency players to short the baht forward. There was some discrepancy between the offshore and onshore rates of exchange, although in general the two rates tended to converge. Abolishment of the two-tier system was delayed until the end of January 1998 out of fear that the baht might plunge further, causing a vicious circle of depreciation and debt-deflation. In addition, policy credibility would be in jeopardy once again if foreign exchange controls had to be re-invoked.

It should be noted that the trade balance has responded favorably to the exchange rate adjustments. In the second quarter of 1997, before the July floating of the baht, Thailand experienced a large current account deficit. By the fourth quarter of 1997, the current account was in surplus. The turnaround of the current account, which began in September 1997, can be attributed to the sharp decline in the value of the baht and the sharp contraction in economic activity. The government and the private sector anticipate that Thailand will experience a current account surplus of at least $4 billion in 1998. While the current account deficit in 1997 was about 4 percent of GDP, the inflation rate was contained at 6 percent. The low rate of inflation rate was due to the fact that tight monetary policy in the first half of the year caused inflation to decline. Nevertheless, the impact of currency depreciation on the domestic price level will be more pronounced in 1998 when all price ceilings are adjusted upward to prevent commodity shortages. The fact that inflation in Thailand has an upward rising trend leads to an anticipation that the baht exchange rate will not rebound above the 40 baht per dollar level. Nevertheless, these cost-push factors will be partially offset by the weakening wage pressure due to a growing pool of unemployed.

Lessons from the Currency Crisis

Thailand's experience of currency crisis shows that capital inflows can have both positive and negative impacts. Thailand should have allowed the baht to appreciate during the boom years and should have been satisfied with a lower growth rate. Even if appreciating currency discourages exports, it is better to live with the resulting lower output growth rate and lower level of foreign debt. In addition, capital control relaxation undertaken when bank supervision and financial regulations are not sufficiently stringent can lead to over-borrowing and inefficient lending. A gradual approach to capital account liberalization should be adopted instead. Furthermore, since international capital flows are many times larger than international trade flows, when a country relies too heavily on short-term foreign debt to finance a current account deficit, it is impossible for the central bank to defend a fixed exchange rate for very long—let alone to inflict wounds on currency speculators. Thailand also learned that accountability should be well established so that the central bank is not tempted to engage in behavior that is akin to gambling in order to get out of a crisis.

January 1998

9

Coping with Capital Flows and the Role of Monetary Policy: The Malaysian Experience, 1990–95[1]

Ong Hong Cheong

CAPITAL FLOWS IN THE 1990S

Slow growth and a decline in interest rates in industrialized countries provided the impetus for an unprecedented surge in capital flows to developing countries and economies in transition from 1990 to 1995. As a small open economy with a track record of strong economic growth and low domestic price inflation, Malaysia was seen as having exceptionally favourable circumstances and consequently was able to attract about 3.5 percent or US$35.6 billion of the aggregate net resource flows to developing countries and economies in transition from 1990 to 1995. Average annual net capital inflows to Malaysia amounted to US$5.9 billion, equivalent to 9.6 percent of GDP (Table 9.1).

There were powerful exogenous, or push, factors for the surge of capital flows to Malaysia. They included less than buoyant growth potential in industrial countries, the cyclical decline in international interest rates, and pressures to seek higher investment income fuelled by the portfolio diversification risk strategy of institutional investors.

Pull factors were equally strong because Malaysia's sound economic fundamentals and growth potential were strengthened by its political stability, business-friendly government, attractive investment policies, adequate infrastructure, booming stock market, high interest rates, and expectations of a ringgit appreciation.

As a developing country, Malaysia has traditionally relied on external finance for its economic development programme. A closer scrutiny of the

TABLE 9.1
Cumulative and Average Annual Capital Inflows, 1990–95

	Cumulative US$ billions	Annual Avg. US$ billions	Annual Avg./GDP %
Current Account Balance	22.5	3.7	6.1
Net Capital Inflow	35.6	5.9	9.6
Official Development Finance	0.5	0.1	0.1
Foreign Direct Investment	25.0	4.2	6.8
Commercial Bank Funds	5.0	0.8	1.4
Cash BOP Reporting System (Cash Basis)			
Net Portfolio Investment (1991–1995)	17.0	3.4	5.1

Source: National Accounts Statistics and Balance of Payments Report, Department of Statistics, Malaysia; Cash BOP Reporting System, Bank Negara Malaysia.

massive inflow of capital during the 1990–95 period reveals a shift in the importance and sources of external finance to Malaysia (Table 9.2). Official development finance declined in importance and foreign direct investment and portfolio equity finance became much more substantial. Commercial bank funds were volatile and foot-loose.

Official Development Finance

During the 1990–95 period, a policy to reduce official foreign loans resulted in gross repayments and prepayments of Malaysian government external debt amounting to US$5.2 billion. This was, however, more than offset by new foreign borrowings of non-financial public enterprises (NFPEs) or state-owned enterprises, resulting in a US$0.5 billion net inflow of official development finance. The NFPE foreign borrowings were for productive investment in large-scale infrastructure projects, transport, telecommunications, energy, oil, and gas. Official development finance averaged 0.1 percent of Malaysia's GDP.

Foreign Direct Investment (FDI)

Over the same period, the cumulative flow of FDI into Malaysia amounted to US$25 billion or an average of 6.8 percent of GDP (Table 9.1). This inflow was more than sufficient to offset the average annual current account deficit in the balance of payments of 6.1 percent of GDP.

The volume of FDI inflows would have been even larger had it not been for a government policy requesting foreign investors to reduce their foreign funding of working capital. Foreign investors were asked to make up the difference from banks in Malaysia.

Commercial Bank Funds

Official data show net inflows of US$5 billion during the 1990–1995 period, based on changes in the short-term external assets and external liabilities of commercial banks operating in Malaysia (Table 9.1). The main components of commercial bank flows were foreign funds held in vostro accounts for non-residents with banks in Malaysia and local funds held in nostro accounts with banking institutions overseas.

The period 1990–1993 witnessed cumulative net inflows amounting to almost US$10 billion, identified as largely foreign borrowings by commercial banks and some repatriation of banks' overseas assets. The following year, 1994, saw net outflows of over US$5 billion. Net commercial bank fund inflows averaged only 1.4 percent of GDP over the years 1990–95 (Table 9.2).

Portfolio Investment

Portfolio investment funds accounted for 88 percent of identified gross capital inflows during the 1991–95 period, as captured on a cash reporting basis by the commercial banking system acting on behalf of the central bank.[2] The magnitude of portfolio investment flows was unprecedented. Over the five years, cumulative inflows amounted to US$221.6 billion compared with cumulative outflows of US$204.6 billion. Portfolio inflows rose from US$7 billion in 1991 to US$67 billion in 1993 and reached an all-time record of US$87 billion in 1994. In 1993 and 1994, the portfolio investment inflows alone exceeded GDP in current market prices. In other words, liquidity from gross portfolio fund inflows was more than

TABLE 9.2
Annual Capital Inflows by Major Category, 1989–95

	1989	1990	1991	1992	1993	1994	1995
				US$ billions			
GDP	37.9	42.8	47.7	57.6	61.0	68.9	87.2
Net Capital Inflow	1.3	1.8	5.6	8.7	10.8	1.3	7.4
				Percent of GDP			
Current Account Balance	0.7	–2.1	–9.0	–3.8	–4.8	–6.3	–8.5
Net Capital Inflow	3.5	4.2	11.9	15.2	16.8	1.6	8.5
Official Development Finance	–2.4	–2.4	–0.5	–1.4	0.6	0.3	2.7
Foreign Direct Investment	4.4	5.4	8.5	9.0	7.8	6.0	4.7
Commercial Bank Funds	1.1	2.0	2.8	6.3	6.6	–7.0	0.1
Portfolio Equity	—	—	–1.5	5.6	14.5	5.7	1.2

Source: National Accounts Statistics and Balance of Payments Report, Department of Statistics, Malaysia; Cash BOP Reporting System, Bank Negara Malaysia.

the value of Malaysia's total annual output of goods and services. Net foreign portfolio equity finance averaged 5.1 percent of GDP.

The massive portfolio fund inflows were for speculative investment purposes. Foreign investors were seeking to maximize capital gains in the booming Malaysian stock market. Their market presence provided the most important push to the Kuala Lumpur Stock Exchange (KLSE) Composite Index, which rose to a record high of 1275 in 1993 from 644 a year earlier. Market capitalization expanded five-fold between 1990 and 1993 to a record of US$230 billion, four times GDP. Three other important motives for the influx of portfolio investment were investors' need to diversify portfolio risk, expectations of a ringgit appreciation, and Malaysia's absence of a capital gains tax.

Foreign investors probably regarded Malaysia as *the* emerging stock market having the most liberal access policy. Non-residents are free to buy and sell stocks on the local market—with the exception of initial public offerings. The general guideline ceiling of 30 percent foreign ownership of KLSE-listed stocks was not a barrier to portfolio investment by foreigners, because they were interested in portfolio diversification. Surveys conducted among stock market participants in early 1995 identified at least 94 major foreign investment and country funds responsible for the portfolio inflows. Country factors such as economic fundamentals, economic growth potential, and political stability were given greater weight by the investors than market factors which included the availability of a variety of quality stocks, risk-return potential, and market liquidity (Table 9.3). About 60 percent of foreign funds were invested in the Malaysian capital market for six months or longer, while 23 percent were short-term, for less than three months. Foreign funds accounted for nearly one-third of total market transactions in 1994, 27 percent of share units and 31 percent of share value, compared with local funds (24 percent and 23 percent respectively) and local retailers (49 percent and 46 percent respectively).

A study by country of origin indicates that the foreign funds came largely from Singapore (54.8 percent) and Hong Kong (33.2 percent). The United Kingdom supplied 7.5 percent of the foreign funds, the United States 2.1 percent, and other countries 2.4 percent. But the fact that Singapore and Hong Kong are established off-shore financial centres suggests that the ultimate origin of the foreign funds entering Malaysia was likely mutual funds, pension funds, and insurance funds in industrialized countries such as the United States, the United Kingdom, and Japan which were experiencing low interest rates and less buoyant growth.

TABLE 9.3
Factors Influencing Foreign Fund Investments
Descending order of importance

Factor Type	Factor Score	Mean Importance
Economic fundamentals	Country	4.72
Economic growth potential	Country	4.72
Political stability	Country	4.51
Variety of quality stocks	Market	4.28
Return-risk potential	Market	4.16
Market liquidity	Market	4.14
Market regulation	Country	4.04
Local interest rate	Country	4.00
Foreign exchange regulation	Country	4.00
Quality of market research	Market	3.98
Price-earnings ratio of stocks	Market	3.97
Foreign exchange risk	Country	3.95
Market capitalization	Market	3.93
Adequacy of company disclosure in annual reports	Market	3.79
Variety of financial instruments	Market	3.77
Trading settlement system	Market	3.77
Timeliness of company announcements	Market	3.75
Transaction costs	Market	3.54
Introduction of financial futures & options	Market	3.44
Companies' divided policy	Market	3.09

Source: Kok Kim Lian and Mansor Md. Isa, "Why Foreign Funds Come to KLSE". *Investors Digest*, July 1996.

MONETARY POLICY AGAINST CAPITAL INFLOWS

The Malaysian economy emerged unscathed from this period of massive investment and speculative capital inflows primarily because the central bank took very strong and decisive monetary measures to mop up the excess liquidity in the banking system.[3] Over the 1990–95 period, real economic growth was sustained at a high level, between 7.8 percent and 9.7 percent, with average annual domestic price inflation held to about 3.8 percent (Table 9.4).

Malaysia has always welcomed foreign capital flows for productive investment. The optimum volume of foreign capital inflows would be sufficient to at least meet the annual savings-investment gap conveniently measured by the balance of payments current account deficit and not so large as to destabilize monetary conditions. It is the conviction of the monetary authorities that a stable monetary environment is essential for business and for steady economic growth, and the central bank has the mandated responsibility to promote monetary stability.

Consequently, during the 1990–95 period there were serious concerns over monetary instability, inflationary price pressure, asset price inflation, and the further overheating of the economy in addition to the problem of the sizeable balance of payments current account deficit. The major concern, which became a crisis-management issue for the central bank, was how to sterilize the highly destabilizing excess liquidity arising from the massive and largely unwanted short-term capital inflows—the speculative foreign portfolio funds and short-term funds coming through the vostro accounts of banks in Malaysia.

In pursuit of price stability, the central bank closely monitors changes in money supply, credit policy, the CPI, and the level of excess liquidity in the banking system for any change in monetary policy. Among these indicators, monthly data on the growth of the monetary aggregates, M1, M2, and M3, provide the most convenient and useful intermediate macroeconomic targets.

TABLE 9.4
Capital Flows and Selected Macroeconomic Indicators, 1990–95

	1989	1990	1991	1992	1993	1994	1995
Real GDP (% Growth)	9.2	9.7	8.7	7.8	8.3	9.2	9.5
M3 Monetary Aggregate (% growth)	20.6	18.2	15.3	19.6	23.5	13.1	22.3
Consumer Price Index (% growth)	2.8	3.1	4.4	4.7	3.6	3.7	3.4
BOP Current Account (% GNP)	0.7	–2.2	–9.4	–4.1	–5.1	–6.7	–9.0
Capital Account (US$ billions)							
Annual Inflow (net)	1.3	1.8	5.6	8.7	10.8	1.3	7.4
External Reserves (central bank)							
Annual Charge (US$ billions)	1.3	2.0	1.1	6.9	10.2	–1.6	–1.6
Ringgit Exchange Rate							
(BNM Composite Index)							
Annual Change (%)	3.8	–5.8	–2.9	5.6	–5.2	1.2	0.4
Ringgit/US$							
Annual Change (%)	0.1	...	–0.1	0.4	–3.5	5.3	0.1

Source: Central Bank of Malaysia Department of Statistics

Policy Options against Capital Inflows

Early signs of a surge in capital inflows became apparent in 1989 and 1990, prompting the central bank to adopt a contractionary monetary stance and to sterilize the impact of capital inflows. Due to a scarcity of government securities as monetary instruments, the monetary measures implemented in addition to accepting deposits from banks were:

- raising the statutory reserve requirement on bank funds on 16 August 1991 by 1.0 percentage points to 7.5 percent of the eligible liabilities base of banking institutions;
- centralising all government deposits placed with banking institutions with the central bank under the Money Market Operations Account, which provided extra liquidity for the central bank to undertake open market operations; and
- direct borrowing from the interbank money market and locking in the perceived amount of excess liquidity with the sale of longer maturity monetary instruments.

In 1992, apart from increased use of market-based instruments to sterilize the destabilising impact of externally induced liquidity and further raising the statutory reserve requirement to 8.5 percent, two new administrative measures were introduced. First, a swap limit up to 2 million ringgit per customer was imposed on non-trade related swap transactions with non-residents by commercial banks (on the bid side). Second, bank deposits of the Employees Provident Fund (the national social security institution for workers' savings and retirement benefits) amounting to US$2.6 billion were centralized with the Bank Negara Malaysia.

As excess bank liquidity entered its fifth year in 1993, the central bank created additional monetary instruments for mopping up excess liquidity, its own version of Treasury bills called Bank Negara Bills, issued on 10 February and Malaysia Savings Bonds, first issued on 16 February. The issue of Bank Negara bills was necessary because the Ministry of Finance had taken the hard view that managing domestic monetary stability was the sole responsibility of the central bank. In line with the government policy, the Ministry of Finance had not issued any new Treasury bills since 1988.With the Ministry of Finance's commitment to fiscal prudence and fiscal balance, the central bank had to carry the full financial burden alone.

Early in 1994 it became evident that the central bank's open market operations using market-based instruments were inadequate to the task of sterilizing the accelerating volume of portfolio capital inflow. Those flows subsequently proved to be larger than the GDP for the year, as they had in 1993. Furthermore, it was no longer financially feasible for the central bank to continue to bear the huge interest burden of open market operations, estimated at nearly US$1 billion in 1993. Consequently, the central bank looked for strong, innovative administrative measures to reduce excess banking liquidity, to discourage further capital inflows, and to compel unwanted speculative capital outflows. Six new measures were implemented in 1994. They were comprehensive and they closed all the loopholes for foreign speculative investors to acquire higher yielding Malaysian assets in exchange for lower yielding foreign assets. They were also perceived as drastic and a few were highly controversial.

Raising the Statutory Reserve Requirement

Between 3 January and 1 July 1994, the statutory reserve requirement (SRR) on eligible liabilities of banking institutions was raised in three steps to an unprecedented high of 11.5 percent. This was the eighth time the statutory reserve requirement had been revised upwards since 1989. The SRR revisions in 1994 absorbed US$1.9 billion in excess bank liquidity.

Broadening the Eligible Liabilities Base for Banking Institutions

Effective from the base period 13–31 January 1994, all foreign funds sourced abroad and previously "reserve-cost free" were defined as eligible liabilities of banking institutions, including commercial banks, finance companies, and merchant banks. Consequently, such funds became subject to SRR and to liquidity requirements. At the prevailing SRR, compliance with this new definition, meant that 11.5 percent of all foreign funds sourced offshore had to be lodged as non-interest earning deposits at the central bank, thereby raising the cost of speculative capital inflows and reducing the gains from interest rate arbitrage operations.

Limiting Non-trade Related External Liabilities of Banking Institutions

Effective 17 January 1994 a ceiling was placed on the net external liabilities position of each banking institution, after deducting funds that were trade-related or meant for productive investment.

Prohibiting Sale of Short-term Monetary Instruments to Non-residents

Effective 24 January 1994 all residents were prohibited under the Exchange Control Act 1953 from selling short-term monetary instruments to non-residents. These instruments included Bank Negara bills, Treasury bills, short-dated Malaysian government securities, Cagamas (secondary mortgage market) bonds and notes, bankers acceptances, and negotiable instruments of deposit. Private debt securities including commercial paper were added to the prohibited list in February 1994. The aim was to prevent non-residents from using these instruments as deposit substitutes.

Placing Foreign Vostro Accounts with the Central Bank

Effective 2 February 1994 the ringgit funds in non-interest earning vostro accounts maintained by foreigners with commercial banks were placed in a special non-interest bearing account maintained with the central bank. Subsequently, statutory reserve and liquidity requirements were imposed on these funds. The restrictions were later relaxed to allow each bank vostro balances up to a maximum of RM10 million for stock market trading and a maximum of RM1 million for other purposes.

Prohibiting Swap Transactions with Non-residents

Effective 23 February 1994, commercial banks were prohibited from undertaking non-trade related swaps (including overnight swaps) and forward transactions with foreign customers. This new measure was to prevent offshore parties from building up speculative, long forward positions in the ringgit which was widely believed to be undervalued. This measure was lifted on 16 August 1994.

Effectiveness of Monetary Policy Against Capital Flows

Evaluation of the effectiveness of the monetary measures implemented by Bank Negara Malaysia to reduce the destabilizing impact of the inflow of foreign speculative funds over the 1990–95 period raises questions of what type of benchmark criteria are relevant, of identifying cause and effect between monetary measures and domestic and exogenous factors, of identifying the net balance between gains and losses, and of timing. Nevertheless, it is interesting to look at available data to gauge policy effectiveness.

Portfolio Equity Flows

According to the central bank's BOP Cash Reporting System annual data on gross portfolio investment inflows and outflows, none of the monetary measures implemented between 1990 and 1993 was effective in stemming the inflow of speculative funds. Malaysia experienced its greatest gross capital inflows and outflows in 1994 despite the fact the KLSE Composite Index peaked in December 1993. It could be argued that the subsequent huge outflow of speculative funds was due partly to the exceptionally strong monetary measures implemented in early 1994. It is equally plausible, however, to attribute the outflows of capital, to increasingly substantial divestment of Malaysian stocks for profit-taking by foreign investors, consistent with the short time-frame of their investment strategy in emerging stock markets and their search for new investment opportunities elsewhere.

Bank Funds

In 1994 bank funds registered a net outflow of US$5 billion following a cumulative net inflow over the preceding four years of about US$10 billion. There is no question that the administrative monetary measures introduced in early 1994 were primarily responsible for the net outflow of bank funds. These measures met with strong negative response from the market, causing the ringgit to decline by over 3 percent against the U.S. dollar and straining the normally cordial relationship between the central bank and the private banking institutions under its supervision.

It can be argued that the imposition of an SRR of 11.5 percent on vostro accounts constituted a variant of the Tobin tax. The opportunity cost to foreign investors of placing these funds in reserve was approximately 0.7 percent based on the prevailing 3-month interbank offer rate which averaged 5.686 percent in the first quarter of 1994. Thus, the imposition of the reserve requirement on vostro accounts amounted to a de facto 0.7 percent tax on foreign depositors. This measure caused foreign vostro balances to fall from US$3 billion to US$1 billion by mid-May 1994, when the tax was lifted, in part because it was too controversial.

Monetary Stability

Official macroeconomic data for 1990 to 1995 suggest that together the monetary measures—traditional, innovative, and administrative—were successful in removing excess bank liquidity, in inhibiting too rapid growth in domestic demand, and in curbing inflationary pressure. The annual growth rate of the monetary aggregate M3 reached a high of 23.5 percent in 1993 and fell to 13.1 percent in 1994, well below the central bank's target range of 14–15 percent. In addition, the annual CPI increase fell from the 4.4–4.7 percent range in 1991 and 1992 to about 3–5 percent from 1993 to 1995.

Economic Growth

Productive investment was not affected by the monetary measures directed at speculative capital inflows. In fact, real GDP growth, rose from over 8 percent in 1991 and 1992 to above 9 percent in 1994 and 1995. For complex reasons, the current account balance did not show any improvement, with the annual external imbalance fluctuating between 4 and 9.5 percent of GNP. The current account deficit, at 9 percent of GNP, remained an issue of concern in 1995.

Exchange Rate of Ringgit

Based on the Bank Negara Malaysia Composite Index (January 1991=100), there was little change in the ringgit value against the currency basket between end–1990 and 1995. The real effective exchange rate, however, showed a 5 percent appreciation.

Financial Cost of Monetary Measures

The central bank incurred a high cost in managing its tight monetary policy from 1990 to 1995 because it had to absorb large interest payments for accepting deposits and for open market operations. The central bank's financial cost is estimated to have been US$1 billion for 1993, based on reported net operating losses for that year and profits for the previous year. In addition, the 5 percentage point increase in the SRR during this period could imply a total cost of a few billion ringgit in lost earnings for commercial banks. It is debatable whether this cost was borne by depositors, by the banks, or by lenders.

OPTIMAL MIX BETWEEN INTEREST RATE POLICY AND FOREIGN EXCHANGE POLICY

At the World Bank Symposium on Monetary Policy Instruments for Developing Countries held in Washington D.C. in May 1990, Charles

Freedman argued that the term "exchange rate policy" is somewhat slippery because it focuses on the variable rather than on the elements of policy that directly influence the exchange rate, i.e., the choice of an exchange rate system, monetary policy, and intervention policy.

Choice of Exchange Rate System

Following the collapse of the Bretton Woods system of fixed exchange rates in August 1971, the ringgit was floated. First it was pegged to the U.S. dollar and then, from 27 September 1975 it was pegged to a currency basket comprising the currencies of Malaysia's major trading partners. In a stable foreign exchange market, the value of the ringgit measured against the currency composite is deemed the appropriate exchange rate because it is determined by the forces of market demand and supply. This trade-weighted ringgit exchange value or nominal effective exchange rate is viewed as the most important relative price for both exports and imports of goods and services.

Monetary Policy and the Exchange Rate

It is self-evident that the exchange rate of the ringgit and its domestic value, or domestic purchasing power, are two sides of the same coin, one influencing the other. In the legislation establishing the Bank Negara Malaysia in 1959, maintaining the ringgit exchange rate ranked as the first priority of the central bank and monetary stability as the third. Now, however, maintaining monetary stability, i.e., maintaining domestic purchasing power of the ringgit, is given more importance.

The central bank faces a perpetual policy dilemma. A higher or overvalued ringgit will lower imported inflation and help to protect domestic purchasing power, but at the same time it will reduce export competitiveness, a factor of crucial importance to an export-oriented economy. Conversely, an undervalued ringgit will lead to high imported inflation but will strengthen export competitiveness. Allowing the ringgit to appreciate too rapidly could be construed as an act of bad faith by foreign investors who have invested in export-oriented industries. Thus, the conduct of monetary policy calls for striking a fine balance between domestic and external considerations. A tight monetary policy characterized by high interest rates vis-à-vis international interest rates will certainly strengthen the ringgit and conversely an expansionary monetary policy and low interest rates are likely to weaken the ringgit.

Intervention Policy and Equilibrium Ringgit Value

Intervention in the foreign exchange market presupposes some decision regarding an appropriate or "equilibrium" rate for the ringgit. According to a recent statement by the central bank governor "a correct ringgit value should reflect price stability with no abnormal capital outflows". In March 1995, the governor also hinted that an appreciation of the ringgit, then trading at RM2.5353 to the U.S. dollar, would not be adverse. In July 1996, IMF managing director, Michael Camdessus, announced that Malaysia could afford a stronger ringgit, then trading at RM2.4900 to the U.S. dollar.

Repeatedly in its annual reports, the central bank has focused on the virtues of maintaining "orderly market trading" of the ringgit in the foreign exchange market. For example, its 1984 annual report stated:

> As a matter of policy, the Central Bank intervenes in the foreign exchange market only to keep the ringgit floating relatively stable against a composite basket of currencies. The Bank also operates to ensure that conditions in the market are conducive to orderly trading of the ringgit, including the availability of continuous rate quotations. It intervenes only when necessary to avoid expectations of excessive changes in the exchange rate, and to provide the necessary counterpart for the continuous operation of an efficient two-way market. The Bank's policy to intervene has been limited to moderating fluctuations, and it does not intervene to prevent the exchange rate from reflecting the underlying trend in the balance of market supply and demand.

Past experience has shown that supporting an overvalued ringgit is futile and costly, eating into external reserves. In particular, the support given, for political reasons, to the ringgit's overvalued bilateral exchange rate vis-à-vis the Singapore dollar between 1973 and the early 1980s illustrated the futility of this policy stance. Indeed, unlike a policy of overvaluing the ringgit, a policy of undervaluing brings such advantages as export competitiveness and more foreign exchange earnings. However, the central bank has declared that the ringgit is not used a policy instrument to maintain export competitiveness or to help resolve the current account deficit in the balance of payments.

ISSUES AND PROSPECTS

Malaysia's extraordinary experience of annual gross speculative capital inflows exceeding total output over the 1990–95 period has taught some lessons about the efficacy of monetary responses and raised some major new issues as well.

Prospects for More Speculative Capital Inflows

Malaysia can anticipate more speculative capital inflows in the foreseeable future in view of the tremendous and rapidly growing funds of institutional investors in search of higher earnings than found in their home countries. The problem will be exacerbated by the process of globalization of financial markets and by the instantaneous transmission of capital flows facilitated by the new information technology. According to 1995 BIS estimates, the total turnover on foreign exchanges world-wide amounted to US$1.2 trillion a day with less than 4 percent directly related to trade in goods, services, and direct investment.

Contagion Effects of a Mexican-type Crisis

Malaysia is unlikely to suffer serious contagion effects because of its strong economic fundamentals, its high national savings rate of 34 percent of GNP, and the fact that the floating ringgit is not the monetary anchor. Ten months before the Mexican crisis of December 1994, the Malaysian central bank had totally banned foreigners from purchasing Malaysian government securities and other monetary instruments. The contagion effects of the Mexican crisis in Malaysia were minimal because the bulk of speculative capital had flowed out by the third quarter of 1994.

Adequacy of Traditional Monetary Instruments to Cope with Speculative Capital Inflows

One lesson from Malaysia's experience in the period from 1990 to 1995 is that traditional monetary instruments proved inadequate to cope with speculative capital inflows. There was a scarcity of government paper because of a policy of fiscal prudence aimed at budget surplus and the central bank's own market-based instruments were inadequate to cope with the huge problem of sterilization. Furthermore, the central bank found it financially costly to undertake open market operations since it had to bear the interest burden of papers used to siphon off the excess liquidity. It was cheaper and more efficient to repeatedly raise the SRR rather than engage in open market operations. For good measure, in early 1996 the central bank again raised the statutory reserve requirement in two steps to 13.5 percent of eligible liabilities. It has not lifted the requirement for banks to place their vostro account balances with the central bank.

Ethical Questions about Administrative Measures for Sterilization

The administrative measures that Bank Negara Malaysia implemented to mop up excess bank liquidity and contain inflationary pressures raised controversy over their stringency and ethics. Malaysia's experience also raises the ethical question of whether it is right to let a central bank, caught in a situation of unexpected and massive capital inflows, bear the full cost of sterilization, while commercial banks, which are direct beneficiaries of a stable monetary environment, are deemed too important to fail and continue to earn larger profits. Another issue is how the market perceives the credibility of a monetary stabilization programme.

Speculative Attacks on the Ringgit

The ringgit came under short-lived speculative attack in January 1995 following the Mexican crisis, in October 1995, and again in January 1996. Speculation against the ringgit is likely to occur again in the future whenever the market holds a different view about the prevailing exchange value of the ringgit.

Tobin Tax on Capital Flows

The strong negative response to Malaysia's de facto taxing of interest on foreign funds in vostro accounts is instructive. It suggests that proposals for a Tobin tax on speculative capital flows are likely to remain academic.

Regional Co-operation among Central Banks to Cope with Speculative Capital Flows

Since Malaysia's experience with massive speculative capital inflows, regional co-operation among central banks has emerged as a new policy tool. Between 21 October 1995 and 17 January 1996 the central bank of

Malaysia signed bilateral repurchase agreements with Bank Indonesia, the Hong Kong Monetary Authority, Bank of Thailand, and Bangko ng Sentral Pilipinas. These agreements, in the form of memoranda of understanding, enable participating central banks to obtain immediate liquidity from each other through the sale of U.S. government securities.

Development Financing from Foreign Portfolio Equity Investment

Malaysia saw a net inflow of US$17 billion of foreign portfolio equity funds from 1991 to 1995. The role of foreign portfolio equity finance in Malaysian economic development is expected to become increasingly important in the coming years in view of the Malaysian government policy that the private sector is the engine of growth, and the government is actively developing a modern and sophisticated capital market in Malaysia.

Notes

1 Based largely on a paper entitled "Exchange Rate Fluctuations and Macroeconomic Management, 1980–1995" presented at the PEO Specialists Meeting, Osaka, 27–28 September 1996.

2 Detailed information on the monthly gross inflows and outflows identified as portfolio investment is available from 1991 onwards as a result of the timely implementation of the Cash BOP Reporting System by the central bank, Bank Negara Malaysia. This is because the standard balance of payments statistics computed on a transactions basis cannot capture such detailed information.

3 Excess liquidity was defined as liquid assets beyond the mandatory 17 percent of eligible liabilities of banking institutions.

References

Bank Negara Malaysia. *Annual Report*, various years.

Calvo, Guillermo A., Leonardo Leiderman, and Carmen M. Reinhart. 1996. "Inflows of Capital to Developing Countries in the 1990s". *Journal of Economic Perspectives*, Spring.

Cornelius, Peter. 1994. "The Internationalization of Emerging Stock Markets". *Intereconomics*, May/June.

Eggerstedt, Harald and Rebecca Hall. 1995. "Measuring Capital Flight: A Case Study of Mexico". *World Development* 23(2): 211–32.

Glick, Reuven and Ramon Moreno. 1995. "Responses to Capital Inflows in Malaysia and Thailand". Federal Reserve Bank of San Francisco *Weekly Letter*, 17 April.

Frankel, Jeffrey and S. Schmukler. 1996. "Crisis, Contagion and Country Funds: Effects on East Asia and Latin America". Federal Reserve Bank of San Francisco *Working Paper*, September.

IMF/World Bank. 1996. "Operation Flood Control". *The Banker*, October.

Kok Kim Lian and Mansor Isa. 1996. "Why Foreign Funds Come to KLSE". *Investors Digest*, July.

Kulessa, Margareta. 1996. "The Tobin Tax: A Tool for Allocative or Distributional Policies?" *Intereconomics* 31, May/June.

Mansor Isa and, Kok Kim Lian. 1996. "How Foreign Funds Invest their Money". *Investors Digest*, August.

Moreno, Ramon. 1995. "Mexico and the Peso". Federal Reserve Bank of San Francisco *Weekly Letter*, 10 March.

Ministry of Finance, Government of Malaysia. *Economic Report*, various years.

Mobius, Mark. 1995/96. "Risks and Rewards: Explaining Investment in Emerging Markets". *Harvard International Review*, Winter.

Ong Hong Cheong. 1996. "Exchange Rate Fluctuations and Macroeconomic Management, 1980–1995". Paper presented at PEO Specialists Meeting, Osaka, 27–28 Sept.

Schioppa, Tomasso. 1995/96. "Flexible Response: The Evolving Role of Central Banks". *Harvard International Review*, Winter.

Sivalingam, G. 1995. "Why Foreign Funds Stay Away". *Investors Digest*, October.

Spahn, Paul. 1996. "The Tobin Tax and Exchange Rate Stability". *Finance and Development*, June.

World Bank. 1990. *Monetary Policy Instruments for Developing Countries*. World Bank Symposium, Washington D.C., May.

______. 1996. World Debt Tables *External Finance for Developing Countries, 1996*.

Zeti Akhtar Aziz. 1994. "Capital Flows and Monetary Management: The Malaysian Experience". Paper presented at the Eleventh Pacific Basin, Central Bank Conference, Hong Kong, 31 Oct. – 3 Nov.

UPDATE

THE 1997 ASIAN FINANCIAL TURMOIL IN MALAYSIA: ORIGIN, RESPONSE, AND LESSONS

THE FINANCIAL MELTDOWN

The Asian financial turmoil which began with the floating of the Thai baht on 2 July 1997 quickly spread to Malaysia, causing a financial meltdown on a scale that was as catastrophic and frightening as it was unexpected. Initial reactions to news of the Thai baht float were reassuring; any adverse contagion effects on Malaysia would be minimal and temporary, such was the unflagging confidence in the strong Malaysian economic fundamentals and the economy being on track to achieve another robust growth rate of 8 percent in 1997.

The central bank, Bank Negara Malaysia, was quick to intervene in the foreign exchange markets to defend the ringgit against speculative attacks. To punish speculators who were shorting the ringgit, it contracted liquidity on 10 July pushing up the overnight interbank borrowing rate almost six-fold to 40 percent and the three-month KLIBOR rate by 70 basis points to 8.60 percent. But currency speculators and hedge funds in the major foreign exchange markets in London, New York, Hong Kong, and Singapore mounted increasingly larger onslaughts against the ringgit, encouraged by their chartists' analyses of the trend of waves of speculative attacks against the currency. Large foreign banks which had monitored the market movements of the currency speculators and hedge funds joined in the attacks with prospects of huge forex profits.

On 14 July after spending an estimated US$3.5 billion in external reserves, Bank Negara Malaysia ceased intervention. The ringgit was allowed to free-float clean for the first time in twenty-two years, since 27 September 1975 when it was pegged to a currency basket, effectively the U.S. dollar. Bank Negara appeared to be unwilling to commit the rest of its US$24.6 billion in external reserves in the face of a seemingly unlimited supply of offshore ringgit for sale.

At a press conference the next day, when the ringgit had fallen to RM2.5710 against the U.S. dollar, the Malaysian Minister of Finance, Anwar Ibrahim, indicated that the ringgit depreciation was temporary as the currency was not overvalued. He added:

> We certainly have to monitor the market and do whatever we can. But we have to be realistic. The ringgit should be maintained at what we consider as an acceptable level, subject to market forces. . . . Ultimately, what determines the value and strength of the ringgit are the fundamentals.

As early as February 1997 foreign investors had started to move funds out of the Kuala Lumpur Stock Exchange (KLSE) for reinvestment in the United States and the United Kingdom. They were concerned over the increasingly unfavourable risk-return profiles of emerging markets in East Asia—the seeming lack of transparency in regulatory controls, property market bubble, questions of bank solvency, wage inflation, balance of payments current account deficits.

Fresh news of negative sentiments and financial deterioration in neighbouring countries put added selling pressures on the ringgit and the Malaysian stock market. On 30 July, the meltdown of the Malaysian stock market began in earnest in parallel with the ringgit sell-down, one affecting the other.

On 7 January 1998 Bank Negara resumed intervention support for the ringgit in the foreign exchange markets. By then, the ringgit had depreciated by 45 percent against the U.S. dollar and the stock market had shrunk to half its previous worth. The major features of this financial meltdown are shown in Table U9.1.

TABLE U9.1
1997 Financial Meltdown in Malaysia

	31 December 1996 – 2 July 1997	2 July 1997 – 31 December 1997	2 July 1997 – 9 January 1998
Exchange Rate			
Ringgit/US$	–0.2%	–35.4%	–45.2%
Ringgit/Yen	+1.2%	–26.4%	–36.8%
Ringgit/UK	–2.1%	–34.9%	–43.7%
Ringgit/S$	+1.8%	–23.9%	–31.9%
Stock Market			
KLSE Composite Index	–12.4%	–45.2%	–54.7%
Market Capitalization	–9.9%	–49.4%	–57.9%
RM billion	–79.6	–359.6	–421.1
US$ billion	–32.3	–193.0	–220.7
PE Ratio[a]	23.74	10.16	9.0*p*

Notes: [a]The PE ratio was 28.56 at end December 1996.
p = preliminary.

Undoubtedly, among the primary contributors, willing as well as reluctant, to the financial meltdown in Malaysia were:

> Currency speculators and hedge funds in major financial centres aided by modern 24-hour real time global forex trading capability and highly leveraged bank loans;
>
> Large foreign banks which monitored and followed the market movements of their clients, the currency speculators, and hedge funds to make huge forex gains;
>
> Malaysian importers, foreign multinationals in Malaysia, and Malaysian borrowers of U.S. dollars who joined in the frenzied buying of dollars to cover their foreign currency positions that they had not hedged because of the seeming stability offered by the long-standing ringgit-dollar pegged regime;
>
> Foreign fund managers dumping their Malaysian investments to avert both exchange rate and capital losses;
>
> Banks in Malaysia making margin calls;
>
> Retail investors who joined in the panic-selling of Malaysian stock holdings, their irrational exuberance turning into irrational hysteria; and reportedly,
>
> Malaysian corporations and high net-worth individuals rushing to seek safe-haven currencies and deposits offshore.

MEASURES TAKEN TO COPE WITH FINANCIAL TURBULENCE

No one anticipated and no authorities were fully prepared for the ferocity and magnitude of the financial turmoil that engulfed Malaysia and other East Asian countries starting from the floating of the Thai baht.

According to the *Economic Report 1997/1998* issued by the Ministry of Finance, Malaysia, the government had to introduce new measures to boost market confidence. These included:

> Declaring all the 100 component stocks of the KLCI as "designated securities" on 28 August;
>
> Announcing a RM60 billion standby facility to stabilize the stock market;

Deferring all "mega projects" not yet started, such as the Bakun hydroelectric dam, a new airport between Penang and Langkawi, the Kuala Lumpur Linear City, the land bridge at the Thai-Malaysian border, and Phase 2 of the new capitol city of Putra Jaya;

Reducing the balance of payments current account deficit from about 5 percent to 3 percent of GNP;

Revising downwards the 1998 growth rate from 7 percent to 4 to 5 percent, to reduce economic overheating;

Cutting 1998 government spending by 18 percent;

Freezing new share issues and corporate restructuring;

Increasing external reserves to cover four months of retained imports; and

Banning corporate bailouts.

As one way of stabilizing the stock market, corporate buy backs were allowed, effective 1 September 1997. To strengthen both the economy and the banking system, Bank Negara introduced five important precautionary measures:

Limiting non-commercial ringgit swap transactions with foreign bank customers to US$2 million per name per day on 4 August;

Slowing loan growth from 25 percent in 1997 to 15 percent in 1998;

Directing banking institutions to give priority to lending to productive sectors such as manufacturing and to those activities which boost exports and foreign exchange earnings;

Shortening the default period defining non-performing loans from six months to three months; and

Raising the general provision for bad and questionable debts from one percent to 1.5 percent of total loans.

Furthermore, to encourage economic growth, Bank Negara refrained from raising the domestic interest rate to strengthen the ringgit, despite the continuing depreciation of the currency.

At the ASEAN Business Forum held in Kuala Lumpur in early December 1997, Mr. Michel Camdessus, IMF (International Monetary Fund) Managing Director, told ASEAN countries that it was dangerous to always take negative market signals as being wrong and that governments should not subscribe to the denial syndrome. Market signals could help point out where changes in regulation and economic structure would be necessary. He said that in the recent turmoil, investor worries were compounded by a general lack of transparency in Asian economies and that it would be a mistake to blame hedge funds as the central agent of the turmoil in Asia. Camdessus added, "I have never seen speculators act when a macroeconomy is strong and government policies are sound." As parting advice to the Forum, Camdessus offered seven pillars of wisdom:

> Maintain an appropriate exchange rate and exchange rate regime;
>
> Maintain an appropriate interest rate policy;
>
> Increase competition and transparency;
>
> Develop regional surveillance and a "club spirit" to put peer pressure on neighboring countries;
>
> Continue to be "market friendly";
>
> Pay due attention to market signals; and
>
> Pursue further market liberalization.

In early January 1998, the Prime Minister, Mahathir Mohammad, announced the establishment of a National Economic Action Council which is tasked to closely monitor the economy, devise strategies to overcome economic problems, and facilitate growth.

LESSONS TO BE LEARNED

Some tentative conclusions or lessons to be learned are:

> The globalized financial market, harnessing the combined power of currency speculators and hedge funds, has the financial power to discipline countries for perceived mismanagement, but not the moral right. The idea of moral right suggests fairness. The savage impoverishing of the Malaysian economy that resulted from the power of speculators and hedge funds does

not seem fair, and an exchange rate of RM4.7000 to the U.S. dollar is an absurd, gross misalignment.

The power of currency traders and hedge funds apparently derives from their very cozy nexus with large international banks and such power if unfettered by a moral purpose and lacking transparency can be grossly and easily abused.

Perhaps more important than the traditional belief that the value of the ringgit is determined by economic fundamentals and domestic purchasing power is the new recognition that the exchange rate of the ringgit as a financial tradable offshore depends on market confidence. Consequently, maintaining market confidence and transparency in regulatory controls should be given strategic priority.

The pegged exchange rate system, with the ringgit hovering at the level of RM 2.5500 to the U.S. dollar for twenty-two years, has finally broken down. This system has been found to be incompatible with an open capital account and a regime of domestic interest rates set at about 400 basis points above U.S. dollar interest rates. This combination of high interest rates and pegged exchange rate encouraged untenably volatile capital movements and over-borrowing in U.S. dollars to fund domestic construction, property development, corporate acquisition, and stock market speculation.

New suggestions that a currency board would have been a more effective monetary institution than a central bank in combating the financial turmoil overlook the fact that the currencies of countries with currency boards were also battered. A necessary condition for a currency board system would seem to be to have a very high level of external reserves of key currencies which earn low interest and, ideally, no foreign debt.

To prevent the re-emergence of another stock market bubble in the future with catastrophic consequences, it may be useful to introduce circuit breakers in KLSE trading so that no market price of a listed stock could rise above a fair and reasonable PE ratio.

If foreign fund managers continue to view all emerging markets in East Asia through one lens for purposes of investment, and if individual East Asian countries are unable to protect themselves against speculative attacks, then the East Asian countries should strive to establish closer cooperation. The countries of East Asia urgently need to establish regional surveillance through peer pressure to encourage more efficient economic and financial management as well as the highest standards of regulatory transparency. The alternative is to remain open to the risk that unfettered currency speculation with its awesome power can again destroy an economy through currency devaluation, stock market meltdown, corporate bankruptcies, bank insolvency, recession, and finally, civil unrest.

January 1998

10

Coping with Capital Flows and the Monetary Policy Framework: The Case of Indonesia

Mochammad Rosul

INDONESIA'S EXPERIENCE WITH CAPITAL FLOWS

Reforms Set the Stage for Capital Inflows

During most of the 1970s and into the early 1980s, Indonesia's economy depended heavily on the country's oil and gas industries. In 1981 about 70 percent of both government and total export revenues came from the oil and gas industries. These industries also accounted for over 25 percent of the country's total gross domestic product (GDP). At the same time overseas funds in the form of foreign aid and soft loans from the Inter Governmental Group on Indonesia (IGGI) were used to balance the government budget deficit and fund development expenditure.[1]

Together these factors led to rapid progress in Indonesia's economy which grew at around 8 percent per year from 1969 to 1980. Economic activity was dominated by the government rather than the private sector. Government efforts to encourage the private sector to take a greater role in economic development and in the financial sector concentrated on enabling the private sector to mobilize the necessary funds to create a basis for sustainable economic development. The capital account was chosen as the first area to be reformed. A free foreign exchange regime was implemented in 1970. This measure was a crucial factor in building and maintaining foreign investors' confidence and creating an environment conducive to investment.

Additional reforms to encourage private sector participation came in the 1980s, when Indonesia's oil and gas revenues declined due to the fall in world oil prices.[2] Indonesia's private sector had depended heavily on domestic funds raised by oil and gas industries rather than on capital from overseas. Indonesia was not able to make up for the decrease in oil and gas revenue from other sources (including private capital inflows), and the growth rate dropped drastically, to about 3.8 percent per year. The government recognized the need for Indonesia to overcome its dependence on official foreign borrowing and to become self-sufficient in financing long-run economic development through the private sector. Increased private loans and other commercial borrowing would provide supplementary funds for Indonesia's development and, because such non-official loans are primarily used to finance export goods production, they would strengthen the balance of payments and Indonesia's economy as a whole.

The government introduced the first phase of its deregulation program for the financial sector on 1 June 1983. Controls on interest rates, direct credits, and subsidized liquidity credits were abolished. In March 1989, ceilings on foreign borrowing by foreign exchange banks and nonbank financial institutions (NBFIs) were abolished and domestic banks were also given permission to borrow more freely on overseas markets. In May 1989, requirements on foreign investment were also relaxed. In addition, the priority list of open and closed sectors used by Indonesia's Investment Co-ordinating Board to approve investment was replaced by a simplified "negative list of closed sectors."

The government also implemented reforms in the capital market to create an attractive environment for investors. Through its deregulation packages of October 1987 and December 1988, the government took steps to energize Indonesia's capital market. Since then, foreigners have been allowed to purchase shares in the domestic capital market and foreign securities houses have been permitted to form joint ventures with local partners. In 1995 a new capital market law was enacted to strengthen the legal foundation of the market. All these deregulation policies coupled with globalization of the financial sector have influenced the shape of capital inflow to Indonesia.[3]

Volume and Composition of Capital Inflows

The deregulation measures succeeded in bringing private capital to Indonesia. The year 1990 marked a significant change in Indonesia's capital account. Through 1989 capital inflows were comprised mainly of borrowing from official sources, but since 1990 private capital inflows have far outweighed official capital and taken over the role of financing Indonesia's savings-investment gap (Table 10.1). Faced with the tight monetary

TABLE 10.1
Indonesia's Capital Account, 1987–96
US$ millions

	1987	1988	1989	1990	1991	1992	1993	1994	1995	1996
Official Capital (net)	2,104	1,965	2,776	633	1,419	1,112	743	307	336	–522
Private Capital (net)	1,548	407	314	4,113	4,402	5,359	5,219	3,244	10,252	11,510
FDI	385	576	682	1,092	1,482	1,777	2,003	2,118	4,345	6,194
Commercial Borrowing	38	–47	–93	2,485	1,892	1,972	1,175	467	3,243	962
Bank	0	0	0	1,948	1,004	1,663	1,340	523	1,953	–1,091
Nonbank	38	–47	–93	537	888	309	–165	–56	1,290	2,053
State Enterprises (net)	1,125	579	–101	–362	422	1,253	717	390	–144	–4
Portfolio Investment	0	0	372	1,961	1,014	1,049	1,805	1,100	1,493	1,648
Other	0	–701	–546	–1,063	–400	–662	–481	–364	1,315	2,710
Capital Account	3,652	2,372	3,090	4,746	5,821	6,471	5,962	3,551	10,588	10,988

Source: Bank Indonesia

policy of the early 1990s, Indonesia's business world set about to meet its liquidity needs by exploiting the 1989 deregulation that permitted banks to borrow more freely in overseas markets. Commercial banks bustled to get more overseas funds. Their activities resulted in an increase in liabilities from Rp 11 trillion in March 1989, to Rp 17.5 trillion in March 1990, and to Rp 31.6 trillion in March 1991. Their heavy borrowing on foreign exchange markets led to negative values of net foreign assets since the third quarter of 1990.

Commercial borrowing, foreign direct investment, and portfolio investment have become the important components of Indonesia's capital account.

Private Commercial Borrowing

Indonesia's net private borrowing shifted from an outflow of US$93 million in 1989 to an inflow of US$2,485 million in 1990 (Table 10.1). The sharp increase was due to the removal of the ceiling on foreign commercial borrowing by banks in 1989, the availability of the central bank swap facility, and the relatively high domestic interest rate. Since the 1990 surge, private borrowing has continued to bring net inflows of capital, although the volume has generally diminished.

During 1995 private capital inflows became stronger and more varied as the needs of investment financing grew and diversified. Foreign loans acquired by banks and other private companies rose and net private commercial borrowing reached US$3,243 million. The increased capital inflows in 1995 might have been stimulated by declining interest rates in international markets (due to easy monetary policy). Foreign borrowing may have declined in 1996 because of the decline in domestic interest rates as Bank Indonesia lowered the interest rate differential with the aim of maintaining internal and external equilibrium.

Foreign Direct Investment (FDI)

Although Indonesia has permitted foreign investment since 1967, flows of FDI have picked up only since the end of the 1980s. Net FDI in 1996 was almost ten times its level in 1989 (Table 10.1). This substantial growth in FDI was helped by the improvement in Indonesia's economic fundamentals, such as macroeconomic stability and deregulation in the real sector, as well as by the lifting of some investment restrictions on companies. The government's seriousness about enhancing FDI was reflected in a series of deregulation initiatives adopted in 1994. The most important measures included permitting foreigners to own a much larger share in companies operating domestically as well as opening several sectors which were previously closed to foreign investment.

Approvals of foreign direct investment were strong from 1994 to 1996. (Table 10.2). Approvals of investments from the United Kingdom, Germany, Australia, and the United States increased significantly in 1995. Approvals for Malaysian and Japanese investment have been increasing while approvals for investments from Hong Kong and Taiwan declined sharply. Higher inflows from FDI also generated larger borrowing by recipient companies.

According to the World Bank, FDI will continue to flow into Indonesia, not only because multinational companies want to tap the rapidly growing domestic market but also because the region is becoming more attractive as a place to base production facilities.[4] Indonesia's capable government, outward orientation, and stable macroeconomic management have been important factors in maintaining the country's relatively high growth for the last two decades. FDI seems to be the most attractive form of capital inflow for Indonesia since it directly benefits the real sector while it causes the least disruption to the monetary sector.

Portfolio Investment

Portfolio investment, particularly purchases of shares of companies listed on the Jakarta Stock Exchange, increased dramatically from 1989 to 1990 (Table 10.1). This flood of portfolio investment followed closely the December 1988 capital market deregulation that simplified listing require-

TABLE 10.2
Approvals of Foreign Direct Investment by Country of Origin, 1992–96
US$ millions

	1992	1993	1994	1995	1996	1968–96 Total Value	1968–96 Total Number
Europe	1,364.6	930.0	3,385.4	8,951.6	5,233.4	33,185.6	705
Netherlands	96.2	311.4	165.7	360.1	1,329.5	4,620.0	157
Belgium	21.7	9.9	0.0	9.3	39.5	325.1	27
UK	978.2	301.1	2,957.1	6,322.1	3,390.6	20,809.2	217
Germany	36.7	120.6	113.1	1,344.6	164.9	3,645.1	101
France	19.9	158.0	37.1	498.4	70.8	1,038.9	59
Switzerland	11.5	17.9	70.8	44.9	160.1	855.3	58
Other	200.4	11.1	41.6	372.2	78.0	1,892.0	86
Americas	942.2	526.5	1,027.0	2,798.2	754.5	8,866.0	333
US	922.5	444.5	977.0	2,770.6	642.1	7962.5	261
Canada	0.1	46.5	39.0	10.5	35.8	135.6	39
Other	19.6	35.5	11.0	14.1	76.6	767.9	33
Asia	4,334.4	3,652.5	14,168.8	9,234.7	18,371.3	78,878.4	3,081
Hong Kong	1,020.6	384.1	6,041.7	1,763.3	1,105.6	14,577.8	358
Japan	1,527.7	836.0	1,562.5	3,792.0	7,665.3	27,778.6	919
South Korea	618.3	661.4	1,849.1	674.7	1,231.4	7,509.6	418
Malaysia	15.8	36.7	421.8	877.0	1,393.3	3,040.1	146
Philippines	0.3	—	35.9	31.2	3.1	89.8	16
Singapore	465.0	1,454.6	1,664.4	1,468.5	3,131.0	13,266.2	595
Taiwan	579.9	131.4	2,487.6	567.4	534.6	8,568.9	506
Thailand	55.8	2.7	11.7	34.5	1,610.6	1,746.6	28
Other	50.9	145.6	94.1	26.1	1,706.4	2,300.8	95
Australia	84.8	158.0	53.3	3,712.4	515.7	5,973.2	259
Africa	4.4	384.0	6.4	0.0	5.7	872.0	19
Joint	3,609.6	2,490. 8	5,083.5	15,221.0	5,050.8	45,861.2	446
Total	10,340.0	8,141.8	23,724.4	39,914.7	29,931.4	173,636.4	4,843
% GDP	1.95	2.47	6.2	8.8	5.7	—	—

Source: Capital Investment Co-ordinating Board

ments and established an over-the-counter market. Further measures to improve efficient operation of the capital market were adopted in November and December 1990.

Net portfolio investment declined in 1991 and 1992 due to an increase in domestic interest rates as the government attempted to cool down the economy. However, it increased by 80 percent in 1993 pushing up stock prices, especially during the second half of the year when the combination of relatively low interest rates abroad and uncertain prospects for the economies of industrial countries attracted foreign funds into the Indonesian market. Improving prospects for some industrial economies and a rise in dollar interest rates in international capital markets in early 1994, caused net portfolio investment to fall back for that year. In addition, the Jakarta Stock Exchange (JSX), along with other emerging markets in Asia, suffered a massive net outflow in December 1994 in the aftermath of the Mexican crisis. Rumours of impending rupiah devaluation prompted foreign investors to move their funds from Indonesia to capital markets in developed countries and to the international money market. However, by January 1995 capital had begun flowing back into Indonesia, resulting in a net positive portfolio inflow for the year.

The sale of Indonesian stocks and bonds on the international capital market is a new phenomenon, with significant growth taking place since 1994. In a pioneering move, the government divested US$800 million equity in PT Indosat in a highly successful offering on the New York Stock Exchange in 1994–95. Some private companies followed suit, so that Indonesian companies raised a total of US$3.0 billion from offerings of stocks and bonds on the international market during 1994–95. In addition, during 1995–96 capital inflows through the JSX rose to US$1.7 billion while capital inflows from abroad declined to US$2.5 billion, of which US$761 million was from the sales of PT Telkom and PT Tambang Timah stocks abroad.

To improve the environment for Indonesia's capital market as well as to strengthen the legal foundation for its future development, the government passed a new capital market act (Act No. 8 of 1995 on Capital Market) which took effect on 1 January 1996. With this act, the government encouraged the establishment of mutual fund companies by permitting 100-percent foreign ownership and with a maximum of 1 percent per investor. The limit on foreign ownership of shares of securities companies was raised to a maximum of 85 percent of paid-in capital.

Impact of Capital Flows on Macroeconomic Performance

Rising capital inflows during the 1990s have allowed Indonesia to grow faster but they have also complicated macroeconomic management. While capital inflows improve the balance of payments, they can also generate inflationary pressure (thus interest rate movements), real exchange rate appreciation, and a deterioration in the current account. Massive capital inflows may contribute to speculative bubbles in stock and property markets and lead to an excessive expansion in domestic credit and threaten financial stability. These problems are likely to intensify if a significant portion of inflows is short term, as the probability of an abrupt and sudden reversal in these flows increases.

The macroeconomic impacts of capital inflows depend on the reason for the influx of funds. Capital inflows may be induced by widening differentials between domestic and foreign interest rates, due to an increase in domestic economic activity or monetary tightening, and they may arise, without any initial change in domestic interest rates, from an increase in the expected return on domestic capital investment relative to returns offshore. It seems that both factors were behind the recent surge in capital flows to Indonesia (Djiwandono 1996a). Although both sources of capital inflows have the same consequences for domestic monetary conditions in the short run, in the long run, only capital inflows induced by a higher expected rate of return stimulate growth in domestic demand, output, and capital stock.

Capital flows, particularly portfolio investment, can affect domestic monetary conditions in the short run because of the openness of capital markets. When Indonesia's market is more attractive than other markets, inflows of capital can exert strong pressure on the rupiah and eventually on the money supply. The greater the inflow of capital, the greater the increase in the money supply. Likewise, any sudden withdrawal of capital can strain bank liquidity.

The large inflows of capital to Indonesia in 1990 caused a rapid expansion in domestic demand that led to an overheating of the economy. Inflation accelerated from 5.97 percent in 1989 to an average of around 9.50 percent in 1990–91. (Table 10.3). Government policies slowed inflation to 4.94 percent in 1992, but with large capital inflows over the next three years the average rate of inflation returned to levels above 9 percent for 1993–95. The increase in domestic demand stimulated by these large capital inflows also widened the current account deficit from US$1.28 billion in 1989 to about US$7.80 billion in 1996 (Table 10.3). Monetary tightening to control inflation using traditional instruments such as open market operations was made less effective because it was counteracted by capital inflows.

Large capital inflows can also lead to appreciation of the real exchange rate, but in Indonesia's case, accelerating economic growth and accumulation of international reserves helped to ameliorate the pressure on the exchange rate. The average growth rate of the economy rose from less than 7.5 percent in 1989 to 8.2 percent in 1995 (Table 10.3). The central bank's international reserves almost tripled from US$6.6 billion in 1989 to US$19.1 billion (five months' of non-oil/gas imports) at the end of 1996. To limit the negative effects of the volatility of major world currencies, the central bank has constantly adjusted the composition of its international reserves to Indonesia's debt servicing and import requirements. The government has also maintained standby loans of about US$2.0 billion to meet unfavourable developments and to maintain balance of payments stability.

MONETARY POLICY AGAINST CAPITAL FLOWS

Policy Options against Capital Flows

In general, monetary policy aims at maintaining macroeconomic stability. The appropriate monetary policy response when capital inflows threaten stability depends on what motivated the flows. In particular, if the flows are transitory, over reaction could destabilize the economy through policy lags and effects on expectations. Furthermore, transitory flows might be symptomatic of basic problems that should be addressed directly, such as policy inconsistency or distortions and rigidities in the system.

Monetary policy options to preserve macroeconomic stability in the face of a surge of capital inflows include:

- Intervening in the foreign exchange market to keep the exchange rate from appreciating while at the same time sterilizing to neutralize the effect of the intervention on the domestic money supply.[5]
- Implementing regulatory administrative measures, including regulation of banks' net open position, regulation of commercial offshore borrowing, and supervision of borrowing, participation, and reporting by financial institutions. (Such banking prudential measures can alter the maturity profile of capital inflows.)

TABLE 10.3
Capital Inflows and Macroeconomic Indicators, 1989–96

Year	Capital Account Balance US$ millions	CPI Inflation %	Current Account Deficit US$ billions	GNP Growth %	BI Reserves US$ billions
1989	3,090	5.97	1.28	7.5	6.6
1990	4,746	9.50	3.24	7.2	8.7
1991	5,821	9.50	4.39	7.0	9.7
1992	6,471	4.94	3.12	6.5	11.6
1993	5,962	9.77	2.30	7.3	12.4
1994	3,551	9.24	2.96	7.5	13.2
1995	10,588	8.64	6.76	8.2	14.7
1996	10,988	6.47	7.80	7.8	19.1

Source: Bank Indonesia. Ministry of Finance.

- Increasing exchange rate and interest rate flexibility. A more flexible exchange rate would reduce the negative effects of capital inflows on management of the money supply.[6] More flexible interest rates would reduce the volatility of short-term capital flows. Encouraging a greater role for foreign exchange and domestic interest rates in the market would not only help reduce the domestic cost of capital but also allow the risk premium on these financial instruments to adjust.[7] Tightening the swap facility would also limit capital inflows.
- Undertaking non-market interventions such as dialogue with parties that influence capital flows or the money supply. Moral suasion includes appeals to financial institutions to implement certain actions that will affect capital flows.

Among these, sterilized intervention has been the primary response of Bank Indonesia (the central bank) to counter speculative inflows (Djiwandono 1996a).

Dornbusch and Fischer (1988) suggest that central bank intervention to affect exchange rates is appropriate:

- when capital flows result from unstable expectations and when exchange rate movements cause erratic changes in output;
- when the central bank wants to affect trade flows; and
- when depreciation of the exchange rate would cause an increase in domestic inflation.

Apparently Bank Indonesia (BI) had reasons similar to these theoretical ones suggested by Dornbusch and Fischer (1988) when it has used intervention policy to counter unstable movement of the exchange rate of the rupiah so far. However, whether BI intervention has been effective or not, depends on whether or not it was sterilized.

With sterilized intervention the central bank breaks the link between its foreign exchange operations and the domestic money supply. Sterilization occurs when the central bank conducts open market operations (OMO) to offset the effect of its foreign exchange intervention on high power (base) money. For example, a country that is facing capital outflows, selling foreign exchange to support the exchange rate, and consequently reducing its money supply, may purchase domestic assets (Bank Indonesia Certificates, SBI, or money market certificates, SBPU, in the case of Indonesia) on the open market to restore the money supply. Thus, with sterilized intervention, the domestic money supply is unchanged, while with unsterilized intervention the money supply changes by an amount equal to the amount of the intervention. Even though base money is unchanged, sterilization does result in a change in the portfolio composition of the central bank's balance sheet.

Coping with Capital Inflows

In the early 1990s alongside stabilizing the exchange rate through intervention, BI employed several measures to sterilize monetary growth stimulated by the surge of capital inflows. It almost doubled the interest rate on Bank Indonesia Certificates (SBI) from 1989 to March 1991 (Table 10.4).[8] In February 1991 it converted a significant amount of state enterprise deposits to claims on the central bank, almost doubling BI's SBI position between the end of 1991 and the end of 1992. The interest burden fell entirely on the central bank. The increase in the SBI rate also led to higher deposit and lending rates at commercial banks. Also in February 1991, the government imposed foreign borrowing limits on state enterprises and adopted guidelines for private sector external borrowing. These steps put a direct limit on capital inflows. It also established a Foreign Commercial Debt Team (FCDT) to give priority to investment projects with state participation and to set ceilings on offshore commercial borrowing for such projects.

TABLE 10.4
Selected Interest Rates, 1986–97
percent per year

End of Period	3-Month Deposits: State Banks	3-Month Deposits: Private National Banks	Interbank Call Money	Working Capital Credit	Investment Credit	LIBOR US$ 3-months	SBIs	SBPUs
12/89	15.50	17.02	12.02	21.00	19.30	8.83	11.60	—
12/90	20.59	21.52	21.20	21.00	20.20	8.06	17.90	—
12/91	20.83	21.92	12.62	25.12	19.28	4.19	18.03	20.19
12/92	14. 83	16.55	11.25	22.09	18.44	3.44	13.79	13.98
12/93	9.00	11.64	6.78	18.73	15.95	3.38	9.08	12.00
12/94	11.07	13.84	11.90	17.00	14.97	6.50	11.59	15.36
12/95	14.86	15.89	13.93	19.28	16.12	5.66	13.34	15.87
12/96	13.93	15.13	12.91	19.04	16.36	5.59	13.75	16.00
5/97	13.50	15.04	12.21	18.82	16.38	5.81	11.25	15.50

Note: Data for 1997 are provisional. SBI and SBPU rates are for end 6/97.
SBI are certificates of deposit issued by Bank Indonesia; SBPU are money market securities.
Source: Bank Indonesia. Ministry of Finance. Republic of Indonesia. *Budget 1997/98*. Monetary Board Secretariat.

With the sterilization, BI could control the growth of monetary aggregates. However, sterilization was very expensive. The cost of sterilization is the interest paid on the intervention instrument (SBIs). The process of sterilization also kept domestic interest rates higher than they otherwise would have been and harmed domestic investment.

The monetary authority gradually lowered interest rates in early 1993 in an effort to stimulate economic activity, but the renewed influx of capital in 1995 prompted a return to restrictive monetary policy. The increased capital inflows stimulated by the resulting higher domestic interest rates added liquidity to the economy and could have disturbed the central bank's ability to control the domestic money supply through OMO. In this more recent period, the government turned to regulatory adjustments as one of its main tools to counter the effect of capital inflows on the domestic money supply.

BI activated the reserve requirement on statutory reserves to help cool down the overheated economy.[9] Under this new regulation, only demand deposits with BI could be used to meet statutory reserves as opposed to the earlier situation in which both demand deposits with BI and cash could serve as reserves. BI raised the reserve ratio, requiring banks to place 3 percent of their funds as demand deposits with BI effective from February 1996. To further contain the economic overheating, effective 16 April 1997, BI raised the minimum reserve requirement for banks to 5 percent. Although the increase in the statutory reserve requirement was successful in the first few months of its implementation, it later led to higher interest rates and to even larger capital inflows.

In addition to raising the reserve ratio, BI raised the paid-in capital requirement and the capital adequacy ratio (CAR) of foreign exchange banks in phases beginning in September 1995. Existing foreign exchange banks were required to raise their paid-in capital and CAR to a minimum of Rp 50 billion and 9 percent respectively by September 1997, to Rp 100 billion and 10 percent by September 1999, and to Rp 150 billion and 12 percent by September 2001. These regulations were aimed at achieving a sound banking system and meeting the minimum capital adequacy requirement set by the Bank of International Settlements (BIS).

BI undertook two other regulatory changes in recent years. First, in September 1994 to provide banks with greater leeway in foreign exchange dealings, the central bank relaxed its provisions on their Net Open Position (NOP). It raised the NOP for on- and off-balance sheet assets from 20 percent to 25 percent of bank capital calculated daily. In addition, it removed the previous 25 percent limit on individual currency exposure and gave banks discretion over the currency composition of their NOP. Second, to support its counter-cyclical ability, BI discontinued its swap facility. This action was expected to insulate foreign reserves held by BI from speculative pressure. Furthermore, since the volume of transactions in the domestic interbank foreign exchange market was more than sufficient to facilitate swaps without the BI's participation, this policy was expected to foster the development of a reliable domestic interbank foreign exchange market.

Coping with Capital Outflows

During episodes of capital outflow in 1995 and 1996 besides using intervention to support the rupiah, the BI undertook monetary tightening to stabilize the exchange rate.

The Mexican crisis triggered alarm over the possibility of a similar monetary problem and devaluation in Indonesia due to the size of Indonesia's foreign debt. The impact of the Mexican crisis in Indonesia was reflected in the movement of the interbank rate, which climbed steadily from 22 December 1994. By 13 January 1995 the rupiah had depreciated about 1.7 percent in interbank trading to Rp 2,223.00 per U.S. dollar, about Rp 5.00 above BI's selling rate. The rupiah depreciation was caused primarily by stronger U.S. dollar buying by foreign investors withdrawing funds from Indonesia. The transaction of interbank foreign exchange also increased sharply during the first two weeks of January 1995 to US$1,200 million, compared with the previous steady daily volume of around US$500 million.

To maintain monetary stability and ease this pressure on the rupiah, on 13 January 1995 BI embarked on a US$580 million intervention in the domestic foreign exchange market through forward, spot, and squaring transactions. The central bank supported the intervention by increasing by 0.5 percent the rate on money market securities (SBPUs).[10] These policies reinforced market confidence in Indonesia and overseas that the government would not devalue the rupiah. The exchange rate was brought down to Rp 2,213.00 per U.S. dollar, or around Rp 5.00 below the BI selling rate. In this case, by effectively stabilising the exchange rate the intervention was instrumental in maintaining Indonesia's export competitiveness.

In another case, in early July 1996 when rumours that President Soeharto was sick and seeing a doctor in Germany caused the exchange rate to weaken, Bank Indonesia did not intervene in the exchange market, since the depreciation was within the allowed spread. Instead, BI conducted an

OMO by selling SBI with higher SBI discount rates. Even without intervention, the monetary tightening made the rupiah scarce, causing it to appreciate and settle at a stable rate.

These two experiences indicate that intervention is not the only way to counter foreign exchange rate movements. OMO can also be used to stabilize exchange rate expectations without previously intervening in the foreign exchange market. The rupiah's stability was also affected by such domestic economic fundamentals as economic growth, inflation, bank interest rates, foreign reserves, and the balance of payments. It is expected that Bank Indonesia will intervene in the foreign exchange market less frequently now that it has adopted a wider exchange rate spread.

A CLOSER LOOK AT INTEREST RATE AND FOREIGN EXCHANGE POLICIES

Indonesia adopted a combination of interest rate and exchange rate policies to tackle the monetary problems caused by capital inflow in the mid 1990s and to support its intervention-sterilization policy. Not only did the monetary authority target exchange rate and interest rate levels, but also it increased the flexibility of exchange and interest rates to allow the risk premium on rupiah-denominated financial instruments to adjust.

Exchange Rate Policy

Exchange rate policy has potentially important effects on capital inflows. The stated objective of Indonesia's exchange rate policy is to create a dynamic and stable macroeconomic environment by maintaining a stable and realistic rupiah exchange rate and by keeping exports competitive. Exchange rate flexibility is one means to reduce the negative impact of short-term capital flows on money supply management. It needs to be implemented by keeping a close watch on at least three factors, namely, developments in domestic and overseas foreign exchange markets; developments in inflation in Indonesia and her main trading partners; and developments in domestic macroeconomic aggregates including interest rates and capital flows.

Indonesia had a fixed exchange rate regime from 1971 until 1978. In November 1978 Indonesia devalued the rupiah by 30.9 percent against the U.S. dollar and introduced a 'managed float' exchange rate system. Initially, the "managed" aspect of the exchange rate system dominated exchange rate policy and the rupiah exchange rate was relatively inflexible until September 1986. Under this managed exchange rate system, rupiah depreciation was not sufficient to make up the difference between domestic and overseas inflation rates. As a result, Indonesia's commodities became less competitive in world markets. The government was forced to devalue the rupiah against the U.S. dollar in March 1983 because of the drop in Indonesia's primary exports in 1982–83 and again in September 1986 because of the sharp fall in Indonesia's oil price. According to Bank Indonesia, since September 1986, the rupiah has been regarded as more flexible and the "managed" aspect in the exchange rate regime has been less dominant. (BI *Annual Report* 1992/1993).

In order to increase the flexibility of the rupiah exchange rate while simultaneously increasing the effectiveness of monetary management, BI widened the rupiah exchange rate band seven times from 1992 to 1997 (Figure 10.1). A wider spread allows the exchange rate to respond to market forces and reduces the destabilising effects of capital flows on monetary aggregates. On 11 July 1997, BI set the intervention band at 12 percent (within a range of 304 points), meaning that BI would only intervene in the market when the dollar traded on the spot market at 6 percent above or below the middle value of its daily conversion rate. In addition to dampening short-term capital inflows, the more flexible exchange rate policy was intended to foster the development of the domestic foreign exchange market. While allowing a greater scope for the market to determine the appropriate exchange rate, the added flexibility also increases the risk premium on speculative capital flows.

A wider exchange rate band provides a greater potential exchange rate differential that should discourage volatile, short-term capital inflows. After the band was widened, however, the rupiah rate in foreign exchange markets tended to approach the lower limit of the intervention band, indicating pressure for exchange rate appreciation, which in turn increased capital inflows into Indonesia.

By widening its selling and buying rates for the rupiah in tandem with a more flexible interest rate policy, Bank Indonesia encouraged the development of the domestic foreign exchange market and also reduced the dependence of banks on BI in foreign exchange transactions. This progress is reflected in the increase in domestic interbank foreign exchange transactions from US$822.7 billion in 1992 to US$1,061.3 billion in 1995. During the same period banks' foreign exchange transactions with BI declined from US$11.0 billion to US$6.7 billion, decreasing fluctuations in money supply that originated from foreign exchange transactions. It is worth noting that the policies taken to widen the spread band did not induce disturbances in the domestic foreign exchange market.

FIGURE 10.1
Spread between Ceiling and Floor for Rupiah Intervention Band

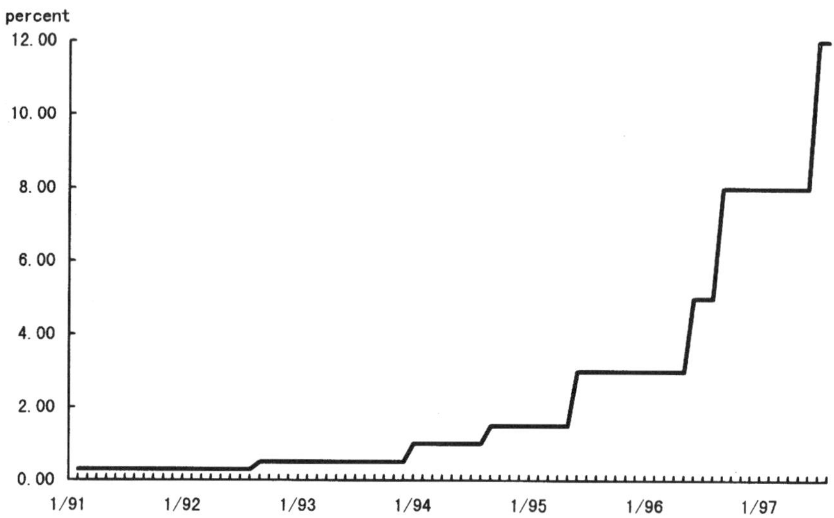

To support the exchange rate policy, a free foreign exchange regime remained in effect to facilitate international trade, particularly to encourage foreign investment (capital inflows) and to promote non-oil and gas exports. Furthermore, establishing a maximum on banks' Net Open Position not only encouraged prudent bank management, but also reduced the risks inherent in exchange rate fluctuations.

Interest Rate Policy

Interest rate policy influences the growth rate of both credit and capital flows. Under a free exchange rate regime, wider differentials between domestic and overseas interest rates will encourage capital flows. Therefore, besides controlling credit growth, another objective of interest rate policy is to avoid excessive capital inflows or outflows.

Through Bank Indonesia, the government controlled deposit and loan rates at all state banks until the first financial deregulation measure in 1983. Since then, state banks have been permitted to set their own interest rates on most categories of deposits except for selected savings schemes and on all loans except for remaining priority loans. As a result of the deregulation, banks, especially state banks, had to compete for funds by offering higher rates on time deposits, particularly short-term deposits. Banks also competed through lending interest rates and the quality of lending services. Time deposit rates, particularly at state commercial banks, responded to the deregulation immediately. Rates on 6- and 12-month time deposits increased by 300 percent and 111 percent respectively within 2 years of deregulation.

In early 1993, lending rates were still relatively high, threatening the quality of banks' earning assets, since high rates tend to worsen debtors' financial positions. Lower interest rates would encourage investment and also relieve banks' burden in implementing the needed consolidation. On the other hand, Indonesia's relatively high interest rates coupled with a stable rupiah exchange rate were responsible for the influx of short-term capital. Considering the above factors, along with manageable inflation, and steady rupiah depreciation, BI encouraged banks to reduce their interest rates in phases. The decline in international interest rates that occurred in 1993 as the industrial countries eased monetary policy to stimulate their sluggish economies gave Indonesia room to lower its domestic interest rates.

BI implemented its more flexible interest rate policy in part through a mid-1993 change in the pricing procedure for SBI auctions. Pricing for the auctions was changed from Cut Off Rates (COR) to Stop Out Rates (SOR). Under the old COR system, the interest rate was set and market demand was satisfied at that rate; under the new SOR system, however, a specific quantity of SBIs was auctioned and therefore the SBI rate could adjust more rapidly to interest rates abroad and was more closely related to domestic assets. The central bank also introduced SBI repos in October 1994 in order to improve the features of SBIs. These changes allowed BI more scope in adjusting domestic interest rates to external conditions.

In 1994 capital inflows to developing countries declined as short-term rates in industrial countries (the United States, Japan, and Canada) increased to more attractive levels. In response to this decline, in April 1994 BI began gradually adjusting interest rates on SBIs upward and it increased the adjustments from mid 1994 as signs of overheating built up. For fiscal year 1994–95, Bank Indonesia raised SBI rates a total of about five percentage points (Table 10.4). These adjustments were undertaken not only to compensate for rising interest rates in international markets but also to avoid any widening of interest rate differentials that might stimulate capital outflows from Indonesia. Between mid July and late August 1994, SBI and SBPU rates were raised by 50 and 100 basis points respectively, compensating for movements abroad during that period. During

November 1994 and February 1995, BI moved even more decisively, approximately matching rate increases by the U.S. Federal Reserve. The increase in rates on SBIs pushed up domestic bank interest rates on deposits and, to a lesser degree, on credit (Figure 10.2).

Having successfully contained inflation with tight monetary policy during 1994 and 1995, the central banks of the major industrial countries began to ease their monetary policies by lowering interest rates in stages during 1995 and 1996. On the other hand, emerging markets adopted tight monetary policies to maintain high interest rates and to cool down their economies. This situation encouraged a surge of capital inflows to developing countries, with intense competition among Indonesia, China, India, Pakistan, and Vietnam. Because of the increased competition for external funds and also to control the money supply, in 1995 BI intervened in the market through OMO bringing about an increase in interest rates on SBIs and SBPUs and eventually an increase in deposit rates. (Table 10.4).

FIGURE 10.2
Selected Interest Rates, 1986–97

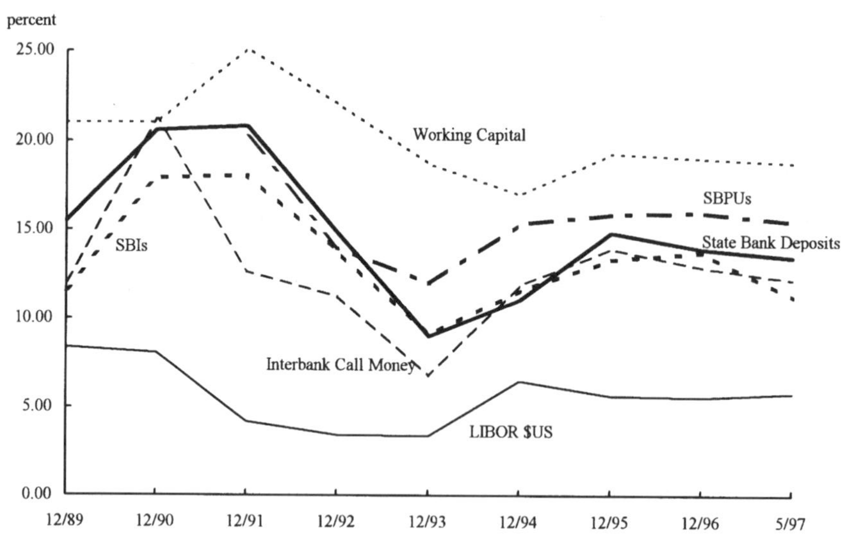

Note: Data for 1997 are provisional.
Source: Bank Indonesia. Ministry of Finance. Republic of Indonesia. *Budget 1997/98*. Monetary Board Secretariat.

CONCLUSION

As with other developing countries, capital flows into Indonesia play an important role in the economic development process. Capital inflows not only represent a vehicle for the transfer of knowledge and technical know-how, but they also facilitate the development of the capital market and strengthen competition there. The prospect for capital inflows into Indonesia, depends, to some extent, on economic conditions in the industrial countries, on their savings rates and perhaps their savings-investment balances in particular, as well as on domestic economic conditions. In the coming years capital flows will likely still be used to accelerate domestic economic development under the free foreign exchange regime and to finance the current account deficit which is currently swollen. The problem is likely to become more severe because a significant portion of the inflows are short-term capital which can reverse course suddenly, because of wild rumours, the contagion effect, or changing conditions in other financial markets. A high volume of capital inflow tends to raise aggregate expenditure and increase inflationary pressure, thereby increasing the current account deficit. Therefore, the government should continue to implement measures to curb short-term capital inflows (such as widening the exchange rate band) and to attract more foreign direct investment. The problem raised by capital inflows can not be prevented by prudential regulation alone, but requires appropriate, firm monetary and fiscal policies.

Indonesia's new policy of widening the exchange rate band will benefit the monetary sector since the added flexibility increases risk for speculators and allows greater scope for the market to determine the appropriate exchange rate. This condition will be supported by the government's policy to encourage capital inflows in the form of foreign direct investment.

Notes

1 The IGGI was dissolved in March 1992 and replaced by the Consultative Group on Indonesia (CGI).

2 The oil and gas sector still accounted for about one-eighth of total output and contributed about 41 percent of government revenue and 39 percent of total export proceeds in 1989 (IMF 1989). By March 1992, the sector accounted for about 17.4 percent of total output and its contribution to government revenue and total export proceeds had fallen to about 29 percent and 36 percent, respectively. Indonesia's

average growth between 1980 and 1987 was calculated from World Table (1989) and Central Bureau of Statistics (1989).

[3] In recent years, most developing countries in the world have liberalized their financial markets.

[4] *Jakarta Post*, 1 November 1996.

[5] Sterilized intervention may be enough to maintain macroeconomic stability in some cases, especially when there is a strong presumption that capital inflows will be reversed quite soon and the size of the inflows is manageable in the interim (IMF 1997).

[6] Greater exchange rate flexibility could be the preferred response to capital inflows provided that the country's overall balance of payments position is sufficiently strong (IMF 1997). Increasing exchange rate flexibility may also discourage some purely speculative (and highly reversible) capital inflows.

[7] Exchange rate policy and interest rate policy are discussed in the next section of this chapter.

[8] Bank Indonesia Certificate (SBI) is an instrument in open market operations. It is a certificate of deposit issued by Bank Indonesia that may be sold to banks or NBFIs and may be traded among them or discounted to the securities houses. Securities houses, in turn, can rediscount the certificates to Bank Indonesia.

[9] This regulation was first imposed on commercial banks in Indonesia in May 1957. Domestic banks were required to maintain a minimum of 30 percent of their current rupiah liabilities in cash and liquid assets. The minimum was reduced to 15 percent in December 1977 and it was lowered to 2 percent in October 1988.

[10] SBPUs, money market securities, are contingent liabilities of the banks or nonbank financial institutions (NBFIs) that first endorsed them. With this money market facility, banks and NBFIs are allowed to trade SBPUs among themselves or with Bank Indonesia.

References

Bank Indonesia. *Annual Report,* various issues.

Dornbusch, R. and S. Fischer. 1988. *Macroeconomics*. Singapore: McGraw-Hill Book Company.

Djiwandono, J. Soedradjat. 1996*a*. "Monetary Policy and Capital Market Development". Paper presented at a conference held by the Capital Market Supervisory Board, Jakarta, 8 August.

______. 1996*b*. "Monetary Policy in a Rapidly Changing Environment: The Experience of Indonesia". Paper presented at Bank Indonesia-International Monetary Fund Conference on Macroeconomic Issues Facing ASEAN Countries, Jakarta, 7–8 November.

International Monetary Fund. 1989. "Indonesia, Recent Economic Developments", 14 April.

______. 1997. "Exchange Rates, Macroeconomic Policies and Private Capital Flows in the APEC Region: Supporting Stability and Sustainable Growth". Paper presented at the APEC Finance Ministers' Meeting, Cebu, Philippines, 4–6 April.

Jakarta Post. 1996. *Business and Investment*, various issues.

Montgomery, John D. 1997. "The Indonesian Financial System: Its Contribution to Economic Performance and Key Policy Issues". Paper prepared for the Conference on Macroeconomic Issues Facing ASEAN Countries, Jakarta, 7–8 November.

PT Data Consults Inc. 1996. "Finance Business in Indonesia: Current State and Prospects until year 2000". Jakarta, April.

Sihotang, Kilian. 1992. "Foreign Direct Investment in Indonesia". Paper prepared for the Asia Pacific TVC Review. Bangkok.

World Bank. 1996. "Managing Capital Inflows in East Asia". Washington D. C., May.

______. 1997. "Recent Trends in the Transfer of Resources to Developing Countries". Washington D.C., March.

UPDATE*

MONETARY CRISIS AND POLICY DIRECTIONS FOR ECONOMIC RECOVERY IN INDONESIA, JULY 1997 – JANUARY 1998

Until mid 1997 Indonesia had generally made good macroeconomic progress, growing at an average of more than 7 percent per year for the last five years, one of the highest growth rates in the emerging countries of Asia. Monetary policy was directed to maintaining internal and external stability. On the internal side, inflation growth had tended to decrease to a safe level. In recent years prudent government policy planning in controlling expenditures, had continually generated fiscal surpluses. On the external side, the current account deficit had been kept below 4 percent of GDP, the lowest ratio in Southeast Asia. The current account deficit resulted from the import growth tied to the high level of economic activity, particularly investment. It seemed possible that Indonesia would be able to reduce its current account deficit in the coming years, since export growth, particularly non-oil and gas exports, had been increasing. This favourable outlook was due to the government's integrated macroeconomic policies that had been undertaken to maintain stability and to support high economic growth. The government had continued prudent fiscal and monetary policy, especially through reduction of growth of domestic demand to a level consistent with national production capacity. On the supply side, the government maintained its policy of deregulation to improve the competitiveness of Indonesian products in both domestic and international markets.

However, speculative attack that started in Thailand in July 1997 was quickly directed at currencies of other Asian countries, including the Indonesian rupiah, and changed this outlook significantly. The exchange rate fell from 2,410 rupiah to the U.S. dollar on 11 July to around 12,900 on 29 January 1998. This drastic weakening of the rupiah shows the

*Editors' note: The situation in Indonesia is still very much in flux. The specific measures described in this update may not ultimately be put in place, but the discussion here highlights the issues that must be addressed to restore Indonesia's economic stability.

negative response of the markets to the Indonesian government's efforts to restore currency stability. The weakness of the rupiah is strongly related to speculation by certain foreign financial institutions (probably a syndicate) aimed at de-stabilizing regional economic performance, particularly the reform commitment undertaken by Indonesia, which was actively supported by international agencies, namely the IMF (International Monetary Fund), the World Bank, and the ADB (Asian Development Bank).

From 1 July 1997 through 20 January 1998 Indonesia suffered a 71 percent decrease in the value of its currency and a 46 percent stock market loss. The government of Indonesia undertook a number of measures to stabilize the exchange rate and turn the situation around (Table U10.1). On 11 July 1997 it widened the intervention band for the rupiah

TABLE U10.1
Rupiah Depreciation and Indonesia's Response to the Currency Crisis

Date	Exchange Rate Rupia/US$	Event
July 11, 1997	2,410	Intervention band widened to 12 percent
July 21	2,445	Intervention in money market of US$ 2 billion
August 4	2,525	SBI interest rate increased
August 14	2,570	Intervention band eliminated
August 19	2,800	SBI interest rate increased
August 20	2,825	SOE deposits transferred into BI
August 29	2,700	Forward transactions limited
Sept. 3	2,775	Liquidity loosened, SBI interest rate decreased
Sept. 16	2,850	Government, SOE, private projects revised
Sept. 17	2,875	Tariffs on 152 items decreased
Sept. 29	3,000	Forward transactions limited
Oct. 3	3,200	Forward transaction swap facility limited
Oct. 6	3,450	Intervention in money market of US$650 million
Oct. 8	3,450	IMF assistance sought
Nov. 3	3,424	16 insolvent banks closed
Nov. 4	3,272	Intervention of Japan, Singapore, and Indonesia
Nov. 14	3,479	Run on Bank Central Asia
Dec. 2	4,000–5,000	Rumours about the president's health
Dec. 8	5,900	Highest in December 1997
Dec. 16	5,500	Bank Indonesia intervention
Jan 2, 1998	7,000	President called for nation's support
Jan 15	9,050	Letter of intent signed by the president
Jan 23	15,250	Government presented revised state budget
Jan 29	12,900	Government guaranteed deposits in private banks

from 8 percent to 12 percent and then on 14 August it eliminated the intervention band, replacing it with a flexible exchange rate management system. This was intended to reduce speculative flows without losing much foreign exchange. During August the government also increased the discount rate on SBI (Bank Indonesia) certificates, and transferred deposits of state owned enterprises (SOEs) into SBI. This tight monetary policy has been gradually loosened in accordance with the current situation.

In addition, the government limited forward transactions by domestic banks with non-residents to a maximum amount of US$5 millions, except for export, import, and investment transactions and provided provide facilities to foster exports of non-oil and gas products including a swap facility for exporters who have foreign currency or accounts receivable in foreign currencies and a forward purchase facility to support imports needed for export production.

On 3 September the government announced other medium- and long-term strategic policy directions including:

Continuing prudent fiscal and monetary policies;
Increasing synchronization of activities of various economic sectors;
Rescheduling some government projects;
Rescheduling state-owned enterprise projects that depend heavily on imported materials;
Requesting private sector understanding to reschedule projects in accordance with their priorities;
Reducing restrictions creating a "high-cost" economy, in order to increase exports and to reduce imports through the increase of luxury goods tax,
Improving the health of the financial system by providing liquidity assistance for healthy banks facing liquidity problems and forcing merger, acquisition, or liquidation of banks that face structural problems;
Eliminating the limitation on foreign investors purchasing shares in the capital market; and
Maintaining price stability and to guaranteeing distribution of people's primary needs.

Exchange rate uncertainty and high interest rates have adversely affected economic activity in Indonesia, particularly activities that are sensitive to interest rate movements and those that depend on imported raw materials and capital. Accordingly, the government has placed highest priority on improving liquidity in the markets and restoring confidence in the rupiah. The government has consistently intervened in foreign currency markets to meet Indonesia's demand for U.S. dollars to fund various economic activities. Recently, such intervention has been carried out cooperatively with central banks and monetary authorities of neighbouring countries that wish to help Indonesia to stabilize the rupiah. In order to add liquidity to the foreign currency market the government also reduced from 5 percent to 3 percent the minimum reserve requirement on foreign currency that comes from third party funding. The government has attempted to restore liquidity of the rupiah in the market by decreasing interest rates on monetary instruments and by decreasing other interest rates, particularly the rate on loans. SBPU facilities that had been temporarily frozen have been reopened to increase credit supply to small- and medium-size enterprises. In addition, funds belonging to some foundations and state-owned enterprises that had been transferred into SBI were returned to their previous deposit status.

Indonesia's financial sector, especially the banking industry, has faced problems caused by high cost of funds. These will adversely affect bank liquidity, return on investment, and solvency. In this regard, on 1 November 1997 the government closed sixteen banks that were considered unhealthy. Healthy banks facing liquidity problems will be assisted by the government.

An unhealthy financial sector, especially banking, can worsen the economic situation. Besides that, private overseas borrowing, especially short term, can worsen the situation. Because of this, in order to avoid undermining market forces, any corrections or adjustments must be market-friendly and in line with market trends.

Faced with continuing depreciation of the rupiah Indonesia sought the assistance of the International Monetary Fund on 3 October 1997. An agreement was reached on 5 November by which the IMF provided stand-by credit in the amount of SDR 7.34 (US$10.14 billion) for a three-year period of which SDR 2.2 billion (around US$3.0 billion) is available for direct use. This assistance from the IMF is to achieve macroeconomic stabilization and structural reform. The strategic policy directions undertaken by the government since that time have been in line with the IMF program and focused on prudent macroeconomic management, financial sector restructuring, and structural reform.

As currency attacks on the rupiah continued in November and December and into January 1998 the initial IMF package proved insufficient.

Rumours about the president's health added to the uncertainty. With the new year, the scope of the IMF bailout had almost quadrupled to about US$43 billion.

On 23 January 1998, in a renewed effort to recover from the crisis, the government announced in parliament a revised state budget for 1998–99 that more realistically reflected Indonesia's economic situation. The revised budget (balanced by law and closely following IMF recommendations) was set at Rp 147.22 trillion (US$11.3 billion) compared to the 6 January estimate of Rp 133.5 trillion. This was an increase of 45.6 percent over the budget for fiscal 1997–98. The new budget was based on projections by the IMF, including zero economic growth in the fiscal year starting 1 April 1998, an inflation rate of 20 percent, and an average exchange rate of 5,000 rupiah to the U.S. dollar. Key among the revisions announced on 23 January was a cut in fuel subsidies to Rp 7.45 trillion from the previous estimate of Rp 10.08 trillion—part of the agreement with the IMF.

The broad macroeconomic objectives of the IMF program are to avoid a decline in output while containing inflation to 20 percent in 1998–99 and bringing it to a single digit level the next year, despite the sharp depreciation of the rupiah. At the same time, the external current account balance is expected to move from a deficit into a sizeable surplus, thereby generating additional foreign exchange to help the country to repay its external debt. The main aspects of the agreement with the IMF are:

Budget

The 1998–99 budget will be revised, to accord with the newly agreed macroeconomic framework, while still adhering to Indonesia's long-standing balanced-budget principle. Based on the IMF presentation, this would imply that the budget would record a small deficit, of about 1 percent of GDP, a level that strikes an appropriate balance between the need to avoid an undue fiscal deterioration, and the need to avoid a fiscal contraction that would further depress economic activity. Nevertheless, to achieve this objective, serious measures will be required. In particular, action will need to be taken to curb energy subsidies, which have grown to unsustainable proportions as the rupiah's depreciation has pushed domestic prices far below world levels. Accordingly, the government will phase out subsidies gradually by raising both fuel and electricity prices, except for those on kerosene and certain diesel fuels, where increases will be kept to a minimum to protect the poor.

Fiscal Transparency

In order to ensure that the public is fully informed of all government activities, the accounts of the Reforestation and Investment Funds will be brought into the budget in 1998–99.

Public Sector Projects

Under current economic conditions, public spending is limited to items that are of vital importance to the country. For this reason, the program envisages curtailment of development spending, including immediate cancellation of the 12 infrastructure projects that had been recently postponed or placed under review; immediate discontinuation of budgetary and extra-budgetary support and credit privileges granted to aeroplane projects of IPTN; and immediate revocation of all special tax, customs, and credit privileges for the National Car project.

Monetary Policy

Monetary policy will need to be kept firm for a sustained period, until confidence in the currency is restored. To signal the government's commitment to this stance, Bank Indonesia will be given full autonomy to conduct monetary policy and start immediately to unilaterally decide interest rates on its SBI certificates. As the program measures take hold and confidence returns, market interest rates should gradually begin to fall, while capital that has moved overseas should return to the country, providing banks with sufficient liquidity to resume their lending activities.

Bank and Corporate Sector Restructuring

It has become vitally important to restore the banking system to financial health and to alleviate the difficulties of the corporate sector. Specific plans to assist the banking system are now being formulated.

Structural Reforms

The program calls for elimination of myriad long-standing restrictions on economic activity. For instance:

> From 1 February BULOG's existing monopolies over the import and distribution of sugar and the distribution of wheat

> flour will be eliminated, leaving it only with a monopoly over rice.
>
> To complement this action, domestic trade in all agricultural products will be fully deregulated, so traders will have the freedom to sell their goods where they want and to whom they want. The Clove Marketing Board will be eliminated by June 1998.
>
> As of 1 February all restrictive marketing arrangements will be abolished, leaving firms free to produce and export their products as they wish, and as the market decides. Specifically, the cement, paper, and plywood cartels will be dissolved.
>
> Another pressing need in the current circumstances is to encourage foreign investment. Accordingly, for instance, by February 1 all formal and informal barriers to investment in palm oil plantation will be removed, while all restrictions on investment in wholesale and retail trade will be lifted.
>
> Measures are also being taken to alleviate the suffering caused by the current, severe drought. The program envisages that community-based work programs will soon be introduced to sustain the purchasing power of the poor. In addition, to ensure that adequate food supplies are available at more reasonable prices, effective 1 February, tariffs on all food items will be cut to a maximum of just 5 percent, while tariff rates on non-food agricultural products will be reduced by 5 percentage points.
>
> Last but not least, particular attention is being paid to the proper financing of small and mid-size enterprises and exporters. To make funds available for this purpose through the banking system, the Asian Development Bank is putting in place a program whose details will be announced shortly.

In responding to the Asian currency crisis, Indonesia has been faced with a national need to formulate economic policies and programs that have the strength and flexibility to withstand economic fluctuations, uncertainties, and risks. To this end, the policies and programs that have been formulated need to be in line with global developments and trends. The substance of these programs and policies is targeted at increasing national efficiency and enhancing economic resilience, as well as improving the global competitiveness of the Indonesian economy. Every sector of the national economy, including private business, must work with the government to achieve these goals. Co-operation between Indonesia and international agencies should be seen within this framework. Although various programs and adjustment measures have been introduced and continue to be implemented by the government, Indonesia frequently consults with the IMF, the World Bank, and the ADB. Considering the international experience of these institutions, and given that Indonesia is in need of technical assistance, the government invited these agencies to provide inputs to the programs which might help the recovery that has just been formulated.

January 1998

11

Capital Inflows and the Philippine Economy: Issues and Policy Options

Emilio T. Antonio Jr., Emilio S. Neri Jr., Teresa V. Taningco[1]

INTRODUCTION

The recent rush of capital into developing countries has been seen in two different lights. The inflows are welcomed by those who see them as augmenting the scarce capital resources of poor countries. They cause concern for others who see capital inflows as sources of instability, bringing wild swings in economic activity because of their variability. These contrasting views of capital inflows are reflected in the disparate policy reactions to them. Policy makers frequently pronounce the importance of attracting foreign investment. However, others propose controls to regulate the inflow and outflow of foreign capital, argue that the monetary effect of such flows should be sterilized, and assert that policy should prevent them from affecting exchange rates.

This chapter looks at the phenomenon of capital flows from the perspective of the realities of the Philippine economy. The objective is to take a close look at the nature of these flows, examine their impact on the economy, identify the policy questions that they provoke, and determine the choices that Philippine policy makers need to make. The chapter is divided into three parts. The first provides a background on capital inflows to the Philippines. The second identifies specific policy issues that capital inflows generate. The final part identifies and evaluates the options open to Philippine policy makers to address these issues.

CAPITAL MOVEMENTS IN THE PHILIPPINE ECONOMY: MAGNITUDES AND COMPOSITION

Capital flows to the Philippine economy have followed the broad trends in international capital movements. As has generally been the case, over a long time horizon, capital inflows to the Philippines have shifted from aid, to loans, to foreign investments. However, the transition in forms of capital inflow was delayed in the Philippines compared with other countries. During the early part of the 1980s when other developing economies were already attracting foreign investment, loans continued to dominate capital inflows in the Philippines. This is understandable because of the political instabilities in the Philippines during the period. In the second half of the 1980s, foreign investment began to gain importance, but political troubles and natural disasters in the early 1990s stalled this trend.

Most recently, improvement in the economic fundamentals of the Philippines has triggered a shift in the composition of capital inflows. Similar to what happened in other countries, investment inflows have grown in absolute and relative importance (Figure 11.1). On a net basis, the largest component of investment flows to the Philippines has been foreign direct investment (FDI, Figure 11.2). In terms of gross amounts, however, portfolio investment has gained greater significance since 1993. For instance, although in 1991 the volume of FDI placements (US$556 million) was more than double the size of portfolio placements (US$227 million), by 1996 portfolio placements (US$6,687 million) had grown to more than four times the placement volume of FDI (US$1,517 million).

The prospects for the continuation of the same trends in the Philippines appear bright. The present level of inflows is still relatively low compared to what other Asian countries experienced when they were initially attracting private foreign capital. In terms of composition, the share of foreign investment in total capital inflows is likely to increase. Nevertheless, it is also likely that foreign loans will continue to play an important role for the coming years as the country's creditworthiness improves.

The potential for attracting portfolio investment is similarly bright. The market capitalisation of the Philippines is less than that of Indonesia and Thailand and well below that of South Korea, Singapore, and Malaysia (Figure 11.3). Portfolio investments have been used productively in the Philippines, helping finance the investments in capital goods (Lamberte 1995).

FIGURE 11.1
Trend in Components of Capital Flows, 1976–96

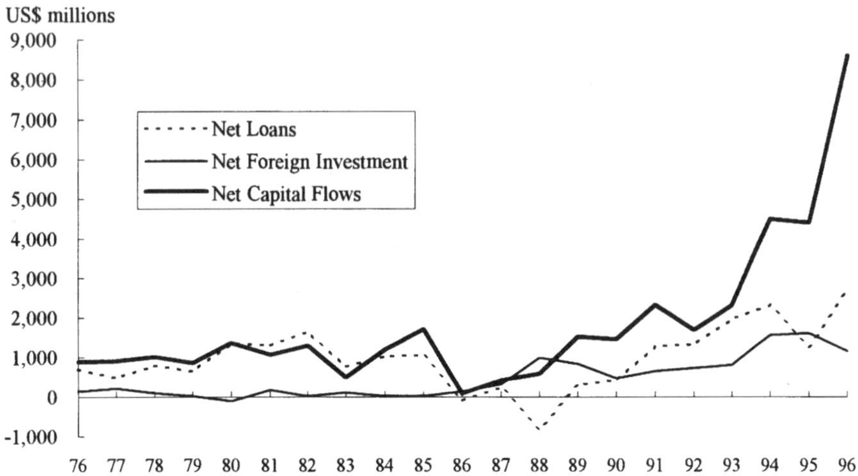

Source: Bangko Sentral ng Pilipinas.

FIGURE 11.2
Trend in Components of Net Foreign Investment, 1976–96

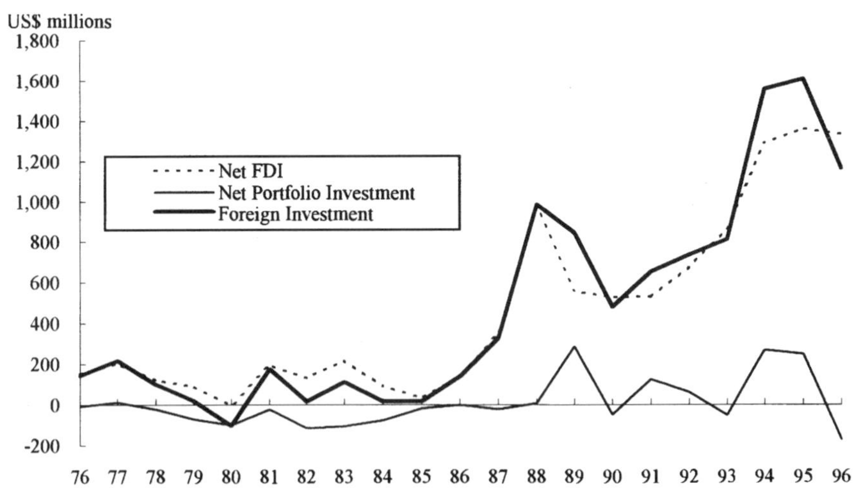

Source: Bangko Sentral ng Pilipinas.

FIGURE 11.3
Capitalization of East Asian Stock Markets

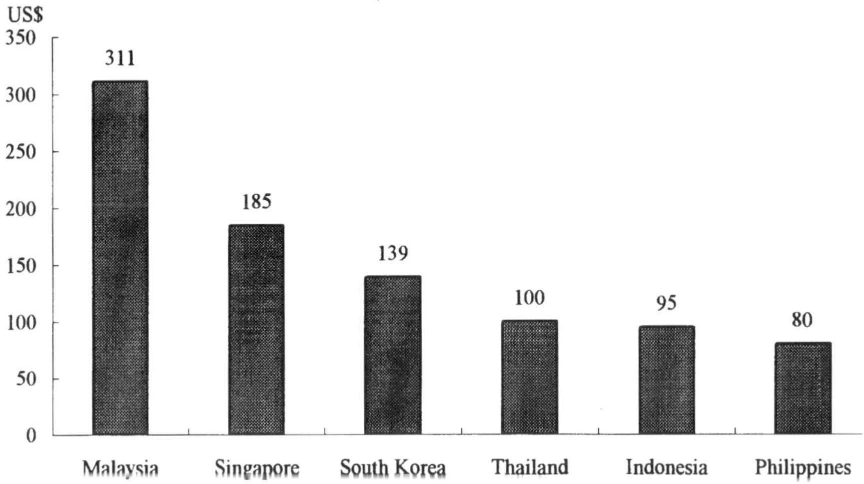

Note: Figures are as of end-December 1996.
Source: *Asiaweek*, 10 January 1997.

Capital Inflows vs. Low Savings Rate

Expectations of stronger inflows of foreign capital should be a welcome development for the Philippines. The flows are important in filling the savings-investment gap; offsetting the foreign exchange gap that originates from persistent trade deficits; and expanding the economy's production possibility frontier which is set by the scarcest production input—foreign currency.

In the Philippines, domestic savings are not sufficient to finance investment requirements. Not only does the Philippines have one of the lowest savings rates among Asian economies, its present rate of savings pales in comparison with the records it posted in the 1960s and 1970s. Political instability and a series of natural disasters that occurred in the Philippines from the beginning of the 1980s to the first two years of the 1990s undermined the incentive to save. In an environment where the future was uncertain, inflation rates were high, and incomes were at a standstill, the savings rate dipped to an all-time low.

Reluctance to save cannot be overcome overnight. Confidence in the future takes time to rebuild. Thus, while the performance of the economy has improved and conditions that are more conducive to savings, such as lower inflation and higher income, have returned since 1993, the national savings rate is still less than ideal. Consequently, the Philippines needs to tap foreign sources to augment its domestic savings. Capital infusions from abroad help finance the investments needed to expand the economy's production capacity.

Capital inflows also help offset the perennial shortage of foreign exchange in the Philippines. The economy usually incurs trade deficits which cannot be fully financed by the earnings from tourism and remittances from overseas Filipino workers. Whenever the remaining shortfall cannot be covered by capital inflows and the level of gross international reserves is low, the price of foreign currencies rises eventually triggering an upward spiral in the prices of goods, funds, and labour. The development of these upward price pressures suggests that the availability of foreign currencies sets the limits to the economy's production capacity. Capital inflows, therefore, can help push out the nation's production possibility frontier.

POLICY ISSUES POSED BY THE PROSPECT OF INCREASING CAPITAL INFLOWS

Basic Realities to Consider

Policy makers should pay particular attention to certain realities of the Philippine economy in proposing policies to confront a surge of capital inflows. The Philippine economy has a low savings rate and is perennially short of foreign currencies because of the propensity to spend more than it earns. Capital inflows should be welcomed because they allow the economy to undertake investments in excess of what domestic savings volume would support and because they augment the supply of foreign exchange. From this perspective, even short-term capital flows (which can become a significant proportion of total flows) can be useful as long as they are kept at a prudent level, their volatility is taken into account, and they are used efficiently to expand productive capacity over the medium term.

To pin down what policy choices arise with capital inflows, we need to make explicit the relationships that govern the macroeconomic performance of the Philippine economy.

Underlying Macroeconomic Balances and Management Policies

We make use of the accounting identity for an open economy, i.e.,

(1) $Y = A - M + X$ where: Y = national income
A = national spending
M = value of imports
X = value of exports

Rearranging this equation highlights the basic reality faced by a small open economy: the nation's balance of trade is just a reflection of the difference between its income and spending. That is,

(2) $Y - A = X - M.$

In other words, a nation that spends beyond its income incurs a trade deficit.

Taking into account that total national spending is equal to the sum of consumption expenditures (C), government expenditures (G) and investment expenditures (I), equation (2) can be reformulated as

(3) $Y - (C + I + G) = X - M.$

Noting that income not spent on consumption (Y – C) is equal to the amount saved (S) plus what goes to taxes (T), equation (3) can be rewritten in terms of the three-gap model usually used to described an open economy, i.e.,

(4) $(S - I) + (T - G) = (X - M).$

Equation (4) suggests how the government may affect the income-spending gap and how various policies are interdependent. By influencing the availability and cost of funds, monetary policy works on the savings-investment balance (S–I); fiscal policy affects the matching of government revenues and expenditures (T–G); and finally, the balance between imports and exports (X–M) can be addressed directly by exchange rate and trade policies and indirectly by monetary and fiscal policy.

In the Philippines, monetary and fiscal policies are closely intertwined. The impact of fiscal deficits is usually reflected in monetary variables. If the government deficit is monetized, the fiscal problem is transformed into excessive monetary growth. On the other hand, if the deficit is financed through domestic borrowings, the loose fiscal policy stance is reflected in high interest rates.

Outside of monetary, fiscal, exchange rate, and trade policies, there are other factors which could influence the trade balance. For example, because the Philippines is a small buyer and seller in the world market, the dollar prices at which the Philippines imports and exports goods are generally determined by world market conditions. These prices are also important determinants of the Philippines' trade balance. Figure 11.4 is a schematic representation of the interdependence among the policy tools and the three components of the income-spending balance.[2]

The most common problem for Philippine policy makers has been to prevent the economy from overheating. This has meant keeping the trade balance within the limits allowed by the available foreign exchange reserves and the inflows of dollars from other sources including capital inflows. If such limits were violated, the peso would depreciate, starting an upward price spiral that would destabilize the macroeconomic environment.

A prospective surge in capital inflows presents Philippine policy makers with the opposite policy problem. If the capital inflows more than offset the trade deficit, the resulting excess supply in foreign currencies would strengthen the peso. This may not trigger a downward price spiral, given the relative stickiness of prices, but it will certainly keep prices of goods, funds, and labour from rising. But, while this may be advantageous at the start, the strengthening currency will increase the trade deficit and

FIGURE 11.4
Policy Tools and the Income-Spending Gap

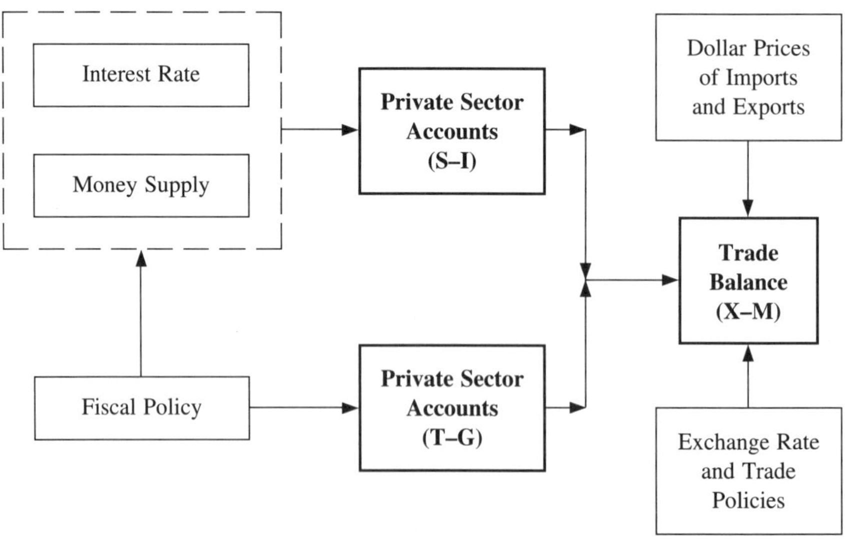

discourage investment that could increase the capacity of the economy to export and to compete against imports. In short, the inflow of capital and the resulting peso appreciation make the economy more and more dependent on foreign capital and undermine its ability to increase productive capacity in the medium-term. The economy's dependence on capital inflows creates a particularly difficult situation if a significant portion of the foreign capital is in the form of portfolio investment and these flows reverse. The essential policy issue that the Philippine economy has to address, then, is to ensure that the short-term effects of foreign capital inflows do not interfere with the longer term expansion of production capacity.

APPROPRIATE POLICY APPROACH

An appropriate mix of macroeconomic policies could make the short-term effects of capital inflows consistent with the country's long-term economic objectives. There are four key policy areas to consider:

- Policy on international reserves should address how much of the capital inflows need to be absorbed as reserves and how much should be allowed to go directly into the foreign exchange market to affect the exchange rate.
- Monetary policy should address how much of the monetary expansion caused by capital inflows should be sterilized and how much should be allowed to cause interest rates to decline.
- Fiscal policy should address how much the public sector can spend beyond its tax revenues without causing the economy to overheat.
- Exchange rate policy should make sure that the exchange rate reflects the long-term scarcity of the domestic currency vis-à-vis foreign currencies.

In choosing the appropriate mix, it is important to recognize the interdependence among policy areas. This complicates the formulation of an optimal mix of policies to reconcile the short-term effects of capital inflows with the longer run objective of building up the economy's capacity. For example, the central bank's decision on how much foreign currency to hold has implications for monetary policies (Figure 11.5). The amount of monetary expansion that is allowed affects the balance between exports and imports and therefore the balance between the demand and supply of foreign currency. Whether a shortage or surplus of foreign currencies is allowed to persist, on the other hand, would depend largely on the amount of reserves held by the central bank. Furthermore, the net trade balance can be influenced not only by the money supply but also by exchange rate movements. The following scenarios highlight some of the dilemmas that could arise in an attempt to manage macroeconomic balances.

FIGURE 11.5
Interdependence of Fiscal, Monetary, and Exchange Rate Policies

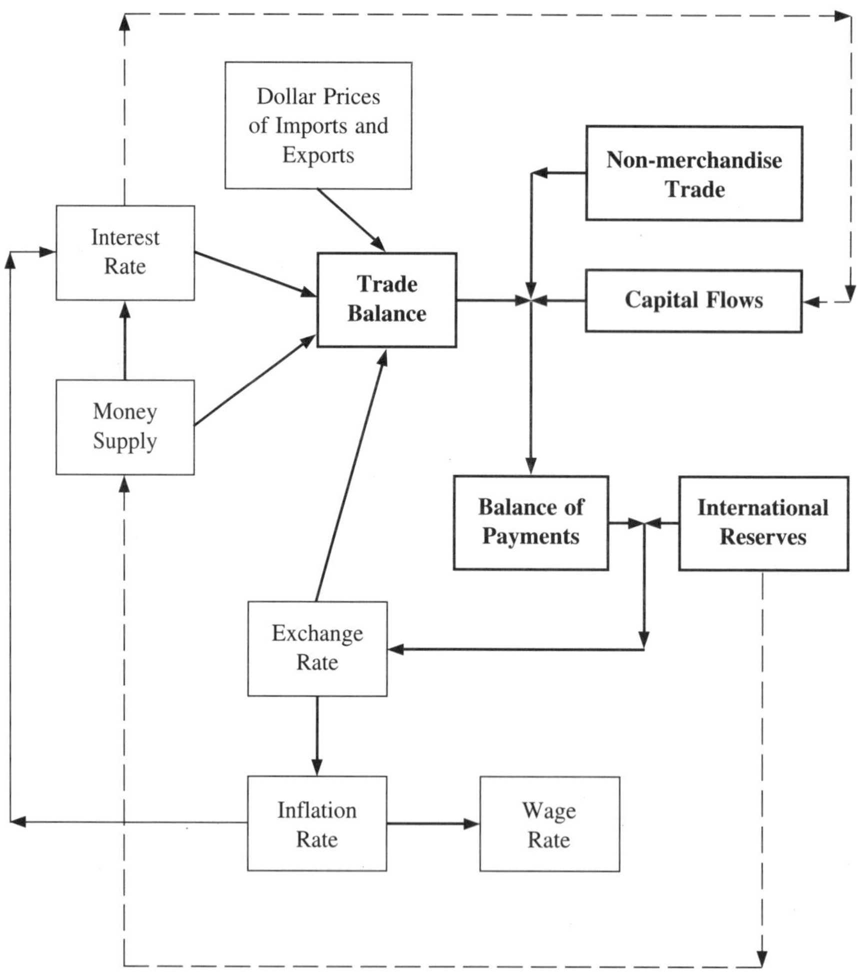

Sterilization Scenario

If policy makers determine that allowing capital inflows to cause the domestic currency to appreciate is inconsistent with the longer term objective of encouraging exports and substitution for imports, they can try to prevent appreciation by accumulating capital inflows as international reserves. This would trigger the following chain of events:

The build-up of reserves causes the money supply to expand and interest rates to fall which in turn provokes fear of inflation. To prevent this from happening, the monetary authorities are tempted to mop up the excess liquidity, preventing a fall in interest rates. By keeping interest rates up, sterilization is likely to affect both the demand and supply of foreign funds. It stimulates the supply of foreign funds because it maintains the interest rate differential. Similarly, it stimulates the demand for foreign loans because of the relatively lower interest rates abroad and because the absence of foreign exchange risk makes borrowing in foreign currencies the cheaper way to finance domestic investment. The stability of the exchange rate in the face of increasing domestic activity is likely to result in a growing trade deficit. The combination of increasing income and stable prices of imported goods is likely to spark growth of imports. The economy requires even more foreign capital to keep from overheating.

Thus, by keeping interest rates up and exchange rates stable, sterilization reinforces the dependence of the economy on foreign funds to finance investment as well as to prevent the economy from overheating. As dependence on foreign funds grows, the economy becomes more vulnerable to painful adjustments should the capital flows reverse. The experiences of Mexico and Thailand suggest the dangers inherent in accumulating capital inflows as reserves and sterilizing their effect on the money supply in order to prevent appreciation of the currency.

Non-sterilization Scenario

Instead of sterilizing the effects of the increased reserves on the money supply, an alternative policy approach is to allow the money supply to expand and to have its full effect on interest rates, causing them to fall. Expansion of the money supply will cause the trade deficit to widen further, but this need not be a cause for concern. The increase in demand for dollars is just a consequence of the increased supply of dollars that caused the increase in gross international reserves. The fall in the interest rate caused by the monetary expansion will bring domestic rates closer to international interest rates. This will dampen the inflow of portfolio investment and could put pressure on the peso to depreciate. Any depreciation in the currency has an impact on inflation, but since this inflation originates more from the higher prices of imported goods, it should also not be viewed with concern. (This is precisely what a depreciation in the currency is expected to accomplish: to make imported goods more expensive.) The fall in interest rates also stimulates domestic investment because capital is cheaper. The new investment is likely to flow, as desired, into the sectors that can build up the long-term capacity of the economy because the exchange rate is not distorted by short-term capital inflows.

In sum, addressing the problem of capital inflows with a combination of policies that allows both exchange rates and interest rates to adjust can create a price environment that could lead the economy along a growth path less dependent on foreign funds.

Existing Policy Preferences

Despite the seeming attractiveness of the second policy scenario, the biases observed in existing Philippine policies suggest that policy makers are likely to adopt the first, sterilization, scenario to deal with the prospective increase in capital inflows.

Preference for a strong currency

Since nearly every bust in Philippine economic history has been brought about by a foreign exchange crisis, there is an unspoken bias among monetary authorities for a strong peso. This has been quite evident in recent years since financial liberalization, when the widening trade gap has been ignored on the pretext of allowing market forces to dictate exchange rates. This preference is also evident in the asymmetry of the authorities' response to pressures in the foreign exchange market: a quick response to forces tending to depreciate the currency; a slower reaction to a currency appreciation.

This preference is understandable in light of the inevitable impact of a peso depreciation on inflation. Since maintaining price stability is the most important mandate of the Bangko Sentral ng Pilipinas (BSP), the central bank will actively oppose any force that would increase inflation. However, in the long run, a strong peso contributes to a widening trade gap. The preference for a strong peso therefore tends to increase the economy's dependence on foreign savings to meet the foreign exchange shortfall originating from the growing trade deficit.

Propensity to use interest rates to prevent currency depreciation

The strong bias against depreciation is combined with an almost knee-jerk reaction to raise interest rates at the first sign of a threat to the value of the domestic currency. Thus, stability in the foreign exchange market is usually bought at a high cost: high interest rates which dampen investment activity.

Monetarist orientation toward inflation

Despite their preference for a strong currency, the Philippine monetary authorities have to contend with the growing influence of exporters. To prevent the appreciation of the currency, the monetary authority is forced to absorb capital inflows into reserves. However, it has also, just as diligently, mopped up the pesos it has released by selling reverse repurchase agreements to keep inflation in check and to prevent a real exchange rate appreciation that could jeopardize growth. Whenever net foreign assets (NFA) surged there has been an offsetting decline in net domestic assets (NDA) to stay within reserve money (RM) ceilings (Figure 11.6). These steps have allowed the BSP to stabilize the peso on one hand and tame inflation on the other, at least in the short run (Montes 1996). However, sustaining this stability is another matter altogether.

Guidelines for Policy Action

The appropriate mix of policies is not easy to pin down. For example, with portfolio capital, the volatility of the flows is an important factor. It means that policy should address both how much of these funds can be used and where they are to be utilized. Prudence requires providing for the possibility of the unexpected pull-out of these funds. Thus, management of portfolio capital inflows should consider: the amount of foreign currencies to be kept in the central bank vaults; the amount of monetary expansion that can be allowed; and how the inflows should affect exchange rate movements.

Policy makers must choose among any number of combinations of monetary, reserve management, and exchange rate policies that could satisfy a given objective. The broad generalizations below should guide them in their search for an appropriate mix of policies.

FIGURE 11.6
Sterilized Intervention 1990–96

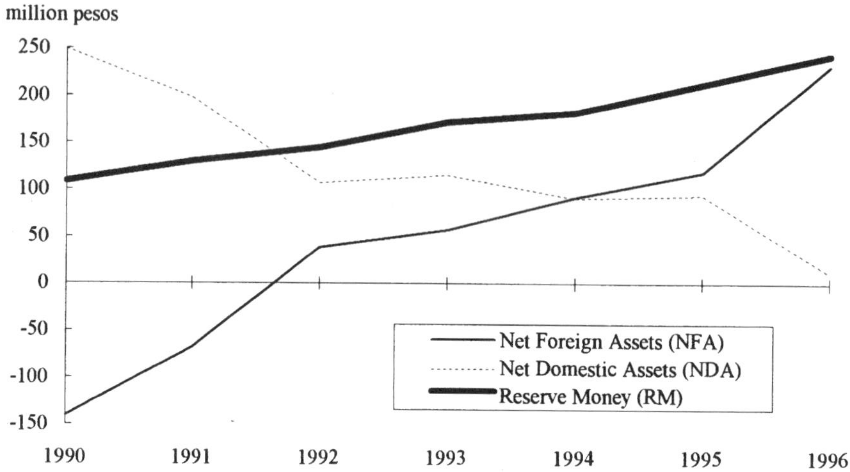

Source: Bangko Sentral ng Pilipinas.

First, the relatively volatile nature of capital flows requires keeping a higher level of gross international reserves than if the economy relied on more stable flows. The central bank's keeping this additional margin of international reserves is similar to a commercial bank's setting aside a certain amount of deposits to meet unexpected withdrawals. At present the Philippine monetary authorities' rule of thumb seems to be to hold sufficient foreign currency to finance three months of imports. Although the actual level of reserves in the Philippines is higher than this, the rule of thumb seems low compared with reserve levels in other countries. Thailand and Malaysia keep reserves equal to about six months of imports while Taiwan, China, and Japan are more comfortable when their reserves can finance their import requirements for about one year. It is also important to keep in mind that when Mexico was hit by its foreign exchange crisis in December 1994, it had reserves equivalent to about six months of import requirements. Monetary authorities in the Philippines should reconsider what level of reserves is acceptable. If the objective is a relatively stable foreign exchange rate that can be sustained over a long period, policy makers should aim to accumulate sufficient reserves to convince market players that they cannot play around with exchange rates.

Second, monetary growth needs to be designed with the limits defined by the availability of foreign currency. Fully neutralizing the effect of capital inflows on the money supply (sterilization) is equivalent to a policy that does not allow capital inflows to affect investment. At the same time, however, it does not seem prudent that the monetary impact of these inflows should be allowed to have its full effect on the trade balance (non-sterilization). Such a policy ignores the volatility of capital inflows. Monetary policy, therefore, must tread a middle ground: some sterilization is desirable but full sterilization would be unwise.

Third, the volatility of capital inflows also suggests that they should not be allowed to be the main determinant of the price of foreign currency. In a relatively thin foreign exchange market, large swings in capital inflows could easily cause the foreign exchange rate to be extremely volatile. This would be bad for business planning. Thus, while the central bank should heed the dictates of market forces, it should also distinguish between permanent and temporary changes in the marketplace. There is no sense in bucking long-term trends, but short-term jerks heavily influenced by volatile moods of market players should be dealt with appropriately.

In addition to the question of how much of the inflows of foreign currency can be spent, an even more difficult issue is how to make sure that these resources are properly used. In the past, the Philippines tried to grapple with this issue through direct intervention. For example, it applied different exchange rates to imports and exports or to different types of imports and exports and it applied different tariff rates to essential and non-essential goods or to capital and consumer goods. Experience has revealed flaws in these theoretically rational approaches. For example, letting government bureaucrats determine what imports are important, strategic, or essential implicitly assumes that they know what is best for the economy as a whole. Even if they do, they may be influenced by lobby groups. Implementation is also a problem. A complicated tariff code is fertile ground for corruption, since it must be implemented by human beings who can persuaded to sell their signatures.

In principle, therefore, it is preferable to let market forces allocate foreign currencies to their best use. This principle must be modified in consideration of the volatility of the supply of dollars coming from capital inflows. For example, if heavy inflows of short-term foreign loans and investments cheapen foreign currencies, then imports become so inexpensive that they are preferred over locally produced goods. At the same time, the dollar cost of production of exports increases, making exporting a less attractive business proposition. This situation does not put foreign funds to their best use in the economy. They should be used to improve export capability and to stimulate the domestic production of goods that would eventually replace imports. Therefore, it seems prudent to meddle a bit in the workings of the foreign exchange market.

Formulating guidelines is relatively easy, but translating them into actual policies is more difficult. The need to balance the management of foreign capital resources with respect for market forces makes the design of policy even more difficult. However, these difficulties cannot be used as excuses for doing nothing to manage capital inflows.

The inflow of foreign savings should be counted as blessing because it supplements domestic sources to meet the investments required for growth. True, the volatility of the investment and loans that are flowing into the Philippines creates a danger, but this danger is best viewed as a challenge to be met with appropriate policies. Furthermore, the dominance of the more volatile types of foreign loans and investments is likely to be temporary. Their predominance could simply reflect the way in which foreign investors have chosen to test the investment possibilities on Philippine soil. Once they become convinced that longer run returns are attractive because economic and political stability have taken deep root, they are likely to commit more long-term funds. At the same time that such transformation is taking place, it is also likely that the domestic savings rate will improve.

Notes

1 The authors and the Institute for Economic Policy Research acknowledge Gilbert G. Garchitorena, Liza L. Glean, Edward T. Gulane, Libertad K. Navarra, and Richard D. Supangan for their invaluable contribution to the writing of this paper.

2 Empirically, the Philippines' trade balance is closely related to the variables suggested by this framework, the peso-dollar rate, the money supply, the interest rate, and to two other variables over which the Philippines has no control, the dollar price of imports and the dollar price of exports. This relationship is shown in the regression results below:

BOT =

−1081	−0.0665 MS1	+ 114.66 Exrate	+ 64.96 Tbill	$-51.94\ P_{m\$}$	$+ 40.51\ P_{x\$}$	+ 11 24 D86	− 1381 D90
	(0.0042)	(24.33)	(17.53)	(10.65)	(12.97)	(375)	(360)
	15.75	4.71	3.70	4.87	3.12	2.99	3.83

$R^2 = 0.991$
SEE = 330
DW = 1.81

where: BOT = balance of trade in million US dollars
MS1 = money supply in billion pesos
Exrate = peso-dollar rate
Tbill = 91-day treasury bill rate
$P_{m\$}$ = dollar price index of imports (1985=100)
$P_{x\$}$ = dollar price index of exports (1985=100)
D86, D90 are dummy variables for the years 1986 and 1990
Time period: 1970 to 1996

References

Lamberte, Mario B. 1994. "Managing Surges in Capital Flows: The Philippine Case". Discussion Paper Series No. 94–20. Philippine Institute for Development Studies, December.

Montes, Manuel F. 1996. "Private Deficits and Public Responsibilities: Philippine Responses to Capital Inflows". Paper prepared for the conference, Macroeconomic Interdependence in the Asia Pacific Region, organized by the Economic Planning Agency of the Government of Japan. Tokyo, October 1996.

UPDATE

CALMING THE FOREIGN EXCHANGE MARKET: HOW THE PHILIPPINES IS COPING WITH THE CURRENCY TURMOIL

The continuing regional currency turmoil has provoked fears that the peso is bound to suffer the same fate as the other Southeast Asian currencies. The Philippines central bank has tried various policy instruments to allay such fears. These moves have had limited success. The most recent tool being tried is the use of the use of non-deliverable forwards (NDFs). It seems that the market has not yet fully grasped the implications of this move but there is a chance that it may calm the foreign exchange market.

CONTINUING TURMOIL DESPITE SIGNIFICANT CORRECTIONS

The continuing upward pressure on the peso-dollar rate can mean only one thing: the demand for dollars still significantly exceeds supply. The demand-supply imbalance, however, is difficult to trace from the traditional sources and uses of dollars. The Philippines has been spending more dollars than it earns, but the size of the shortfall relative to dollar earnings still seems manageable. The current account deficit is about 12 percent of total export earnings. Judging from historical relationships, to wipe out this gap through a 12 percent cut in imports would require only a 20 percent depreciation of the peso, or an exchange rate of about 32 pesos to the U.S. dollar. Thus, the depreciation to 40 pesos per dollar, and fears that the exchange rate could even go up to 50 pesos per dollar, seem overblown.

In a fundamental sense, the exchange rate adjustment that has already taken place should have corrected the demand-supply imbalance in the foreign exchange market. The fact that the imbalance still persists suggests that we need to look beyond the inflows and outflows of dollars to explain the imbalance still unsettling the market.

Regional Currency Turmoil Creates Uncertainties

The nervous state of market players has often been cited as the reason behind the present situation. The triggering mechanism was the currency turmoil in the region which provoked market players to think that the Philippine peso would suffer the same fate as the other Asian currencies. Because of the prevailing uncertainties, some are holding on to their dollars in expectation that the peso equivalent of their dollar holdings will continue to increase given shortage of supply in the market. Those who need dollars for future use are also rushing their dollar buying spree hoping that they can store up their dollar requirements now before the price of the dollar gets higher.

The Central Bank's Reaction

Since the crisis erupted in July 1997, calming this nervousness has been the central concern of the central bank (Bangko Sentral ng Philipinas, or BSP). Thus far, the BSP has resorted to three sets of tools. During the first few days of the foreign exchange market turbulence, the BSP tried to augment the supply of dollars in the market by drawing from its reserves. Unfortunately, the surge in demand was too great to be satisfied by the available reserves. Realizing that it was just wasting precious dollars to pursue a hopeless battle, the BSP gave up this defense almost immediately.

The second set of tools tried to influence the demand side. Attempting to cool the speculative fever by clipping the capability of market players to buy dollars, the BSP tightened money supply and limited the amount of dollars banks could hold. Interest rates were also raised to make peso assets more attractive than dollar assets. During normal times, these tools usually work. Given the abnormally high-strung environment engendered by the regional currency turmoil, however, these tools failed to reverse expectations. Worse, the prolonged regime of tight monetary policy and high interest rates had severe side effects. It dampened investment activities and raised production costs. If this regime becomes even more prolonged, it could provoke a stagflation—a high rate of inflation while economic activity slows down.

Given the backlash of opinion against the high interest rates and tight monetary policy, the BSP was left with little choice. As its third tool it was forced to allow more substantial adjustment in the peso-dollar rate in order to restore a balance between the demand and supply of foreign currencies in the market. Under normal circumstances, this should also have stabilized the foreign exchange rate. Unfortunately, the upward pressure on the peso-dollar rate remains, suggesting that a demand-supply imbalance persists.

PINNING DOWN THE ROOTS OF THE NERVOUSNESS

Why does the nervousness in the market continue despite the substantial peso-dollar rate adjustment that has already taken place? A large part of the answer lies in the unabated turbulence in the foreign currency markets of the East Asia region. With the baht, rupiah, and won taking a heavy beating in the foreign currency markets, it has become difficult for the market to believe that the Philippines will be spared of the same fate. With fires raging in the neighborhood, it has become increasingly difficult to convince the market players that the Philippine economy is indeed fire-proof.

While the turbulence in the regional currency markets is a valid reason for nervousness in the Philippine foreign exchange market, it is important to pin down more specifically why fear of further depreciation of the peso has precipitated such an extreme reaction that the supply of dollars in the market practically dried up. Depreciation of the peso, after all, is not 100 percent evil. There are sectors that are likely to be hurt by depreciation—the import-dependent firms catering solely to the local market. But there are also those who will benefit from it—exporters, families of overseas Filipino workers, and firms that compete with imported products. With these latter sectors making up more than 50 percent of total national output, the net impact of a devaluation on the economy should be positive.

Unreasonable or Ignorant Market?

Is the nervousness, then, purely psychological? Is it rooted in ignorance of economic realities? It is very tempting for economists to jump to such a conclusion, but they should be reminded that they are the first to assume that markets are rational. It is more prudent, therefore, to search for the possible rational reasons why the market is behaving in such way before condemning the market as crazy.

The question to ask is: Which sectors are likely to be made nervous by the prospect of a runaway depreciation of the peso? There are two key sectors: those using imported raw materials and those holding large amounts of dollar-denominated debt. The Philippine balance of payments records suggest that the mismatch between dollar earnings and dollar spending is not yet at a crisis level, since the ratio of the current account deficit to dollar earnings is still manageable. Thus, it is highly likely that the real root of the nervousness is a problem of the mismatch between the denomination of assets and liabilities. A number of companies that were lured by cheap dollar loans in the past two years went to a short position (i.e., their dollar assets are less than their dollar liabilities) and their attempts to square their positions are placing tremendous pressure on the demand for dollars in the market. The BSP estimates that the existing unhedged dollar loans of the corporate sector amount to about $2 to $3 billion.

The Story—Long and Short

If the main root of the Philippines' problem is the overexposure of companies to foreign currency- denominated loans, is it in the same rocky boat as the Thai economy? It seems not. The big difference lies in the fact that Thai companies owe their dollars to foreigners. In contrast, the bulk of the dollar obligations of Philippine companies can be traced to loans sourced from foreign currency deposits (FCDs), the majority of which are deposits of local residents. The regime of a stable exchange rate and high domestic interest rates induced companies in the Philippines to borrow foreign currencies while what they actually needed was domestic currency to finance their operations. What happened, then, was that Philippine banks borrowed from FCD accounts, sold the dollars to the BSP, and gave the pesos to the local companies. In effect, as the corporate sector was shifting to a short position, the BSP was moving into a long position in terms of dollar assets. In other words, the long position of the BSP was just the mirror image of the short position of the corporate sector.

Under such circumstances, should the Philippines require an exchange rate adjustment of the same magnitude as Thailand to correct the demand-supply imbalance in the foreign exchange market? Two key considerations suggest that this need not be the case. First, from a macroeconomic perspective, squaring the dollar asset-liability mismatch of the Philippine corporate sector does not require a massive amount of dollars from foreigners. Second, a realignment of the peso-dollar rate in excess of what is needed to correct the dollar income-spending mismatch could be counterproductive because the one-time impact on corporate balance sheets would have serious implications on their profit-and-loss positions over the medium term given the mismatch between their dollar assets and dollar liabilities. It is tempting to say that those who engaged in unhedged dollar borrowing during the time of cheap foreign currency should be made to pay for their own mistakes. Nevertheless there is also a need to recognize that ultimately everyone in the economy will be forced to pay for these mistakes if the unhedged borrowing results in a massive wave of corporate failures.

HOW NON-DELIVERABLE FORWARDS WORK

From this perspective, the recent attempt of the BSP to calm the market by opening up the facility for non-deliverable forwards (NDF) for foreign exchange offers some hope that the upward pressure on the peso-dollar rate will abate even while the turmoil in the regional currency market continues. What does this instrument do? NDFs are similar to ordinary forward contracts which are agreements between two parties to buy and sell dollars at a prearranged price and on a prearranged date. The only difference is that what is actually delivered is the amount of pesos representing the difference between the prearranged price and the actual spot price at the time of settlement. The instrument, therefore, allows those with foreign liabilities to fix the peso implications of their dollar debts at a specified date. The contract effectively shields them from the impact of a runaway devaluation. This is accomplished without depleting further the dollar reserves of the BSP.

In effect, the NDF foreign exchange facility is aimed at easing the pressure in the foreign exchange market by addressing the needs of those with unhedged dollar liabilities. This is likely to calm the jittery nerves of a significant sector of the foreign exchange market. Consequently, moves of the corporate sector to square their positions will no longer strain the foreign exchange market, because the corrections will not involve the use of scarce dollars. Once corporations' needs are flushed out of the foreign exchange market what will remain will be the buying and selling more directly related transacting business with the rest of the world. Historical trends suggest that the depreciation of the peso thus far is already in excess of what is needed to maintain a healthy balance between the inflows and outflows of foreign currency for such transactions.

Will the NDF accomplish what the other policy tools have not? As of now, it seems that market players have not yet fully grasped the implications of the BSP's new policy instrument. This is understandable. For one thing, the market is not too familiar with the use of hedging instruments. For another, this is the first time the instrument will be used. Nevertheless, this policy tool is likely to be effective in calming the market because it addresses the sector that seems to be at the root of the market uneasiness.

December 1997

12

Management of Capital Inflows in China's Opening Economy

Zhao Jinping

INTRODUCTION

The massive flow of foreign capital into China since the late 1970s when the country shifted to an open door policy has boosted China's economic growth. In particular, the surge in foreign direct investment has contributed to expanding industrial capacity, fiscal revenues, employment opportunities, and international trade.

China has been very successful in minimizing the adverse effect of volatile capital flows. The share of foreign direct investment has increased sharply while that of short-term capital has been reduced. The amount and composition of foreign debt have been closely monitored and kept under control. Direct controls on credit availability, supplemented by indirect measures that act through interest rates, have helped maintain macroeconomic stability in the face of rising capital inflows.

The yuan became a convertible currency for current account transactions in December 1996 when China accepted the obligations of Article 8 of the International Monetary Fund (IMF). However, China is following a very gradual and cautious approach to realizing its long-term goal of liberalizing capital account transactions. During the transition period, effort is being made to develop the domestic capital market and improve the mechanism of monetary control.

DEVELOPMENT OF CAPITAL INFLOWS

Capital Inflows Since the 1980s

Attracted by favourable policies, the flow of foreign funds into China has been increasing at a rapid pace since the late 1980s. The amount for 1996 alone was almost 28 times that for 1983 and greater than the total for the 10 years from 1979 to 1988. By the end of 1996, China had actually utilized foreign funds totalling US$284.0 billion, of which foreign direct investment was US$174.6 billion (Table 12.1). China ranks at the top among developing countries in terms of the amount of foreign capital introduced.

China has experienced three stages in absorbing foreign capital. The start-up stage was 1979–85. During this period, the Chinese government formulated a number of laws and regulations regarding foreign capital, set up special economic zones, opened coastal cities to the outside world, and carried out a series of preferential policies toward foreign direct investment. All these steps improved the investment climate for foreign investors in the coastal areas. At the same time, a program to develop infrastructure was launched with loans from foreign governments and international financial organizations. During this period the volume of capital inflows was small, at US$2 to 5 billion per year. Foreign borrowing was two times the volume of foreign direct investment.

TABLE 12.1
Foreign Capital Actually Utilized, 1979–96
US$ millions

Year	Total	Foreign Loans	Foreign Direct Investment	Other Investment
1979–82	12,457	10,690	1,166	601
1983	1,981	1,065	0,636	280
1984	2,705	1,286	1,258	161
1985	4,647	2,688	1,661	298
1986	7,258	5,014	1,874	370
1987	8,452	5,805	2,314	333
1988	10,226	6,487	3,194	545
1989	10,059	6,286	3,392	381
1990	10,289	6,534	3,487	268
1991	11,554	6,888	4,366	300
1992	19,202	7,911	11,007	284
1993	38,960	11,189	27,515	256
1994	43,213	9,267	33,767	179
1995	48,133	10,327	37,221	285
1996	54,804	12,669	41,726	409
Cumulative 1979–96	283,940	104,106	174,884	4,950

Source: *China Statistical Yearbook* 1997.

The second phase, from 1986 to 1991, was a period of steady growth in capital inflows. With the inflow of foreign capital increasing, China introduced another series of policies specifically on foreign investment directed to certain sectors. More special economic zones and economic development zones that enjoyed preferential policies were established. In this period, despite the economic sanctions imposed in China after the Tiananmen incident, the inflow of foreign capital exceeded US$10 billion in most years, increasing at an annual average rate of 9.7 percent. Still, foreign loans remained the major form of capital inflows.

The third phase, from 1992 to the present, has been one of rapid growth. Deng Xiaoping's urging the people to speed up the pace of economic reform during his trip to the southern region in early 1992 spurred a boom in the utilization of foreign capital nation-wide, with annual inflows averaging US$41 billion a year between 1992 and 1996.

The composition of capital inflows into China has shown the following changes in recent years. First, foreign direct investment has grown in importance. It exceeded foreign borrowing for the first time in 1992. Foreign direct investment accounted for 76 percent of total capital inflows in 1996 (Table 12.2). More and more foreign direct investment in China takes the form of wholly owned subsidiaries ("foreign enterprises") instead of joint ventures. Second, loans from foreign governments and international organizations have always been the main source of China's external debt and their share of total foreign loans has been on the rise. Third, in terms of maturity, the share of short-term loans has declined sharply from about 40 percent in the mid-1980s to 11.2 percent in 1995. This has made China less vulnerable to volatile capital flows. Finally, foreign funds raised through issues of equities and bonds have increased sharply. In 1992 China issued B-shares (shares of Chinese companies opened to foreign investors) for the first time. Later, H-shares were issued in Hong Kong and N shares in New York. The total outstanding volume of bonds issued overseas reached US$10.7 billion in 1995, accounting for 10 percent of China's total external debt.

The Effect of Foreign Capital Inflows on China's Macroeconomy

According to economic theory, the expansion of a country's production capacity depends upon the rate of domestic investment and the quality of the newly added capital. Foreign capital inflows can boost economic growth by making up for a shortage of domestic funds, stimulating domestic investment, and increasing capital accumulation Over the past 10-odd

TABLE 12.2
Amount and Composition of Foreign Capital Inflows

	1985	1990	1995	1996
		US$ millions		
Foreign Loans	2,690	6,534	10,327	12,669
Foreign Governments	490	2,521	2,773	3,451
International Monetary Organizations	600	1,066	2,707	2,997
Chinese Stocks, bonds		3	783	3,399
Foreign Direct Investment	1,660	3,487	37,521	41,726
Joint Ventures	582	1,886	19,078	20,755
Foreign Enterprises	13	683	10,317	12,606
Other Foreign Investment	300	268	285	409
Total	4,650	10,289	48,133	54,804
		% of Total		
Foreign Loans	57.8	63.5	21.5	23.1
Foreign Governments	10.5	24.5	5.8	6.3
International Monetary Organizations	12.9	10.4	5.6	5.5
Chinese Stocks, Bonds	0.0	0.0	1.6	6.2
Foreign Direct Investment	35.7	33.9	78.0	76.1
Joint Ventures	12.5	18.3	39.6	37.9
Foreign Enterprises	0.3	6.6	21.4	23.0
Other Foreign Investment	6.5	2.6	0.6	0.7
Total	100.0	100.0	100.0	100.0

Source: *China Statistical Yearbook* 1997.

years, the large inflow of foreign direct investment has relieved the capital shortage in China. Foreign direct investment actually utilized has increased in importance, from 2.3 percent of total domestic fixed investment in 1985 to 16.1 percent in 1995. Most foreign loans were put into such bottleneck sectors as transportation, telecommunications, and energy and into technical improvements in medium and large-sized enterprises. In 1995, for example, foreign borrowing helped to finance 3.2 percent of the total investment in infrastructure construction. By improving the supply of infrastructure facilities such investment greatly expanded the production capacity of basic industrial sectors and created conditions for further economic growth.

Another contribution of foreign capital inflows is reflected in increases in industrial capacity, fiscal revenues, and employment opportunities. In 1995, foreign enterprises accounted for 14.5 percent of China's industrial production and contributed 12.3 percent of China's total industrial and commercial tax revenues. Taxes on foreign investment represented the main source of local revenues, particularly in some coastal areas. In addition, the increase in the number of foreign investment enterprises has created employment opportunities for China's abundant labour resources. According to preliminary statistics, some 17 million workers were employed by more than 120,000 foreign investment enterprises in operation by the end of 1995. Employment also increased in medium and large-scale infrastructure and renovation projects that had foreign investment.

The large inflow of foreign capital has promoted the opening of China's economy. First of all, diverse forms of foreign investment have motivated a rapid increase of foreign trade. From 1983 to 1995 the total volume of imports and exports carried out by foreign investment enterprises shot up at an annual average rate of 78 percent, 5.5 times the annual average growth rate of China's foreign trade as a whole. Forty percent of China's exports are attributable to foreign investment (Table 12.3).

Although China has set balance of payments equilibrium as a target for its economic development, in the early 1980s slow development of exports led to a trade deficit. The flow of foreign capital into the country was small, so that the surplus on the capital account was not large enough to cover the trade deficit. This made it difficult to balance foreign exchange receipts and payments (Table 12.4). The situation changed in the 1990s, however. The capital account balance has been in surplus in most years due to large inflows of capital, the major portion of which were in the form of long-term investment in capital projects. The surplus from capital inflows has contributed to a small surplus in the overall balance of payments. Capital inflows generally lead to a current account deficit, but this has not always been true in China. Thanks to increases in exports, China has maintained a sizeable capital account surplus while also keeping its current account balance in surplus. This has greatly eased the long-term shortage of foreign exchange and increased foreign exchange reserves. China's foreign reserves reached US$105 billion at the end of 1996, placing it just behind Japan among countries with the largest reserves.

TABLE 12.3
Exports by Foreign Funded Enterprises, 1988–96

	1988	1990	1992	1994	1995	1996
Exports by Foreign Funded Enterprises (US$ billions)	2.5	7.8	17.4	34.7	46.9	61.5
Share of Total Exports (%)	5.2	12.6	20.4	28.7	31.5	40.7
Share Contribution of Foreign Funded Enterprises to Increase in Total Exports (%)	18.1	30.2	40.5	32.4	43.8	608.3*

Note: *Export growth for local enterprises was negative.
Source: *China Statistical Yearbook* 1996.

TABLE 12.4
Balance of Payments, Selected Years
US$ billions

	1985	1990	1991	1992	1993	1994	1995	1996
Current Account Balance	–11.42	11.99	13.27	6.40	–11.90	7.66	1.62	7.24
Foreign Trade	–13.12	9.17	8.74	5.18	–10.65	7.29	18.05	19.54
Non-trade Account	1.46	2.56	3.70	0.06	–2.42	–0.97	–17.87	–14.42
Transfers	0.24	0.27	0.83	1.16	1.17	1.34	1.44	2.13
Capital Account Balance	8.97	3.26	8.03	–0.25	23.47	32.64	38.67	39.97
Long-term Capital	6.70	6.45	7.67	0.66	27.41	35.76	38.25	41.55
Short-term Capital	2.27	–3.20	0.36	–0.91	–3.94	–3.11	0.43	1.59
Errors and Omissions	0.09	–3.13	–6.79	–8.27	–9.80	–9.77	–17.81	–15.56
Change in Reserves	2.35	–12.12	–14.51	2.12	–1.77	–30.53	–22.48	–31.65
Foreign Exchange	2.51	–11.57	–14.07	2.27	–1.76	–30.42	–21.98	–31.43

Notes: Imports and exports are free-on-board. Reserve increases are negative.
Source: *China Statistical Yearbook* 1997.

Theoretically, capital inflows, either through direct investment or through loans, would be expected to stimulate investment demand and consumption, lead to an increase in the money supply, and, in turn, add to the possibility of inflation. Large capital inflows have indeed pushed China's inflation rate up in recent years. However, we have estimated that capital inflows accounted for only 3 percent of the inflation rate in 1994 which reached 24 percent.

REGULATION OF FINANCIAL AND FOREIGN EXCHANGE MARKETS

The large volume of capital inflows over the past decade has greatly boosted China's economic growth. Although they have added some inflationary pressure, they have not had any severe detrimental effect on the economy nor have they created financial disorder, despite turbulence in the international capital market.

China's positive experience with capital inflows is due to four factors. First, a large proportion of China's capital inflows have taken the form of foreign direct investment which enhanced domestic production capacity and increased exports. This is quite different from the situation in Latin American countries which have a high percentage of speculative, short-term capital inflows that stimulate consumption, raise asset prices, and restrain domestic savings. Second, more than 60 percent of foreign direct investment is supplied in-kind in the form of equipment and materials. As a result, the capital inflows have not created excess demand or generated substantial inflationary pressure. Third, China's moderately tight monetary policy also has contributed to restraining inflation. Since 1993, reducing inflation by controlling the money supply has become a major macroeconomic target. To this end, the government has adopted policies to control the scale of credit, thus relieving the pressure of capital inflows. Fourth, limits on capital transactions and foreign exchange controls have played a part in stabilizing the exchange rate and the capital market, so that China has avoided the shocks to its financial order caused by volatile exchange rate fluctuations and capital flight, as happened in Mexico and other countries.

Control over Aggregate Investment

In order to prevent investment fever which could lead to severe supply-demand imbalance and inflation, China has retained a certain amount of regulatory control over total investment. Such control proved to be necessary in the economic reform and opening process even after planning of investment, production, and sales were eliminated in most economic sectors. While state ministries and local governments have been granted approval power over their investment projects, planning departments at various levels have retained the right to examine and approve certain investment projects, including those that supplement foreign investment and construction projects financed by funds borrowed from abroad.

This planned management system is, of course, fundamentally different from China's traditional planning system. Economic means such as credit limits and tax rates are used to implement the plan in most cases. As projects funded by foreign investments and loans generally need immense amounts of supplementary funds, controlling the supply of supplementary funding indirectly regulates the size of capital inflows. This was most apparent during a period of economic austerity in 1994–95, when China restricted capital construction and credit. The shortage of domestic funds to supplement joint venture projects meant that the annual growth of foreign investment slowed from about 150 percent in 1992–93 to 10–20 percent in 1994–95. On the other hand, local authorities often have strong motives to undertake investment projects and may blindly introduce foreign capital even if the central government expressly controls the investment scale. This discretionary power of local authorities affects the efficacy of the central government's control of the economy. That is one reason why M2 increased sharply by 34.4 percent despite the restrictive credit policy in 1994.

Policy toward Foreign Direct Investment

In the earliest phase of capital inflow, China had no explicit policy regarding the composition of foreign direct investment by industry, and these funds were primarily used in labour-intensive processing and tertiary industries, including hotel and service projects. In late 1987, China formulated regulations on foreign investment and adopted policies regarding which industries were to be developed and supported by supplementary funds, tax exemption, land use rights, and other concessions. Since then, there has been a great change in the structure of foreign investment, particularly since 1992 when foreign investment accelerated. More and more trans-national companies began to enter the Chinese market, capital- and technology-intensive projects and large-scale infrastructure projects increased significantly, and the level of investment expanded remarkably.

On the other hand, excessive growth in property investment bloated China's overall investment scale and disturbed the financial order, increasing inflationary pressure in 1993–95. Inefficient investment in redundant projects and in non-priority sectors aggravated the problem. In response, in June 1995 the State Planning Commission promulgated Interim Regulations Guiding Foreign Investment which clearly set forth the scope of projects for which foreign investment should be encouraged, limited, or prohibited. Meanwhile, supportive measures and policies were formulated and the flow of supplementary domestic funds was adjusted to meet the requirements of China's industrial policies.

Since 1995, these policies have succeeded in channelling foreign investment to priority sectors. Among these projects, infrastructure, energy, and transportation are new hot spots for foreign investment, while high-tech projects such as electronics and machinery are also growing in number. In contrast, investment in property and some other projects has been brought under control, with a drastic fall in their share of investment funds (Table 12.5).

Limiting Access to China's Capital Market

After roughly a decade of development, China's capital market has become the most dynamic and attractive aspect of the economy. The government bond market has grown in breadth and depth. Government bonds are issued in many forms and types, for different terms, and their value has increased from 4.8 billion yuan in 1981 to 151.1 billion in 1995 (Table 12.6). The stock market has also made much headway. According to the *People's Daily* (8 November 1996) by the end of 1995, there were 467 companies listed at home with over 100 billion yuan in book value and 980 billion yuan in market capitalization. There were seventy-three investment funds, of which thirty-one were listed. In addition, markets have developed for corporate bond issues, futures, and interbank lending. As China's capital market has only a short history, it is still immature and needs further improvement.

TABLE 12.5
Contracted Foreign Direct Investment by Sector, 1993 and 1996

	1993		1996	
	Value US$ billions	Share %	Value US$ billions	Share %
Total	111.4	100.0	73.3	100.0
Farming	1.2	1.1	1.1	1.5
Industry	51.2	46.0	50.5	68.9
Construction	3.9	3.5	2.0	2.7
Transportation, Post, & Telecommunications	1.5	1.3	1.6	2.2
Commerce, Food Services	4.6	4.1	2.3	3.1
Real Estate, Public Residential	43.8	39.3	12.9	17.6
Health Care, Recreation, & Social Welfare	0.5	0.4	0.4	0.6
Education, Culture, & Arts	0.5	0.4	0.2	0.3
Scientific Research	0.6	0.5	0.2	0.3
Other	3.8	3.4	2.1	2.9

Source: *China Intertrade*. March 1997. *China Statistical Yearbook*. 1995.

TABLE 12.6
Domestic Securities Market, 1995
Yuan billions

	Issues	Repayments	Year-end Balance
Total	261.19	87.75	593.33
Stock	3.10		30.23
A-shares	0.53		11.39
B-shares	1.03		6.16
H-shares	1.54		1.03
N-shares	0.00		0.24
Bonds	258.09	87.75	563.10
Government Bonds	151.09	49.70	330.03
Enterprise Bonds	21.62	32.55	36.44
Financial Bonds	85.39	5.50	167.52

Note: Issues of stock are publicly held stock only.
Source: *China Financial Yearbook* 1996.

In order to prevent financial disorder from undermining the stability of the whole economy, China has opened its financial and stock markets to foreign financial institutions and investors very gradually. Many limits to market access are still retained. First, foreign financial institutions applying to enter the Chinese market are strictly limited to those with good reputation, sound performance, and economic strength. Second, the scope of business for foreign financial institutions already operating in the country is restricted. For one thing, foreign banks are only permitted to handle foreign exchange business and cannot engage in yuan banking transactions. Third, foreign financial firms face tight controls on the number and scope of branches they may open. Apart from these limits to access and differential treatment, foreign financial institutions have been restricted in extending their market area. Initially, they were limited to the special economic zones; in 1990 they were granted permission to operate in Shanghai, in 1992 in Dalian and other cities. By 1995 altogether 13 coastal cities had been opened to foreign banking institutions, and 11 inland cities including Beijing had also been opened.

With the public placement of B-shares by Shanghai Electronic Vacuum Valve Company on 21 February 1992, China's securities market took a big step toward internationalization. This issue provided the first channel for foreign capital to access China's stock market. As of today more than 30 foreign banks and securities companies have won seats on the Shanghai Stock Exchange where they can directly trade B-shares. However, there are still some limits, such as a ceiling on the number of shares that foreigners can hold. Also, B-shares and domestic yuan A-shares are strictly segregated and foreign investors are not able to enter the A-share market, where the bulk of the shares of Chinese companies are traded. China's securities market, particularly the stock market, is still only partially open (Table 12.6).

China's control of the entry of foreign capital has effectively enabled the domestic financial market to avoid external shocks and ensured its orderly expansion. With the deepening reform of China's financial system, access limits will be relaxed and replaced by more open policies. Some headway has been made in this respect. In 1995 approval was granted to 18 more foreign banks, 2 foreign insurance companies, 1 Sino-foreign joint venture bank, and 82 representative offices of foreign financial institutions. As a result, the number of foreign financial institutions has increased to 137, representing more than 30 countries and regions, and the number of representative offices has increased to 519.

Major steps were taken in December 1996 to open China's financial markets further. The People's Bank of China announced that foreign investors would have partial access to the A-share market through authorized investment funds, starting in 1997. In addition, selected foreign banks were granted permission to engage in yuan-based business in Shanghai's Pudong district.

Foreign Exchange Control Under Conditional Convertibility of Current Account Transactions

Prior to 1979, all foreign exchange transactions were handled by the Bank of China, the sole authorized foreign exchange bank in the country, and foreign exchange was controlled by plan. With the start of the economic reforms in 1979, however, the foreign exchange system was revised. A foreign exchange retention system was adopted for export enterprises, and foreign exchange quota swap markets were set up in various localities, allowing enterprises to buy and sell quotas and introducing some aspects of the market mechanism to the foreign exchange system.

In 1994 the dual exchange rate system was eliminated and an interbank foreign exchange market was established. Thereupon, a foreign exchange settlement and sale system was implemented for Chinese enterprises and the yuan was made conditionally convertible for current account transactions. The swap market was maintained so that foreign investment enterprises could purchase and sell foreign exchange, if necessary. All this made China's exchange system more market-oriented.

Despite the conditional convertibility of the yuan, the foreign exchange system remained under tight control. First, demand and supply of foreign exchange were restricted. Under the new system, Chinese enterprises must sell to banks the foreign exchange that they earn through trade and they must buy foreign exchange with yuan against presentation of valid certificates. In principle, foreign enterprises were supposed to balance their foreign exchange receipts and repayments and, thereupon, their foreign exchange account and revenue and expenditure were placed under state supervision. They could not settle their accounts with banks but were required to buy and sell foreign exchange at the swap centre subject to approval. Foreign banks could only make one-way settlement of accounts.

The second main control was through the limits on market competition. The central bank was the main institution for foreign exchange dealings, so authorized foreign exchange banks had to bid for deals and to trade foreign exchange between the official floor and ceiling rates. This requirement restrained these banks from taking full part in the market.

The controls over China's foreign exchange system offered two distinct advantages. One was that, despite a flood of foreign capital into China and expansion of foreign trade, the system ensured an adequate supply of foreign funds, balanced demand and supply, stabilized the exchange rate, and insulated the domestic financial market from violent fluctuations of world interest and exchange rates. Since the elimination of the dual exchange rate system in 1994, the value of the yuan has risen only slightly (from 8.7 yuan per dollar at the beginning of 1994 to 8.3 yuan per dollar in mid-1997), despite the massive capital inflow and a rapid accumulation of foreign exchange reserves (Table 12.7).

The other advantage of the exchange control system was that it supported the rapid increase of foreign exchange reserves and enhanced China's debt-servicing and import-paying capability. At the end of 1994 China's foreign exchange reserves amounted to US$51.62 billion, 1.44 times above their level the previous year under the dual exchange rate system. At the end of 1996 reserves had grown to US$105 billion (Table 12.7). Furthermore, the ratio of foreign exchange reserves to external debt outstanding more than doubled from 25 percent in 1993 to 56 percent in 1994 and reached 69 percent in 1995.

Nevertheless, the existence of limits on the convertibility of the currency for trade and non-trade current account transactions kept the market from fully mirroring demand and supply. To some extent it also limited foreign enterprises from conducting normal operations. On the other hand,

TABLE 12.7
Exchange Rate and Foreign Exchange Reserves, 1985–96
end of term

	Official Exchange Rate		Exchange Reserves	
Year	100US$/ Yuan	% Increase	US$ millions	% Increase
1985	320.15	—	2,644	—
1986	372.21	16.3	2,072	–21.6
1987	372.21	0.0	2,923	41.1
1988	372.21	0.0	3,372	15.4
1989	472.21	26.9	5,550	64.6
1990	522.21	10.6	11,093	99.7
1991	543.42	4.1	21,712	95.7
1992	575.18	5.8	19,443	–10.5
1993	580.00	0.8	21,199	9.1
1994	844.62	45.6	51,620	143.5
1995	831.74	–1.5	73,597	42.6
1996	829.97	–0.2	105,000	42.7

Source: *China Statistical Yearbook* 1997.

the requirements of mandatory settlement and conditional sale of foreign exchange had the practical effect of driving up supply and dampening demand, so that supply of foreign exchange exceeded demand. To reduce the resulting pressure for revaluation of the yuan, the People's Bank had to make large purchases of foreign currency. This in turn led to a surge in China's foreign exchange reserves. The resulting increase in the supply of high-powered money has caused inflationary pressure. In order to solve these problems, in July 1996 the People's Bank began introducing additional market-oriented measures to the exchange control system.

Newly instituted reform measures included permitting foreign enterprises to settle and sell foreign exchange through banks and removing limits on the supply of foreign exchange to settle current account transactions. Meanwhile, the People's Bank eliminated limits on money exchange and remittances for non-trade transactions, so that Chinese residents going abroad for personal reasons can now purchase foreign currency. On 1 December 1996 yuan became fully convertible to settle current account transactions, meeting the requirements in Article 8 of the IMF Agreement.

External Debt Control and its Effect

China's controls on external debt aim to utilize foreign capital through various channels and in diverse forms to meet the needs of economic development while at the same time limiting the total amount of foreign borrowing. In addition, the composition of external debt must be optimized to reduce exchange risks. With this target, China has drawn up a unified external debt plan and has instituted a strict registration system that is centrally managed. First, all borrowings from abroad must be incorporated into the State Plan, and the state draws up annual and longer term plans to control and co-ordinate borrowing. Second, under the leadership and co-ordination of the State Council, individual departments guide and manage the sources and disposition of foreign borrowings in their functional areas. Third, a dozen or more banks including Bank of China, CITIC Industrial Bank, China Investment Bank, and Bank of Communications are designated to act as special windows for commercial borrowing from abroad and for issuing bonds on the international market. Only authorized institutions are permitted to borrow commercially or to issue medium- or long-term bonds abroad. Finally, since 1987, all foreign loans managed by the functional departments and by designated Chinese banks must be registered on a regular schedule. In January 1996 China introduced a reporting system for international payments and receipts. This system provides the government with reliable statistics for monitoring external debt, including short-term capital inflows and outflows, as well as for formulating macroeconomic policy.

Since 1979 China has had almost two decades' experience borrowing from abroad, and its outstanding balance has grown as much as 31.7 percent per year. By the end of June 1996, China had become the third largest debtor country among developing nations, with an outstanding balance of US$109.8 billion. External debt has two effects on the economy. On the one hand, it increases investment and boosts economic growth. On the other hand, it adds to the debt burden and may hinder the country's sustained and healthy development if it becomes too large or if the borrowed funds are not used efficiently. The serious debt crises encountered by some Latin American countries in the 1980s illustrated the dangers of external debt.

China's accumulation of external debt began to slow in the 1990s. From 1979 to 1984, the outstanding balance of external debt rose at an average annual rate of 26.8 percent and from 1985 to 1988, debt growth speeded up to annual average rate of 36.2 percent, a rate far greater than the total increase in GNP. From 1990, though, debt growth tended to moderate. Although the balance of external debt outstanding was larger during the 1990-95 period than in the previous periods, the average annual growth rate had dropped to 19.3 percent, below the rate of growth in exports for the same period. By source, loans from foreign governments and international financial institutions make up about one-third of the total, with the rest accounted for by commercial and other loans (Table 12.8). By term, the share of long-term loans has increased sharply in recent years.

China has always maintained its outstanding external debt balance at a moderate level. This has been due to strict external debt controls, limits on total volume, and close supervision over debt service and structural readjustment. China's debt indicators have always been kept within state targets and below the internationally recognized critical levels. In 1995 for example, both China's debt-service ratio of 7.3 percent and its debt ratio (foreign debt/foreign exchange receipts from exports) of 69.9 percent were far below the critical levels of 20 percent and 100 percent (Table 12.9). Overall, China's external debt situation has been a healthy one in terms of both scale and structure.

Nevertheless, there are three main problems with China's external debt management. One is that foreign borrowings are not used efficiently, due to such factors as the shortage of supplementary domestic investment.

TABLE 12.8
Composition of China's External Debt by Type and Term, 1985–96
Percent Share

	By Type of Debt		By Term	
Year	Official	Commercial and Other	Long-term	Short-term
1985	30.5	69.5	59.5	40.5
1986	35.2	54.8	27.8	22.2
1987	29.0	71.0	81.1	18.9
1988	26.2	72.8	81.7	18.3
1989	29.7	70.3	89.7	10.3
1990	28.0	72.0	87.1	12.9
1991	27.4	72.6	83.0	17.0
1992	28.7	71.3	84.4	15.6
1993	29.6	70.4	83.8	16.2
1994	35.1	64.9	88.8	11.2
1995	34.6	65.4	88.8	11.2
1996	33.1	66.9	87.9	12.0

Source: *China Statistical Yearbook* 1993–97.

TABLE 12.9
Foreign Debt Indicators, 1985–96
Percent

Year	Debt-Service Ratio	Liability Ratio	Foreign Debt Ratio
1985	2.8	5.6	53.4
1986	20.3	7.8	70.0
1987	12.7	9.4	75.2
1988	6.3	10.0	84.4
1989	8.0	11.5	83.1
1990	8.5	14.8	87.0
1991	8.0	15.0	87.0
1992	7.3	14.1	90.7
1993	9.7	14.0	94.5
1994	9.1	17.6	77.8
1995	7.3	15.5	69.9
1996	6.7	14.3	75.6

Notes: Debt-Service Ratio is the ratio of repayments of principal and interest on foreign debt to foreign exchange receipts from exports.
Liability Ratio is the ratio of foreign debt to GNP.
Foreign Debt Ratio is the ratio of foreign debt to foreign exchange receipts from exports..
Source: *China Statistical Yearbook* 1997.

Another is that debt-service in certain areas and for certain projects suffers from poor planning and management. The third is that because the lion's share of the outstanding balance is in U.S. dollars and Japanese yen, the debt burden fluctuates with the exchange rates of these currencies and there is risk in the currency composition. As a matter of fact, in the first half of the 1990s China's yen debt increased by 70 percent or more in dollar terms due to the sharp rise of the Japanese yen, although it has declined a little recently. China's vulnerability to increases in its debt service requirements due to exchange rate movements is a problem to be solved in the days to come.

PROSPECTS AND POLICIES FOR INTERNATIONALIZING CHINA'S CAPITAL MARKET

Effectively utilizing foreign capital for infrastructure improvement and economic development is a policy target of China's medium-and long-term economic development program. The traditional practice of relying solely on preferential policies and offering access to the domestic market in exchange for foreign capital does not suit the requirements of today's international investors. Therefore, the only choice for China's development is to carry through financial structure reforms to make the capital market more market- and outward-oriented and consistent in all dimensions with the international economy. With a more open capital market, however, domestic financial order and economic development will become more exposed to the risk of international financial fluctuations. In order to prevent a shock like the Mexican financial crisis, to ensure stable economic growth, and to utilize foreign capital effectively with minimum negative effects, China has to adopt the following comprehensive policies with respect to its financial and foreign exchange systems:

- open securities and exchange markets to foreign investors while strengthening the mechanism of monetary controls;
- limit inflows of short-term funds to stabilize the capital market; and
- enhance foreign exchange earning capacity in order to improve the balance of payments.

Gradual Opening of the Securities Market

Issuing B-shares on the domestic market and directly placing international bonds abroad is consistent with China's transformation from a system of unitary investment by the state to pluralistic investment and conforms with trends in the international capital market. At present, around 80 percent of the funds China raises in the international capital market are securities issues. Financing by international securities issue will become an increasingly important means to absorb foreign capital once China's medium- and large-sized enterprises have set up a modern enterprise system and the domestic securities market has matured. The potential for opening the Chinese capital market is great.

The stock market offers the greatest potential. China's stock market is far more volatile and risky than international markets because it lacks sound mechanisms and standard procedures among stock issuers. Also, share prices in the domestic market are not based on expected return and normal investment criteria, but are determined largely by the speculative activities of investors. The first steps to increase the market's openness are to establish mechanisms for bond issuance, to standardize marketing procedures, to improve the management of listed enterprises, and to properly control market speculation.

In this respect, China will pursue a policy of improving selected stock market mechanisms and step-by-step opening of the market to foreign issuers and investors. Until the yuan becomes fully convertible for capital account transactions, foreign investment in China's A-share market will be limited to authorized funds managed by institutional investors. Foreign investors will have access mainly through increased B-share volume and overseas placements. A- and B-share markets will remain strictly segregated. During this period, as quickly as possible, China will create a suitable operational framework to improve the functioning of the securities market, develop intermediary organs for securities investment, open the securities market further, raise the share of stock issues available to foreign investors, compel listed companies to improve their operations and management, and reinforce their international competitiveness. When the system has adjusted to these changes and the yuan has been made fully convertible for capital account transactions, most, or even all, A-shares can be made available to foreign investors. Then the Chinese securities market will be entirely consistent with the world capital market.

With the gradual development of the securities market, financial instruments for foreign capital inflows can be diversified. Driven by a worldwide liberalization, the number of new financial vehicles and derivatives has mushroomed. Some of these vehicles may be used in conjunction with existing financial instruments. The increased diversity and complexity of financial instruments can more readily meet borrowers' requirements, but those instruments also entail more risk. China has already tested some new investment modes, such as BOT (Build-Operate-Transfer). But China needs a more sound market system and macroeconomic environment before it relies heavily on financial derivatives as a form of foreign capital.

Continued Liberalization of the Foreign Exchange Market

The complete opening of China's foreign exchange market depends upon the full convertibility of the yuan which is the ultimate objective of reform of the foreign exchange system. The extension of yuan convertibility in late 1996, has paved the way for relaxing limits on foreign investors' access to China's capital market and for granting them resident status. The adoption of this freer foreign exchange control system will improve the operational environment for foreign investors, provide full legal protection of their legitimate rights and interests, and reduce risks in the outward remittance of profits. Since the yuan has become freely convertible for current account transactions, enterprises can now easily acquire foreign currencies for importing goods and services. Demand and supply distortions in the foreign exchange market have been largely eliminated. This should help China open its economy wider and increase its participation in international trade and investment.

On the other hand, opening the foreign exchange market brings potential dangers, such as the risk of a credit crunch due to massive capital flight. China will take the necessary measures to prevent a crisis such as Mexico experienced. One important prerequisite to maintaining a stable foreign exchange market when yuan accounts are freely convertible, is to ensure that the supply of foreign exchange from reserves and export earnings satisfies the demand for import payments and outward remittance of profits. China's current accumulation of US$100 billion in exchange reserves is due largely to restraints on demand rather than to rising export earnings. As outward transfers of dividends, interest, and debt-service payments increase, export earnings will need to become a reliable source of foreign exchange. Therefore, China's trade policy must persistently encourage exports and expand the country's share of world markets. Another policy imperative is to ensure that the progressive opening of the foreign exchange market proceeds in an orderly manner. Free convertibility of the yuan is an inevitable step in opening China's capital market, but China may still exercise policy control over capital flows, particularly short-term funds. In order to prevent excessive capital inflows from causing domestic financial instability because of imperfect and unsound market mechanisms, strict control over capital accounts will still be necessary for some time to come. Convertibility of capital account transactions will be realized first for long-term and then for short-term transactions. Still another task is to further improve the external debt control system to guard against shocks from speculative capital inflows. Debt capital, especially short-term capital inflows, will be included in the monitoring statistics and the volume of external debt will be strictly limited.

Progressive Marketization of Interest Rates

The most essential element in financial system reform is the liberalization of interest rates. However, China's imperfect market mechanisms require that this liberalization take place incrementally.

Enterprises, particularly state-owned enterprises, that have not yet thoroughly transformed their operations to market practices present one obstacle to immediately freeing interest rates to be determined by demand and supply. Once interest rates are liberalized, some of these enterprises will go bankrupt as they have no way to offset the higher cost of borrowing if interest rates rise. The higher interest rates may also be passed on in higher product prices, potentially triggering inflation.

Another obstacle to immediately setting interest rates free lies in the fact that not all of China's commodity prices have been liberalized. For example, price controls still remain in agriculture, energy, materials, and other basic industries. If interest rates were to be determined in the market, these basic industries would be unable to obtain needed funds and this would create bottlenecks for China's continued economic development.

Finally, China needs to maintain some control over interest rate adjustments in order to conduct monetary policy effectively. Because China's financial market was late in starting and the central bank has limited securities assets that it can use to adjust interest rates, it relies to a large extent upon direct regulation of the base interest rate to control the money supply. Convertibility of the yuan for current account transactions has made it difficult to manage short-term capital flows which are supposed to be still under strict control. In recent years, some of China's immense capital inflows have been comprised of short-term debt capital that is induced by interest rate differentials and expectations of exchange rate changes. Under such circumstances, the central bank will need to retain some control over interest rates in order to maintain its ability to control the money supply.

Given these obstacles, the process of freeing China's interest rates to market determination will likely take place in the following way. Development of the money market will be promoted first, because it provides the basic conditions for a market-determined interest rate. In the last few years, China has made some breakthroughs in establishing markets for interbank lending, treasury bond trading, and bill discounting. Second, liberalization of the interest rate on interbank lending is the starting point for overall market determination of interest rates. As the interbank lending market is a funding pool among banks, the change in the interbank rate can best reflect money market conditions, and the interbank lending market can transmit conditions from other parts of the money market, such as securities and bill business. Effective 1 June 1996, the People's Bank eliminated the ceiling limit on the China interbank rate (CHIBOR) and set it free to be determined by banks in accordance with market demand and supply. This is no doubt an important step toward further development of the interbank lending market and interest rate reform. The central bank can control commercial banks' capacity to supply funds by adjusting its lending rates, the rediscount rate, and the deposit reserve rate. In this way it can influence market rates and the money supply. Thus, on the basis of effective development of the money market, particularly the interbank lending market, reinforcement of transmission mechanisms with the rediscount interest rate as its core will enhance the role of market forces in determining interest rates.

UPDATE

CHINESE FINANCIAL REFORM IN THE CONTEXT OF THE ASIAN CRISIS

The Southeast Asian financial crisis which began in July 1997 has aroused world-wide concern. It reiterated the lesson from the 1994 Mexico financial crisis that financial system reform and preventive measures to reduce systemic risk are of urgent importance for developing countries. Despite the Asian financial crisis, the Chinese financial sector remained relatively stable in 1997. The yuan exchange rate rose steadily with a consistent increase of foreign exchange reserves and a sharp decrease of inflationary pressure. Furthermore, there was not much fluctuation in the stock market.

China's relatively stable financial situation is due to institutional and policy factors. It owes much to China's perseverance in promoting financial marketization, gradual restructuring, and opening capital markets in line with the strategy for financial development, as well as to the stable macroeconomic environment. The yuan is convertible for current account transactions preparatory to its full convertibility for capital account transactions. Meanwhile, strict controls have been placed on foreign loans, stock investment, and foreign exchange transactions by Chinese residents. Consequently, there is little scope for buying and selling in currency and capital markets by foreign investors or speculators to affect China's financial stability.

Like Japan, Korea, and other East Asian economies, China has adopted a government-guided market economy, uses high savings as the driving force for economic growth, and has an immature securities market. Hence, China's economic system and structure have some problems and potential financial risks similar to those of other Asian countries. At the same time, China is making a transition from a traditional planned economy to a socialist market economy and from an extensive economic growth mode (by increasing inputs) to an intensive one (by raising productivity). The transition is not yet complete and the economy is still subject to influences of the traditional system in many ways. China has not adapted to the development of an open economy and the trend of economic globalization. How to address these problems appropriately has become the key for the improvement of the financial risk prevention system and for financial reform in the years ahead.

KEY ISSUES IN FINANCIAL REFORM AND PREVENTION OF FINANCIAL RISK

Over-Reliance on the Banking Sector

According to some western experts, the recent Asian financial crisis is directly related to over-reliance on bank financing. The problems exposed by this crisis, such as currency fluctuations, bank bankruptcies, and the bursting of stock and real estate bubbles, are similar to the problems facing the Japanese economy. Analysis of Japan's financial system reveals two important factors—unstable securities markets and high concentration of savings in the banking sector. In the past, the Japanese government restricted the development of the stock market to protect the banking sector's control over capital. For many years, Korea and some Southeast Asian countries followed similar practices. As a result, capital markets in these countries are immature and cannot provide stable, long-term backing for economic growth. This is the biggest risk confronting these countries. It follows that only mature securities markets can successfully resist speculative pressures.

China also still relies too heavily on bank financing because of the late formation and underdevelopment of its capital market. At present, securities issues and shares provide only 1.1 percent and 0.7 percent respectively of funds for gross capital formation. With an over-reliance on indirect financing and the underdevelopment of direct financing through securities markets, China's problems of financial market structure are similar to those of Japan and some Southeast Asian countries. Improving and vitalizing the securities market, including encouraging bond and share issues, should become a major orientation for reform of China's financial system.

Non-Performing Loans

At present, the greatest concern in China is not an unstable currency, but the increase in non-performing loans in banks' portfolios. Several factors contributed to this situation. First, the weakening of the real estate sector following the over-investment in the overheated economy in 1993 has brought about large amounts of bad debts. Second, the burdens of restructuring and institutional transition are resulting in growing operational losses for state-owned enterprises (SOEs) which are the main clients of state commercial banks. Third, commercial banks in China have accumulated huge amounts of non-performing loans because of poor management. Countermeasures to reform the banking system comprehensively, address non-performing bank loans appropriately, and establish a sound financial market are needed to avoid a potential financial crisis in China.

Poor performance of SOEs is the likely source of a financial crisis for China. The Fifteenth National Congress of the Chinese Communist Party, held in September 1997, called for SOEs to adopt share-holding systems. It also established a three-year target for large and medium-sized SOEs to get out of their economic difficulties. These guidelines will bring about great progress in SOE reform. Nonetheless, many problems, such as the re-employment of laid-off workers, are still to be addressed.

Risks of Opening Capital Markets

With economic globalization, many countries have opened their commodity and capital markets to allocate domestic and international resources rationally, and China is no exception. Opening capital markets is often accompanied by increasing financial risk, as is shown in the recent crisis in East Asia. Since the fourth quarter of 1997, China has taken many risk-prevention measures to strengthen its financial controls and normalize its financial markets. However, it will still be a long time in the future before China meets the requirements for a sound capital market in an open economy. With economic globalization and the liberalization of capital markets, once a financial crisis occurs in one country, there is a great possibility that it will affect an entire region and even the whole world. Therefore, it is essential to set up a strict risk prevention system in each country and to establish a joint co-ordinating mechanism.

Controlling Current Account Deficits

The deterioration of current account balances was one of the basic triggers of the Southeast Asian crisis. Keeping a balance of payments equilibrium should be adopted as a long-term policy to prevent future currency crises. From a short-term point of view, China has an export structure similar to that of many East Asian countries. China will face fierce competition in exports as a result of the substantial currency devaluation in Korea and other Asian countries. Competitiveness of China's exports to Japan, which is China's biggest export market, will be weakened and China will lose some market share. The growth rate of Chinese exports has already begun to fall and this situation may continue in 1998. Deficits on China's current account will exert pressure on the exchange rate. Accordingly, how to adjust trade policies and promote steady export growth will become one of

China's policy priorities. There is still room for China to enhance the international competitiveness of its exports, including speeding up reform of the foreign trade system, increasing the access of industrial enterprises to the international market, and streamlining the system of tax refunds for exporters.

The huge capital account surplus in the 1990s helped China maintain its balance of payments equilibrium in recent years. However, the capital account surplus may become a negative factor in China's balance of payments in the longer term. Over time, repayments of foreign loans and outward remittance of direct investment earnings will put pressure on the balance of payments. If the inflow of capital should drop, it would be difficult for China to avoid an overall balance of payments deficit. Thus, China should adopt a long-term policy of encouraging exports, promoting the restructuring of domestic industry, raising international competitiveness of Chinese products, and maintaining balance of payments equilibrium through a combination of industrial and trade policies. In addition, to improve the efficiency of utilizing foreign capital, it is necessary to put priority into infrastructure and high-tech industries that can expand economic capacity.

CHINA'S RESPONSE TO THE SOUTHEAST ASIAN CRISIS

China has reacted to the crisis in Southeast Asia with great seriousness, taking another look at the major issues of financial reform and development and adopting a series of measures to reduce the influence of the crisis. In November 1997, the National Finance Conference called for setting up a sound financial order, modern financial institutions, and financial market systems over the next three years. The measures taken by China as a result of the crisis fall into five areas.

Strengthening Supervision of Financial Institutions

As early as July 1997, the Supervisory Commission on Securities Transactions (SCST) prohibited margin trading of overseas futures and foreign exchange in order to eliminate high-risk speculation and violations by Chinese enterprises in overseas markets. Meanwhile, to strengthen control over stock exchanges, on 14 August 1997 the State Council declared that both the Shenzhen and Shanghai Stock Exchanges would be put under SCST. On 22 September 1997, the People's Bank of China (PBC), along with the Bureau of Industry and Commerce reiterated that financial agencies including insurance, securities, currency, and futures must obtain a license from the PBC and that individuals are forbidden to engage in brokerage. They also re-emphasized that financial institutions without PBC approval are illegal.

PBC has taken some steps to improve the supervision of financial institutions. On 11 December 1997, authorized by the State Council, PBC created a supervisory committee for state-owned commercial banks. The main functions of the supervisory committee are: to audit financial statements of state-owned commercial banks; to evaluate and supervise the quality of credit assets, management of asset-liability ratio, preserving and increasing of state bank assets; to evaluate and supervise performance of chairpersons and presidents of state commercial banks; and to make suggestions concerning appointments and removals, rewards and punishments. In order to safeguard the institutionalization and efficiency of financial controls, PBC issued Regulations on Financial Controls.

Improving the Mechanism for Monetary Policy Formulation

Since July 1997, China has increased the responsiveness of the mechanism for monetary policy formulation in order to meet the needs of the socialist market economy, enhance macroeconomic regulations, maintain domestic economic stability, especially financial stability, and prevent the influence of international financial crises. On 1 August 1997, a PBC monetary policy committee was founded. The committee is supposed to regularly discuss issues concerning the draft and adjustment of monetary policies, policy targets, the use of monetary policy tools, and co-ordination between monetary and other macroeconomic policies. In addition, it is also supposed to make suggestions on monetary policies. The proceedings of the PBC monetary policy committee have been in effect since 31 August 1997.

Current Chinese monetary policies as published by PBC are: to adhere to an appropriately tight monetary policy, to adjust economic structure through credit policies, to promote the restructuring of supply and demand, and to co-ordinate supply and demand to curb inflation. In line with these principles, PBC reduced interest rates on deposits and loans by an average of 1.1 and 1.5 percentage points respectively on 23 October 1997.

Speeding Up Capital Market Reform

Many lessons for capital markets and market operations can be learned from the Southeast Asian crisis. In a speech on 25 August 1997 a PBC official stressed the importance that the Chinese government attaches to the development of capital markets and described the guidelines for their "legalization, supervision, self-discipline, and normalization." The government is determined to cultivate and develop capital markets through the following measures: speeding up the legal framework for capital markets; gradually improving the structure and function of capital markets; strengthening law enforcement, market supervision, and the information management of listed companies; actively and prudently exploring new financial products; and helping enterprises find new sources of financing.

The promulgation of regulations concerning capital markets is under way. On 12 December 1997, SCST published enforcement regulations establishing norms for the management of securities investment funds.

Improving Management of Foreign Exchange Transactions

In December 1996 China agreed to Article 8 of the International Monetary Fund (IMF) and permitted full convertibility of the yuan for current account transactions. Since then, effectively managing foreign exchange settlement while the currency is not fully convertible for capital account transactions has become an important project to ensure the stability of exchange rates and improve the functioning of the foreign exchange system. The Southeast Asian currency crisis has made this issue more urgent.

On 30 October 1997, the State Administration for Exchange Control (SAEC) issued regulations to prevent foreign exchange under capital accounts from entering exchange settlements under current accounts. On the other hand, SAEC raised the ceiling on conversion of yuan into foreign currencies by domestic individuals and allowed Chinese enterprises to keep certain foreign exchange revenues from 15 October 1997. These measures were intended to stabilize exchange rates and reduce the pressure of both foreign exchange settlement expansion on the supply of domestic base currency and yuan appreciation resulting from the trade surplus and increasing foreign direct investment. According to the guidelines published by PBC, China's foreign exchange system will be reformed step by step. The first step was to allow convertibility of yuan for current account transactions. The next step is probably to allow a few commercial banks and enterprises to invest abroad under the state macro-regulations. The steps after that may be to allow a few foreign companies to purchase Chinese A-shares or permit the convertibility of some loans into yuan.

The existence of "hidden foreign debts", or foreign liabilities that escape government supervision, may confound China's controls on foreign debt, causing statistical distortion and leading to uncontrolled accumulation of external debt. The State Planning Commission (SPC) emphasized that such hidden foreign debt must be put under government monitoring and control.

Cleaning Up Non-Performing Loans

Quite a number of measures have been instituted to limit the growth of non-performing loans and to ensure financial safety. PBC demanded that commercial banks accelerate the reform of credit control systems, set reasonable credit time limits, lay down systematic methods for asset classification, and create a reserve fund system for bad debts. A reserve of 30 billion yuan will be drawn on in 1997 to write off bad debts. On 9 November 1997, the government announced standards to strengthen investment credit management. After that, Industrial and Commercial Bank of China (ICBC) issued regulations to monitor outstanding loans and set up a sound management system.

ICBC, China's largest commercial bank, has made the reduction of non-performing loans and avoidance of credit risk its priority in the years ahead. These objectives will be carried out through prevention, control, transfer (by merger), and writing off.

All of the above measures have played a significant role in stabilizing China's financial order and macroeconomic situation during this period of regional financial turmoil. They will play an even more important role in financial reform and the prevention of financial risk in the years ahead.

January 1998

THE EDITORS

C. H. KWAN is senior economist at the Center for Knowledge Exchange and Creation at Nomura Research Institute in Tokyo and author of numerous books and articles on the Asian economy.

DONNA C. VANDENBRINK is economist at the Center for Knowledge Exchange and Creation at Nomura Research Institute and formerly at the Federal Reserve Bank of Chicago.

CHIA SIOW YUE is Director of the Institute of Southeast Asian Studies in Singapore and was previously Associate Professor of Economics at the National University of Singapore. She has published extensively on regional economic integration, trade, industrialization, and foreign investment in ASEAN and East Asia.